The
Runaway

The Runaway

When her stepfather came back,
Janice's only option was the streets…

Janice Erlbaum

EBURY
PRESS

1 3 5 7 9 10 8 6 4 2

Published in 2006 by Ebury Press, an imprint of Ebury Publishing
A Random House Group Company
This edition published 2008
First published as *Girlbomb* in the United States by Villard Books in 2006

The Random House Group Limited Reg. No. 954009

Addresses for companies within the Random House Group can be found at
www.randomhouse.co.uk

A CIP catalogue record for this book is available from the British Library

The Random House Group Limited supports The Forest Stewardship
Council (FSC), the leading international forest certification organisation.
All our titles that are printed on Greenpeace approved FSC certified paper
carry the FSC logo. Our paper procurement policy can be found at
www.rbooks.co.uk/environment

Printed in the UK by CPI Cox & Wyman, Reading, RG1 8EX

ISBN 9780091944735

To buy books by your favourite authors and register for offers visit
www.rbooks.co.uk

For Judith

Perhaps someday it will be pleasant

to remember these times.

— VIRGIL

PART ONE

Shelter Happens

1
INTAKE

November 18, 1984

Where do you think you're going?

Forty-seventh Street and Tenth Avenue – that's what the lady on the phone told me. "The building has a big sign with a cross on it," she said kindly. "We'll be looking out for you."

I hung up the pay phone and hoisted my book bag. I was fifteen years old, it was ten-thirty on a windy November night, and I was somewhere in Hell's Kitchen. I'd been marching uptown since Washington Square Park, not knowing where I was going, my hands swollen and tingly from swinging furiously at my sides, my book bag denting my hip with each step.

"Yo, where you goin', miss? I could walk with you?"

No, papí. I was walking alone tonight. I was going to a shelter, which was on Forty-seventh and Tenth, and I wasn't stopping for anybody – not the hustlers hawking nickel bags, not the Italian homeboys in their tricked-out IROC catcalling me. Not even a break in stride for the two boys passing me, shoving each other and laughing, then yelling, "Hey, miss, you dropped something!"

"Hey, miss!"

You miss me yet, Mom? The way you missed Dave so much you just had to take him back? It's only been a few hours, maybe you think I'm walking around the neighborhood, burning off some steam, I'll be coming back any minute. Or maybe I went to one of my friends' houses – what were those girls' names again?

"Pssssst. Over here, girl."

I was on a bad block, a gauntlet of drunks, hookers, and bums, leading nowhere. I'd been walking quickly, but now I started really hoofing it, still trying not to out and out run, red-eyed men hissing at me from every shadow. I was almost at the address the lady gave me, but I didn't see the building with the cross. *Don't panic*, I thought, panicking, faint tears blurring my sight. *Maybe it's across the street.*

Across the street was a rotting industrial plant. Catty-corner was a diner and a church. But right here was a building covered in scaffolding, and a man approaching me from a driveway, asking, "Are you looking for someplace?"

"No," I said quickly, moving away. "I'm fine."

"You sure? Because this is a shelter here."

I stopped, took in the man's blue windbreaker and badge. His face was impassive, but his hand was outstretched.

"You need to come on in here tonight?"

I sat in a plastic chair and waited. The place looked like places look, I guessed. Linoleum. Windows that probably didn't open. A lot of taped-up construction paper on the walls, memos on bulletin boards. NO HATS OR DO-RAGS INSIDE THANK YOU. PRAYER GROUP 7:30 CHAPEL. *Prayer group*, I thought – *Oh Christ, not Jesus*.

An older woman with short gray hair and a black smock came out of her office and nodded at me. A nun. I didn't know any nuns. I thought nuns were spooky. This one appeared human. She looked like a middle-aged gym teacher in a smock.

"Come in," she suggested. I rose and followed her.

The entire inside of the nun's office was papered with MISSING posters, ghostly kids smiling down in smudgy, high-contrast black and white. Shameeka Wells, age 16, missing from Brooklyn since September. Ebony Johnson, age 15, missing from the Bronx since July. Ebony's fax had curled and yellowed, but her eyes burned bright from the center of a black splotch. Her picture looked like it had been drawn by a seismograph. Ebony was not smiling.

The nun sat at her desk, engulfed in this cage of missing kids. She looked concerned, and busy.

"How are you tonight?" she asked.

I was . . . How was I? Disoriented. In shock. Just two hours ago, I was heating up some lentil soup at my mom's in Brooklyn, thinking I'd eat it and maybe read some Edith Wharton before bed. Now here I was at a runaway shelter, staring at a nun's mustache and wondering where I was going to spend the rest of my adolescence.

"I'm okay," I said.

She nodded and tried to meet my eyes. "Is there a reason you came here tonight?"

I didn't want to cry, so I kept my eyes averted. "I can't live at home anymore."

She nodded again, like she agreed. "Can you tell me about it?"

"I . . ."

Where to start? *I was born, and . . .*

"My stepfather . . . he's crazy. He's . . . abusive to my mother. And he's creepy. And they have a baby, and he shakes the baby." I winced, thinking about Dave handling baby Jake, panged with guilt over leaving my brother behind.

The nun bobbed her head seriously, like, *Yes, you're right, that sounds bad.* I was heartened to continue.

"So . . . my mom and him fight all the time, and he gets crazy and violent, and she throws him out – like, ten times in the past two years. And every time, it's the same. She calls the cops on him, and then she changes the locks, and we go to court to get an order of protection . . ."

The nun's nod knew what was coming next. It knew before I knew. I still couldn't believe it.

"And then she takes him back."

She was taking him back. She swore she wasn't going to do it this time, and here she was, doing it again. I told her, after the last time, "That's it. If you take him back this time, I'm leaving." She swore to me, "Jan, I'm not taking him back."

Until tonight. There I was, heating up some soup, and my mother came into the kitchen, and she said we had to talk. And I knew what that meant, so I turned off the soup, went into my room, and got my bag.

And I left.

"So here you are," said the nun, like something was settled.

I shook my head yes. I looked her in the eye. Then my eyes welled up again, and I looked at my lap.

I didn't know what else to say. The nun wasn't questioning me, she wasn't jotting down notes. I didn't have to go on with my story, didn't have to back it up with dates and details the way I did in depositions with my mother's endless divorce lawyers. She wasn't asking me for proof that I wasn't lying, or exaggerating – *Yes, we know your stepfather* threatened *to hit you, but did he ever actually* strike *you?* She just believed me.

"What about your father? Do you have a relationship with him?"

Ugh. Another case history, in twenty words or less: "Not really. He's abusive. He hit me when I was a kid. We don't talk anymore. I can't live with him."

Case closed. "Any other family you'd like us to contact?"

"No." No grandparents, no aunts. No godparents, no friends' families. No friends. Nobody.

Nod. She closed her eyes for a moment and drew in a breath. I got the crazy idea she was saying a prayer for me.

She opened her eyes and said, "We're glad you came to us tonight."

The fifth-floor lounge was crowded. Twenty or thirty girls were sitting or lying on thin foam mattresses on the floor of the large rectangular room, some curled up with their jackets over their heads like they were trying to sleep, which clearly wasn't going to happen with the ruckus under way. Two girls argued loudly over the custody of a Walkman; another hollered at her neighbor to *move the fuck over before I wreck you, ho.* Several animated conversations dropped to whispers as the nun escorted me to the supply closet and pulled out a pallet for me. I distinctly heard the word *white* more than once, and I knew, from a quick scan of the room, that it had to be directed at me.

"We just did head count," said the nun. "It's almost lights out. Here're toiletries for you. We'll take you over to the minors' wing after breakfast. It's in a separate building. It's a little quieter over there." She handed me a Baggie with a toothbrush, a small tube of paste, and a hotel-sized soap. I put it in my book bag, which I clamped to my side. "Have a good night."

The nun walked away, and I was left to my foam mattress. I was in the furthermost corner by the closet, right up against the wall. The girl to my right was sleeping with her coat over her head and her sneakers on; either she or somebody else had tied the laces together. How could she sleep in here? People were cursing one another out, shrieking with laughter, stomping around the room looking for the *bitch who took my fucking comb.* The girl on my other side gabbed in Creole to her neighbor.

I was too wired to sleep anyway. I leaned back against the wall and looked around the room. Several people looked back at me, some frowned. I lowered my gaze, dipped my head, and gently closed my eyes as though I was exhausted.

My mind raced, as it had been racing all night, since I stepped out my mother's door, *What now what now what now what now.* I didn't know. So far I'd been running on instinct and adrenaline, following my feet. They took me out of the apartment, down Flatbush Avenue to the D train, through cold, empty Washington Square Park, to a pay phone in Hell's Kitchen. Now we were here. What now? What now? What now?

I heard someone say, "What that white girl doin' here?"

Quiet.

Then, "Same as you, bitch, she ain't got noplace else to go."

Laughs.

Welcome to the asylum, to the first night of the rest of your life. I stayed with my eyes closed and my back to the wall until the lights went out. Then I curled up with my jacket over my head and my sneakers on, put my thumb in my mouth, and stared at the darkness for hours, until I finally fell something like asleep.

2
OUTTAKE

It was all Dave's fault.

Okay, maybe life wasn't perfect before Dave came along, but it was definitely way better. It's true that my mom had picked some crappy husbands before, including my own father, an abusive tyrant she left when I was five. My father used to scream and hit and break the furniture, and he was *still* better than Dave, who did all of that, *plus* picked racist arguments in movie lines and threatened to burn down the dry cleaner's. I mean, at least my father kept his temper tantrums in the family.

Dave Malley was crazy. He *smelled* crazy. He smelled like bad soup and aluminum foil, and his unfiltered Camels left murky stains on his fingers and teeth. I was introduced to Dave when I was twelve years old, and I wrote down that he was *itchy*. He was tall and wiry, and he pointed stagily with his cigarette as he spoke – "Very valuable skills to have, computer programming skills, very lucrative field." He smirked at me, as though I should be impressed with him, which I wasn't. My mother was. God only knew why. My mother could have done a million times better than Dave Malley.

My mother, Barb Rosen, was thirty-five years old, with a twelve-year-old daughter, but she looked like she was twenty-three. She was about five foot six, and model thin, with glossy auburn hair, green-gold eyes, bisque skin, and a wide smile, next to which lived a perfect little mole. Sometimes I sat and watched her, dressed for the office in her cowl-necked sweaters and high-heeled boots, and I could not believe how gorgeous she was. Meanwhile, I had a puffy, freckled face with a schnoz like my dad's. It hardly seemed fair.

I had, I guess, sort of a crush on my mom, in that I thought about her a lot, I wanted to spend time with her, and I wanted her to like me. Any time she was paying attention to me, I was elated. I wanted more than anything to live just the two of us, just me and my mom. I'd been waiting for this blessed arrangement since I was five years old, when we left my father in the middle of the night and drove to my grandma's in the Bronx, and my mom told me gravely, "It's just us now, Jan."

But it wasn't just us, it was never just us. As soon as we left Grandma's for our own Manhattan apartment, my mother met Joe, a droopy-eyed guy who stayed over in her room a lot. I had no use for Joe, and he had none for me. Then after Joe came Barry, the leisure-suited salesguy from New Jersey. Barry had curly hair, a gold Star of David around his neck, and three daughters, all older than me, all of whom despised me on sight. Within weeks of their first date, my mother moved us to the suburbs and married Barry, making him Crummy Husband Number Two, though he was probably the best of the lot. He was a "putz," according to my mother – "I don't know why I put up with him," she'd confide to me, age eight, any time we were alone in the car. "He lets his ex-wife bleed him dry, and those girls of his are little nightmares."

I agreed with everything my mother said. Even if I didn't know what it meant. I developed a repertoire of sympathetic responses: "No. Really? Wow. Uh-huh?" The important thing was to keep her talking to me, feeding me information, making me indispensable.

"So I said, 'Barry, you're paying your ex-wife child support and *you're* stuck raising them? Send them to their mother's if she loves them so much!' " She punched the dashboard lighter, impatient.

I bobbed my head. "Yep. Mm hmm. You're right."

I prayed every day for this marriage to end, wishing on every dandelion puff, fallen lash, face-up penny, and airplane masquerading as a shooting star. Maybe Barry wasn't as scary as my own father, but he was kind of slimy, with his exposed chest hair and his incessant mom-fondling, and my stepsisters were like evil characters from a fairy tale, who delighted in pulling my index finger backward until it met my wrist. It took Mom and Barry almost three years to break up, by which point I was ten years old and didn't really believe in wishing anymore; still, I was as gratified by their divorce as if I'd arranged it myself.

My mother and I moved back to Manhattan – "Just the two of us, Jan, won't *that* be a relief?" – but then she immediately started dating again. First there was Sam the stuttering WASP, then Irv the importer with the pinkie ring, and then Richard the retiree, who was *sixty-five fucking years old*, for god's sake. I really saw no rationale for any of them; they were charmless compared to my brilliant, adorable mom. It was like she just dated whoever was standing right in front of her at the time. Fortunately, Sam, Irv, and Richard lasted only a few months apiece. They were temps. They were like goldfish that died and got replaced, and nobody ever stopped to ask, "Hey, do we really want another goldfish?"

Sometimes my mother's boyfriends overlapped a little, but sometimes there were a few delicious weeks in between them, when it was just us. We'd get up late on weekend mornings, me humming to myself over my fruit and yogurt, my mother in her bathrobe with her hair in a crown of curlers, her eyebrows not yet penciled in, smoking. "What do you want to do today, Jan?" she'd ask. "I have to stop by the office this afternoon, but we can go by the library and get you a book beforehand." Great, super, hum hum hum. I was happy enough to sit in the anteroom of my mother's one-woman events-planning office in Midtown, reading one of the Narnia books, listening to her droll, knowing voice on the phone with her clients, basking in her glamorous, efficient near-presence.

"Then maybe afterwards we can go to the Peacock for an éclair." Well, that would just be cloud nine. To eat pastry in a café with my mom, and talk like adults, like good friends. She'd tell me interesting things about other grown-ups, for instance, did I remember her old boss, Dan McDonough, from when I was six? He was a terrible alcoholic. He passed out and peed his pants in the office once. Really? Sweet cream on my fingers. Oh yes. Of course, his business collapsed when my mother left him and went out on her own. It was a shame.

My mom always spoke the frank truth around me. Regarding Richard the retiree: "Honestly, Jan, if someone is always too tired to, you know, make love, then really, that's . . ."

I nodded knowingly – she didn't have to go on. Sex was an important part of a healthy, loving adult relationship! I was twelve, I'd read plenty of books. I totally understood.

"Richard was boring," I added, shifting the subject a little. "He didn't even like to do anything, like go to the movies."

"I know, I know." She exhaled, annoyed. She knew I didn't like Richard, that I didn't really like any of them, but I wasn't supposed to express it outright. Disliking her boyfriends was her exclusive domain. Besides, I'd already won this battle by default; she'd dumped Richard the retiree last month, when he did not make a big enough deal out of her birthday. And now she was left, thirty-five years old, contemplating the oily skim on her cold coffee, alone.

For about a minute. Then she met Dave. Who was thirty years old and lived with his mother in Westchester. "Temporarily." Dave was temporarily living with his mother in Westchester while he sought employment as a computer programmer. Within weeks, he was temporarily living with us.

Dave was six four, skinny, and balding, with glasses. Not only was he *itchy*, but he was sarcastic, critical, bossy, moody, and obnoxious. I watched him shove our elderly cat, Sausage, with his leg in an unkind manner, watched him castigate a meter maid in the street and then fume all night about "the Hispanics." *Definitely temporary*, I blustered to myself, eyeing him with suspicion from the outskirts of the living room. *Surely this goldfish will die quickly.*

I tried to catch my mother's eye to confirm, but she wasn't looking at me. She was looking up at Dave, nervously ensconced under his gangly arm like she was along for the ride. What was it about him that kept her there? Once out of range, she tried to explain it to me. "He's very bright, Jan, extremely high IQ. *You* know how hard that can be to negotiate."

I didn't like this explanation at all, first because it compared me to him, and I was *not* like him; second because it alluded to the difficulties I'd been having in school of late – skipping assignments, stealing a book from the library, "acting out" in class – which were all being blamed on my frustration with my own brain-busting intelligence. Yeah, too smart for my own good. That was me.

I sulked and waited for my mother to crack. Okay, so Dave was "bright," and "sensitive," and he was good company for her when she was feeling manic, as she often was these days – when she wanted to tear apart the kitchen for a full-scale reorganization, AM radio blaring, Dave was right there with the black coffee and cigarettes, egging her on. Dave could surprise her with tickets to see Neil Diamond in concert, which was something I could not do. But I could tell she didn't enjoy the snide tone he sometimes took with her – "Well, who do you *think* runs the government, huh? *Think* about it, Barb. *Think*." It flustered her, especially when he did it in front of me, and I got so anxious I put my thumb in my mouth. And then they both turned to me and said, "Don't do that." He embarrassed my mother by talking too loud, and taking issue with random people on the subway – "You can buy your own paper, buddy, and stop leaning over mine." It bothered her that she couldn't shop at the deli closest to the apartment anymore because Dave had called them "Paki cheats." I sensed that whatever tense, desperate bond they had forged was fraying, and that it wouldn't be long before my mother took me out for coffee and filled me in on a few vital facts about our new friend Dave.

I was sucking my thumb in my room one night before bed, and my mom came in, eyebrowless, in her curlers and robe. She looked peaked – there was a crease between her hooded eyes, and some wrinkles in her forehead I wasn't used to seeing. I'd heard a lot of heated conversation from the master bedroom lately, noticed a lot of hushed voices and guarded looks between my mother and Dave, and my fingers were crossed for the complaining to begin. I thought, *She's going to tell me they're breaking up.*

She sat on my bed. "Jan, I have something to tell you, and I don't expect it to be easy at first, but I think you'll understand that it's best for everyone."

I must have been actively trying not to smile.

"I'm pregnant, and Dave and I have decided to have the baby."

Gong. Like someone put a bell over my head and hit it with a hammer. Like an elevator cable snapped, and I was plummeting, dashing to my death underground. Stunned. Nauseated.

"Now, Jan, I know it may seem sudden, but this is the right decision." Her tone was warning.

Now, Jan, don't fuck me up here. Don't protest. Don't say anything. I can always send you to live with your father, like I did during the Barry Marriage, when you were nine. Remember that? You didn't like Barry, you didn't like the girls, so I got your dad to take you for a while – that didn't work out too well, did it? The hitting, the choking, the yelling – scariest six months of your life, right? You said you never wanted to go back there again as I recall. So don't push it.

I tried to suppress the cry rising in my chest, tried to keep it down like vomit. This was the worst news I'd ever heard. Not only was she *not* going to get rid of this obnoxious weirdo, she was going to have a baby with him, and start a whole new family. I was being permanently displaced. It would never be just us.

"Jan." My mother sounded impatient as I began to out and out sob. "Janice! This is a good thing, and I expect you to be happy about it." I heard Dave lurking in the doorway, a malevolent bat. I pulled myself into a ball on my bed with my arms over my head. She reached out a hand and dully patted my shoulder. Softer now, she insisted, "Jan . . . honey, come on."

We sat like that for a minute or so, her bony hand limp on my heaving shoulder, and then she removed her hand and turned away. I heaved and hiccupped, but her hand did not return. She sighed deeply, as though this was very hard for her.

"Jan," she said, finally. "I understand that this is sudden. But this is the decision that both Dave and I have made, and you're going to have to get used to it."

I kept my arms over my head, chest hitching, as I felt her rise from her seat on the bed. She stopped by the door.

"I'm sorry you can't see this as a good thing right now, but you will."

She left, and I balled up even tighter, dense as a star, and wished one of us, any of us, was dead.

Then the fighting started.

Dave wasn't happy about a few things around the house. My mom spent too much time at the office on weekends. She cut him off in the middle of a twenty-minute rant about judiciary conspiracies in small claims court. She took too long saying good night to me in my room, and I overheard him berating her in the kitchen – "She's thirteen years old, Barb, and you treat her like a baby. And I'm sick of seeing her suck her thumb. And she doesn't treat anybody with any respect, and frankly, it's pissing me off."

Sometimes she actually sat there and defended herself, explaining to Dave why, for instance, she had to go to work, as though all he needed was a refresher course on the concept of exchanging labor for money, and then he'd stop being insane. "Now, Dave, you know I have several key events coming up, and I have got to make *at least* ten or fifteen phone calls tomorrow or I will not be able to pull any of this off. I'm sorry you feel neglected, but this is my business, and – "

It never worked. He always started hollering at her, mid-sentence, "Bullshit! God, Barb, you are so full of shit. You know *perfectly well* that you *swore* to me . . ."

When the explaining failed, she skipped straight to yelling back at him. "Dave, calm down!"

I'd be crouched behind my bedroom door, listening as it escalated like a bad fever. Dave screaming accusations and threats at my mom – "I know you're up to something, and when I find out what it is . . ." – shoving the furniture and taunting her. "Is this what you want? Is this what you want, Barb?" Then her voice, sharp and furious, like she was commanding a dog. "Stop it, Dave! Stop it!" And me, hiding behind my bedroom door on my knees, never protecting her.

If there was a dandelion puff handy, I would have blown its head off, wishing for Dave to go away. She had to break up with him sometime, I prayed, baby or no. I took all the pills out of the medicine cabi-net and held them in my hand until the easy-swallow coating left mottled stains in my palm; then I put them back in their bottles. They were Plan B.

One night when my mother was five months pregnant, they were in the living room arguing – "Dave, the man is a *client* of mine! You're being completely irrational!" "Don't tell me I'm being fucking irra-tional, *I know you're fucking around!*" It was almost midnight, they'd been at it for hours, and I was sore from kneeling in my usual spot behind the door, in the prayer-vomiting position.

"How do I know this baby is mine!" Dave demanded, like on a soap opera.

"That's absurd and you know it," she spat. "You're out of control, and I'm not going to – "

"Out of control? You want to see *out of control?*"

I heard a table overturn and my mother yelling, "Stop it, Dave, stop it!" Less commanding now, more shrill, like when my father would start to lose it on her. I cried out without meaning to, "Mom!"

The action stopped. I cringed, pressing myself further into the door hinge. Dave had given me enough warnings – "Don't get smart with *me*, missy, or I'll show you what's what." Now he was going to come in here and kill me. I heard his heavy footfalls – *which way?* – going toward the front door. There was a *thunk* as he kicked the plastic umbrella stand, then the door ripped open.

"*Fuck* you, Barb," he hissed, and he let the door slam hard.

Ten. Nine. Eight. Seven. Six. Five. Four. Three. Two. One.

Nothing.

In horror movies, the dead psycho usually popped up again around "three."

Maybe Dave was not coming back.

My mom called, "Jan?" Very concerned. I popped up from my shin-hugging cringe right away. My head swam.

"Mom?" I stumbled into the living room, where the coffee table was now on its side, drinks seeping into the rug along with ashes and butts, and pieces of the *Times* everywhere. She was muttering, trying to scoop up the worst of the broken glass before the cat could get to it.

She didn't look at me. "I'm sorry you had to hear that."

I bent down, dazed, and started blotting at the carpet with the newspaper.

She said, "Honey, get paper towels."

My mother was moving briskly, but I was clumsy from shaking. *Is the door locked?* I wondered. *Did she put on the chain?* I kept blotting stupidly, dripping tears. She blew past me and flung a sopping handful of crap into the garbage.

"Well, he's certainly not coming back after that little display. You don't have to worry about that."

She flicked her hands, finished. I nodded gratefully at the news, still shaking. Maybe I'd prayed for it to end, but not like this.

"I'm sorry about this whole thing, Jan. I really am. Come here."

I didn't know how to hug my mom now that she was pregnant. I approached her side, and she took me under her shoulder.

"It'll be just us now," she promised. "Just us and the baby."

Just us and the baby. That didn't sound so bad. As long as Dave wasn't around anymore. I burrowed deeper into her side. "What about Dave?"

"He's gone now," she assured me. "And good riddance."

Two days later, Dave was back.

He came back for his things, and they wound up talking. "Jan," my mom explained, "Dave and I have a lot of stuff we have to work out."

Obviously. They spent almost the whole weekend behind closed doors. I got sent out with money for ice cream and video games, which I spent on cigarettes, which I smoked on nearby stoops until I was dizzy.

My mother and Dave reconciled. What could I say? There was no evidence I could present against him that she didn't already have. He was awful. He scared the shit out of me. I hated him. She knew.

She told me, "The fact is, Dave and I are going to have a baby, and we are going to try to be a family." She sounded like she was speaking from notes. "Now, we've talked about getting couples therapy, and that's definitely something we're going to think about. But for right now, I want you to pitch in a little more and help us all get along better."

I hung my head in despair, which she could construe as a yes if she wanted. It was futile, I might as well take the pills.

Their next breakup: She was eight months pregnant, and they were arguing, because he wanted them to get a bigger apartment, and she said they couldn't afford it. This sent him into a boiling rage – "That's *bullshit*, Barb! I know how much you've got socked away!" – matched only by hers – "Without *my savings*, we'd all be out on the street!" She paid for everything these days, as Dave had become unemployable for more than two weeks at a time, and she was sick of it, on top of being very pregnant. "We can't afford it, and that's final!"

It went on like this forever, as I crouched behind my bedroom door, hyperventilating into my clasped hands. The sound of the chair scraping across the floor as he shoved her down – "Sit down! You're going to listen to me now!"

"Get off of me!"

"You're going to *sit down* and *listen to me!*"

Don't butt in, she'd warned me. *If I need you to call the police, I'll shout. Otherwise, stay in your room.* I rocked back and forth on my burning heels, panting, bladder ready to burst.

"Sit the fuck down, Barb!" The honk of the chair against the floor, the groan of a familiar ghost.

"Stop it! Stop it, or I'm calling the police!"

Is this me? Is this my cue? Does she need me?

My eyes were squeezed shut behind my steepled hands, I saw only a blistering red field. Heard something clatter across the room – the ashtray. The sound of the phone off the hook – "I'm calling them right now!"

His heavy stomp out the door. *Slam.*

This was their second breakup. This one was serious – she was going to go to court this time and get an order of protection against him, that was how serious it was. "We'll write you a note for school tomorrow, you can come with me in case you need to testify." I nodded, or my head shook up and down with nerves, whichever. She called a locksmith, who came in his coveralls and changed the locks, even though it was around one in the morning. I was impressed. My mother smoked and rubbed her round belly as he worked.

"It was a mistake to think he could act like a human being." Puff, puff. "I am *very* sorry about this, Jan. You should *not* have to put up with this."

We did not hug this time. We watched the locksmith drill the bright brass fixture to the wall. We went to court the next day.

Five days later, they reconciled.

A month later, she gave birth to my half brother, Jake, a healthy, beatific baby boy with features just like his dad's. She and Dave were married. We moved to a bigger apartment, in the cracked-out neighborhood of Crown Heights, Brooklyn. We were a family.

In other news: I turned fourteen. I grew breasts – first the left one, then the right. I moved from a small private middle school in the East Village to one of the city's most competitive public high schools, where I started cutting class, drinking during the day, and smoking as much pot as money, time, and lung power allowed. I hung an Adam Ant poster in my new bedroom, and my mother glanced at it suspiciously as she hurried past the doorway, on her way to dealing with Jake. "I don't know what's happening with you lately, Jan, but you'd better get straightened out."

Things could not have sucked more at home. As bad as the fights were, the times in between were even worse, because that was when Dave and my mother were aggressively trying to pretend they weren't both fucking nuts. God, how I loathed her when she was with him. She adopted all his mannerisms, his sarcastic sneer, his "sociological" observations on "those kinds of people." Together, they made these desperate, ridiculous plans – "Dave and I are talking about having another baby." "Next year, we're thinking of moving to France" – and my internal eyeballs rolled so hard they practically bounced.

My mom and Dave became manic about putting a good face on things, both seething with paranoia and rage, and I was often the proxy target of their mutual hatred. They'd call me in for a "family meeting" and tell me that I wasn't doing my part around the house, that they hated my clothes, and what was I doing with those hickeys, missy? "You need to cool it with the boys." My disgusting stepfather leered as my mother imperiously agreed. "You're really stacked. The boys must be on you like dogs."

His eyes flicked over me like a tongue. It was around this time that I started to think about leaving.

. . .

It was summer, and they'd "broken up" again – by now, I knew I had to add invisible quote marks to everything my mother said, as though it were hypothetical. She'd kicked Dave out a few days earlier, but tonight she'd picked up the phone when he called, and I heard her voice rising in anger, then dropping, dull and sad. Then she was sobbing, then she was mad again. "You're not being fair, Dave! That is not true!"

Hang up, Mom. Just hang it up.

I sat at the kitchen table facing Jake in his car seat, where he was happy to sit and gurgle at me, an unnaturally good-natured baby, especially considering who spawned him. At fourteen months, Jake was the best thing in my life right now, my single favorite person on Earth. My new game was to pretend that Jake was mine, and we were just visiting my mom, and any minute Jake and I would be going home to our own apartment with our husband-father, Matt Dillon. I made blubbery boo-boo lips at Jake, and he spat back nonsense at me. My mother wailed and declaimed in the other room.

She exited the bedroom around eight o'clock, limp. "I just don't know, Jan . . . I mean, he is Jake's father . . . he's entitled to see his son . . ."

I didn't even listen anymore. Jake's spit bubbles made more sense than whatever was coming out of her mouth.

"Jan," said my mom, sternly.

"What." I hung my head, hiding my mascara-smeared eyes under my hair.

She exhaled hard, frustrated. "You know, *you're* part of this family too . . ."

Ucch. No I wasn't. I had nothing to do with any of this. I never wanted to be dragged in.

She stood in front of me, arms folded, lips in a line. "Jan, I'm trying to do what's right here, and this is very hard for me. I'd appreciate your support."

I didn't say anything. I removed my finger from Jake's miraculous grasp, went into my room, and closed the door.

. . .

Within two hours, Dave arrived, and the screaming began. *Fuck them*, I thought. *Fuck them both*. I wasn't hiding on my knees anymore, waiting to call 911. I was in bed with my arms folded over my chest and my headphones blasting. *Fuck them*. I could hear them shouting, even through the music, then Jake started to wail. *Jake! – god fucking damn them.* I pulled off the headphones and went to listen at my bedroom door.

I heard Dave tearing through the apartment. "I'm taking him, and I'm not coming back!"

My mother yelled, "Jan, call the police! Call the police! He's taking the baby!"

Oh no, he was not. Jake was *ours*, he was *mine*. *I* helped feed and bathe and burp and diaper him; *I* sang to him, rocked him in my arms. Dave treated him like the prize in a game of keep-away. He was not *touching* Jake. A primal switch flipped in me: I would kill him first. I grabbed a six-inch pair of sewing shears off my dresser and ran into the hallway, shrieking, "Put him down!"

Dave was already halfway out the front door, Jake squalling in one arm, my mother clinging to the other. She dug in with her bare feet, pulling at Dave as he pushed her away. "Jan! Help!"

"Put him down!" I raised the scissors like Norman Bates in *Psycho*. "Put him down right now!"

"Jake is *my son*!" Dave pushed hard against my mom and broke free into the hallway, dashing down the two flights of stairs to the lobby. My mother and I ran after him, half-dressed and shoeless.

"Police! Help! Police!"

We spilled out onto the sidewalk – Dave, practically foaming at the mouth; Jake screaming in his arms; my mother, screeching, barefoot in her robe; and me, in only a T-shirt and underwear, with a pair of scissors in the stabbing position, yelling, "Put him down! Put him down!" There were plenty of people on the street, enjoying the warm night in lawn chairs, playing dominoes outside the bodega – some of them pointed and laughed as we ran by, a bunch of foolish white people running down the street yelling, "Stop him! Stop the man with the baby!" "Police, help!"

A cop car swung around the corner and whooped its siren. Dave froze, and I dropped the scissors to the ground. My mother caught up to us, gasping, as the officers got out of the car. "What's going on here? Sir, stay right there. Ma'am, what's the situation?"

I was in a daze. All the flashing lights, the endorphins. A nice officer gently shielded me with his jacket and led me into the squad car. What was happening? Was I in trouble? In a minute, my mom got in the car, Jake in her arms, bawling. Poor Jake. "Shhhh," I told him, petting his head and back. "Shhhhhh."

Two cops drove us the two blocks back home, and then Dave was escorted in by two other cops. He hurled his clothes into a bag, spewing his customary potpourri of threats and accusations.

"She tried to kill me," he said, indicating me with his head. "Did you see those scissors she had? They should be marked into evidence!"

The cops were unsympathetic. "We didn't recover any scissors," said one.

"You just pack," said the other.

Jake needed to be put down into his crib, but I wanted to stay in the same room as the cops. I wanted to make sure that they were taking Dave away with them, and that we were locking the door behind them, with the chain, and the police bolt, and that he was never getting back in.

"All right, hurry it up, let's go," said Cop Two.

"Thank you, Officers," my mother said, shaking her head. "I don't know what he would have done . . ."

"Oh, *fuck* you, Barb." A cop grabbed each of Dave's arms, and the cop from the kitchen grabbed the suitcase. They shoved him out the door, and he yelled back at us as it slammed behind him. "This isn't over! Barb? *This is not over!*"

"Oh, it's over," she swore.

A week passed, and she didn't take him back. She'd never stayed away from him this long. Then it was two weeks, then a month. A month! I didn't dare believe it. She wouldn't speak to him on the phone. She spoke only through her new attorney, Steinman. Dave left frantic clusters of messages – warnings, taunts, suicide threats. My mother recorded the messages on her new Steinmaninstalled phone recorder, logged them on a legal pad, then firmly deleted them.

She stood glaring at the phone and shook her head. "I can't believe I let this go on this long, Jan. When I think what this has done to you, to Jake . . ."

She teared up briefly, her green eyes glassy, then composed herself. I didn't say anything.

"I know you don't believe me anymore, Jan, and I don't blame you. I wouldn't believe me if I were you. You'll just have to see for yourself how serious I am."

Yep. That was about the size of it. I remained silent, arms folded, head down.

"Jan."

What? Did she want me to say it wasn't true? That I still trusted her? Maybe I should fetch her a crocodile handbag to match those crocodile tears? Either she would stay away from him or she wouldn't; I wasn't laying any bets, and I wasn't coddling any hopes.

"Jan . . ."

Her voice was less warning than usual, more pleading. I sneaked a look at her – her slender frame, slightly bent so that one shoulder was always higher, the circles under her eyes covered over with tan makeup.

I broke. "All I have to say is, I'm not living with him anymore. If you take him back, that's your choice, but I'm telling you now, I'll leave."

My mother's high chin wobbled, and her eyes filled again. The silence was like a vacuum, sucking all the air from the room. I was hit with the urge to rush in and equivocate. *Look, Mom, I didn't mean it, I just meant . . .*

No. I meant it.

She crossed her thin arms and nodded, tears dripping down her face. "I understand. I'm so sorry, Jan."

For a second there, I believed it.

"I know," I said. Before I could say more, I got up and left the room.

.   .   .

October. November. Sophomore year, 1984. I was fifteen, and not a virgin anymore, thanks to a lifeguard I met out at Rockaway Beach that summer. I'd failed out of one of the city's most competitive public high schools and was now attending a regular public school in Chelsea, where I continued my campaign of truancy, drug use, and casual sex. Jake was one and a half, toddling determinedly on his doughy, hot-dog-bun legs, and my mother was divorcing Dave. It had been three and a half months since the cops escorted him out. Dave was finally gone for good.

I relaxed into my old role as my mother's partner, schlepping the groceries with her, Jake strapped in his stroller, and I caught myself admiring her again, her determination and toughness, the nape of her neck straining as she picked up two full bags in each hand. My mother was thirty-seven, with two kids, three ex-husbands, no living parents, and nobody to lean on but herself. She'd been through a lot, I was now willing to admit – a lousy childhood with my crazy dead grandma, an abusive first husband, a baby when she was barely out of her teens. Unfortunately, she got mixed up with the wrong guy. She didn't ask for what happened.

And then she took him back.

It was a Thursday night in November, a week or two before Thanksgiving. I'd been working a cash register at a gourmet market after school, when I wasn't skulking around Washington Square Park; I got home from work around quarter to ten. The apartment was strangely quiet.

I called, "Hello?" Softly, so I didn't wake up Jake.

My mom was in her bedroom. "I'll be right out."

I dropped my book bag and went into the kitchen to make the soup. I'd already decided not to do my chem homework because it was too hard and I could probably copy it from someone the next day. The soup sputtered. I thought, *Ooh, maybe I'll take a bath.*

My mother came into the kitchen, still dressed in her patterned shirtdress and pantyhose. Work clothes, this late at night? She carried her cigarettes and an ashtray. This meant she wanted to talk.

"Jan," she started.

I knew right away.

"Oh, no."

"Listen to me, Janice."

My stomach flipped. I choked on a laugh, like I'd inhaled a dandelion puff. "You're not . . ." I couldn't speak. I backed away from the stove.

"Jan, you may think you know what I'm going to say, but I want you to understand . . ."

Oh my god. "I don't believe this." When did this happen? My mother's face was guilty, defiant. She must have been talking to him from work. Since when? A week? Just last weekend she was telling me how grateful she was going to be when the divorce papers were finally ready, and Dave was "permanent history," and it was just me and her and Jake, "for good."

"Jan, I need for you to at least listen to me . . ."

And I felt like I was staring into the sun, like my eyes were burning and my head was melting and everything inside was aflame. "Oh my god. Oh my god." I couldn't catch my breath. I had to get out right away.

"Janice!"

Dave was coming back. I had told her I was leaving if she took him back. And she was taking him back. This math only added up one way.

I walked out of the kitchen and into my bedroom, grabbed my book bag, and headed for the door. My mother stood by the door, arms folded.

She said, "*Where* do you think you're going?"

I had no idea.

"Out," I said. And I walked out.

3
THE REGULAR

Now, three weeks later, here I was, sitting in the TV room at the shelter's minors' wing like I'd been here all my life, watching a repeat of *Friday Night Videos* with eight other girls, two of them pregnant, all of us smoking. These days I was smoking Newport 100s instead of Marlboros; Alice and Hope, my girlfriends at school, wrinkled their noses and complained, "Now we can't bum cigarettes off you."

No such problem at the shelter, where the elongated Newport 100 was especially preferred because two people could go halfsies on it. Thus, the minute you pulled out a cigarette, someone said, "Gimme halfsies," and somebody else said, "You got another one of those?"

If you had three cigarettes or fewer in your pack, you could decline – "I only have one more after this, and my wish" – which was your "wish cigarette," the one you turned upside down as soon as you opened the pack while saying to yourself, for instance, "I hope I'm not, and I hope to god I never get, pregnant." You smoked your wish cigarette last, ruminating on the wish, and if you gave it away, you risked not finding your perfect new boyfriend or magically receiving a thousand dollars.

Because I was the white girl, people smoked all my cigarettes. "White girl, Jenny, Jane. Gimme one." I resented it but went along with it, griping to myself. If I didn't act friendly, it was confirmed that I was a stuck-up racist bitch. I'd been fighting a losing battle on that front ever since I "dissed some brothers" outside the Orange Julius while coming back from a shelter-sponsored trip to Forty-second Street to see *A Nightmare on Elm Street*. What did I do? I didn't even know. We were strolling down the Deuce, making crazy killer razor-claw fingers at one another, and a swarm of guys launched right at us, sucking their teeth and muttering suggestions, so I tried to skirt past them. Not two blocks later, the whole group's cutting their eyes at me and hissing, "Bitch. Stupid white ho."

Still, life here in the minors' wing was marginally more comfortable than at Main, where I'd spent my first night and morning. Whereas Main held maybe seventy-five girls at a time, half of them sleeping on foam mattresses on the floor, the minors' wing housed only fifteen girls in shared bedrooms in a private, four-story brownstone, with two nuns or counselors on duty at all times. My new bed was in a room on the third floor with two other girls, Big Perla and Treece. Big Perla was the size of a sumo wrestler, and she never spoke. Treece was a square-headed girl with square-rimmed Cazal glasses who hated my guts.

Treece's friend Sherri also hated my guts, and Sherri was psycho. Her fists were always clenched, her neck veins strained, and her nostrils flared; she was like a charging bull with cornrows. Sherri was about six months pregnant, her belly stuck out like a load of laundry in front of her, and she was determined to miscarry – often, when the nuns weren't looking, she'd take a flying leap at the arm of the sofa or smash her belly into the stair banister.

I'd already had a run-in with square-head Treece and Sherri the pregnant psycho, my very first week at the minors' wing. They were hanging out in our room one night after lights out, dancing by the window, fucking around with some guys standing down on the street, flashing them and miming blow jobs, whooping it up like it was Disney World. I was tired, and I knew Big Perla was trying to sleep too, and if the nuns had to come upstairs to shut us up, we would all get punished.

"Oh my gawd!" screeched Sherri, her big belly throwing distended shadows as she lurched around the room, heaving with laughter. I wasn't interested in a 7:30 P.M. curfew, or cleaning the stairs with a toothbrush, so I pulled the pillow over my ear and grumbled, "Shut up."

The men on the street were forgotten. "Shut up?" said Treece, suddenly behind me. She reached out and slapped me on the head. "I *know* white girl didn't just tell me to shut up."

"Oh yes she did," said Sherri, at the foot of my bed.

"Hey!" I said, as Treece jumped on top of me, pushing the pillow hard on my face. "*Mmmph!*"

I flailed in panic, the feet of the bed scraping and bumping on the floor as we thrashed, and the nuns immediately called up the stairs, "Ladies!" They were on their way. Treece got me with a fist to the side of the head, then scrambled back across the room to her bed as Sherri fled to her room. Sister Thomas Rita opened the door and hit the lights. Treece and I lay there panting, pretending to wake from a deep sleep. Perla lay there with her eyes and mouth shut, as usual.

"What just happened here?" demanded Sister Thomas Rita. She was a tall, broad-backed woman, formidable even in her sixties.

"Nothing," I said, my heart drumming loud in my ears. "I don't know, I was asleep."

"I didn't hear nothin'," said Treece, grumpy. "Sound like it came from upstairs."

Perla showed us her silent back, pillow over her ear.

Sister Thomas Rita wasn't buying it. "I *know* I heard something. In *this* room. Who else was in here?"

I shook my head and shrugged, mouth innocently agape. Treece continued to act affronted. "Nobody! We was sleeping!"

I could feel a tender spot throb where her fist had hit my head. "Honestly," I said, "we were."

Sister Thomas Rita squinted at me. She was a tough old nun, and she had no problem throwing you out for breaking the rules. No fighting was the first rule; fighting would get you thrown out of the shelter right then and there – both of you. Even if you were just defending yourself. I looked up and blinked at her, blameless.

Sister Thomas Rita left, unsatisfied, and Treece and I sank back in our beds. "I'ma catch up with you later," she promised me.

"Look, I'm sorry I said shut up, I apologize." *Jesus.*

I had not slept easy since that night. I was way on the tips of my toes. I waited until the last person was finished in the bathroom so I could be the last person in bed. I stayed out after school until dinner, and after dinner I stayed in plain view in the TV room until it was time for lights out. But if I ever happened to cross Treece or Sherri coming from the bathroom, or going down the stairs to the kitchen for chores, they'd press right up against me in my face and flex.

"White bitch."

And I'd do my best not to flinch, even at the fake punch that often followed, or the real shove. Just scurry away, get past it. I wouldn't be here forever.

Where was I going to go? That was the burning question. The counselors determined that "family reunification" was not a viable solution in my case – they were talking to me about foster care, or a group home. Scary, but exciting to think about a new life, one that didn't include any of my ostensible parents. As long as the shelter wasn't sending me back home, I'd go just about anywhere.

My mother had called the shelter twice so far. The first time, I called her back, revving up my indignation in advance so I wouldn't immediately cave in when she told me that Dave was gone and begged me to come home.

Which she didn't. "I don't know *what* is the matter with you," she said coldly, her heels echoing on the floor as she paced. "This is *unacceptable* behavior. You'd better get your butt home, pronto. You have *a lot* of explaining to do."

"*Me?*" Blood rushed to my face, swirling in my ears. There must have been some kind of mistake, I must have misdialed the phone – the lady on the other end was supposed to be crying right now, apologizing, swearing to make it up to me if I'd forgive her again. Instead I heard Dave in the background, clearing his throat like a bad actor, making his presence known. "You said you weren't taking him back, I told you. . . !"

She rolled over this like a tank. "You don't set the rules around here! Now you can come home right now, or I can throw away all of your belongings. If you don't live here, your stuff doesn't live here either."

I hung up the phone, went to the bathroom, and cried for about an hour.

I didn't return her second call.

. . .

Girls came in and out of the minors' wing. A girl named Bernadette, gawky with a big, flat nose, locked herself in the pantry with a knife – they had to call the nutwagon to come and get her, straitjacket and everything. Two girls, both named Tina, got thrown out in one night, after fighting each other over a bisexual boy hustler named Angel. A small, bow-backed Chinese girl came in one afternoon, stayed for about an hour, and sneaked out, never to be seen again.

Then my scary, square-head roommate Treece got bounced when she showed up two hours past curfew, trying to get in the door. Everybody knew, if you were even fifteen minutes late, the counselors were already packing your stuff in a plastic bag and people were claiming your leftover toiletries. You missed curfew, you didn't get back in the house, period, ever.

So Treece's ousting could not have been even remotely my fault, but of course Treece's hate mate Sherri tried to put the blame on me. I heard her talking loud about me in the room next door: "You can't trust that white bitch. She always running to the nuns, complaining out her neck. Watch, she gonna get me thrown out, too. Watch."

Sherri wasn't even waiting to catch me alone anymore, now she'd try to fight me right there in the TV room. "I hate that white bitch. She know I'm talking about her, but she too scared to look over. Bitch can't even look at me. Hah." Then she'd punch herself in the stomach. There was no possible response to this; I'd tried everything – laughing, scowling, leaving the room, addressing her: "I don't know what your problem is with me, Sherri, I never did anything to you."

Somebody mocked me from the corner, my corny white girl enunciation: "I *dewn't* know what your *per-ob-lem* is." I excused myself from the TV room.

Fortunately, not everyone hated me quite so much. This new girl, Roxanne, seemed very mellow. She and I found ourselves walking to the A train together one morning, and somehow we started talking about books. There were no books at the shelter except some old coverless Michener paperbacks, a World Factbook from 1973, and a beat-up copy of the Bible, which failed to grab my interest the one time I deigned to skim it.

"Who do you like to read?" Roxanne asked. "Who's your favorite author?"

I had to think about it so I didn't say Jackie Collins. "I guess . . . Kurt Vonnegut, or Khalil Gibran."

She nodded. "My favorite author is James Baldwin, you know him?"

" 'Sonny's Blues,' " I said. "He's really good."

"You know he's gay," she offered.

Aha. I should've figured. "That's cool."

Roxanne smiled wide. She had a broad face with a big, cheeky smile, which was purple and white against her dark brown skin. She had earring holes but no earrings. Her hair was short and natural, and she wore a blue workman's coat. "You all right, Jane."

I didn't correct her on my name.

Roxanne and I went to the laundromat together on the weekend, traded stories. She was from the Bronx, where she said she used to be a "Five Percenter."

"What's a Five Percenter?"

Roxanne rolled her eyes and shook her head, like I didn't want to know. "Girl, Five Percenters is the blackest black people there is. They're Islam, and they preach that the white man is the devil." She broke into her wide smile. "You don't want to come visit me in my neighborhood."

We watched our laundry turn in the dryers, all the clothes we owned except what was on our backs – my black sweater, purple with wear; the jeans and T-shirt I got from the donations room at the shelter. Everything else had been left in a bag on the curb in front of my mother's apartment.

"So, what are you doing here?" asked Roxanne, curious but not critical. Everyone else who asked seemed a little critical.

I gave her the short answer: "Stepfather." Roxanne nodded. It was a common answer. "How about you?"

"Mother," she said, sighing. "And father."

Yeah.

There was a pause where the next question would go, if the next question were said out loud. *So . . . how bad was it?*

"Your stepfather ever try anything with you?" she asked, raising her eyebrows like she was amused.

"No, he's . . . I mean, he's definitely crazy, but . . . no." Another pause.

"My father's been trying to have sex with me for years now," she said. "But he and my mom got divorced when I was little."

"Jesus." She was so nonchalant, I didn't want to overreact, but – Jesus. I mean, say what you want about my own crazy dad, at least he never tried to have sex with me.

"Yeah, he's always coming around my school, trying to talk to me. Telling me he wants to take me to a hotel, buy me things." She made a flapping puppet mouth with her hand. "Talking all this crazy stuff."

"That's crazy. They're all . . ." I shook my head.

She shook her head too. "Yeah."

Roxanne liked to keep a low profile at the shelter, where her "gay ass" was not embraced. She wanted to spend evenings downstairs in the kitchen doing homework, and I was only welcome to join her if I was going to be totally quiet, and not clowning or kicking her ankle. Sometimes I managed to calm down enough to work alongside her, with the hiss of the brownstone's steam heat shushing me. Other times the lure of the TV room was too great; I wanted to smoke or use the pay phone. I got restless, shuffled my papers too loud, and got a scowl that sent me upstairs.

What can I say? I was bored. In between being scared, and being angry, and feeling sorry for myself and deprived, and then feeling really proud of myself and full of adrenaline, I was bored. The shelter was dull, it was ugly, it was uncomfortable – wherever you sat was saggy and smelly. There was no privacy. There was nothing to do. It was like waiting at a bus station for days. People lolled around, enervated and cranky and hungry, hoping something or somebody interesting would distract them until it was their time to get shipped off someplace else.

Vondell was a distraction. She was one of the most beautiful women I've ever seen, and she was only twelve years old. When she came into the minors' wing, she lied and said she was seventeen, and she looked like it – she had a woman's face, full, round breasts, and a curvy waist and ass – but the counselors eventually came up with her legal name and birth date, and Vondell was busted. She was furious – she could have had a 9:30 P.M. weekend curfew. Instead, she had to be home by 7:00 every night.

Baby Vondell was a sensation in the house. She was everywhere, hanging off people's arms, laying front and center across the couch in the TV room, sucking her thumb, and I quickly became her favorite – well, one of her favorites, at least. She called me Mamma, as in "Mamma, you love me? Am I pretty? You gonna give me thirty cents?" Asking was she pretty – like she didn't know. She was a living, breathing plum, and she smelled like cocoa butter, sprawled out there on my lap.

I had to wonder if maybe Roxanne's tendencies were rubbing off on me, or if I was really this pathetically happy just to be liked by another girl in the house, even if it was insincere. Either way, I was acting like a chump. Roxanne came with me to buy a Klondike bar at the corner store, then laughed at me when I threw in a bag of Bon Tons for Baby Vondell. "Oh, no. That little girl is playing you."

I scoffed. I knew full well what Vondell was up to. I *chose* to let her play me, so I wasn't getting played. "She's not *playing* me. I *offered* to buy her some chips."

"Oh, you *offered*. After she went on for twenty minutes about how she's dying of hunger, and won't somebody bring her chips . . ." Roxanne did an apt impression of Vondell, with her lower lip pouted out, and I cracked up.

"Shut up, you're just jealous."

"Of who? Vondell? Pshoo." She punched my shoulder, grinning. "Get over yourself, girl, you ain't all that. And besides, I know you always love me the best."

"Friends," rapped Whodini over the radio. "How many of us have them?"

I'd given the number of the residents' pay phone to some people from school, but the phone never rang for me. Which was fine, whatever – they were new friendships, most of us were new sophomores at the school that year. It wasn't like we'd all been friends since the seventh grade. I didn't even have any friends since the seventh grade – I was a pariah in middle school, and my freshman year at Competitive High hadn't been much better. But this year, since I'd started at this new school in Chelsea, things were significantly different. I'd dropped into a decent-sized crew of new-wave party kids – skateboarders, art punks, potheads, and mods – that covered a full two tables in the lunchroom. The girls wore tight, pegged, purplish, black pants and shirts with cutout necklines; the guys doodled checkerboards in pen on their white high-top canvas sneakers. After school, we slouched around Washington Square Park, trying to mooch one another's pot; on weekends, we went to keg parties or dive bars or nightclubs like Danceteria. This was all recapped at the lunch tables on Monday.

"We stayed out *so late* on Friday," said my friend Alice, flipping her long, famous black hair. "We were having *such* a good time, we did *not* want to leave."

"That sounds fun," I said, over a mouthful of school lunch. School lunch was a shameful thing, but it was free with my voucher, and I was hungry.

"It was *really* fun," added my friend Hope. "Totally."

Alice continued playing with her mesmerizing hair, which fell straight down like waterfalls from both sides of her perfect part, like the Chinese girls' over in their corner of the lunchroom. Guys loved Alice's hair. They loved *Alice*, even though she was only a gawky sophomore, baby fat still apparent under her sharp chin – she acted way older than fifteen. Hope sat next to her at the chipped Formica table, chewing absently on her raggedy nail polish. She was shorter and curvier than Alice, with a strawberry blond bob and a sweet, kittenish face, usually set in a look of jaded disdain.

Alice and Hope and I were in the same homeroom together, and we shared the belief that everything about school was beneath us, so we had grouped up pretty quick. We ran around to parties and bars together, cut first period and got bagels, kept up on who the others hated and liked. On paper, Hope and Alice were my best friends. Sometimes, though, it was like they weren't even thinking about me.

"You should have come out with us," said Alice. Was she laughing at me? It was hard to tell with Alice; she had a habit of pursing her lips in a little pout when she came to the end of a sentence. "We missed you."

"Yeah . . . I have that curfew."

"That's right, oh my god. What is it, like nine o'clock? That totally sucks."

"*Totally* sucks," Hope agreed. Hope was more empathetic; she got grounded by her mom all the time. She usually went out anyway and suffered for it later. Sometimes I thought Hope was tougher than me, because she stayed at her mother's, while I ran to the shelter for protection. Her mom was at least as bad as mine.

Alice grabbed Hope's wrist. "I can't believe Ollie Wythe was there, he is so gorgeous."

"Oh my god, Ollie Wythe is *so* gorgeous."

Hope and Alice had a little shudder and whinny over gorgeous Ollie Wythe, a member of this pack of hot, alcoholic upperclassmen who called themselves "the Boyses." Coming in contact with any of the Boyses for any reason made Hope and Alice neigh like horses – "I saw Leland Banks in the stairway after fourth, *bbbrrrrrrr!*" "Ollie Wythe almost ran me over with his skateboard before first, *huhhhhhh!*" I had no encounters with the Boyses to report. I just kept shoveling in the Salisbury steak.

"So, what'd *you* do this weekend, Janice?"

NununUNununun, Nanice? I didn't want to be extrasensitive, but suddenly I was in a shit mood. I bit the inside of my cheek and tried to sound casual.

"Not much. Hung out. Went to the park on Saturday."

"Oh."

Yeah. Here's what I did that weekend: On Friday night, I ate a Klondike bar on a stoop with Roxanne. We sat outside in the cold December air until exactly 9:00 P.M., then we went back inside, where Baby Vondell smoked all my Newport 100s, and Sherri crossed her eyes and spat at me.

On Saturday I looked for a job. In the afternoon, I went to Washington Square in the cold, hoping someone would be hanging out and smoking pot. I watched the Rastafarians bounce soccer balls like hackey sacks and envied their customers. On Sunday it rained and I stayed in. It was my turn to sweep and mop all five flights of stairs and the hallways. That took about an hour and a half. I even did some homework. That's how bored I was.

I needed a new boyfriend, or some guy to spend time with. Me and the girls aimed high in our dating careers, but there were only two or three really top-status guys at school, and we couldn't all go after the same ones. Maybe, I thought, I should broaden my criteria. There was a guy from the basketball team in my computers class who was exceptionally well-built, though he had a skin problem. He was conservative and dull, with his collared sport shirts and his too-short hair, but he seemed interested in me, and he had that upper body.

I floated the notion by Hope over a cigarette in the fourth-floor bathroom. "What do you think of Andrew Winkler?"

Her nose wrinkled. "I don't know, dude . . . I guess he's got a nice body, but . . . he's not that hot . . . and he's not even that funny or anything."

"Oh, I know. He's totally in love with me. I'm like, 'No thanks, I only want to have sex with your shoulders and chest.' "

"Hah." Hope appreciated my toughness, as I did hers.

Despite the veto, I pressed on. I needed something to do after school. I was tired of sitting in the TV room at the shelter like a political protester, always passively resisting a beating. I deserved a little hands-on affection.

We should study together sometime, I proposed to Andrew via note. His reply: *I like to study naked.*

And that was what we called foreplay.

It was quickly arranged that I would go over to Andrew's on Friday to study naked. "We have to go right after school, though, because my mom gets home at five."

I rolled my eyes at Andrew's mommy. People who lived with their parents were such suckers. They had even less freedom than I did at the shelter. When I got my own apartment, they would all be jealous. "Whatever," I said, dismissive.

"And we can't smoke pot or cigarettes or anything in the house."

"Okay." Some date this was shaping up to be.

Still, I went. The bell rang after eighth period, and we both left by the back exit, as agreed – better not to parade down the block, lined with friends who would just stall and embarrass us. We walked briskly back to his apartment in the West Village. We didn't have anything to talk about on the walk. The only thing we'd ever really discussed was the logistics of this date, and now here we were, on it. Andrew was a nervous person, I realized, trotting beside him down Greenwich Avenue. Besides missing obvious answers in computers, and taking teasing way too personally, he was also a little bit of a granny. Oh well. I didn't respect him, I didn't even like him, but I didn't *dis*like him yet, so here we were.

He hustled me into his building, then the elevator, then the apartment, then his bedroom. No grand tour, no orientation. His room was dark blue with white trim. A desk, a basketball, a pile of laundered and folded clothes. A big boy's room.

"So," I said coyly, sitting on his bed. "Are we going to study?"

He said something like "Unh" and fell on me. This was the first kiss, the climax of all the waiting. It was wet and flabby. Our chemistry was inert, all the molecules dropping straight to the floor, refusing even to roll. I thought, *Ugh.* I wondered what he was thinking. He was in his own world, eyes squeezed shut, pimples pulsing. "Take off your shirt," I said seductively, as he blindly humped my upper thigh.

Ah yes, there they were, the pectoral muscles. The shoulders, the upper abs. Something to focus on while this nasty operation was under way. God, he really didn't know what he was doing. Stab, stab. "Here." I realized, *He's a virgin. He's just using me to have sex for the first time, so he can say he did it.* And why was I using him again? For the romance?

I thought, *Let's just get this over with.*

It didn't take long. It never did. The cleaning up was gross. I splashed water everywhere, trying to bathe in the sink like a pigeon in a puddle. Spruce myself up before I bolted up to the shelter. I caught myself in the mirror, eye makeup smudged, hair mussed, neck bitten, face red. Busted.

Here we are again, I said.

The regular, my reflection replied.

We smirked at each other and turned away.

4
CHRISTMAS

Mid-December, and tinsel wreaths hung all over Times Square. Drunks yelled "Meh Kissmiss!" as they shoved their worn cups in your face. It was snowy, cold, and dark by five. My feet were consistently wet. I didn't have a winter coat. I'd walked out of my mother's apartment wearing my denim jacket over a sweater, and that was what I was still wearing, every day, until people couldn't help but notice.

"Aren't you cold?" asked Alice, stomping her feet and frowning as we smoked on the corner before school.

Hope stomped and frowned beside her. "Dude, you definitely need a new jacket."

Yes, *apparently*. But I'd refused the ugly doofus winter coat they offered everybody free at the shelter – I took the free socks, underwear, and sweatshirts, plus some donated sweaters that were kind of cool, in a retro way, but I was not going to walk around in public in an ugly doofus shelter coat. I'd rather freeze in my denim jacket, with its safety pins and marker scrawls and cigarette smell. And I kept planning to get myself something warmer at the Salvation Army, maybe a men's overcoat.

"Yeah . . . I'm probably going to get one this weekend. I have to Christmas shop anyway."

Hope and Alice swapped looks, like, Christmas shop? Who was I kidding? I ignored the looks and regarded the toe of my sneaker, twisting as it crushed the butt of a cigarette.

I *was* going shopping. For Jake, if no one else. I had money. I still had some in the bank from my old cashier job. And I was going to get another job, too, it was part of my new plan: drop out of school, get my

GED, become a secretary or something, and get my own place. Even if I had to be a cashier full-time, at five dollars an hour, that was still two hundred a week, eight hundred a month – I could make it work. I could get a room at the Y, or one of the flophouse hotels in Hell's Kitchen. The Hotel Mansfield Hall had semiprivate bathrooms, and they didn't care if you had a small fridge and a hot plate; I asked. Of course, the place was crawling with jittery freaks. And the guy in the Plexiglas booth in the lobby gave me the hairy eyeball.

"Aren't you a little young?" he asked, folding his meaty arms over his greasy T-shirt.

"No," I said, insulted, like when I got carded at bars, like, *how dare anyone question my maturity?* "I'm nineteen, I have my ID at home."

"Uh-huh."

The guy didn't buy it. Well, fuck him, "a little young." I could go down the block to Fascination on Broadway and get a fake ID for five dollars, they'd make it say I was sixty-three if I wanted. What did that prove? Age was just a number. I was already on my own, looking out for myself, more grown-up than any grown-up I knew. So what if I was only fifteen?

My guidance counselor, Ms. Glass, shook her frizzy head at me. "Hon, you're only fifteen! You're too young to take the GED. You've got to stay in school or you're a delinquent. It's the law."

I sat in her plastic chair and felt my throat close, tears of frustration forming. "But listen, Ms. Glass, I have to move out of the shelter, because I've been there more than thirty days, and you're only supposed to be there thirty days, and they keep saying they don't know where I'm going to go, and I'm just trying to . . . to take care of myself, to survive, you know?"

She didn't get it either. "Hon, you can*not* take care of yourself, you're too young! You have to work with them at the shelter to find you a placement. You can't live on your own!" She barked – *hah!* – and shook her head some more. "For god's sake, you're my daughter's age."

Well, what the fuck that had to do with anything, I didn't know. Ms. Glass was seriously no help to me at all. As a matter of fact, Ms. Glass was a useless dingbat, and her stupid pig daughter could go fuck herself too. I left her office and slipped quietly out the back entrance of the school, headed for Washington Square Park, done with school for the day.

I'd been at the shelter for about six weeks, almost two weeks past the deadline, and they still hadn't found me a bed. I didn't fully understand what was going on behind the scenes with my case. When I asked, the counselors told me, "We should have something for you soon. Just hang tight."

There was a lot of comparison shopping among the girls waiting for placement. Some people knew a lot more than I did about the various options. Foster care was the worst, they agreed – a girl named Yvette told me, "They just stick you with whatever stranger they got, like a dog from the pound. You don't even know them. They could be real strict, too. It's worse than living at home. I ran away twice from foster homes. Fuck that. I'm trying to get into a group home, otherwise, I don't know. They could arrest me, I'm not going back to foster care."

Group homes were supposed to be better than foster care, but they were also supposed to be strict, especially the religious ones. I'd heard from the start that they were thinking of sending me to a group home, and I knew Roxanne was in line for one, too.

"This place is bad enough, I'm not going to live in some convent," I told Roxanne, huddling next to her on a stoop. "I don't care. I'll go live with my boyfriend from school." He didn't technically exist yet but would surely materialize any day.

Roxanne was more practical. "I just want someplace where I can still get to my school. They're talking about putting me way out in Brooklyn, in Canarsie – that's too far. I don't want to switch out of my school. And how'm I supposed to get to you from Canarsie?"

I leaned into her and pushed her with my shoulder. She pushed back. We did this a lot – pushed each other, leaned on each other – to punctuate a comment. Sometimes we just stayed arm to arm, mooshing against each other in a kind of Greco-Roman shoving match. Then I'd go to light a cigarette, and she'd push me away, coughing exaggeratedly and waving her hand in front of her face.

"Well, I have to find something soon. I'm past thirty days here. They could throw me out anytime."

Roxanne pooh-poohed this. "They're not throwing you out. If they were gonna throw you out, you'd have *been* thrown out. They're probably gonna send you to a group home, and they're just waiting to see where a bed opens up."

Easy for her to say. She had ten whole days until her deadline, and nobody was actively trying to beat her ass. I pulled away and lit a cigarette. "I'm just saying, they better find me something soon."

Roxanne leaned over and smooshed me. "You'll be all right."

I wasn't so sure. Roxanne wasn't home much these days, between school and her new job – things were changing at the shelter, and not for the better. My nemesis Sherri was still there, way past her own deadline, waiting for a bed to open up in one of the scarce group homes for teen mothers. Now seven months pregnant, she was angrier than ever, slamming into walls and beating her legs with her fists, pounding her hand down at the dinner table to make the plates jump.

"That fucking white bitch make me so sick I can't even eat!"

Everybody around her at the far end of the table laughed. Sister Thomas Rita glared at them.

"We will have *none* of that," she ordered. "I will give everybody a warning."

Stuff like this made things nine or ten times worse for me. Now I was a nun's bitch, on top of the already established racist, snitch, cracker, and ho.

Sherri had lost the support of my erstwhile roommate Treece, but now she was backed by two newer girls, Earletta and Cookies. Earletta was tall and mean, and she asked upon first sight of me, "What *her* white ass is doing here?" – not in a friendly, interested way, either. Cookies was short and pregnant, and equally militant in her approach. Together, the three of them went out of their way to make my life suck.

If I put something down and left the room, that thing was gone. My chem book, my fresh pack of cigarettes, my sweater. I kept my shoes on at all times; I couldn't afford to lose them. And if Earletta wanted to come up right behind me in the TV room and literally breathe all over the back of my neck, I had to sit there and pretend that it wasn't happening, or that it didn't bother me.

"Whatever you want to do," I muttered to myself.

"You say something to me, white girl?"

Nothing. Just kept watching the TV like there wasn't nasal slobber on me.

It wasn't just the three of them, either; it was the whole house. Popular sentiment had shifted against me, not that it had ever shifted toward me at any point, and whatever status I might have once had as a novelty – See how white girl looks with cornrows! Watch white girl dance! – had worn off. Even Baby Vondell didn't love me anymore, or not in public, anyway. Sometimes when nobody was around, she'd still latch on to my arm. "Mamma, you wanna hear about my new boyfriend? His name's Justice, and he's so fine, he a real proud black man . . . Mamma, you got a cigarette for me?" Then ten minutes later she'd be blowing smoke in my face, laughing at me.

Roxanne wasn't catching most of this, and if she did, there wasn't much she could say. She wasn't afraid to defend me; she just knew, as I did, that it would only make things worse. She'd heard that she was on her way out, shipping off to the group home in Canarsie right after New Year's. That was almost two hours away from her school on the subway, but what was she going to do?

More to the point, what was *I* going to do?

At least Christmas Eve at the shelter was festive – raucous, even, in the overheated house, but genially so, because there was an extra-big meal of fresh turkey and ham and all good holiday things, plus extra desserts. Everybody got three dollars cash, and they were giving us gift bags and having entertainment after curfew. It was a rare good night to be at the shelter.

"Where's Vondell?" asked Sister Thomas Rita, counting heads at the dinner table. "Has anybody seen Vondell?"

Quietly, from the end of the table: "Seen her suckin' a dick on Tenth Ave." Snickers, muffled by the general din.

"Sister, I di'nt seen her, but if she miss her curfew tonight, she said I could take her shampoo."

Somebody muttered, "Dumb bitch is missing out, because this food is for real."

No kidding. Turkey and gravy, sweet potatoes and stuffing, green beans and cranberry sauce – this was *food*. Not the frozen spinach and Cream of Wheat we usually made do with. I took myself another helping of everything. Too bad for Vondell.

After dinner, me and Roxanne and a few other girls lugged over to Rockefeller Center to look at the tree. I had planned to be unimpressed – so what, it was a *dead tree* – but it turned out to be pretty spectacular, the sheer mammoth size of it, twinkling like an arcade game.

"Damn," said VeeVee, her head tipped all the way back to her neck. "That shit is real?"

All of Fifth Avenue was lit with white lights, all of Central Park South. Well-dressed people came out of the hotels, rode by in carriages, smiling and looking happy. There was a sparkling fresh coat of snow on the ground, and the night was crisp and thrilling on our faces.

"It is so beautiful tonight." Roxanne turned to smile at me, wet-eyed. "I can't believe it."

I reached out my hand. She took it and put both our hands in her pocket, pulling me close alongside her.

Back at the house, there was cocoa with little marshmallows in it, but *real* little marshmallows – not the dehydrated package kind – left over from the sweet potatoes. Then they gave us all gift bags. Inside were sweaters, some nail polish and lipstick, and these educational video games that nobody had a player for. The video games got tossed around the TV room and mostly ended up under the couch, as everyone shrieked and started their manicures.

One gift bag sat unclaimed – Baby Vondell still had not returned. Now she had blown her curfew by two hours, and girls were excited.

"Where she at?"

"She think they not gonna discharge her because it's Christmas Eve?"

"That's some messed up shit, if a nun throw you out in the snow on Jesus' birthday."

"So what? That bitch ain't the Virgin Mary."

Roxanne offered me her tube of Lady Ebony lipstick. "Here, make yourself look nice for a change." I mooshed her, and she sat on me. Sherri cut her eyes at us and stage-whispered to Cookies. *Fuckin' dykessss.*

The entertainment that night, besides Vondell's absence, was three hippies with guitars playing Christmas carols and Beatles tunes. "This shit is corny," complained Yvette, but soon she was singing along to "Frosty the Snowman." The hippies stayed past midnight, way past the regular lights-out time, until the counselors finally broke it up and sent us to bed – bellies swollen, nails tacky with new paint, visions of secure housing dancing in our heads.

5

RESOLUTION

Finally, the news came down from on high – delivered by a nun, no less – there was an opening at a group home on the Upper West Side. "You're lucky to get this placement," Sister Thomas Rita advised me, peering severely over the tops of her glasses. "Make sure you pass your interview."

Roxanne was impressed. "Upper West Side," she said, eyebrows high. She could get to her school in thirty minutes from the Upper West Side; why was she getting sent out to Canarsie instead? Because I was white and middle-class? I ducked my head, ashamed of my unfair advantage, but Roxanne chose to be happy for me. "I'll come visit you," she declared. "We can chill in Central Park."

I demurred. "I'll probably fail my interview anyway."

Roxanne had passed hers the week before. She was leaving in a few days, packing her two small bags' worth of stuff, taking the A train down to the L train and sitting on that L train until the end of the line. Pulling up to a group home eight long blocks from the subway, and checking in with a whole new set of counselors and roommates and rules. Dumping her two small bags' worth of stuff on the bed, still warm from someone else's half-homeless ass.

"You'll do all right," she advised. "Just smile at them, and tell them how much you like school."

This was never going to work. I leaned forward and buried my face in my hands. A horrible thought jerked me upright again. "They don't test your pee for drugs, do they?"

"You better hope not," she said, laughing at me. "Pothead."

Roxanne could laugh all she wanted; I was serious. I declined a lunchtime joint behind the auditorium with Hope. "I might have to take a drug test for this group home."

She nodded, mouth full of escaping smoke, and generously waved her arm in front of me to clear away the pot molecules. "Sucks," she croaked.

"Yup." It smelled like decent pot, too, like syrup and sweat, not like the harsh schwag we usually scraped up.

Hope took another big hit, held it, and blew it professionally out the corner of her mouth. "My mom threatened to drug-test me. She thinks I'm stealing her pot. I'm like, 'You're crazy.' " I nodded. Hope pinched from her mom's pot all the time, but only tiny bowlfuls here and there, the occasional bud – nothing anybody would notice. "I think she's weighing it. She's so fucking paranoid, I hate her."

The pungent smoke was alive, curling into my nose and throat. I caved, extending my fingers in an open pinch. "Just one hit."

Hope was on record as hating her mother, as was I. Alice was mostly annoyed by her mom, who she considered flaky and dippy and an obstacle to anything fun, but Alice's mom still did nice things for her sometimes, which made Alice roll her eyes in discomfort. She just wanted to hate her stupid mother without remorse.

Hope wheezed out another slow lungful. "We should totally move in together. My mother's driving me crazy. I'm dying to get out of my house."

"We totally should." I thrilled at the idea. With Hope onboard, I could really put a plan into action. "Seriously, I'm not even kidding."

"I know, me neither. We just have to get jobs . . ."

"We could get, like, a loft in SoHo. . . ."

"We should ask Alice, too. She'd prob'ly be down."

"Oh," I said. "Yeah."

"I know her mom is driving her nuts, too."

Yeah. I didn't usually like to compete over shitty moms, because Hope's mom still smacked her with a hairbrush, or whatever she could throw at her. Hope was definitely in the race. As was Roxanne, whose mother beat her up and threw her out into the street when she caught her with another girl. As was Vondell, whose mother beat her up and threw *her* out into the street when she caught her with her forty-year-old stepfather, like it was Vondell's idea to be twelve years old and sucking his dick. As for Alice, she was not so much in the running.

"Yeah," I agreed, deflated. Hope wasn't serious about moving out, I realized, she was just baked. And now I was baked, too, and I was probably going to fail my group home interview for having big chunks of pot in my pee, and I had to go to chem and I didn't have my homework. "I gotta go. I'll catch up to you later."

Hope stubbed the end of the joint out against the wall and knocked my fist with hers. "Later, J."

It was the worst interview of my entire life.

First, there was the special anti-drug-test tea I got from the health food store, which made me jiggle my leg like a maniac and run to the ladies' room every five minutes. Maybe it was going to mask the pot in my system, but first it was going to make me look like an incontinent cokehead.

Then my mom showed up. And if I had to pee before, I really almost wet myself when I saw my mother, Barb Rosen herself, stride on into the waiting room of the group home's administrative offices in Midtown, in her work clothes with her briefcase, all dolled up like Super Professional Working Mom. Nobody had warned me she was going to be here – I was baffled, totally thrown. I hadn't seen my mother in months, not since the night I left home, and I hadn't planned on seeing her, maybe ever again.

She announced herself to the receptionist, then sat down a chair away from me, grimly smiling.

"What are you doing here?" I hissed, incredulous.

She flipped open her briefcase and sighed, annoyed. "Trust me," she said drily. "There are plenty of other places I'd rather be."

I couldn't get over the sight of her – her same old camel-hair overcoat, her new, shorter hairdo. I'd kind of thought that she'd wither and die without me, that she'd be too racked with guilt and worry to get out of bed in the mornings, but look at her – she was up and around and getting her hair cut. "They called you?"

She addressed the inside of her briefcase. "The home? Oh, yes. We had a loooong talk."

She sounded like Dave again; I felt the antipathy wafting off her. My leg went from jiggling to jackhammering, and my bladder swelled until it felt like I was going to weep pee.

A pointy-faced brunette woman in a red pantsuit came into the waiting room. "I'm Miss Poulos. Are you Barb?" She smiled and extended her hand to my mother like they were old friends. I sat unacknowledged in my chair like an imbecile.

"And you must be Janice." She turned to me. Her hawkish face was icy. No extended hand. "Follow me."

Within minutes, it was clear: I'd been blindsided. Whatever I'd been expecting – a quick Q and A, an inkblot test, maybe a conversation like the one I'd had with the nun the first night at the shelter – I was grievously mistaken. The next forty-five minutes were like a military interrogation.

"Your mother tells us you have problems with drugs and promiscuity, Janice. What do you have to say about that?"

"There's also the matter of the truancy," my mom added.

"I missed school going to family court with *you*," I protested, bewildered, gripping the arms of my chair.

"Obviously, Janice is a very angry young girl . . ."

"*And* she has a problem with acting out . . ."

"Poor impulse control," Poulos agreed.

Really? Because I was doing a heroic job of controlling the impulse to pick up the letter opener on Miss Poulos's desk and stab them both. The interview continued in this vein: "It's best to address the root of the problem as early as you can." "My *husband* and I couldn't agree more." I stopped defending myself and sat with my arms folded, declining to answer Miss Poulos's pointed questions.

Until: "Why do *you* think you've found yourself in this situation, Janice?" Then I couldn't resist.

"Because my stepfather's a psycho. Ask her, she called the cops! A bunch of times! And then she took him back!"

"Mm-hmm. But the question is, What's *your* role in all this?"

My mother threw up her hands. "Oh, *she's* the wounded innocent."

I turned to her, agape. "This is *my* fault?"

She looked me dead in the forehead, her chin high. "You never should have left home!"

Miss Poulos was smiling. Sometimes ugly people look nicer when they smile, but not her. She looked uglier. She looked like she had bugs in her teeth. I held my aching stomach full of pee. I said, "I have to go to the bathroom."

"We'll be finished here soon. I'd still like you to answer my question."

The sisters at the shelter were going to kill me. "I don't think this is the right place for me," I squeaked, tearing up. I rose partway from my seat, painfully, trying not to leak.

"This is exactly the right place for you," said Miss Poulos. "And right now, this is your only option."

I sank back into the chair, limp. Poulos smiled all the way to her back teeth. I shielded my face with my hands as I started to cry.

"Now I think we're getting somewhere," she said.

I'm fucked, I wrote to Alice during English. *I'm so fucking fucked, it's not even funny.*

Alice tossed her hair, looking back at me with sympathy and alarm. The note came back a minute later. *What happened now?*

They want to put me in a juvie home. I might as well go to fucking jail.

Alice tossed her hair again and shook her head, copying some stuff off the blackboard. Mr. Tschudy was going on about Mark Twain and the picaresque and a bunch of useless shit as always. School was beyond irrelevant; these days, it functioned mostly as a clearinghouse for drumming up drugs, sex, or shelter. I doodled a skull and some flowers on my note to Alice, pretending to copy like everyone else.

I need to find someplace to stay.

Maybe Alice would invite me to crash at her place. That would be so great. Even if it was for a few weeks – we would have so much fun. I'd only met Alice's mom once, and she was chill enough, drinking her mint tea in a peasant skirt, listening to Olivia Newton-John. And she seemed to like me all right; I always put on a little show for other people's parents, acting superfriendly and polite, and it tended to work, except with Hope's mom, who hated all of Hope's friends on principle. Alice's mom was much sunnier, and often absent, and that made her an ideal foster mom to me.

The note came back from Alice. *That sucks. What are you going to do?*

Um, I don't fucking know, Alice, that's what I'm saying. She turned back and made her pouty face at me to indicate concern. I crumpled the note, shook my head, and dragged my finger across my throat. *I'm dead.*

Poulos was right, I had no other option. Hope's house was out, so was Alice's. Andrew Winkler, my erstwhile fling, was now going out with a tall, pretty girl who had once been pictured in *Seventeen* magazine. She was a virgin, and they were in love. I would not be living at Andrew's.

I could take off, I supposed. I could take all my stuff with me one day, miss curfew, and never come back, the way Vondell did on Christmas Eve. The shelter filed a runaway report on her and closed her case – she wouldn't be going into foster care after all. Then, not two weeks later, Roxanne and I saw Vondell hanging around the men's bathroom at the Port Authority with some pit-faced guy in zebra-striped weight lifter's pants.

"Nice," Roxanne observed. We watched Vondell wobble over to a commuter in her stilettos, sniffling. She looked like either her ass or her feet hurt her very much.

"Jesus Christ, you think she's . . . ?"

Roxanne gave me the world-weary look she reserved for moments of extreme naïveté on my part.

I shuddered. "Jesus Christ."

Maybe I would not take off.

Roxanne left that Friday. She had her two bags' worth of stuff packed, and she was taking her shampoo, thank you, so bitches who wanted to scam on it could just step off.

"Help me carry all this to the train, woman." It wasn't even that much stuff, she just wanted to say good-bye. We trudged through the slush to Fiftieth Street.

"I hope it'll be good," I said. "At your place."

"It'll be all right," she grumbled. "It's no Upper West Side, but . . ."

I mooshed her. "Shut up, man, that place is a jail. I'm not going. I don't know what I'm going to do. I'm going to come out to Canarsie and hide under your bed."

"Any time, baby. Any time."

We got to the subway, the station we walked to together most mornings. She turned to me and extended one arm. I came in for a hug. I felt her bury her face in my neck, the wet of her breath as she kissed me.

"I'ma miss you, Cracker."

"I'ma miss you too. Bitch."

She broke from me and looked at me, mock-stern. "I'm serious, now, you take care of yourself."

"You too."

She turned to go down the subway stairs, bags slung heavy across her chest. I wanted to say, "Wait!" have her turn around like in a movie and run back to me. But there was nothing to wait for.

"I'll see your white ass later then," she said over her shoulder, and descended. She didn't turn around. I watched her disappear, then I walked back to the shelter, alone.

Sherri came for me the next day.

It was another cold, wet weekend afternoon, and I was spending it inside. I cleaned the kitchen, as instructed by the chore roster, then settled in to watch some TV, except nobody could pick a channel, and the inevitable argument that followed was boring. I didn't feel like calling anyone. I wandered into the far corner. It was overly hot in the brownstone, but residents weren't allowed to open or close windows or blinds. We weren't allowed to take things out of or put things into the fridge. We weren't allowed to touch the stove, the lights, or the counselors' phone. We had to walk around like amputees.

I thought about going out. I got the tweed overcoat I'd liberated from the donations room, put on my sneakers, and grabbed my bag, but when I looked outside at the sleet, I lost my enthusiasm for trolling

Washington Square. There were only so many times I could walk up and down West Eighth Street, MacDougal Street, Sixth Avenue. Nobody was going to be out smoking pot in the sleet, and I couldn't afford a bag of my own. I couldn't even afford the subway downtown. I was finally broke. I'd get another job when I moved to . . . wherever. To the group home, I supposed. It was better than a bench in the park.

Now that I was resigned to going to the group home, I just wanted it to happen. It was way past time to get the fuck out of the shelter, as Sherri and her girl Earletta reminded me every day. "Ain't there supposed to be some kind of deadline on you? You ain't pregnant, why you got an extension? 'Cause you white?" Other girls agreed, it was totally racist. "And you in here taking up a bed from a sister! From a pregnant girl! Some black pregnant girl probably out in the street because you got her bed, how you feel about that?"

I felt like shit about it. I felt like a fraud. Obviously, I did not belong here, I was out of my league. My stepfather never tried to molest me. I wasn't abused in foster care. I was not pregnant, and I had no kids. I had nothing to complain about. My life was great.

The afternoon thickened around me, the oppressive heat mingling with the rat-a-tat of the sleet on the roof until I was hypnotized. The TV was so loud it became a drone, and the sharp rise and fall of voices – "You ugly, with your face scars, you ugly face-scar bitch." "Shut up, you uglier, you ugly dark black cocksucker" – was as predictable as ocean waves. I sat, then lay down, on the patch of rug in the corner behind the sofa, resting my head on my schoolbag like a pillow, pulling my coat over me. It was warm and muffled inside my little coat-tent, about as peaceful as a room full of shouting, cranky, pregnant, or premenstrual teenage girls can get. I dozed off.

Next thing I knew, someone was sitting on my chest, my coat pressed hard against my face, and I was choking.

"Mmmph." I rocked my body violently, swinging at the crushing weight on my ribs. I couldn't breathe in. I pedaled my legs spastically and swung. The weight moved, and the coat shifted. I sucked in air.

It was Sherri. She scrambled on top of me again. I smothered underneath her as she kneed me in the side, landing random punches to my head and arms. "Mmmph!"

I struggled, half under my overcoat, flopping like a desperate fish, rolling and swinging blindly. I got a knee in her stomach and pushed, and I felt her fall to the side. I scuttled backward like a crab. She swung a hand at me, and I saw a flash – a tiny knife, no bigger than her finger – as it came toward my face.

Something just scratched my brow – her nails? the knife? – as I scrambled, gargling with panic, feeling her grab for my shins. I kicked her off me; she came back strong. "*Hey!*" I screamed. She was everywhere, her legs and arms engaging me on all fronts – going for my throat, my face, my knees. "*Hey!*"

The TV was on too loud, the counselors' office too far, and if anyone else in the room noticed what was happening, I was just lucky they didn't jump in. Sherri lunged at me with her stabbing hand, and I kneed her hard, twisting away. "*Hey!*"

I was on my feet, bag and coat in hand, flying, flying over the stair banister, down the stairs, barreling right past Sister Thomas Rita and out the door – running for two blocks as fast as I could before I dared slow down to breathe.

I stumbled around Times Square. It was still sleeting, and now it was dark. I was missing dinner – in an hour and a half, I'd be missing curfew. I didn't know where to go. I stopped at a pay phone and called Hope.

"She's at Alice's," Hope's mom snapped. "I'm on the other line."

I didn't have another quarter on me to call Alice's.

I kept my hand in front of my face to block the stinging ice, slogging through the spreading puddles of slush toward Port Authority, the closest shelter from the weather. Lots of other people, I saw, had the same idea. There were two kinds of people at Port Authority – people who were in a hurry to get somewhere, and people who had no place to go. It was easy to tell who was which.

I went into the women's bathroom and looked at the scratch on my forehead. It wasn't anything, but it kind of burned. I washed my hands and face, and the scratch bled a little. I stared at myself in the mirror, pale and trembling.

Behind me, I could see an old woman approaching, hunched and shambling, a scarf tied around her thick, swollen face and crumpled newspapers stuffed between her layers of shirts and pants. She smelled like the bathroom, but more so. She stopped in front of me, and her gums worked hard to get the sound out over her wobbling jaw. "Gah quarter? Gah quarter?"

I swallowed a gag. "I'm sorry."

Her gray lips trembled, spit thick in their corners; she reached out a cupped, withered hand in my direction. "Miss, 'm homeless; 'm homeless, miss."

Yeah – me too. I started breathing through my mouth, practically panting in the humid chill of the bathroom. "I'm sorry," I said again. Her cracked red palm stared at me like a bloody eye.

"Help, miss."

I was going to faint and crack my head open on the floor; I was going to die an indigent in the bathroom at Port Authority if I did not get out right away. "I'm sorry," I said and took off in a blind stagger – out the door, back into the street, and toward the shelter, the only place I knew to go.

It was chaos back at the house – nuns shouting, girls cursing, counselors storming up the stairs. I came in and skirted the wall, hoping to be invisible. "Says who!" I heard Sherri yelling from the third floor. Someone slammed a dresser drawer. "You can't send me to another shelter, I didn't do nothing!"

The crowd in the TV room was rowdy. "They sayin' she had a knife on her?" "How'd they find it?" "They discharging her right now?" "They referring her to Bellevue, I heard." "That pregnant bitch is crazy anyway."

From upstairs: "I never even touched the bitch!" Slam! "That's enough! You're going, now!"

Before I could duck away, they were thundering down the stairs – Sherri, surrounded by a swarm of nuns and counselors, her one suitcase worth of stuff packed into a clear plastic garbage bag, a ragged brown bear visible on top. They swept past us, down another flight and out the front door, and then I heard the door slam and Sherri howling on the sidewalk.

"I didn't do nothing! You can't discharge me! It wasn't my fault!"

Sister Thomas Rita came huffing back upstairs, face dark and flushed. She spied me cowering in the corner.

"Get your things from your room," she told me, brusque. "You're sleeping in the office tonight."

The entire TV room turned to look at me. I kept my head down and nodded to the nun. The entire TV room turned away. I heard them as I clomped up the stairs to get my things.

"That white girl was out to get her." "That's a damn shame, they throw a pregnant girl on the street like that." "She lucky she sleeping with the nuns tonight."

I was lucky to be sleeping anywhere, or I would have been lucky, had I been able to sleep. But all I could see when I closed my eyes was the toothless crone haunting the Port Authority bathroom; Sherri, trudging through the slush; and the sad, glassy eyes of her ragged brown bear.

Two days later, I packed my stuff and took the subway uptown to the group home on West Seventy-fifth Street. I didn't say good-bye to anyone at the shelter, nor did I leave any forwarding address.

I spoke to Roxanne one more time. I'd been at the group home for six weeks, and I'd sort of blocked out everything that had happened before. My scratch had mostly healed. I stopped touching the spot. Then one night after dinner, me and my seven new housemates were sitting around the living room watching TV, and when the residents' phone rang it was somehow for me.

"What up, woman?"

That unmistakable lilt. "Roxanne!" As good as it was to hear her deep, mellow voice, I felt suddenly guilty, caught out, like I'd welshed on a debt. "I'm glad you found me."

"Yeah, me too. How you doin'?"

"I'm all right," I said. "How are you?"

Roxanne was good. Spending a lot of time on the subway. "I got a girlfriend here," she bragged. "She's cuter than you."

"Hah, impossible."

"No, true."

"That's awesome," I said. "That's really great."

"Yeah." She chuckled, dry. "And they arrested my father again. He kept on coming by my school, trying to talk to me, and it turns out he was bothering some of these younger girls, too. Exposing himself."

"Jesus."

"Yep. I think they're locking him up for a while this time. He won't be bothering me anymore."

"Congratulations," I said.

"Thanks." She sounded pleased.

By all accounts, Roxanne was thriving – a group home, a girl-friend, and her father safely in jail. We chatted for a few minutes more, then her change started to run out, and the recorded voice interrupted us. "*Please de-po-sit ten cents for the next five min-utes.*"

She gave me her number, and I promised to call. "You better," she warned me. "I don't want to have to come up there and kick your white ass."

"I will," I swore. "I'll talk to you soon."

I never spoke to Roxanne again.

PART TWO

Loco parentis

6

GROUP THERAPY

"What *is* your problem, child?"

I was sitting in a circle with my seven new housemates for our weekly group therapy session, watching wide-eyed as one of our counselors, Mavis, chewed out my roommate, Genie the JAP, for throwing her schoolbooks on the floor. Mavis was a large, regal West Indian woman with a booming voice. Her tall batik head wrap remained erect, even as she waved her finger like a baton.

"You have *nuh* respect for yourself, you have *nuh* respect for others, and you have *nuh* excuse for that kind of behavior!"

Genie the JAP's voice was too loud, as usual, and her plump, ivory face was getting red. "What! I didn't do anything! I went like this with my arm" – *swoosh* – "and now I'm in trouble? You hate me! You're just trying to send me to Treatment!"

"Do you *want* to go to Treatment, girl? Is that what you're trying to tell us?"

Me and the six other girls who weren't getting roasted – Becky the Baby, Shirley the Nympho, Indira the Bully, Julie the Snitch, Gladys the Quiet One, and Shanita Who Could Squirt Breast Milk – gaped around the circle at one another, wincing in sympathy. Nobody wanted to go to Treatment. Treatment was when the group home had you legally pulled out of school and placed in an all-day "attitude adjustment program" at a nearby rehab center, where you had to spend eight hours a day cleaning toilets and chanting slogans alongside a bunch of kids who used to inhale paint fumes *on purpose*. Even if you didn't do drugs, even if you'd never done them, the group home could still elect to send you to Treatment, just for your behavior, which blew my mind nearly inside out. To be sure, I was being extra careful not to throw any books on any floor, à la Genie the JAP.

Genie folded her arms over her prodigious boobs. "No, I don't want to go to fucking Treatment!" There went another quarter for the swear jar. Genie was really asking for it tonight. "I don't *need* Treatment, I'm not a fucking retard!"

Becky the Baby piped up from her folding chair, whining. "*I'm* in Treatment, and *I'm* not a retard!"

Our housemate Becky was in Treatment for being a baby. Becky was fifteen, but she acted like she was eight. She usually talked in baby talk and cried if you touched any of her stuffed animals. In Treatment, they made her wear a cardboard sign around her neck that said BABY, in order to increase her sense of personal responsibility.

"Yes you *are* a retard, so shut up, because nobody's fucking talking to you!"

Becky the Baby's mouth unfolded like a box, her lower lip flopping down and her top lip flipping up, then both lips flattening into a grimace as she started to bawl. Becky the Baby was an amazing bawler. She could turn from pinkly, quietly snuffling into a heaving purple fountain of snot in under a minute. The rest of us duly turned our attention to Becky the Baby.

Group therapy was always a clusterfuck. Every Monday, we trekked down to the group home's administrative office in Midtown, sat around a conference table, and completely dismantled one another. The dreaded Poulos would come by randomly. She'd nod at the counselors – fat, mean Mavis, her ass spread out over two folding chairs; Bronx-bred Sandy, who was slightly less rotund than Mavis but not a bit less mean; and skinny, old, dessicated Grandma Dolores, a forty-year veteran of social work, who'd sometimes slip you one of her long, brown More cigarettes if you begged hard enough. Poulos would stand in the doorway for a few minutes, observe the carnage with her squinched-up eyes, and vulture away. Then the rest of us would get back to the business at hand, which was yelling, "You're a JAP!" "Well, you're a baby!" "Well, you have no respect for yourself!" at one another.

When we'd ripped on one another back at the shelter, the nuns made us cut it out. Here, it was practically encouraged. The counselors had contempt for us – well, Mavis and Sandy did; Grandma Dolores was an old pushover – and if we saved them the trouble of constantly articulating our faults by doing it to one another, so much the better. The more our fundamental personality defects were hammered home to us, the more likely it was that we'd become successful adults, which we were definitely not going to be unless we admitted that we were total useless shitheads first.

Here's how things worked at the group home:

Me and Genie the JAP were roommates. I took the bed of a girl named Chita, who'd recently turned seventeen and gotten a room at the YWCA with her cashier wages from Love's Discount Beauty store. Chita was my new hero, for finding a way to move out before her eighteenth birthday. Genie didn't like her much. "Chita was boring! She never did anything but work and hog up the pay phone and go see her boyfriend. She didn't even fuck him or anything! I was like, 'At least tell me you're fucking him.' She tried to ignore me." And here Genie laughed. "Hah! Ignore me. As if you can."

Genie the JAP, who liked to be described as a "luscious brunette," attracted most of the attention in the house. If she wasn't fighting with the counselors, she was fighting with one of the other girls. Genie liked to think of herself as a serious badass because, back in junior high, she smoked pot, and did coke a few times with some older guys around her neighborhood in Staten Island, until her hothead dad and her shopaholic mom threw her in a lockup facility upstate, where she was beaten by a girl wielding a combination lock in a sock. This was the story I got from Genie on my first night, as she sneaked a smoke out our bedroom window – "Where'd you live before you came here? I was in a lockup upstate. You ever get hit with a lock in a sock? I got the shit beat out of me by a spic."

"Wow," I said appreciatively.

"You're lucky, 'cause I'm the best roommate." She ducked her head two feet out the window for another drag of her cigarette, then popped back in, arm still dangling over the sill. "You know why? Because I would never tell on anybody. Even if I didn't like somebody, I would never tell on them. That's because I'm loyal."

I nodded vigorously. This was my half of any conversation with

Genie – me nodding vigorously, and Genie popping in and out of the window, chattering about loyalty one minute, showing me her big mute ass the next. "But I'm only loyal to people who are loyal to me. That's why I wouldn't want to be roommates with Becky. She always goes running to the counselors, she's such a fucking baby."

I nodded vigorously.

Becky the Baby was the second-biggest attention getter in the house. If we weren't talking about Genie in group, we were talking about Becky. Why Becky refused to act her age, why she wheedled and cried to get her way. *Maybe,* I thought, *it's because her parents stuck her in a fucking group home, with all-day Treatment, for no reason at all, except that she's annoying.*

Becky the Baby wasn't a drug addict, she wasn't even a slut, and if she ever cut school or drank a beer at the age of fourteen, it was because somebody else told her to. But she still got sent to live in a group home, where she spent all day in Treatment, because her personality sucked so bad. And okay, she could be annoying – sometimes she'd drag on your arm too hard, or guilt-trip you if you wouldn't sit in on a game of hearts – but she was essentially a good kid. And yet every week at group, every night at dinner, it was, "Becky! Stop acting like you're helpless! Becky! Why are you crying? Becky!"

Becky's roommate was Shirley the Nympho, who I liked a lot, and not only because she made me look relatively chaste and choosy, with her bizarre string of "conquests," mostly gross older guys in their thirties. To me, Shirley was a sweet, spiritually innocent neurotic who sincerely wanted to love and be loved, and if everybody used that to get sex from her, that was their shame, not hers. But it was frustrating at the same time. Sometimes I just wanted to shake my head for poor, hapless Shirl, who didn't understand men the way I did – how they used you and ridiculed you for it later; how only the powerful ones were worth it.

Shirley was just lucky that she wasn't sent to Treatment, that she was allowed to go to school and did not have to wear a sign around her neck that said NYMPHO, though she did have to attend biweekly family therapy at the Midtown offices with her creepy looking dad and spooky, silent mom. She was superpolite to the counselors, almost to the point of being obsequious, which irritated Mavis and Sandy. Grandma Dolores ate it up.

"Lord, that child is so sweet," she said, as Shirley the Nympho skipped off to retrieve her sweater for her from the other room. "Why can't the rest of these girls be more like her?"

The counselors were similarly split on reedy, dark-haired Julie the Snitch, in the next room. Grandma Dolores doted on her; Mavis and Sandy used her services regularly, then abused her for snitching. "You need to keep your eyes on your own paper," Sandy advised Julie the Snitch with a wagging finger. "None of us is perfect, and you need to remember where you came from before you start thinking you're past it."

Julie the Snitch kept her chin up but cast her eyes down. She wanted to be proud of being good. Julie'd been at the group home since she was fifteen and she took off from her mom's to follow the Grateful Dead. Now, after a year and a half of cleaning toilets and wearing signs, Julie had graduated Treatment, receiving a diploma and a key chain that commemorated her moral journey from acid-dropping slut to joyless busybody. Now Julie wanted to enjoy her position in the cult.

"I'm just pointing out your self-destructive behavior," she would say to Becky primly in group, as Mavis sucked in her cheeks in disgust.

"Julie, the point is that Becky needs to learn for *herself*. You are not helping her, and you are not helping yourself."

Julie sat, arms crossed, and tapped her foot. It must have sucked to work so hard and still be so unpopular.

In a neat bit of coincidence, Julie the Snitch's roommate was Gladys the Quiet One, a light-skinned black girl with a neat corona of relaxed hair. Gladys managed to upset people just by being quiet. The counselors would try to draw her out at dinner, but the most they ever got was a wispy "fine" or "okay," directed at her plate. Mavis and Sandy found this intolerable. I found it quite pleasant, compared to some of the other girls, who never shut the fuck up. Sometimes we tried to discuss "Gladys's anger" in group, but it was like trying to discuss a funny noise in the room that nobody could really hear. I thought Gladys was more depressed than angry. Gladys had eyes like paisleys, sad-shaped.

In the last room were Indira the Bully and Shanita Who Could Squirt Breast Milk, both of whom made me afraid, for different reasons. Indira was tall and gorgeous and mean, and almost as contemptuous as the counselors. She wasn't an overt bully – she'd draw her fist back, but she wouldn't hit – mostly, she'd just shut you down with a scathing look if you didn't do exactly what she wanted. I couldn't always guess exactly what Indira wanted, though I valiantly tried, and she was scornful of me for it. "You think you're so badass," she told me, more than once, "but you're a *pussy*."

Shanita had suffered a miscarriage six months ago, and she was still goddamn angry about it, which she often expressed by shooting milk out of her giant, floppy breasts. Both Indira and Shanita had jobs, so they weren't around much – I, too, was angling for an after-school job, so I could make myself scarce like them – but when we did see Shanita, she was usually fired up about something: "Whose goddamn clothes is these in the dryer? Move your damn clothes out the dryer!" In a room full of big personalities, Shanita could make herself the biggest, and if she felt challenged in any way, she'd just whip out a boob and fire milk at you. The counselors chastised her for it, but what were they going to do? Shanita was almost eighteen. She'd be "aging out" of the home soon, leaving whether she wanted to or not.

Thus I found my new sorority: Genie the JAP, Becky the Baby, Shirley the Nympho, Julie the Snitch, Gladys the Quiet One, Indira the Bully, and Breast-Milk-Shooting Shanita. And me, the eighth dwarf. Janice the Liar. The one who lied to everyone, all the time. Hoping, *nobody knows*.

"Too bad you can't sleep over tonight," said Alice, puckering at the mirror. "We're gonna stay out until – "

"I don't even know when," finished Hope. She made a sad clown face as she applied mascara to her bottom lashes. "Prob'ly, like, dawn."

Alice's mother was gone for the weekend, off to Miami with her new boyfriend, leaving Alice alone in the apartment, so Hope was sleeping over at Alice's tonight, and they basically had no curfew.

This was one thing you could never, ever do at the group home –

sleep over at a friend's house. No way. They were not going to let you that far out of their sight, not while they were legally responsible for you. As long as the group home was in loco parentis – a legal term I'd read on the intake form and often recalled – you could count on missing a lot of sleepovers.

And here I'd been so grateful that the group home gave me an eleven-thirty curfew. I swigged my beer, grimacing at the sour, pukey taste. Well, it was still better than getting back to the shelter at nine.

"We *could* even bring guys back here," Alice noted. "Like if we saw the Boyses."

"Or Brian Cooper," Hope volunteered.

"Ucch, Brian Cooper is *so* hot."

Brian Cooper was Hope's latest obsession; she'd staked him as soon as she saw him, the first day he transferred into our school. Now she arched her thin eyebrows as she glossed her lips, catching Alice's eye in the mirror. "Step off, bitch, I liked him first."

"I know, bitch," Alice rejoindered. "I'm not trying to scam on your man, I'm just agreeing he's hot." She stepped back to appraise herself, tugging the waist of her skirt so the hem went higher, then lower, then higher again, frowning at her mother's high-heeled boots. "Are these too, like, dowdy? My mom has the lamest taste."

I said, "I'm just happy to be out of the fucking group home for a few hours."

"Totally," Hope agreed. "My mother's such a bitch. We got in a huge fight because she wouldn't give me three dollars for a new notebook. Look at this bruise! She grabbed me and I pushed her, and then she punched me right in the arm. I hate her."

"Ucch," groaned Alice. "I'm *so* glad my mom is out of town. I hope she just stays in Miami with her stupid boyfriend."

"Yeah," I said, like I was joking. "Then me and Hope can move in with you."

"Yea-uh!" Alice's voice broke strangely in the middle. "Totally."

I sat back and drank my pukey beer, my third in an hour, watching the abstract geometry of the room reversed in the mirror, the way Alice and Hope moved and laughed on their axis. I noticed: If me and Alice and Hope made a triangle, that triangle had no equal sides. We were scalene. We were a thirty-sixty-ninety wedge. I was the thirty, the constricted, critical angle in the corner, with the longest lines between me and everybody else; Alice was the sixty on top, the point of the triangle, the peak. And Hope was the ninety, the base, the support. The one that made us right, so the ratio of our sides always stayed the same.

Both Alice and I were measurably closer to Hope than to each other, but Alice and I shared our own special hypotenuse, in that we were both little divas, in different flavors – Alice was an Ice Princess Diva, while I was going for Femme Fatale. Hence, we understood things about men that Hope didn't; at least, that was the impression I sometimes got from Alice, when she flashed me a knowing look or a wink over Hope's mussed strawberry bob – *There she goes, talking to that* freshman *again.*

And I smiled back, superior. *At least he's cute.*

With Hope, I could be more mortal. She didn't rib me about smoking other people's cigarette butts, or sleeping with Andrew Winkler, the way Alice did. Hope knew sometimes you had to fudge it just to get it done. She didn't call me on obvious lies, like when I'd said I was starring in a benefit production of A *Streetcar Named Desire* at the shelter, and Tom Cruise was probably going to play Stanley. She just nodded, passed the joint, and let it ride.

Alice and Hope trotted ahead of me on the sidewalk as we approached tonight's party, held at a loft somewhere in Flatiron. We were attending a lot of these three-dollar keg parties lately – a mix of kids from the better public high schools and the worse private ones, crammed into some big square room with ungodly loud music, drinking beer and smoking pot, getting into fistfights and puking on the sidewalk. It was a circuit. You saw the same guys at every party (unless they were at a club that night – *club* beat *party* in the hierarchy of fun things to brag about on Monday), and they saw you, and proximity made you more attractive to each other – "There he is *again*. It's like he's following me."

God, I missed so much while I was at the shelter. I had to scout guys and gulp beer with one eye on everyone else's watch. "What time is it?" Swig. "What time is it?" Puff. I loitered by the keg, concentrating on taking in the maximum amount of beer and pot possible until exactly 11:15 P.M., at which time I would take off and fly back to the group home, dose myself with eyedrops and breath mints, rip off my smelly outer clothes in the hallway, and cruise in five minutes before curfew – "How was the movie, Janice?" "Great, fun. Thanks. Good night."

By 10:45, I was obliterated. I was sitting on the windowsill near some people from school, and I realized that I was extremely warm, and woozy, panting like a dog in a locked car. "I'm hot," I interrupted. I leaned my head out the window and caught a blast of the cold February air, dusting the inside of my nose, exhilarating. "I gotta go outside a minute."

I took a rough stumble through a packed, slippery room, dizzier and more claustrophobic with every step. The stairwell down to the street was jammed with people. I spotted Hope fighting her way up the stairs, and she yelled to me, "Dude!"

I pointed up toward the roof. "I gotta get air," I slurred.

"Where's Alice?"

"I don't know, I gotta . . ."

I staggered up another flight of stairs, past a few girls I knew from Competitive High, heart thudding way too hard. Another flight up. Dizzy. I could just puke right here in the stairs, nobody would see. "What up, J?" Well, except that one guy from school. I kept climbing. People came banging out the door to the roof, nearly knocking me over as they passed. I made it outside and sank gratefully into a seated position.

I was as clammy as chowder. Bile rose in my throat, burning the inside of my nostrils. I half-crawled over to the ledge where the roof met the roof next door, and I crouched next to it.

Not three feet away, Alice was making out with Brian Cooper.

I threw up over the ledge for about five minutes – spat, coughed, rinsed my mouth with my beer and spat it out again. Then I threw in a mint, brushed the loose gravel off my knees, stopped in the washroom for a quick sink bath, and stumbled back down the stairs, out into the street, heading home.

· · ·

"And how is our newest resident doing?" asked Poulos, over a folder full of notes about me that only she could read.

"Good!" I chirped, perky with nerves. "I think it's going really well, so far."

"Mm-hmm." Poulos looked suspicious, but she couldn't disagree. My grades were good – better than anyone else's at the house – and I hadn't been busted cutting class since I stole the guidance counselor's stamp and forged myself a handful of passes. I got home on time every night, kept my side of the room clean, did my chores, obeyed the rules. I didn't argue with the other girls. I maintained a chipper, efficient air of goodwill, even when I was ridiculously baked. Even Mavis and Sandy grudgingly liked me. They let me know they didn't trust me for shit, but I didn't cause them active grief on a daily basis, so I was somewhere in the top of the pack for them – wherever that was.

"I get along pretty well with everybody," I ventured. "And school's good, so – "

Poulos interrupted me. "Mavis says you're tired at night. You don't like to get up on time on the weekend." She narrowed her eyes at me. "What's making you so tired, Janice?"

Um, that would be the hangover. I smiled weakly, stalling. "Sometimes, I guess . . . I don't know, I guess . . . there's a lot of pressure at school . . ."

Poulos's sharply angled eyebrows shot up. "Pressure to do what?"

"Oh, nothing! I just mean . . . there's a lot of work. And stuff." Jesus! I was glad I drank more drug-test tea, I was going to need it. They were totally onto me.

Poulos paused and assessed me some more. I tucked my thumbs inside my palms and squeezed a little, thighs pressing tight against each other – her silences always made me want to babble. "And . . . I've been looking for an after-school job. I'm trying out for the spring play."

"Mmm-hmmm," she said again. I had to shut up before I said something stupid.

"I guess . . . sometimes I try too hard, and that's . . . tiring, sometimes." I wrinkled my forehead like a puppy, attempting to look sincere.

"Mmm-hmmm."

Poulos had one of those swinging pendulum toys on her desk, with the five steel balls that smack against one another like clockwork. I loved those. It was nearly impossible to sit there and not smack the balls, but I was sure that if I touched them she would cut off my hand. The ball-smacking toy was for her use only, for hypnotizing kids into confessing everything – puking on roofs, smoking pot on stoops, giving clandestine, ill-advised blow jobs behind the auditorium at school. I tried to tear my eyes from the toy lest I lose my shit completely and fold like a cheap, three-legged card table.

"There's also the matter of your haircut."

"Um, uh-huh." *What the fuck?*

The counselors and Poulos didn't like my new haircut. I'd given myself what we called "whitewalls," two-inch stripes shaved on either side of my head. It wasn't even close to a Mohawk; it was barely noticeable if I wore the rest of my hair down and covering my ears, as I wore it now. Poulos gave my haircut a look that made my scalp crawl.

"It's antisocial," she decreed. "It sends a hostile statement."

"I . . . I didn't mean . . ." Could they put me in Treatment for a haircut? Mavis and Sandy threatened us with Treatment all the time, and with Bellevue, and with a lockup facility upstate, for offenses as minor as throwing a magazine, or smoking out the window of your room when you'd been warned a hundred times already. Sometimes they even mentioned Spofford, the juvenile prison, which seemed pretty preposterous, that we got threatened with jail because we didn't clean the tub. Still, it stuck with me – they could do with me what they wanted; I was in their "care." I started to feel extremely claustrophobic in my chair, sweaty hands gripping the arms. "It was . . . an experiment, it'll grow . . ."

"It's apparent that you're angry, Janice. Your behavior says it loud and clear."

"My *behavior*?" I gawked at her, gripping tighter. My behavior was fucking *perfect*, as far as they knew. I didn't find a goddamn dish in the sink that I didn't wash, dry, and put away. I didn't throw tantrums or hissy fits; I didn't try to fuck the guy at the bodega. I was *unfailingly* fucking polite. "What am I doing wrong?"

Poulos liked this question a lot.

"That's something we can discuss in future sessions," she said. "We'll meet again in a month and talk more about what course of treatment we'll be pursuing from there."

I flushed, completely agitated and trying not to show it. Was that Treatment with a capital T, or was it lowercase treatment, like family therapy? Poulos wouldn't really put me in Treatment, would she? She was just fucking with me. I imagined a forest of cardboard signs around my neck: LIAR. DRUGGIE. SLUT. THUMBSUCKER. I would kill myself first. I might kill myself anyway.

"You can leave a urine sample at the desk on your way out."

"Okay."

I rose unsteadily, woozy from the brightness of the light, the chemical smell of the carpet, the gleaming blackness of her black-hearted hair.

"And grow your haircut out," she added. She was back to looking at the files on her desk, done with me.

I gulped, nodded, and rose, done with.

SEXUAL IDENTITY

"My friend Domenic's in love with you," said Genie.

I joined her at our bedroom window. We'd learned, over the past two months of rooming together, that if we squished alongside each other, we could both stick our heads out and smoke at the same time. "Move over. Give me a drag. Who?"

"You know, that guy we saw on the way to the store that night? Domenic? In the flight jacket?" She hiked her eyebrows at me and grinned. "I *told* you I'm the best roommate."

"Oh my god, *that* guy? Really? What'd he say? Give me another drag."

We'd seen Domenic on Broadway while on a cigarette run the other night. He hailed Genie from the other side of the street, ringing her name like a doorbell – "Gen*ie!*" Genie stopped dead in the middle of the block, spotted him like prey, and indifferent to eight lanes of traffic, dragged me by the arm across the street to chat.

The guy was adorable, with a fuzzy, near-bald head, sleepy green eyes, and a slight wicked grin. He wore maroon combat boots, a black flight jacket, and jeans with a pen-drawn anarchy symbol on the knee. He went to Genie's school, this private school for fuckups her rich parents paid for. They talked – rather, Genie talked – "Oh my god, you don't have any pot, do you? I wanna get high so bad! They'd kill me if I failed a drug test, though, I would get in so much trouble" – and I stood staring off in the distance, a practiced look of bemusement on my face, arms crossed underneath my breasts to maximize their appeal.

Evidently, it had worked.

"You totally owe me now," Genie gloated.

"Oh my god." I was too excited to smoke. I pulled back into the room and bumped my head on the sash. The prospect of having a *boyfriend* was astonishingly good – I hadn't had one since my first, botched affair in Rockaway Beach – and *this* boy in particular . . . it was like Billy Idol himself had climbed down from Genie's poster on the wall and started telling me he loved me.

Genie made the phone call, and that weekend I went for a walk with Domenic Burns through Central Park. It was early March, the leafless trees still gray and brown, patches of scum around the edges of the lake. We were both surprisingly shy.

"Let's get some weed," he suggested.

Weed, I noticed. *He must be from California.* He had a slow, almost self-mocking way of speaking that gave him away.

"Great." I tried not to beam, tried to look like this amazing date was the world's most natural thing. "That sounds great."

We hiked over to the Sheep Meadow, a grassy field in the middle of the park that attracted a year-round community of hippies and dealers, and Domenic flagged down a guy in a fake leather bomber. I stood a few feet to the side as he made the deal.

"Got it," he said proudly. He flashed that slight grin and tipped his head toward the lake. "Wanna go?"

"Great," I enthused. "Awesome."

I strayed a few steps behind him, grinning into the turtleneck of my sweater, watching his jeans crinkle under his butt. *It's working*, I delighted to myself – the skull I'd drawn in eyeliner next to my eye, the way I tossed my head back before laughing – one of my many manufactured affectations must have been doing the trick, because he turned and smiled back at me, tipped his head like he wanted me to catch up and walk closer to him.

We sat in one of the gazebos by the lake, and Domenic pulled out a brass one-hit pipe from his jacket. He opened the Baggie of brown shake, packed the pipe, and offered it to me. "Hang on." He patted his chest pockets, then his pants pockets, and his sly grin turned sheepish. Then his hand landed on his lighter, and he held it up to light the pipe for me like he was Humphrey Bogart.

"Thanks," I said demurely and pulled in the smoke.

He took a hit for himself and smiled some more. I smiled back.
He was younger-looking than I thought he was the night I first met
him with Genie on Broadway – without the scowl, his forehead was
smooth, his cheeks round and ruddy; his teeth looked soft as gum.

I said, "So . . ."

"So."

We kept smiling. I kept looking at him, at the few short, stray hairs
stuck to his forehead. He must have just gotten a haircut, for our date.
My smile got wider on one side.

"What," he said, lifting his chin like a friendly challenge.

"Nothing."

"What."

I wasn't going to go first. "You say something!"

"I am!" He laughed.

"No you're not. Tell me something."

"Like what?"

"Like . . ." *Who are you? Where have you been all my life? What do
you like about me so far? Be specific.* "Why are you at Genie's school?"

He reared back a little, tilted his head down. "My dad put me
there. My mom threw me out last year – I was living with her in
Oregon, and then she threw me out."

"Why."

"Um, for being a bum." He ran his hand over the top of his freshly
buzzed hair, and the smile went sheepish again.

For someone who dressed so hard-core, he was remarkably tender.
The hard-core guys I knew didn't smile like that. Smiling was not
punk rock. And they didn't ask you what you wanted to do, they
ordered you. They weren't sweet, as Domenic was. I had an urge to
reach out and pet his fuzzy head like a puppy's, to kiss him and press
his cheek to my breast.

I said, "You don't seem like a bum."

"Yeah . . ." He shrugged one shoulder as he tapped more pot into
the pipe for me. "What about you? Why are you at the group home?"

"Because my mother's crazy, and my stepfather's a total dick."

"Yeah?" He passed the pipe back to me, lighting it again. "Your
stepfather ever . . . try anything with you?"

"No." Why did everybody ask me this? I always felt like they were disappointed when I said no. "Just . . . violent."

Domenic nodded. "My mom's pretty violent, too. She freaks out a lot, she'll start throwing things, dishes and shit – it's scary."

We weren't smiling anymore. He moved closer to me. My breath sped up, and I scraped my teeth over my bottom lip.

"So," he said.

"So."

His baby face blurred as he came in for the kiss. "You wanna do this?"

"We should get married," I told him, three weeks later.

I hadn't planned on asking, I just blurted it out. We were naked in his bed at his dad's apartment in Brooklyn, sweaty and content. It was about eleven in the morning, game shows flickering on the mute TV. We'd been screwing around and smoking pot since nine, and we still had hours to go before we even had to think about getting dressed and acting legitimate.

Domenic continued to nuzzle my neck, unfazed by the big pitch. "You wanna?"

"Well . . . sure, don't you? Then we could move in together, and do this every day."

"Uh-huh."

"We just have to wait until I turn sixteen in August. But we can get engaged now. And we can both get jobs, and then we'll have two incomes, and we can get a really nice place together and just . . . chill, all the time." Not that I'd been thinking about it much.

"Mmmmm." Domenic gave me a dreamy smile and pressed his erection into my thigh. He was not taking me seriously.

"I love you," I reminded him.

"Oh, baby, I love you too." He squeezed me tighter. "I do, baby."

"Well, that's why we should do it."

I sat up and reached for the roach in the ashtray. Domenic sighed and rolled off me. I noticed that he did not light the roach for me, I had to light it myself. So much had changed in three weeks.

He propped himself up on his elbow and set his eyebrows to "cute," regarding me as I smoked. Poor Domenic. He was just lucky that he met me, and that I put up with him. He had no idea how to plan. His idea of planning was to get two six-packs when we cut school instead of only one. I didn't even like beer that much. God – were we right for each other after all?

I ticked through my list.

Pros: Adorable. Excellent arm candy, made me look great. Got new respect from Alice and Hope for landing supercute hard-core intramural boyfriend. Also, sexy. Nice in bed. Not rough or jerky. Very sweet. Loved me – that was a big pro. Was something other than indifferent to me, unlike other guys. Picked me up after school on the days we didn't cut together, and asked me how my day was, and kissed me like it had been a week since we'd kissed last. Also: could rescue me from the group home, if we were legally married. Loved me.

Cons: Um, not smart. No! I didn't mean that. Just . . . not on the ball. Was a brilliant genius, really, and very creative – I could tell. Just not ambitious, was all. Didn't read for fun. Didn't think at all about the future, or consequences. Often flaky, often lost or forgot things. Qualified to one day be the father of little Janice Jr.? Jury still out.

I sneaked a sideways look at him, his barely shaded jaw slack as he gazed past me at the TV. I cleared my throat. He snapped to attention.

"Well, we could get engaged, right?" He tried to smile at me, that goofy, harmless smile, an edge of doubt in his voice. "I mean, if it's that important to you . . ."

To *me*? What about to *us*? He didn't realize, apparently, how grateful he should be to have me – I was the best thing that ever happened to him, he'd said so a hundred times, his brown eyes shining: "I don't know what I'd do without you, babe; nobody gets me like you do." *Don't do me any favors*, I thought, tears ready to spring. "Well," I muttered. "Not if you don't want to."

Domenic tried to look at my face. I pressed it into his chest and wouldn't budge. He wrapped his arms tighter around me. "Aw, hey baby, don't cry, I love you! We'll get engaged! Okay?"

His voice was a half octave too high, and it warbled, but he said it nonetheless: *I love you; we'll get engaged*. No diamond ring, no bended knee, just a quavering capitulation. I should have been grateful, if not elated – Domenic was going to rescue me, my halfhearted knight.

"Baby, I said let's do it! Okay? Baby?"

I squeezed my eyes shut, nodding yes against his chest. "Okay." I sniffled. "Yes."

He sighed, relieved, and kissed the top of my head, rocking me back and forth. "Okay! Great. I love you, baby." I heard his smile go sheepish again. "But listen . . . I don't know about a job . . ."

I suppose I might have pressed too hard. I got too angry. Whenever it was time to talk about Janice in group therapy, that was what they said – *You're angry*. And nothing makes a person angrier than being told she's angry – "I'm not angry! I'm shouting because I'm not angry! If I was angry, I wouldn't shout! I'd just agree!" – especially when that person is working her ass off to hide it and be nice.

I wasn't *angry*. I was *tense*. I was tense at school, where my excuses for absence had worn vapor-thin ("I was at the guidance counselor's office." "I had to go to family court again." "I had a nosebleed and the nurse sent me home"). I couldn't let my grades slip, so I took caffeine pills and wrote papers off the top of my head, copied my homework, cheated on tests. I bit Alice's head off after an English exam, all essays on books I'd only skimmed. "I *fucked it up*, that's how I did. Okay? I fucked it up."

"All *right*," she retorted, hand on hip. "Excuse *me*."

I was tense around Alice, ever since I saw her on the roof at that party with Brian Cooper; I was even more tense around Hope, who was now officially dating Brian Cooper; and when forced to be in the company of all three of them, say, smoking a cigarette before school, I was practically chewing through the inside of my own cheek. I was tense at the group home, my fake smile cracking at the edges. I snapped at Genie: "I *owe* you for Domenic, I know, thanks a fucking lot!"

Genie looked hurt, her dark eyes sparkling. "Fuck you," she decided and went back to looking at her zits in the magnifying mirror.

Things had changed with Domenic since the day of our engagement. He was flakier than usual, and I took it personally, sulking because he would rather spend his afternoons hanging out in Washington Square than looking for gainful employment on our mutual behalf. I'd already started working afternoons and weekends at a snack stand in Central Park, and what was he doing? Taking up collections for a nickel bag he'd smoke without me?

I blew up at him outside my job one afternoon when he made the mistake of coming by to mooch food while spare-changing outside the park. "Spare-changing is not the same as working!"

"Yes it is, baby! It's doing work for money!"

"It's not a job!"

"It's hard work!"

I bugged my eyes, shut my mouth, and tried to catch my breath. I wasn't *angry*. I wasn't *disappointed*. I wasn't *acting like a mean asshole*. I was just *tense*.

Domenic and I were rarely together anymore. We'd both run out of excusable absences – no more luxurious school days in bed – and now I was busy with my after-school job – no more afternoons spent smoking pot and groping in the park. When we saw one another, we'd fight. Then he'd call me on the residents' pay phone and apologize and cry.

"I don't know why I act this way," he told me, his voice wracked and helpless.

I was giving up hope for our marriage. I pressed my forehead to the wall by the phone. "Maybe we should . . ."

"No," he insisted. "I love you. I'm just confused."

Then I saw him with another girl.

I thought I was supposed to be working at the snack stand that day, but I screwed up my schedule and showed up when it wasn't my shift, so I threw my visor and T-shirt back into my book bag and jumped on a downtown A for Washington Square, hoping I'd find him there – my Domenic, my gentle, fuzzy Dom Pérignon. Maybe today would be the day that everything got better and we felt like we used to feel in the beginning, like our heads were full of carbonated gas and our skins were sunburned.

The sun was stronger than it had been in a while, and I opened my coat as I breezed into the park, headed for the fountain in the middle. And then I saw them together: Domenic in his black flight jacket, leaning toward a pink-haired girl in a ripped plaid skirt, gallantly touching his lighter to the brass one-hitter at her lips.

She took the hit, put her lips to his, and blew the smoke back to him.

The gas in my head caught flame. I turned and backed out of the park. I started walking as fast as I could, legs scissoring the empty path in front of me. It was the only thing I knew how to do. Walk away.

What *do* you do when your fiancé cheats on you?

I took LSD. It helped. It was a distraction, something to do on balmy weekend nights in Washington Square Park besides watch *my ex-fiancé*, Domenic Burns, stick his tongue down the throat of a pink-haired girl named Jennifer. A girl who lived, I happened to know, with her appallingly wealthy parents in a six-story town house on the Upper West Side. I'd seen the happy family more than once, up by the group home, getting out of their gigantic Mercedes together, so what the fuck she was doing panhandling for schwag in the park with a bum like Domenic Burns was beyond me.

"God, I fucking hate Domenic so much," I perceived, with my altered powers of consciousness.

Alice breathed, gulped, and nodded. Hope brooded next to her on the concrete bench, playing with Alice's hair, lost in the blues and purples and oranges of its enthralling blackness.

Thwack! Skateboards landed on the benches next to us. We swigged our brown-bagged beers and smoked cigarettes like they were Pixy Stix. I breathed in, gulped, and breathed out, staring now at a fallen leaf. There was so much meaning in a single leaf, so many new leaves budding on just this one tree.

"I loved him." My ribs broke, my heart cracked.

"I loved Brian Cooper," monotoned Hope.

Their three-week affair was over – who knew why? Boys grew cold. They leaked heat, like science. I could see the heat. I saw every footprint on the asphalt, the blue-orange heat of every footfall for hours past, sparkling like oil. I heard the heat in Alice's voice. She breathed, gulped, and said, "Men are weak."

"Hear hear."

Did Hope say that or did I? Did I say that out loud? Was it stupid? *Hear hear.* That's a stupid thing to say. I was ashamed of myself if I said that out loud.

Yeah, acid was a good distraction, but nothing was going to distract me better than a new boyfriend. And I'd make sure this one wasn't a spineless fuckup in a flight jacket. Hope and Alice could swoon over the Boyses and the Brian Coopers, the skateboard-thwacking party kings. My priorities had changed.

I began to pay extra attention to the nice boys at school. And I know – me and a *nice* boy – what a laugh! But there were a few cute ones, if you looked past the button-down shirts and the reeking wholesomeness. Some of them were even funny, or charming. Their virginity was endearing, their enthusiasm palpable. Perhaps I would boldly condescend to date outside my social set and go out with one of them.

From the ranks of my drama class, I chose a sensitive lad named Jimmy Wilson. He was gangly and WASPy, with sandy blond hair and pretty features. I enjoyed perching on his lap and making him blush, brushing against him as we painted backdrops. He was the anti-Domenic if ever there was one.

"Jimmy," I drawled, like Dorothy Parker, draping my arm over him like a feather boa, "when are you and I going to get married?"

Jimmy blinked his blond lashes a few times, gaped. "Anytime you want," he said, in his squeaky-clean voice.

That's a good boy. He didn't think I was serious, of course. I was categorically out of his league, and everyone knew it. Even Mr. Sheldon, our drama teacher, raised an arch eyebrow over our nascent affair.

"*This* should be interesting," he smirked.

I laughed. Mr. Sheldon was a trip. "I'm a nice girl at heart!" I swore.

"Mm-*hmm*," he intoned. "Just don't *hurt* the poor boy."

Alice and Hope laughed at me outright. "You can't be serious. Jimmy Wilson?"

Hope shook her head: Veto, veto, veto. "Seriously. You can't. You seriously can't."

Now I was the sheepish one. "I know! I know. But he's nice to me!"

"So what?" Alice laughed. "He looks like he belongs on a toothpaste commercial!"

"I know!" Jesus! Couldn't they just cut me a break? I was heartbroken, my ego was wrecked; I was having a tough time, I needed an easy score. "I know, he's a geek. Whatever. It's not anything."

I turned and tossed my head, deflecting further comment. *It's not anything. Yet.*

"We should get married," I told Jimmy Wilson, three weeks later.

We were naked in his bed in his parents' apartment in the West Village, sweaty and content. It was four-thirty in the afternoon; videos flickered on the mute TV. We'd come right from school to bed, where we'd been screwing around for an hour, and we still had about twenty minutes before we had to get dressed and act legitimate.

"Gee," said Jimmy, holding my hand. "You think?"

I reached for my pack of cigarettes, though there was no smoking in the Wilson household — at least I could suck on one unlit. "Well, yeah, don't you? Then we could live together, and do this all the time."

Jimmy frowned. "I don't know . . . I think my folks would want me to finish school first."

Ugh, his *folks*. Jimmy Wilson just loved his folks, and the Wilsons loooved Jimmy, so much so that his mother, a museum administrator, left him fresh-baked cookies on a plate with a note in the afternoons — "Jimmy, Hope you had a great day! Love, Mom." His mommy baked him cookies! How did he stand it? How did he manage to walk to the fridge and get the milk and pour it into glasses and stand there in front of me, offering me milk and cookies his mommy baked for him, and not die of shame?

"We could finish school. We could get jobs and finish school at the same time. Except we'd be married." I smiled seductively and nibbled his ear.

Jimmy didn't seem convinced, his hand detangling itself from mine to run through his sandy mop of hair. "Well . . . what about college?"

"We can both go to college. We can do whatever we want. That's the great thing."

I remained patient and reasonable with Jimmy, speaking gently, as though to a young child, even as I wanted to yell at him, *Just fucking say yes! It'll be good! Jesus Christ! Do you love me or not!*

"I love you," I reminded him.

"I love you too," he said, dutifully, kissing my hand. The whole hand-kissing thing did nothing for me.

"I know," I said, dubious.

"Aww, honey. Come on. You know you're my princess . . ."

Oh, spare me. I turned my head and pouted. After all I'd done for Jimmy Wilson – taken him to keg parties, babysat him through his first unfortunate experience with pot ("We have to go to the emergency room!" "Jimmy, it's just paranoia, drink this beer!") – after I'd devirginized him, and socially legitimized him, he couldn't do this one little thing for me?

They all want to fuck me, but nobody wants to marry me. Tears leaked silently out of the corners of my eyes. I'd even kind of grown to like Jimmy, his childlike devotion, his fawning consideration. It was tragic, my lot: Even naked in bed, with a man's arm around me, a man who swore he loved me, I would always be, ultimately, alone.

"Aww, honey . . ."

I wiped my eyes and pushed off from the bed. I'd be damned if I was going to let *Jimmy Wilson* – the joke, the geek, the monthlong experiment in sociocultural slumming – see me cry. "I'm all right," I said bravely. I pulled on my red bra.

Jimmy cooed helplessly from the bed. "Aww, baby, princess . . ."

I threw on my ripped tights, slashed T-shirt, holey sneakers, and jeans. I kissed his cheek.

"It's okay. I'm not upset. I just have to get home."

And once again, I walked away.

. . .

I'm becoming a lesbian, I wrote.

I shoved my notebook two inches to the left on my desk so Hope could see it, as Ms. Wong rattled on about the sine and the cosine. Hope wrote a reply in her own book, shoved it my way.

Gross.

Men suck.

She rolled her eyes. *Tell me about it.*

I'm breaking up w/ Jimmy.

Didn't you already?

Not officially. Why?

Saw him w/ Karen Newfield after 6th.

"Hah!" It escaped me, too loud. Ms. Wong paused at the chalkboard.

"Does somebody need help?"

I lowered my burning face to my notebook. Karen Newfield wore pastel sweaters. She was on the Student Association. Her favorite group was Journey. Karen Newfield was the anti-me.

KAREN NEWFIELD FUCKS DEAD DOGS.

Hope snickered. *You're way hotter any day.*

AND JIMMY WILSON HAS A TWO INCH DICK.

Brian Cooper is a scumbag. Alice says he hit on her while we were going out.

Oh, does she now? I'm not surprised.

Me either. Men suck.

Hope looked up at the clock. Twenty minutes to go. She rolled her eyes again and dropped her head to the side, tongue stuck out like she'd hanged herself.

I wrote, *Get back to me in a few years on that lesbian thing.*

DRAMA CLUB

Whatever. The show had to go on.

"This is *not* going to interfere with your working relationship with Jimmy," Mr. Sheldon instructed me backstage before rehearsal.

I adjusted the waist of my rented skirt and gave him a withering look: *Sheldon, we both know I'm a pro.* Jimmy Wilson was a bit player, just another boy from the chorus. *I* was the star of the show. Since Mr. Sheldon had given me the leading role in our school's spring production of *Guys and Dolls*, boys didn't matter anymore. I'd found my true love – dramatics.

Mr. Sheldon tugged the hem of his blazer. "All right. I just need you to stay focused."

"I'm *focused*," I stressed. "Let's rehearse."

"Good girl." He redimpled his tie and strode onstage, clapping loudly. "All right, people, places!"

Drama Club had become my life. I cut back on shifts at the snack stand, gave up afternoons in the park with Alice and Hope, passed up all manner of recreational drugs – "No thanks, I have to *perform* later." I sang exuberantly around the group home – "Ask me *how* do I feel, ask me *now* that we're *cozy* and *cliiiiin*ging!" – grabbing Becky the Baby in a tango dip, dancing past fat, mean Mavis's suspicious eye.

"What drug is that girl taking now?" Mavis said.

"I'm *happy*," I replied, pirouetting around Shirley the Nympho. "Don't worry, I'm sure it won't last long."

Poulos noted my success at our monthly meeting, looking over her notes. "It seems you're quite the young actress," she observed.

Was she praising me or accusing me? Poulos was crafty – I'd seen her pick secrets out of girls like a safecracker, wielding only a double-edged statement ("It appears that Shirley's quite . . . *popular* at school").

I kept up my smile, sweating and full of anti-drug-test tea. "I, uh . . . yeah."

She smiled her ugly smile back at me, waiting for more.

"I really like my drama teacher, Mr. Sheldon."

"Mm hmm."

"He says I'm a natural."

"I'm sure you are."

Okay, that was it. I was clamming up. Poulos wasn't going to trick me into self-incrimination. I'd been at the group home for four months, and I'd managed to evade Treatment thus far – nothing was going to trip me up now. She could put bamboo shoots under my gnawed, half-polished fingernails. I wasn't talking.

"Will you be inviting your mother to the spring play?"

Um, my who now? I got a tight feeling in my chest. I might have actually preferred the bamboo. I hadn't seen old Barb since my intake interview, when she'd made sure to emphasize to everyone what a druggie slut I was. "Yeah . . . I guess I didn't think about it."

Poulos looked pleased and scribbled a note to herself. I hated when she did that. I wanted to whip out my own notebook and start writing things about her: *Hateful witch; probably sterile*. She assessed me again, eyes narrow, head cocked. "You know, your mother called last week and requested a home visit with you."

"She *did*?"

I couldn't keep the shock off my face. She called? I'd half-expected never to hear from her again. And a home visit – like me going to visit her at home? Why did she want me to come home? She knew I wouldn't set foot in that house with Dave there, no matter how badly I wanted to see Jake. But maybe . . . maybe she'd canned him again! *Of course!* How many months had it been since I left, six? That was their record for staying together. She must have dumped Dave, and now she wanted me back.

Or maybe that was just my insane, zombielike hope, killed and buried a dozen times but always rising from the grave again. I dug my nails into my thigh, trying to maintain an impassive mien.

Poulos watched me like a scientist watches a rat. "How would you feel about a home visit?"

Um, freaked out? Exhilarated? Homicidal? "I don't know," I mumbled. "Depends."

She scribbled another note. *Gah.* I tried to peer over and see what she wrote, but I couldn't. The longer she wrote, the harder I gripped my thigh. Finally she quit it, looked up, and smiled at me.

"I think a home visit is an excellent idea," she pronounced. "You can call your mother tonight."

My body said *flee*; my pulse sped and my temples pounded. I didn't want to call that house. Dave could answer. I wanted to shudder just thinking of the outgoing message on their answering machine, his hateful voice sneering, *Weeeee're not here right now.* I didn't want to go home. *He* would be there. And even if, by some miracle, he wasn't there now, he'd be back. He'd always come back, and I'd just have to leave. There was no point in visiting a home I could never go home to again.

"All right," I lied.

"Good." Poulos sat forward in her chair, squinting at me like a suspicious cop. "And I want you to get your mother tickets to the show. Get tickets for the girls and the counselors, too. We want to see this talent of yours on display."

It took all of my talent to stand up and smile. I delivered my line – "Okay, thanks, Miss Poulos" – and exited, stage left.

Mavis hovered within earshot as I dialed my mom on the phone in the counselors' room. I put my back between Mavis and the phone and held my index finger over the hang-up button. Just in case Dave answered.

Three rings. I was thinking I'd get the machine, then my mother picked up. "Hello."

Her voice was higher than normal, and tense. I heard Jake burbling in the background, and my throat stuck for a second. "H-Hi. Mom. It's Janice."

"Hi, Jan," she said, relaxing, voice dropping back to its customary key. "I'm *really* glad you called."

Like I'd never left home. Like the past six months hadn't happened. Like she hadn't sat there in Poulos's office with her nicotine-stained finger pointed at me, saying *I* was the one to blame for fucking up the family. The bile rose in my stomach, even as the old zombie hope started clawing its way out of its grave in my chest.

"What's up," I asked, wary.

She sighed, preparing for a speech. "Look, Jan, I know things haven't been the best between us lately . . . I really regret that things got to this point. I know I've made some mistakes . . ."

"Uh-huh." I knew this speech by heart – *thud thud* – this was the speech she used to give while we were waiting for the locksmith to change the locks. She'd made some mistakes, she needed my support . . . *Just say it, Mom. Say it. Dave is gone, and you want me to come home.*

"Jan, Dave is gone, and I want you to come home."

I let out a huff like I'd been punched. *Not again!* I thought, and *Finally!*

"I know you've heard it before, but this time, it's really true. Jake and I are moving out. I should have an apartment by the end of the month."

"Uh-huh," I wheezed. "Okay."

She lowered her voice, like she was girding herself for a big admission. "Jan, you were right. You never should have had to go to that shelter in the first place. I know we've had our differences, but I think we can work through them. I'd really like you to come home."

I could feel Mavis staring holes in my back as I bent over the phone. I wondered how it would feel to go home, to be normal, to never feel those eyes on me again. Jake called *ba-ba!* in the background, and I pictured bringing it to him, walking across the Dave-free apartment to the fridge, warming it up, and putting it in his grabby little mitts, his stubby fingers all working as one.

"Jan?"

Her entreating tone – I'd heard her use it on clients over the phone. My mouth felt suctioned dry, like I was waiting in the dentist's chair for a root canal. "I'm here."

"Look, Jan, I know it's sudden. But will you at least say yes to a visit? To lunch? You don't have to come here. I can come meet you."

And oh, I'd been waiting for this. The whole time I'd been away, I'd been waiting for her to beg my forgiveness and ask me to come home – thinking, since that first phone call at the shelter, about the speech I'd give, and my conditions; about how I'd laugh in her face, how she'd cry. No, I'd say, *I'm not coming home. I'm never coming home again.*

The word came out small and faint. "Okay."

"My mother wants me to come home," I told Hope.

"Really?" We huddled in her tiny bedroom in the afternoon, cutting seventh and eighth periods on a whim, listening to KISS FM on the radio, and smoking her mom's pot. Hope broke up a small bud and put it in the glass pipe. "My fucking mom wants me to move out."

"No kidding." I'd already admired her new bruise. "Hey, there's a bed opening up at the group home. Shanita's leaving next month."

Hope made the gas face. "Is that the girl with the breast milk?"

"Yep."

"No thanks."

"I figured."

It wasn't a serious suggestion anyway. There was a line of girls already waiting for Shanita's bed. And Hope wasn't stupid enough to put herself into a group home; I was an object lesson in what happened if you turned to the system for help. Nobody wanted to live like me.

The lock clicked on the front door, and we froze.

"Holy shit," hissed Hope. "Hide the bowl, hide the bowl."

Her mom. My stomach pitched. We were fucked. It was two o'clock in the afternoon on a school day, and the whole apartment stank like pot – *her* pot. The door opened and slammed shut, and Hope's mom bellowed. "Hope!"

"Shit!"

I tried to dive under the bed, a stupid impulse, but there was no time. Hope's mom, a tall, broad, sandy-haired woman wielding a magazine like a cudgel, appeared at the bedroom door. She charged in and grabbed Hope by the upper arm, whipping her back and forth.

"What the hell are you doing here! You're supposed to be in school!"

"Mom, stop, there was an assembly! They said we could leave early!"

"This place *stinks of pot!*"

"We weren't doing anything!"

Hope's mom slapped her hard across the face. "Don't you fucking lie to me!"

"Ow!" Hope caught the backhand and started to cry. "Ow! Mom, stop it! We weren't doing anything!"

Hope struggled against her mom, shoving and kicking; I cringed from where I was trapped, in the corner between the bed and the wall. *Stop, stop!* I couldn't get out of the room, I couldn't get between them. Her mom raised the rolled-up magazine in her hand, slammed her with it, and Hope yelped in pain; I yelled without thinking, "Stop!"

Hope's mom turned her head to me. She was a red-eyed Gorgon, her face contorted with hate.

"*What the fuck are you doing here?*"

"I'm sorry, I'm sorry, I'm – "

"*GET OUT.*"

"I'm sorry, I'm really – "

I'm really a coward. How humiliating, for everybody. I couldn't protect Hope, couldn't even look at her, shielding herself and crying – I was too busy running away. I scurried for the door, grabbed my book bag, and ran.

I heard a loud *thump!* as something heavy hit the wall.

I flung open the front door and flew through.

Alice and I waited for Hope on the corner before school, Alice swiveling her head like a periscope on a very lost submarine, tapping her ashless cigarette.

"What time is it?"

I peered into the window of the deli.

"Eight-twenty," I reported. The herd of students was starting to migrate down the block toward first period, the stragglers taking one last drag before they stomped their cigarettes and moved on.

"Let's wait," she said. "I don't feel like going to first anyway."

"Yeah, me neither."

Alice stared off toward the subway, like she could make Hope appear through her superior mind power. "Hope's mom is just so fucked up."

I shook my head. "It was ugly, dude. I feel bad, I just ran out, I didn't even . . . I don't know."

"Yeah . . ." She tapped her smoke, pensive. "I can't believe you guys cut out without me yesterday."

I looked at her sideways – was she kidding? She seemed kind of serious. Alice didn't like it when I hung out with Hope without her, which was preposterous – everyone knew that they were the primary bonded pair, the proton and the neutron; I was just the electron, loosely orbiting. Alice continued to stare down the block, smoking and tapping. I turned my head and stared after her.

"Well . . . it was kind of last minute," I allowed.

"You guys should come get me next time."

Well, don't worry, Alice, you didn't miss anything good. "Yeah. No, we should have. It's just, I heard Sheldon was sick, so rehearsal was canceled, and then Hope was coming out of sixth, and I said – "

Alice perked up. "Hey, girl!"

There was Hope, coming toward us with her head down and her fists clenched. Either she'd been punched in both eyes or she'd been up all night, both of which were equally likely.

"Hey," I said, hangdog. "I'm sorry I ran out, I didn't – "

She shook her head – it wasn't important. "*MY FUCKING MOM THREW ME OUT.*"

"Oh my god! Hopey!"

Alice embraced her stiffly. Hope just stood there and fumed. "I hate her fucking guts so much. She's totally psycho! You saw her, right? She went crazy on me!"

I nodded emphatically. "She did! She just started whaling – "

"I know!" interrupted Alice. "I was just saying to Janice, your mom is so fucked up."

Hope could barely light a match, her hands were shaking so hard. I passed her my cigarette, and she lit hers off mine.

"What are you going to do?" I asked.

Her eyes weren't black, but they were bloodshot, and wet with tears. "I don't know. I should call the fucking cops on her. I'm serious. That shit is child abuse."

"Oh, Hopey!" Alice exclaimed again.

Hopey? I wondered. *When was this one coined?* "Do you want to go down to family court? I could take you."

Alice put her hand on Hope's arm. "Yeah, you know, you can totally sleep over at my house for a few nights. My mom's at her boyfriend's this weekend anyway."

"Can I?" Hope turned to Alice gratefully. "Thanks."

Understood. Alice's offer was better than mine. Nobody wanted to go to family court when they could just go to Alice's house, eat celery sticks with peanut butter, and watch afternoon TV. Also understood: Alice could offer Hope a place to stay, but she couldn't offer it to me. Because when I needed a place, it was for the rest of my adolescence. Whereas we all knew Hope would go home in a few days.

"Okay, well . . . if you did ever want to go to court," I said.

"Thanks," said Hope.

Alice picked up Hope's book bag and handed it to her. "Let's go get breakfast. You must be totally in shock."

"Yeah," said Hope. "Thank god I have you guys. I seriously don't know what I'd do."

Alice stepped in and hugged her again. "We love you, Hopey."

"Yeah," I added, off to the side. "We do."

I knew something was wrong when my mother didn't call.

I tried to brush it off. *She's busy,* I thought. *She's busy packing all their stuff to move. She said she'd probably have to go to court again – she's probably in court. She never actually said, "I'll call you Wednesday" or "I'll call you by next week," she just said she'd call.* I was mad at myself for feeling so impatient, for waiting by the phone – I mean, if my mother didn't call, so what? It wasn't like I was dying for a home visit or anything. I wasn't the one who requested it.

But I was the one who cracked.

"I thought you were going to call," I said over the phone in the counselors' room, gently accusing. "I thought we were going to have lunch." Mavis lurked behind me, pretending not to listen.

"I was. We are." My mom sounded distracted. "I'm sorry, Jan, it's been . . ."

A difficult time. Uh oh. My stomach sank. I rotated slowly around the phone, keeping my back to Mavis. "How's the new apartment?"

"Well, I don't have anything yet, but I should have something soon."

I closed my eyes, groaning inside like a rusty hinge. *Come on, Mom. I told everybody you want me to come home. Don't make me look stupid again. Please.*

I said calmly, "Mom, if something is happening with Dave . . ."

"Jan . . ." She exhaled, harried. I wasn't the good client she wanted to woo anymore; now I was the pushy client whose calls she screened. "I don't know what's happening."

My voice got smaller and higher. "You don't know?"

"Jake and I are going to move, Jan, we are! I mean that. It's just taking me longer than I thought. I – " She stopped short, casting about for a shred of credibility. "Look, Jan, I still think we should have lunch and talk about your coming home."

"Whatever," I told her, weary. "Maybe I'll see you at the play."

"Jan . . ."

I kept my back to Mavis and her audible smirk. "Bye, Mom." I put down the phone and turned to leave the room.

"So, Juhneece." Mavis tilted back in her chair behind the counselors' desk, hands resting below her bosom, satisfied look on her face. "When are you going home?"

Whatever. The show must go on.

Sheldon put both hands on my shoulders and looked into my eyes. "You are going to go out there, and you are going to give everything you have," he told me. "No matter what else happens, no matter what you do, you go out there, and you *give. Use* what you're feeling, Janice. I know you're going to be great."

I nodded, still sniffling. The auditorium was packed, we'd peeked from backstage, and you could hear the audience, murmuring like a well-trained group of extras in their seats. The group-home girls and counselors took up almost a whole row by themselves. They bitched about the mandatory field trip, but before I left for the final tech rehearsal that afternoon, they gave me a card that said, YOU'RE A STAR, and everybody wrote something personal. Genie wrote: "Don't forget me when your famous, bitch. You're beautiful. I love you."

I didn't see my mom.

Sheldon was right, that didn't matter now. I had to redo my eye makeup so I didn't look washed out, had to open my throat and stretch my palate, had to *embody* the role, the woman, Sergeant Sarah Brown, the virginal Salvation Army doll who risks her virtue for the love of a man's soul. I saw my Sky Masterson backstage, and he winked at me, gangster-style. I cold-shouldered him, as I would for the entire first act. That was me, Sarah Brown. I was noble and upright, my longing for love held firmly in check.

The music started. "Five minutes," whispered Sheldon behind me. He dabbed sweat off his pale brow with his pocket square. I nodded primly his way.

He darted off to whisper something to Sky. I retreated to the corner and watched the opening scene begin. I couldn't help it – my eye was drawn to the crack in the curtains.

No mom.

I stood straight and fixed my hat. I took my place. I heard my cue. I strode proudly onto the stage and began to sing. "Follow the fold and stray no more, stray no more, stray no more . . ."

9

SUMMER

All in all, an inauspicious sophomore year.

"I'm fucking jolly well glad *that's* over," I swore, passing Alice the official first joint of the summer. We'd just come from our last day at school – well, *half* our last day at school, really – we only went in to get our report cards, trade some last-minute party info, and collect a few more scribbled tributes in our yearbooks ("Stay high, sexy!"), then we took off after lunch, dashing out the back door to the familiar shriek of the fire alarm. Now we lounged in the grass in Sheep Meadow with the rest of the last-day cutters, including charter Boyses member Leland Banks, a.k.a. the Black Bulldog of Love, a pug-faced hardbody whose résumé included a recent ejection from the basketball team for partying. I had been brave enough to rest my head on his lap today, and for some reason he was tolerating this. So far, the summer was going great.

I lifted my head briefly to squint at passersby and caught sight of the snack stand, where I'd been picking up shifts again. I gave it the mental middle finger. *Fuck you, snack stand. I'm not working today.*

I said, "I hate having to *see* my job every time I hang out."

The comment went unacknowledged, as I said the same thing every time we came to Sheep Meadow, which was almost every day, now that the weather was nice and the dealers were out in droves. In summer, Sheep Meadow shared duty with Washington Square Park as the social nexus of the high school universe. It was the uptown annex – like Washington Square but with more preppies.

I was actually quite lucky to have scored a job at the snack stand, in the center of all the action. I got as many free zucchini sticks as I could cram into my face during a given shift, and I could dispense *beer*. And *ice cream*. For *free*. Alice and Hope were heavily invested in this plan, serving as waitstaff to our entire hungry clique. "We need four beers, two mozzarella sticks, a tuna salad pita, a chicken salad pita, and a bunch of brownies and shit." I cheerfully rang it all up. "That'll be two dollars, please. Thank you!" After my shift, I'd pour a beer for myself, peel off my T-shirt and visor, and head into the grassy field, where I'd be welcomed like a war hero, a joint passed my way. Not a bad job at all.

Work also made me look good at home. I turned over half my pay every week to Grandma Dolores, who put it in a savings envelope with my name on it, clucking with approval. "You work so hard, Janice, you know you do us proud. Why can't the rest of these girls act more like you?"

"Oh, Dolores," I protested, "you know *all* of us girls here are trying our best."

I didn't mind handing over half my pay, as I was stealing twice my salary in cash from the register. It was a trick I learned from my colleague Star. Star was a gregarious, talkative girl, always smiling and engaging everyone – management, prep crew, customers – and one day I asked her if I could borrow ten bucks until payday. She looked at me like I was a whole can of nuts.

"Take it from the register, fool."

Obviously, I wasn't as smart as I thought. I was already stealing food, why didn't I take some money while I was at it? "Uh, how?"

"You didn't figure it out?"

I admitted that I hadn't. Star broke it down for me.

"What you do is – they order, like, a chicken pita and a large soda. So you say, 'That's four dollars plus two dollars, that's six dollars, please.' Then they give you six dollars, and you put it in the register, but you only ring up four dollars, and you remember two in your head. Then when you get to twenty in your head, you take out a twenty and you put it in your bra. 'Cause if they search you, they can't search your bra."

Wow. And here I was, thinking I was getting everything I could out of life. Stealing money made things infinitely better. Suddenly I had money for pot and mushrooms, for dinners and drinks at Mexican restaurants, for some clothes from the vintage resale place on West Seventy-eighth Street. I bought actual hair dye instead of my usual homemade bathroom sink mixture of hydrogen peroxide and ammonia. I could take taxis when I went out with Alice and Hope, which meant I could stay at Danceteria until 11:15, which was still way too early even to get there, much less to leave and go home and play cards with a bunch of nymphos and brats, but it was at least fifteen minutes funner than 11:00.

I even had money for a little bit of coke. Me and Alice and Hope loved coke, but it wasn't easy to get. They didn't sell it openly in either of the parks, and we didn't know any regular dealers. Sometimes a guy at a club would mention that he had some, and the three of us would follow him around, waiting for him to dole out a little sniff, perking up every time he feinted toward the pocket of his suit jacket, but more often than not it was a huge tease; we wasted our time and went home frustrated.

But now that we were becoming established on the scene, we were meeting more people, and sometimes those people were holding coke. And I could take two twenties out of my bra and hand them over, still warm, while Hope and Alice lurked on my case like the Secret Service, ready to hustle me to a secure area.

"Awesome, so cool. I'll totally give you ten bucks on Monday."

"Don't worry about it."

"Are you sure?"

Sniiiifffffff. Yes. I am positive about everything. Would you like to hear all about it? Only I can explain.

The prop for cocaine that summer was iced coffee. I walked in the door at curfew holding a half-empty cup, and if I seemed hyper during the opening of *Saturday Night Live*, I blamed it on the coffee.

"I'm addicted to this stuff!" I exclaimed, rubbing the tops of my thighs like I was trying to start a fire. "Oh my god, I'm *never* gonna get to sleep tonight!"

My thoughts came too fast – *I can't let . . . So good . . . Never tell . . .* – crashing into the backs of other thoughts, piling up; bloody thoughts crawling out of their car windows, trying to reach the top of the pile. Whirling helicopters of thought swooping over the scene. I had to talk to someone.

"Come smoke with me." I dragged Genie by the arm into our room, lit two Newports, and stuck my head out the window. She squeezed in beside me. "I'm so fucking wired right now, I can't even . . . Holy shit."

Genie's eyes widened. "You are? You lucky bitch! Do you have any more? You have to give me some!"

"What, are you crazy? I didn't bring it here! We did most of it tonight; Alice is holding the rest. Dude, it's *so* good. I am *flying* right now."

"Oh my god, I want to do coke so bad! That would be so fun! You better get me some!"

"I will! I will!"

"Ucch!" Genie made a grumpy face at me. "You're so lucky."

I pressed my arm against hers, heat surging inside me, overpowered by the urge to tell her I loved her. "Dude, it is *so* good, and I'm totally going to hook you up. Because, seriously, Genie? You are the best roommate. You rock. You are totally loyal, and you have hooked me up so many times, and even if Domenic Burns turned out to be a worthless scumbag, you still hooked me up – No, you did, Genie, I'm serious. You're like . . . my sister. No, you are. I always know I can trust you. I don't care what everybody says about, like, you're a JAP or whatever – you're awesome. You're like the best person. I love you."

Genie twisted her mouth, trying not to show her smile. It was true, I loved her. She was bossy, loud, and obnoxious, she had seventeen pairs of shoes; whatever, I didn't care. Genie was fierce. She took her lumps in group therapy and hollered for more. She led midnight raids on the supply pantry and shared the pilfered applesauce with me. She was a superstar, with a big gold heart under her fluorescent pink sweatshirt. I loved Genie, and she loved me.

Genie French-inhaled smoke through her flared nostrils and snapped her thick fingers in the air. "That's *right*," she croaked, pleased. "And don't you forget it."

. . .

It was my least favorite housemate, Indira the Bully, who busted into our room the next day, eyes flashing as she bore the hushed good news: "Mavis is going on vacation next week. Sandy's going to be on two nights, and the rest of the week it's Grandma Dolores."

Yes. Genie and I tightened our fists and grimaced with joy. Even better than a vacation from school was a vacation from Mavis. Indira nodded seriously, her wizened eyes trained intently on us. "You *know* I'm breaking curfew on Friday night, and Grandma won't do shit about it either, watch."

The house was quietly but definitely abuzz with similar plans. We usually had two counselors on overnight; they never left us alone with only Dolores – this was just a beautifully curtained, lushly landscaped window of opportunity to get away with some fucked up shit. Genie procured several airline-sized bottles of peach schnapps, all of them hidden in various pairs of socks, and begged me to get some mushrooms or some coke – "something *fun*," she implored – but I didn't want to take the risk of Genie getting us busted, so I pretended there was a drug drought that weekend.

"I tried," I told her, showing her my empty, upturned palms. *Oh well.* "But everybody was dry. Sucks. I totally wanted to trip together, too."

We had to content ourselves with the peach schnapps, which we shared with Shirley and Becky in their room after lights out on the first night of Dolores's solo reign. Becky made churlish faces over the liquor – "Eww! Tastes like poo-poo!" – and Shirley regaled us with tales of her latest affair, with a guy she met playing guitar on the subway. "He's like twenty-four, and he's a totally genius musician, and he lived with his mother in the Bronx until, like, last week, and now he's sleeping in Riverside Park while he gets a place of his own. I want to move in with him *so bad*."

Genie toasted her with a miniature bottle. "Go 'head," she slurred approvingly. It had been a while since she'd been drunk, and she wasn't wearing it especially well, her voice having climbed precariously over the past hour.

"Shhh," I warned her. "Whisper."

"*Why?*" she bleated, full voice. "Grandma's not waking up. Have you *seen* her napping on the couch?"

Becky giggled, grabbing her feet and rocking. None of these girls could handle their booze; while I was out binge drinking every weekend, they were watching Go-Go's videos on Channel 68. "Okay," I whispered. "I just don't want us to get in trouble."

"*Neh neh neh neh neh neh,*" Genie singsonged. This was supposed to be her impression of me. "I'm Janice, I'm a suck-up, I never want to get in trouble."

"Hee hee!" Becky rocked and giggled like she was being tickled. Shirley put her finger to her lips and shushed her, giggling almost as hard. "Shhh! Shhh!" I was missing the humor in it myself.

Genie's eyes were slits, and one of her hands supported her head unsteadily as she reclined on the floor. "None of you bitches would last a minute in lockup. I ever tell you about lockup? They tie you to the bed the first night, you know that?"

Shirley nodded, wide-eyed. We'd all heard Genie's superscary tales of lockup before; Shirley wanted to talk more about the subway guy, but Genie was gearing up for a roll. She knocked back the last swig of her third schnapps, lids heavy, and tucked in her chin like she was going to belch. "Yeah. And they shave your head, too. They don't even care if you're a girl!"

Shirley clutched at her own thick, brown mane. "I'd *die,*" she swore.

"Yeah, it's bad shit. You're scared of *Treatment* – try *lockup.*"

I cringed – her voice was way too loud and indignant. If Dolores didn't wake up, Julie the Snitch would, and our asses would be fried.

"No thanks," I whispered meaningfully, pressing my hands down as if to muffle the sound.

As if. "*God,*" said Genie. "What's your problem?"

I thought I heard something in the hallway, and the stubble on my legs stood on end. "I'm sorry," I whispered. "I just don't want to get busted."

"You think *I* wanna get busted?" She sat up and pointed at herself, her head wagging back and forth like Mavis's. "Because *I* don't. I've been worse places than you can *imagine* – "

"I know!" I whispered, explosive. "I'm not trying to say anything. Calm down!"

"Don't tell me to calm down!"

Becky stopped giggling, and Shirley bit her lip, alarmed. Noise in the hallway? Hard to tell, with all the noise Genie was making. She reared back and frowned, recomposing herself. "You're such a Goody Two-shoes, it's disgusting," she hissed, hushed.

"Me?" How did this conversation get started? I mean, I knew we all loved to fight, and everybody had to participate or it was no fun, but couldn't we all just dump on Becky, like usual? What had I done to warrant this?

Genie's red face was all up in mine. "Yeah, you. You get away with more shit than anyone in the house, because you're such a suck-up fake."

"Okay." I started to back away, hands out in front of me for protection. "I don't know what I did, but – "

"*Neh neh neh neh neh neh.*" Genie sneered at me, and Becky started giggling again. Shirley's eyes flicked back and forth between the three of us, an uncertain smile on her face. "You're just Little Miss Perfect, aren't you?"

No, that would be Julie, who was probably listening with her ear against the door, transcribing the conversation in eyeliner on her knee. Genie and I could discuss this later, when she wasn't quite so hammered – right now, I wanted to get back to my bedroom while the getting was good, stick my head out the window and smoke, let the humid air swell around my head until my ears clogged and I forgot where I was.

"Something like that," I said under my breath, and tiptoed out of the room.

We didn't discuss it again, me and Genie. I got up before everybody the next day and went to work, then spent the afternoon in Sheep Meadow with Hope and Alice, clocking Hope's new crush, Jay Finster, with his flattop haircut and his practiced smirk. We plucked blades of grass and chewed their white roots, watching Jay move from clique to clique in the grass, massaging the girls' shoulders and fist-pounding the guys. I couldn't ditch the aftertaste of peach schnapps.

I stared at Jay's broad shoulders, barely even appreciating their glorious sashay as he strode by. "Do you guys think I'm a Goody Two-shoes?"

"Hah," said Hope, genuinely amused.

"Not at all," Alice assured me. "Maybe, like, a *Slutty* Two-shoes."

"Oh my god, he's coming over." Hope spoke out of the corner of her mouth, a bad ventriloquist.

"Ladies . . ." Jay approached and crouched down next to Hope, arm on one knee. "How are we today?"

We're brooding. Or I was, at least. Alice and Hope made blasé chitchat with Jay – "*Nothing* going on, *everyone's* away for the summer, *no* good parties, *sucks*" – and I chewed blades of grass like a cow, ruminating on my relative popularity at the group home. I'd thought that Genie and I were best friends – sisters, cellies, loyal for life – then I saw her red, triumphant face, telling me what a two-faced suck-up I was. She couldn't really go from loving me to hating me like that, could she? Maybe she was just jealous. Or drunk.

I was morose at dinner, sitting next to Quiet Gladys and staring at my frozen peas.

"What's wrong, child?" asked Grandma Dolores, gesturing my way. "You feeling all right?"

"I think I have my period," I mumbled. It was the all-purpose group home excuse.

Dolores wrinkled her forehead. "You need some Midol?"

Genie smirked at Becky from behind her napkin, and I lost my appetite altogether. I shook my head. "I'm all right. Just not hungry. Can I please be excused?"

I crawled into bed, hiding behind my copy of *The Fountainhead.* I could hear the rest of the girls playing hearts in the living room, Shanita on the pay phone talking to her boyfriend, the laugh track on the TV. *Two more years,* I told myself. *Just a little over two more years, and I'll turn eighteen, and I will never see any of these treacherous bitches again.* I kept my lamp trained on the page, and when Genie came in for lights-out, I held the book in front of my face like a shield.

"Good ni-ight," she sang.

I grunted a reply. "Mnugh."

No smoking out the window tonight, no ghost stories from lockup, just the faint buzz of Genie's glottal snore coming within minutes from across the room. I tossed for a while, thumb in mouth, then read some more by flashlight until I started to feel drowsy and turned off my light. Someone padded softly past the door to our room; it was probably Becky, going to pee. Except it sounded like she was wearing shoes and heading for the front door.

The *balls* on whoever it was! Nobody had ever successfully sneaked out of the house after lights-out; there was only the legendary incident when Shanita tried to slip out the back entry one night and wound up tripping all over the garbage cans in the hall, a cacophony even Dolores couldn't sleep through. That was before my time. She got three months of Treatment, and then she had a miscarriage. Shanita was definitely not the one sneaking out.

The sneaker-outer was almost at the front door, and then I heard her pause. *The locks.* Should she turn them slowly and quietly, wincing with every pin, or snap them open and fly? She went for the chain first, then the first snap of the lock –

– and then a door creaked from the other side of the apartment. I froze in my bed like it was *me* sneaking, my back plastered against the hallway wall, heart knocking like an angry neighbor against my chest.

"Who is that?" Dolores's voice was scratchy and faint from sleep and cigarettes, echoing in the still halls. "Who's there?"

A band of light appeared under the door; I heard the other girls murmuring from their rooms. Genie sputtered awake and blinked at me, gawking. "What's going on?"

From the hallway: "Shirley!"

Genie swung out of bed and ripped open our door; I was right behind her, the rest of the girls shuffling into the hall, Dolores hustling toward the door in her pilly robe. "Shirley Segal, where do you think you're going!"

Shirley squirmed in the light, arms protecting her face, which was made up like a cancan girl's, her skimpy outfit and heels belying her protestations – "I was just going to the bathroom! I wasn't doing anything!"

"Then what is this purse you're carrying!" Dolores reached out one of her twig arms and snatched Shirley's bag, her voice shaking with outrage. She was elderly, but she wasn't blind. "What is this in here?"

An extra day's worth of clothes. A strip of condoms. And an unopened airline-sized bottle of peach schnapps. Julie gasped from her bedroom door; "Oh, *no*," exclaimed Indira, ecstatic. I goggled at Genie, and she goggled back, her eyes wide, her lips smashed shut. "It's not mine!" cried Shirley. "I found it! I didn't do anything, I was just – "

"You are coming in this room, and we are calling Miss Poulos *right now*."

"Nooooo!" Shirley wailed like a dying calf as Dolores fixed her claw on her arm, dragging her into the counselors' office. "*Noooooo!*"

The door slammed behind them, and the rest of us stood there blinking, mouths hanging open, stupefied.

"What's going to happen to her?" asked Becky. She clutched her Boo-Boo Bunny to her chest, scrunching up her face like she was ready to cry.

"She *really* needs Treatment," clucked Julie.

"Oh *no*," repeated Indira. "That shit is *hilarious*."

"Oh my god," I muttered, stunned. "Oh my fucking god."

The door to the counselors' office flew open, and Dolores's head snapped out like an angry turtle's. "Now the rest of you girls get back into bed *right now*, and I had better not hear a single peep out of anyone!" *Slam*.

Genie and I turned and floated back inside our room, the unreal feeling hanging like mist in the air between us. She went over to the window without speaking and stuck her head out, leaving room for me. I picked up two cigarettes and a book of matches and joined her, my arm pressed up against hers. I handed her a smoke.

She took it and lit it, then lit mine. We dragged, wordless, staring at the brick wall of the air shaft across from us.

"Well," said Genie, at last. "It's a good thing Shirley likes fucking. Because she sure is fucked now."

10
FALL

And then, because things weren't crummy enough, I went and slept with Jay Finster.

It was a terrible way to start the school year, fooling around with Hope's new man. It was like I *wanted* to lose all my friends. Why else would I sleep with a guy who was already sleeping with Hope? What possible motive could I have for fucking her over like that? I trudged down the street after school with my head low, heels dragging, trying to come up with any explanation besides the stupid truth:

I did it because he asked me to.

"He *asked* you to?" Alice was incredulous. She followed me down the block, repeating it – "He *asked* you to?" – just a little too loud, considering the proximity of the rest of the clique.

I reshouldered my book bag and kept heading down the block. "Um, I'm not going to talk about this here."

Alice trotted right alongside me. "Why not, *Janice*."

"Because it's none of anybody's business."

"Uh, it's Hope's business, and Hope is my friend, and that means it's my business."

She got in front of me, and I stopped short to avoid plowing into her. "Well, I'll talk to Hope about it."

Alice looked inordinately smug, even for her. The Hair glared at me blackly. "She doesn't want to talk to you, *Janice*."

I didn't like the way she kept saying my name. "Well then, I'll write her a note, *Alice*."

I started down the block again. She caught my arm, and I turned around. "She doesn't want you to write her a note. She's really pissed at you. And so am I. What you did was totally fucked up."

I know. Okay? I got it. She was right. I fucked up, and it must have been completely intentional. I knew it was fucked up while I was thinking about it, I knew it was fucked up while I was doing it, I knew it was fucked up afterward when we were smoking a cigarette talking about how fucked up it was. I knew Hope would be really hurt if she found out, and I knew that I loved Hope, and that she didn't deserve to be hurt. And I did it anyway. What was wrong with me?

Alice looked like she had something delicious in her mouth and she was sucking the life out of it. I really wanted to punch her right in the kisser, that hypocrite – I mean, what about Brian Cooper? I saw her practically sucking his dick on the roof at that party last year! I wanted to throw that in her face, but I knew she'd just deny it – *What? You don't even know what you're talking about. You were drunk. And besides, Hope wasn't even dating him yet.*

"Whatever," I said instead. "Fine."

I turned away and trudged toward the subway, hating Alice, hating myself. Hating Jay for telling everyone when he swore he wouldn't. "It'll just be between us," he'd assured me. "Come on, I know you want me as much as I want you."

He wanted me. So I went. He was Jay Finster, for chrissakes, he was practically a celebrity! What was I supposed to do, say no? Alice would have done the same damn thing if he'd come up to her after trig and started rubbing her back, rapping that Finster rap – "You look too good today, you know that? How's a man supposed to learn anything with you looking like that?" I was heroic for holding out against this treatment for a full five days before agreeing to meet him after seventh period behind the gym.

What a naïve idiot I was. I stood on the subway, blinking hot tears of rue, reliving homeroom, everybody laughing – "Hey, Janice, I heard you really blew Finster's mind yesterday!" "Yeah, it wasn't just his mind she blew!"

The next few hours were excruciating. I should have cut out after homeroom, but I had a history test with no makeups last period, and I needed that grade. I ran into Hope on the stairs before sixth, her eyes puffy – as soon as she saw me, she turned and walked away. Then I saw

Jay Finster preening in the fourth-floor hallway. The guys around him groaned as I walked by and pointed. "Uhhhh ooohhhh!"

"What," smirked this girl I barely knew. "Aren't you even going to say hi to him?"

I tossed my head and walked by. I took my history test with my stomach crawling up my throat. It didn't go well.

I got off the subway and stopped at a pay phone, called the snack stand and said I was sick. My manager, Alfredo, was surprised – I never called in sick, even when I had a bad summer cold – the cash was just too good to pass up. "You sound awful," he said. "It's slow today anyway. We'll see you on Friday." I plodded home, nauseated with stress and regret.

"You're home early," Mavis observed.

I should have gone to work, I realized too late; I should have gone someplace – a library, a church – someplace where they just let you sit and be quiet. Any place but here. "I'm off work today."

Mavis tilted her head back, the better to peer at me. "You never come home right after school. What's the matter."

"Nothing."

She narrowed her watery eyes. Maybe I could hide being stoned – I had plenty of practice at it – but I could not disguise how I was feeling. "Something is going on," she diagnosed.

"I'm just not feeling great."

"Mm hmm. Let me smell your breath."

I let out a little grunt of frustration. This was a disgusting ritual, even more disgusting than peeing in a cup. Mavis leaned forward, her huge face right up in mine, the smell of her floral skin lotion cloying as I opened my mouth and huffed. *Nothing.* Nothing but cigarettes and coffee, and a blow pop, that's about all I'd put in there today. Should have smelled me yesterday, bitch.

Mavis leaned back and stared at me some more. She and Sandy were being extra vigilant since the night Shirley the Nympho tried to sneak out of the house. We girls were being extra vigilant too since the day after, when they put Shirley the Nympho in a lockup.

None of us were forgetting what Shirley looked like when they took her away, how desperately she begged not to go, how the transporters took her by the arms and dragged her out of the apartment into the van downstairs. They would shave her head the first night, and tie her to a bed. Her roommates would beat her with a lock in a sock. We had a new housemate now, a girl named Angelique, whose single mother died of breast cancer and left her an orphan. Shanita the Milk-Squirter was gone too. The house was a sober place.

I barely looked up from my book when Genie came in.

"Hi, *Roomie*." She put her big bag down and wiped her face with her hands. "What are you doing here?"

"Reading."

"Well, duh." She started taking off her turquoise-striped shirt and dark-wash jeans. I could smell the cigarette smoke and sweat coming off her even through my own. "Why are you home so early? Why aren't you out having fun?"

"Reading is fun," I deadpanned.

"Whatever. I wanna do something fun. You keep saying you're gonna take me someplace, but you never do."

Genie and I were best friends again, at least tacitly; we'd never officially made up after our one-sided spat, but everything was nominally okay between us, as long as I remembered which of us was the boss. I could continue my campaign of illicit sexing and drugging, but only if I included Genie – *that* was what being a loyal roommate was about.

I sighed and put my book down. "Where do you want to go?"

"I don't know. I want to go to Studio 54!"

Studio 54 had long passed its peak, though the girls and I still went sometimes, if we had free passes and there was nothing else to do. These days it was mostly filled with the bridge-and-tunnel crowd. Genie would fit in perfectly there.

"Studio is over." I went back to my book.

Genie flopped onto her bed in her bra and panties. "Well then, you pick! I just want to go someplace fun, where I can meet a lot of guys. And I want to do coke. And smoke pot. Anywhere!"

I sighed. Clubs were hard enough to get into without a JAP in a turquoise-striped shirt hanging off your arm, yelling, "I wanna see Simon Le Bon! I wanna do coke!" I could not bring myself to be socially liable for Genie.

"Uh, okay, let me just find the right night."

"That's what you always say! It's pissing me off!"

She was too loud, but I didn't dare shush her or she'd get louder. I dropped my own voice low, whispering to a drunk. "Okay, well, it's been hairy here lately! I don't want to get us in trouble."

Genie moaned and fell backward. "Oh my god! You're so frustrating." She sat up again and fixed me with her most determined glare, like Shirley Temple ready to stomp her foot. "We're not gonna get in trouble! Okay? I'll get you in trouble if you *don't* take me."

I closed my book and looked back at her. "You'll what?"

She smiled. "You heard me."

I did not smile in return. "And I know you're kidding."

She better have been. Genie knew far too much. I'd kill the bitch before I let her get me sent to lockup.

Genie batted her lashes at me, coy. "Am I?" She picked herself up off the bed and sailed over to her closet. "Well, I probably am," she mused. She flicked through the hangers for something she could wear to Studio 54. "But you should take me anyway, just to be sure."

I glared at her half-naked back, grousing as she hummed over her wardrobe.

"I *said* I'd take you, I'm *going* to take you. I never said I wasn't going to take you, I just didn't know *when*."

She hummed like she didn't hear me and held up a glittery silver blouse.

"We'll go Friday," I promised.

"This Friday?" She abandoned the blouse and flung herself onto my bed, grinning. "You swear?"

"I swear."

Genie grabbed my head and gave my cheek a big, sloppy smooch. "You're the best roommate ever! Besides me."

"I know," I said. She danced back to her closet, and I wiped off my cheek.

I was well past sick of living like this. As adept as I was, lying all the time was taxing, like living on camera. I was tired of residing with antagonists, people provoking me all day and all night, waiting for me to fall. There was never any respite, either – no privacy, even in the bathrooms – which didn't lock, of course, because then some girl might successfully swallow an entire bottle of Tylenol and need to have her stomach pumped, which happened anyway (Angelique the Orphan). My home life was just a flushing sinkhole of stomach pumps and lockups and drug tests and treatments, and people telling me I was angry, and threatening me, and giving me early curfew for smoking cigarettes with Genie out the window in my room.

I was looking at two more years before I turned eighteen. Two more years of liver and onions every Thursday, of smelling Genie's shit in the bathroom every time I brushed my teeth, of arguing through a cloud of stale smoke over who cheated at hearts, of cringing against Mavis's shrill, backward pronunciation of my name – "JuhNEECE!" Two more years of high school to go. It hardly seemed worth it. Next year, if I wanted, I could take my GED, drop out and get a job, and apply for independent living. Or I could stick it out, as Mr. Sheldon encouraged me to do, and apply to college.

Or I could go home. Wherever that might be.

It had been four months since my mom asked me to come home, then changed her mind. I got a card and a gift certificate for my birthday at the end of August, and she called on the counselors' phone that night, but I missed it, and I didn't call back, because I swore to myself after last time that I wasn't going to call her again. Not even from a pay phone during the day just to hear the answering machine. I wasn't doing that anymore.

Then one night Grandma Dolores came into the living room and beckoned me to the counselors' room. "Honey, it's your mama on the phone."

Mama. It sounded so sweet, the way Dolores said it; it fooled me. *Mama!* I wonder if I would have taken the call if she hadn't put it that way. I was already on my feet, moving toward the phone, even as I realized it was just another bullshit phone call from my mother. Right on schedule, too.

I picked up the phone, my heart sinking, beating in my stomach. "Hi, Mom."

"Hi, Jan. How are you."

"Fine." *Better off without you.* I kept it clipped, neutral, like she was the pushy client. I didn't ask how she was doing, and it threw her.

"Well, that's good, I'm . . ."

She was at a momentary loss for words. I thought of some that might apply:

1. Sorry. I'm so sorry that I faked you out yet again last spring, that I made you think Dave was gone *yet again,* when you didn't even care anymore, when you'd finally stopped hoping. I know you hadn't even been thinking about coming home, not until I proposed the idea, and then to pull the same old practical joke on you – that was just cruel. And then I didn't even call until your birthday. Not that you wanted a call, but I still should have called and tried to explain what I did to you last spring. I'm sorry.
2. Embarrassed. I'm embarrassed by my own behavior. It's mortifying to be (a) so totally crazy, and (b) so totally predictable about it. I can't believe that I have done the many stupid things I've done, repeatedly, and in public, with such drastic, shitty repercussions. It's hard to admit that you, my sixteen-year-old daughter, were right all along, that you've been right since you were twelve. Dave is an utter, filthy asshole. What the hell was I thinking? I'm ashamed.
3. Alone. I'm calling you because I'm alone. Dave is gone, and I need somebody here with me or I'll go berserk. I need somebody to comfort me. I need help with Jake. You're supposed to be here with me, Jan, until I send you away. Jan, come home, I'm alone.

My mother didn't go with any of these. She said, "I'm calling to let you know that Jake and I have moved into a new apartment, and Dave went back to his mom's in Westchester. He's gone. It took longer than I hoped it would, but it's true, Jan. It's really true this time, we're getting a divorce. He's gone."

My heart started rising from my stomach to my throat. I crammed my finger in my free ear and bit my lip. "Good," I offered.

"I'm serious, Jan. We moved out. No more Dave. It's done."

"Congratulations," I said, swallowing my heart. So she moved out – okay, I was a little impressed. She'd changed the locks before, but she'd never gone so far as to change the whole apartment. "When?"

"Well, we moved out last month, and Dave has been at his mom's for almost two months now. I guess we've been here about six weeks. It's right off Flatbush Avenue, it's so easy to get to. Jan, I really want you to come visit us soon."

I needed a prepared speech for times like these, the way my mother had her speeches, a laminated index card in my pocket that read: *Mom, you've been dishonest and unreliable too many times, and whatever you're saying to me right now is probably bullshit. So, I'm sorry, but no, and good-bye.*

"Uh-huh," I managed, speechless. "Uh . . ."

She pressed on. "A lot has changed, Janice. It's been almost a year since you left, and it's forced me to see things a lot differently. It took me far too long, and I'm sorry about that, but I am really and truly separated from Dave, for good. No more."

No more. For good. I'm sorry. All phrases right off my mother's laminated card. I patted my mental pockets, looking for mine.

NO. Just say no.

I could not possibly be falling for this again. I was like Charlie Brown and the football. Like a duckling who could never be retrained. I would waddle straight off a cliff, following her. *She threw away your clothes when you left home,* it said on my index card. *She told Poulos you were insane. She's done this to you eight hundred times already. A new apartment doesn't mean shit.*

But there was no card in my hand, just sweat.

"Just come for a visit, overnight. We miss you, Jan. Jake wants to see you, and so do I." Her voice dropped, urgent and dear. "It's been far too long, honey. I miss you, and I love you."

Whoosh – the sound of me getting sucked back in. *Sucker.*

"A visit," I agreed, crumpling nothing in my empty palm.

My mother's new apartment was about ten blocks from the old one in Brooklyn, on a bustling, tree-lined street. It covered the top two floors of a turn-of-the-century brownstone, loaded with detail – I admired the carved wood banisters on the stairs, the bits of stained glass in the kitchen and bath, the original crown moldings everywhere.

"And this is Jake's room."

Jake, now two and a half, toddled behind us on the tour. He was so big – a long-limbed, fully mobile entity with well-defined features and a head of sandy hair – I couldn't stop looking at him. I'd missed him so much since I left last year, I'd missed a whole year of watching him, carrying him, putting my nose on his soft-smelling head. And my mom had said that he missed me, but he didn't even recognize me when I first came in, slinging my weekend bag of clothes and books. He hid behind his mommy's legs.

"He'll get used to you, Jan. Right, Jakey? You remember your sister, Janice?"

I crouched down and widened my eyes. "Hey, Jake. Hey, Jakey-boo. Remember me? Remember Janice?"

He looked suspicious, hid his face with his chubby arm. I stood up again, panged.

"Give it some time," said my mom. "He'll catch on."

I looked wistfully at the pale blue walls of his room, the blond wood crib, the stuffed lamb, gray with wear, by his pillow. She picked up Jake and led me into the next room.

"This room's yours, Jan."

I nodded, noncommittal, like she was a realtor and I wasn't fully sold. "Nice," I said. It was gorgeous. It had two big, sunny windows and a dressing alcove with a marble sink. My mom had arranged my old furniture in here – my old futon, my dresser, my desk. My record player sat on the dresser, no records. The room was otherwise bare.

I couldn't help but picture myself here. I could already see a future me, like an acid phantasm, a 3-D green-and-red ghost zipping around the room. Getting ready to go out for a night with the girls. Sitting on the bed, reading a picture book to Jake. Closing the door at night, sucking my thumb, doing whatever I wanted with myself in bed. Going downstairs to that big fridge full of food and pulling out anything I felt like eating, whenever I was hungry.

My mother looked at me, expectant.

"It's nice," I said again. I tore myself away, into the hall. "Nice skylight."

She laid Jake down in his crib with his stuffed lamb, and we sat together at the kitchen table, her with her coffee, me with a mug of mint tea. She pulled the ashtray toward her and took out her cigarettes; I pulled out mine. She gave them a disapproving look.

"I wish you wouldn't, Jan."

I shrugged like, *Yeah, but what are you gonna do?* She sighed and lit her own. I lit mine, blowing the smoke off to the side.

"So what do you think?" she asked.

I shrugged again. "It's a nice place. I'm glad you got it."

She nodded, lips taut. "Well, I hope you can see how serious I am."

I had to admit, I was impressed. "How long has it been?" I asked.

"Almost two months. He moved back to his mother's in September. I haven't seen him since, except in court. I pressed charges on the last complaint, and he spent the night in jail. Then his mother bailed him out." She shook her head at Dave and his crazy, codependent mom. "Now he's holding up the divorce. He says he wants custody of Jake."

My eyes flew open wide.

"Oh, he'll never get it, don't worry about that. It's just making things take a little bit longer than I'd hoped."

Ucch. I hated that phrase, *take a little bit longer than I'd hoped . . .* It usually meant, *This will never happen, so stop hoping.* "So what does that mean?" I asked, pointed.

She frowned but nodded – fair question. "It means that Dave and I are getting a divorce, Jan. And it can't happen soon enough."

I sipped my tea, eyes down. More dialogue straight from her scripts – "We're getting a divorce, Jan. I can't wait." But something was different about the delivery.

My mom shifted in her chair.

"And . . . I'm going to a doctor," she said. "A shrink. He gave me an antianxiety pill."

So that was what was different. I'd felt it as soon as I walked in the door. She wasn't nearly as anxious as usual. I thought maybe she was tired, but that wasn't it. She was calm. I'd seen her happy, I'd seen her furious, but I didn't know if I'd ever seen her calm.

"Is it . . . Do you feel better?" It was hard to imagine her on downers – my manic, workaholic mom, who never even drank a glass of wine, whose drugs of choice were coffee and cigarettes.

"I do, Jan. I feel a lot better. It's allowed me to really think for a change, instead of just responding all the time."

I nodded. "That's good."

"It's allowed me to see a lot of the mistakes I made, especially when it comes to you. You really don't belong in that place, Jan. It's been a terrible year for you, I know. And I'm the one who put you in that situation. I can't tell you how sorry I am . . . If there was any way I could undo what I've done . . ." Her voice got squeaky, and she teared up.

"I know, Mom."

This was the part I wanted to avoid – the forgiving. I'd have been just as happy to skip straight to the forgetting and never talk about it again. To not have to tell my mom that it was all okay, to just ignore that it wasn't okay and start fresh anyway. I didn't want to see her cry; I didn't want to hear her apologize. The more she apologized, the worse I felt.

"Mom, stop. It's okay."

She blotted her tears with a napkin, carefully dabbing the corners of her eyes. "Well . . . it's not. But I want to make it okay."

"I know, Mom."

She reached out, put her thin hand over mine. "Will you think about coming home? We need you here, Jan. This is your home, too. This is where you belong."

My hand was a fist under hers. "I'll think about it," I said. "I will."

In the morning, she made blueberry muffins. Jake dismantled one, gurgling happily, and pitched pieces of it at my leg. I laughed and caught them.

"Hi, Jakey. Is that your muffin? Is that your muffin, Jakey-boo?"

My mom smiled wanly. "You remember your sister now, Jake? Remember Janice?"

"Jan-sis!" said Jake, pointing.

"That's right," I said. "Jan-sis."

He waddled over and handed me a damp, spit-covered piece of muffin. "Jan-sis," he said.

"Thank you, Jakey-boo." I accepted his present.

My mother smiled at us from the kitchen, wet-eyed like a new bride. Jake clambered up onto my lap, squirming and giggling. I kissed the top of his soft, warm head.

My decision was made.

Poulos was not sure I was ready to go home.

"Janice has benefited greatly from the structure she's been getting with us. Do you think it's wise to disrupt her again, in the middle of the school year, when your own situation isn't entirely clear?"

My mother's chin was high, her hair impeccably coiffed, her slight smile steady. "It's not a disruption. She can move over the holidays. She's not switching schools."

"Mm hmm. But do you feel that the situation is stable? Will you be able to provide Janice with the kind of supervision she needs in order to stay on the right track?"

My mom smiled at me, then back at Poulos. "I think Janice and I are both ready to do whatever it takes to ensure that things work out this time."

I nodded emphatically. "I think I can, like, apply the lessons I learned . . . and stuff . . ." I trailed off under Poulos's glare. It was amazing how she could smile with the lower half of her face while the top half gave you a look to chill your guts.

"Mm hmm," she said, openly skeptical.

My mother's tone shifted, and she lost her slight smile. "Look, Miss Poulos, the goal all along was to bring Janice home. We're very grateful for the opportunity she's had here, but she and I both agree that it's time for her to come home."

Poulos lost her smile as well. "Of course, Barb. We're just trying to keep Janice's best interests in mind."

I flashed my mom an alarmed look. Why in the world would they want to keep me at the group home? What vested interest could they possibly have? They hated me – wouldn't they be glad to see me go?

My mother and I reconvened on the sidewalk.

"I think it's bullshit, Jan. I think this review process is a formality, and I don't even know what this 'waiting period' is about. Legally, you should be able to come home tomorrow if you want to. I'll check with Steinman. In the meantime, just hang tight, and we'll get you home over the holidays."

"Okay." I had to trust her. It was her, or nobody, and I was tired of nobody.

Mavis and Sandy also doubted the decision. They cornered me in the living room, Mavis folding her big arms in front of me. "You think things are going to be different this time? Why?"

"Well, a lot changed . . . my stepfather is gone . . ."

Mavis peered at me. "But did *you* change, JuhNEECE? Or are you still the same girl that was taking drugs and messing around with boys?"

"Well, yeah, I changed." Before, I did all that stuff mostly out of boredom; now I did it at least partly out of spite.

"And how exactly have you changed?" asked Sandy, arms similarly crossed. "You know we know about all your little adventures, don't you? Takes more than a urine test to fool us. We know you've been running around."

She gloated at me, registering the shock and panic I vainly tried to suppress. "What are you talking about?"

"I think you probably know," said Mavis. "All the other girls seem to know about it."

"Mm hmm," added Sandy. "We're gonna have a *good* group therapy this week."

Surely this was just a new flavor of psyops they were trying out on me. "I don't know what you're talking about," I maintained. "I'm gonna just . . . go to my room." I barged past them and through the door.

Genie was on her bed, flipping through a copy of *Cosmopolitan*.

"What the fuck," I hissed at her. "Mavis and Sandy just told me I'm in trouble."

Flip. Genie ignored me. She'd been ignoring me all week, since she heard I was going home to my mom's. What, like that made me two-faced? That was a betrayal? She'd go home in a fat second, if her stupid nouveaux riches parents would let her. It wasn't my fault they didn't want her around.

"What the fuck," I repeated. I nudged the bed with my knee.

Flip. Flip. Genie smiled at her *Cosmo*, blinking her cow eyes innocently.

"Genie." I nudged the bed again. "Don't fucking ignore me, Genie, I'm serious."

She tented the magazine on her breasts and tossed her head back. "Mavis, Janice is kicking my bed!"

"Girls!" called Mavis. In her accent, it sounded like "Gulls!"

I paced back to my side of the room, standing just behind the invisible border, Billy Idol sneering at me from the poster over her bed. "What the fuck is going on?"

Flip. Genie looked somewhat less than innocent now. Her big fake smile was belied by her real evil squint.

"Did you fucking *tell on me*?"

Genie the Fucking JAP flipped her *Cosmo*. "Well, *I* didn't say anything," she said, smarmy as a game show hostess. Her smile got wider and smug. "But I think maybe Julie did."

I got a pain like a bullet in the side of my head. "If I get in any fucking trouble . . ." I warned her. My hands flexed at my sides, ready to exact revenge.

Flip. Genie studied the results of her skin-care quiz. "When you get to lockup," she said, offhand, "say hi to Shirley for me."

I wasn't going to lockup. I was going home. But just barely.

"You have endangered yourself and everybody at this home!" thundered Mavis. Poulos sat at the head of the circle for this special Kafkaesque edition of group therapy, hands folded like she was the head of the parole board. Julie the Snitch glared at me, arms across her flat chest, her vicious yap set in a prim slash, as Genie ingenuously studied her nails – still faintly bloody, no doubt, from *stabbing me in the fucking back*.

I sat shaking my head no, my hands up in front of me, a drunk driver stumbling in the headlights. "I didn't do anything!"

"You had *sex* with *multiple partners*," scolded Sandy. Grandma Dolores shook her head sadly. "That's a risk to your own health, and to your housemates."

"Some of us have to share a bathroom with you." Genie sneered.

"Yo, that's disgusting," said Indira the Bully.

Mavis's voice rang out over everyone's. "And what about the drugs! JuhNEECE! Listen to me. What about the drugs you've been taking, hmm?"

I stared across the circle at Genie, who I'd loved, talking late into the night, our butts squeezed together out the window of our room. I scanned the rest of the girls, the counselors, a whirling circle of hateful faces. "You need to get some self-respect!" yelled Julie the Snitch. Indira the Bully pointed and laughed. Mavis kept tolling out the charges – "You're a liar! You come home drunk! You've been cutting school!" Poulos frowned at the head of the circle, perturbed. Why wasn't she happy? She was right about me, she knew it all along. I was no good, I deserved everything I got.

"I don't care," I told them, shaking my head. "I don't care. You can't do anything to me. I'm going home." I repeated it, heels clicking under the table like ruby slippers. "I don't care. I'm going home. I'm going home."

PART THREE

The Babe

11

THE SQUAT

"Is that you, Jan?"

I was home. It had been a long day – a long year and two months, when I thought about it – but here I was again, finally home. I locked the front door of the brownstone behind me and trotted upstairs to the living room, where my mom sat knitting a sweater in front of the TV, Jake playing at her feet with his toy cars. Knitting was my mom's new obsession – now she came home from her office in the evening, put on her bathrobe, popped an antianxiety pill, and started knitting. Dinner was catch-as-catch-can in front of the TV.

"Hey," I said.

She didn't look over; her eyes were riveted on the TV, the needles moving without her notice. "Are you hungry?"

I let my bag slide off my shoulder. "I had a burger after school. Maybe I'll make some soup later." I bent down to mess up Jake's hair. "Hi, Jakey-boo."

Jake stood, diaper drooping, as he held up his car. "Jan-sis, issa car. Issa car."

"That's right!" I enthused. "It's a car!"

He puffed with pride at his own astute remark. "Issa car," he repeated to the car.

"How was your day?" my mom asked, still staring at the screen, fingers clacking away. She was in that post-medicated phase of the evening, when she'd moved beyond calm and into zombified, her attention glazedly fixed even as her hands twitched and knit. This was her Zen place, the place between breaking down and freaking out, neither of which she could afford to do right now. It was weird to see her this way – my knife-sharp mom dulled to a plastic spoon – but this was where she needed to be.

"Boring. How about you?"

"Oh, fine." She stopped and counted stitches, transferring some onto a big safety pin. She kept offering to teach me how to knit – like, every night since I'd been home she offered, as though she didn't remember offering the night before. Every night I said, "Yeah, I'd like to learn sometime," and that was the end of it.

I sat down next to her on the couch for a minute, warming up, happy to be home. This winter was as cold as the last one, but this year I had a brand-new wool peacoat, as well as new boots, new sneakers, a bunch of other new clothes, and two new chunky hand-knit sweaters from my mom. When I went upstairs to my very own room, there were no other people there; nobody wanted to stab me, or fuck me over, or beat me with a lock in a sock. I could close the door – or even leave it open, listen to the TV and my mom's needles clicking and Jake's car sounds downstairs – and lie on my bed, thumb in mouth, luxuriating in the privacy. Compared to where I was last winter, things were very, very good.

Jake drove a car over my foot and up my leg.

"Who stinks, Jakey-boo? Who stinks? You do. It's almost bath time. Right? Bath time for Jakey."

"You mind, Jan?" My mom's hands went *clack clack clack*. Her brow was slack, eyes glassy, voice low and weary. She'd developed a habit of sighing deeply after she spoke; I don't think she even noticed.

"No problem."

"Thanks," she said. *Sigh*.

"Sure thing." I raised myself off the sofa.

"Are you going out later?" she asked.

"Yeah. Just to the park. I'll be home by twelve-thirty."

"It's cold out," she noted. "Come home earlier if you get cold."

"I will."

I grabbed Jake by his armpits, swinging him up the stairs to his room, where I helped him out of his sweaty T-shirt and diaper while his bath filled. He wanted to bring his Matchbox cars into the tub, but I wouldn't let him. "No, Jakey, they'll break in the water. Play with your boats. Brrrrrrr!" This was the sound I told him boats made, because a vehicle without sound was essentially useless.

I looked at myself in the mirror while Jake soaked the walls and floor – "BRRRRRRR! BRRRRRR!" – turned and sucked in my stomach, making my sultry model face. I looked all right. I was back to being a redhead – it just made more sense with my freckles than the bleached blond – and I'd recently added some black streaks, which didn't really come out the way I'd planned, but whatever. Maybe I'd cut my bangs before I went out. I definitely planned to wear my new low-cut Lycra top underneath my layers. It was Friday night, and I had a date with a guy named Dougie Paradise.

I'd met Dougie Paradise in typing class, the first day back at school after winter break. I'd been called to the front of the class to get my Delaney card, which is this card the New York City public school system has you fill out, with all of your information on it – name, address, parents' names, date of birth, et cetera – it even had a space for you to write down your nickname, or what you wanted to be called, like sometimes a girl wanted to be called Elaine instead of Xao Mei. This was a treasured opportunity for people to put down answers like Stud, King Darnell, or Bond, James Bond. I filled in my mom's address in Park Slope and paused over the nickname, thinking, *White Girl. Jane. JuhNEECE.* I didn't fill in a nickname.

Dougie Paradise wolf-whistled for me – *twee twoo!* – when I went up to get my Delaney card. "Boys," scolded Ms. Gerber. I pouted as though hurt and vamped back to my seat, delighted. I *was* looking extra-good these days, with my new clothes and a bathroom all to myself in which to primp; it was nice of somebody to notice. Within a minute, the girl next to me was passing me a folded note.

What up? it said in an abstract curlicue. I looked over at this ridiculous blond kid, mugging at me from the back row. Ms. Gerber glared at him as well. "Douglas?" she asked, referring to his card.

"Dougie Paradise," he corrected. "That's my real last name, yo."

"So it is," noted Ms. Gerber with consternation. "Please focus your attention up here."

He did not. He continued to stare at me, hiss *pssst!* at me, pass me notes, and make faces in my direction for the entire forty-minute class, as I sat with my back perfectly straight, paying the most studied attention I'd ever paid to Ms. Gerber. Finally, the bell rang, and before I could rise from my desk, Dougie was there, his unformed, ill-shaved face inches from mine.

"Yo, what's your name? How come I ain't seen you before?"

I raised my eyebrows at him, smiling. Um, probably because I was on the honors track, and he was mostly vocational. Or because he hung out with the hip-hop kids in the lunchroom, and I was over with the new wave club–party crew. Didn't he notice how I was dressed, my pointy black boots with the extraneous silver buckles, the carefully shredded shirt? I was certainly aware of his powder blue sheepskin coat and matching hat, his thick-laced sneakers, his gold chain. I knew how ridiculous he'd look to Hope and Alice, but he was sort of cute under the sheepskin hat, and persistent, so I let him walk me to class anyway.

The next day Dougie bought me a box of assorted chocolates from the drugstore and a bouquet of red carnations, and presented them to me before typing class with a card that pictured a couple standing on a bridge looking at a rainbow. On the inside, he wrote, "Janis, my feelings for you are true. I want for you to be my girl and for me to be your guy. You tell me if you want this too."

I looked up at him, like, *What?* He stood in front of me, face as serious as a firing squad. "Hey, Doug . . . I think you're a nice guy, but . . . I don't even know you. I mean, we haven't even been on a date."

"I know! That's why I want to know, will you be my girl, *before* we go on a date." He put his hand to his heart. "Because I don't want to fall in love with you and then you say no."

This was charming and bizarre in equal amounts. I certainly loved being pursued, and I *loved* the l-word, but . . . so soon? "Why don't we just go out this Friday and see what happens?"

He considered this compromise. "Okay, yeah, we'll go out Friday, and then you'll be my girl. And I don't want you dating no other guys, either."

"Um . . ." Yeah, I'd think about that. Before I could say anything else, he leaned in and kissed me, then took off down the hall.

"You have a good day, angel love, I'll check you later."

For our first date, Dougie Paradise was taking me to a squat on East Fourth Street, a high-status destination if ever there was one – a windowless, waterless hovel where chunks of crappy yellow insulation fell from the ceiling onto the kids who congregated there, sitting on milk crates and watching TV with electricity hijacked from a lamppost outside. I'd heard plenty about the Squat in the past – one of the peripheral members of the Boyses, the insanely charismatic Mike Shanahan, was living there, ever since his dad kicked him out – but I'd never been invited to go. I plucked Jake from his bath, diapered and dressed him, put him in his crib, and started putting on makeup. And then Alice called.

"What up, girl?" Alice was crisp and businesslike, no doubt putting on her own makeup for the night. The radio was on in the background, and I heard Hope pipe up, faraway: "What up, J?"

"Hey, what's going on?"

I wasn't hanging out with Alice and Hope so much these days. I made up with both of them almost right away after the Jay Finster affair, but it was a tenuous rapprochement. Hope's official statement was, "Whatever, shit happens, let's just not talk about it." Alice's was "You're just lucky Hopey's such an awesome friend." I still hung out and wrote notes and smoked in the bathroom at school with them, but I knew they passed separate notes about me that I didn't see, and the one time I got to sleep over at Alice's when her mom was at her boyfriend's, it was totally by the grace of Hope.

"We're going to the thing on Broadway and Houston," Alice informed me. "You can come with us, if you want. I think the Boyses are going to be there."

She dangled that last part like a hypnotist's watch. I still had a useless crush on Leland Banks, the love dog, and she knew it. I regretfully declined. "Thanks, but . . . I'm going to the Squat."

I could almost hear Alice's antennae buzz and wave; I pictured her mandibles opening and closing in confusion. What was I doing, making plausible Friday night plans without her? "With who?"

"With . . ." I didn't want to say. ". . . that guy Doug."

Alice laughed, relieved. "Dougie Paradise? The white homeboy?"

"Yeah." I laughed too, as though we were sharing the joke. "He's crazy."

"Well, maybe if the party's lame we'll check out the Squat." Her voice was friendlier than it had been in a month, the hierarchy re-established – *if* the party was lame, *then* they'd catch up with me.

"Great," I said. "Say hi to Hope."

I assessed my outfit one last time – exposed cleavage, *check*; flash of stomach, *check* – then threw on my mom's latest handiwork, a chunky black turtleneck sweater that disguised the entire look. I went into the living room and twirled in front of the TV for her.

"It looks nice, right?"

My mom lifted the corners of her tired smile, her needles clicking absently. The curlers on her head made her look like an android – a knitting android. "It does. Very nice."

"All right, well . . . I'll come in and turn off the alarm when I get home."

"Okay, hon. Have a good time."

She stared straight ahead, mesmerized by a sitcom as the sleeve between her needles grew longer by itself. She'd sit there exactly like that for another two hours, then she'd go upstairs and get ready for bed, alone. The cold draft from the front door made me shudder.

"Thanks, Mom. You too."

I tore myself away and chased the draft.

I met up with Dougie in Washington Square Park, where he took me stiffly in his arms and drew me toward his lips. "How you feelin', my angel love? You look so beautiful and precious tonight, what's going on?"

"Nothing," I said, though he did not seem to require an answer. He chattered the entire way to the Squat – ". . . me and my boys, you know how it is . . ." – I wasn't able to follow or add much. *Nerves*, I thought. *He's nervous. Or brain damaged. One or the other.*

Dougie and I climbed our way up to the top floor of the Squat, where Mike Shanahan was playing host for the evening, flashing the wide grin I'd seen him employ cadging free food at the snack stand every summer – "Aw, come on, let me get a pita, you're the bomb." Mike grabbed Dougie in a man-hug, then broke away to admire me.

"And look who you brought with you," he said, his toothpick becoming erect between his teeth. I was suddenly superconscious of Dougie's hand, manacled around my wrist. I resolved to keep Mike Shanahan in my sights as we got down to that evening's order of business, which was smoking some PCP.

"You ever get dusted before, baby?" Dougie threw his arm around me and kissed my cheek. There were three or four other guys, none of whom I recognized, hanging around the apartment; they duly noted Dougie's ownership of me. We pulled up our milk crate seats to an industrial wood spool table, where a friend of Dougie's poured inky, gummy powder into a pipe.

"Yo, let me hit my girl first," ordered Dougie, self-important. He passed me the pipe, and I held it to my lips. He lit it, and I inhaled. Immediately I sputtered and coughed, holding the pipe at arm's length so I didn't blow out the contents. Everybody laughed, including me, through my coughing. Dougie took the pipe and took a hit for himself. The pipe went around the circle. And then everything went black.

Black, and silver. Like an eclipse. I was used to hallucinations, but these were different. These were other dimensions. Flat worlds with rubber walls, and sounds that entered your head through the top of your skull. "Ha ha," I said, for no reason. *Ha ha*, I heard, like chanting, like my pulse. *Ha ha, ha ha, ha ha, ha ha.*

Dougie's face pressed over mine. Somewhere, something was happening – something around my lap, very far away. Not connected. "Let's go downstairs." "Okay." I stood up and swooned. It was like diving into cold water. I stumbled after the back of Dougie's neck, following the patch of glowing pink between his powder blue hat and coat. Each stair swayed like a swing when I stepped forward on it.

On the second floor of the Squat was an abandoned theater, and behind the stage was a dressing room with a carpeted floor. The dressing room had actual windows in the wall instead of plastic; it was ten degrees warmer than it was upstairs. Dougie took off his coat like Sir Walter Raleigh and spread it out on the floor.

"You feeling that dust?" My head wobbled yes from atop its marshmallow neck. "Word. Me too." I didn't feel like kissing him, but there he was, smelling of burnt paint, all in my face. I had no reaction to anything he did, except to marvel at my lack of reaction, at how perfectly this drug removed the capacity to give a fuck. I could have put my hand in fire, watched it blister and char like wood, and not felt a thing. Apparently, Doug and I had some kind of sex, and he climaxed, without my full awareness. I noticed that PCP definitely didn't make sex better, but it did somehow make it less worse.

Somewhere in the haze of my gray-out, we got our clothes back on. Doug could operate while dusted, I could not. He helped me on with my tights, my shoes, half-singing, "Here we go, here we go," like someone's dad. It was very funny, and I laughed until I drooled. "Okay, okay, angel, we're going upstairs, all right? Up the stairs. Up the stairs." I leaned on his back, panting. "Okay, you gotta stand up, all right? You gotta get it together, all right?"

"Right." All right. I could be cool. If I could talk my way past Mavis while coming down off mushrooms, I should be able to act all right tonight. Everybody seated around the spool table was just as dusted as me. Except now there were a few more people there – strangely familiar outlines, saying dialogue I recognized . . .

"Hey, Janice." Alice smirked, her hair tenting behind her like a black triangle, a radiation sign.

"Holy shit, look at you." Hope frowned at me. She looked like a bad green witch. "What the hell?"

I furrowed my brow. "What . . . How did you guys . . ."

Alice and Hope – they weren't here before – were they on TV? Was I imagining things? All the important Boyses seemed to be there too – Sam King, Ollie Wythe, and Leland Banks – unless I was just fantasizing him, as usual. The fantasy Boyses tipped their forty-ounce beers at me in greeting. I nodded like I understood.

"She's dusted!" crowed our host, Mike. He was one to talk. His grin stretched his mouth to three times its normal size. I clung to Dougie like wet moss. I felt gritty and drippy and raw. Alice and Hope shook their heads, associatively ashamed by me. I'd try to remember to care about that later.

"I gotta go," I said, in what I hoped was a cogent way.

Dougie helped me down the stairs and put ten dollars in my hand.

I watched the bodega across the street turn white as he put me in a cab. "Yo, I'ma call you tomorrow, angel, okay? And I'm gonna need that ten bucks back, it's Felipe's. I love you, angel. I love you."

"Unh," I said, or something, and braced myself for the ride home.

My mother slept a heavily medicated sleep, the clock in her bedroom flashing 12:27. Three more minutes – if I wasn't home in time, the alarm would ring. I shut off the alarm and put my hand on my mom's shoulder. This was our ritual, a bedtime story in reverse.

"Mom," I said. The word echoed in my head like in a concrete tunnel. "Mom, I'm home."

"We should get married," said Dougie Paradise, three weeks later.

"You're high," I told him.

We lay on his laid-out coat on the floor of the dressing room at the Squat, clothes askew, dusted out of our minds. The stains on the ceiling looked like the continents on other planets, the light coming in yellow through the plastic-covered windows like burning fruit. I was getting more used to being dusted by now, after six or seven times. Or eight, or ten. Hard to count. Probably no more than ten. Or twelve.

"I'm serious. I love you. I never loved anybody before you. Let's have a baby."

Dougie's eyes spun around like errant wagon wheels in his head, his thoughts rolling downhill faster than he could run and catch them. I didn't understand Dougie at all. Even when he wasn't dusted, even at eleven-thirty in the morning before typing, when we were both stone sober, he was unintelligible to me: "What up, my angel, are you keeping my love close to your heart today?" I'd given up trying to talk to him on the phone; it was clear to me, if not to him, that we had nothing to talk about. He refused to discuss anything but the miraculous fact of our love, which I was still not sure existed. And now he was talking about having a baby? That was the last thing I wanted in the world, and lastly with him.

"You're a dust case," I said.

He drew his smooth, babyish face into a scowl. "Yo, you're a slut. Why you fucking with me if you don't really love me?"

I pulled my bra and shirt down over my chest, baffled. What kind of question was that? *Um, for the hell of it? For the sex and drugs? Because you asked me to?* "I'm trying to love you," I said, and it was true, I honestly wanted to love Dougie Paradise – he was cute, in a half-baked, puppyish kind of way, and well-connected to sources of a variety of drugs, and attentive beyond belief. But on the one hand, he never said anything, and on the other, he never shut the fuck up.

He sprang unsteadily to his feet. "You supposed to be my *girl*, yo, through thick and thin, you don't even know if you love me?"

"Dougie, calm down." Too much motion around me made me seasick – riding the elastic floor was fun only up to a point.

"Naw, I gotta go talk to my man Felipe."

"Dougie . . ."

He jammed his legs into his pants, his stocking feet into his sneakers, pulled his sweater down, and grabbed his coat. I followed carefully, moving through the syrupy wake of his disjointed energy. He hustled upstairs, where Felipe sat on a milk crate near a few other dust cases, watching snow on the TV. There were no Boyses there tonight, no Alice and Hope – the girls had declared themselves "over" the Squat, with its lack of heat and windows, and its grimy clientele. Dougie lurched over to his friend Felipe's crate and draped his arm over him.

"I'm going home," I said thickly. "Bye."

Dougie shot me a wounded look from across the room. I couldn't be bothered with all that right now. I made my way out of the building, palming the spackled hallways for balance, walked down to Broadway and Houston, and got on the tinny, magnetic train to Brooklyn.

The clock in my mom's room said 12:15. I turned off the alarm and nudged her shoulder.

"Mom, I'm home."

"Jan, wake up."

My mom stood over my bed, impatient. Jake toddled around the room, imitating an airplane. My dry eyes wouldn't focus; I couldn't make heads or tails of any of it. I felt like someone had poked my brain with a twig and held it over a campfire.

"Jan, it's almost two o'clock. Get up. You've been sleeping for almost fourteen hours. What's the matter with you?"

"Hunhhh?"

"Are you sick? What's the matter?" My mom was annoyed. It was a Saturday, chore day, and she needed all hands on deck. She only had until 6:00 or 7:00 P.M. before it was time to take her antianxiety pill and she lost the ability to do anything but sit in front of the TV and knit. Helping around the house was an unspoken condition of my residence; if I was going to live here, I would have to pull my weight. "Come on. I already did the laundry, but we still need groceries, and I have to stop by the bank, and refill my prescription."

I raised myself partway up from my lumpy futon, and the room fell away from me like on a roller coaster. Jake made dizzying loops around the bed. "All right," I managed. "Give me a minute, I'll get in the shower."

She frowned, arms folded. "I don't like this sleeping until two thing you've been doing lately. Every weekend, you sleep like the dead."

"Sorry," I said. I could feel the empty space in my skull, from where my brain had shrunk to the size of a shriveled jalapeño. I dragged my cement ass into the bathroom.

I could see it in the mirror – dust was taking a toll on me. I had a dazed, beaten look on my face, and my skin was breaking out. The shower helped, but I still wanted more than anything just to sit quietly in the dark for a good number of hours and see if I could regrow some neurons. I emerged from the shower and threw on some layers. Jake airplaned into the room and tackled my leg, giggling, and I nearly fell on him.

"Goddamn it, Jake!" I smacked his hand, and he howled.

"What just happened!" called my mom from downstairs. "What's going on!"

Jake bawled, pointing at me with reproach. *Jesus Christ, I just hit Jake.* I fell to my knees in front of him. "Jakey, I'm sorry, I'm so sorry, Jakey-boo, it was an accident, I'm sorry, don't cry . . ."

My mom sighed and puffed her way up the stairs. "Are you two ready? Jan, get his coat. Come on, Jake. Stop crying."

I shambled behind my mom all day, Jake pouting in his stroller, my mom nibbling the sides of her fingers, anxious without her meds. I could barely lift the groceries, much less carry them up the stairs. My mom was alternately concerned and pissed off. "Are you sure you're not sick? You could have a sinus infection. Jesus, will you hurry up? I can't hold this door open forever."

There was a message waiting on the answering machine; my mom played it back as I stuffed the perishables in the fridge. "Yo, what up? It's Dougie P. Call me back, okay? Aiight."

"Who's Dougie P?" my mom asked, frowning.

"That kid from my typing class. He's called a few times."

"Right. What does he want?"

"I don't know. I'll call him back." *Go take your pill, Mom, I've got it covered from here.*

"All right." She nibbled the side of her thumb. "Can you put away the rest of this stuff? I want to take Jake upstairs and get him changed."

"Sure thing."

I unloaded the soup into the cabinet, Jake's jars of applesauce and little boxes of juice. Handling them made me well up with tears. I was so exhausted and demoralized and fucked up. I managed to put everything away without falling down weeping, then I sank into one of the farting vinyl-covered kitchen chairs and let my head droop down to my knees.

The phone rang, alarmingly loud. "I got it!" I picked it up. "Hello?"

"Hello, Janice. It's Dougie Paradise." He was even stiffer and more formal than usual. I groaned inside.

"Hey, Doug, what's up."

"Yeah, well, unfortunately, I'm going to have to say that we can't be together no more, due to some unfortunate circumstances . . ."

"Oh . . . I'm sorry to hear that," I said. I knew I should have been insulted; instead I was bathed in soothing relief.

"Yeah." His voice was far away, like he was holding the phone at a distance, but I could hear it – he was choking up. I felt a sudden rush of tenderness for Dougie Paradise, white homeboy, would-be player.

"Hey," I said gently. "Are you okay?"

He cleared his throat, and his tight voice got tighter. "Well, I am, but . . . actually, after you left last night, me and some of my boys, we went out, down by the park, where they got that construction site."

"Uh-huh."

"And, uh, my man Felipe – he was messing around, walking on them beams, you know . . ."

Oh no.

"And he fell, five flights, and he broke all his pelvis and his legs, and his collarbone, and one of his arms. He's crushed up, yo. I mean, he's gonna live, thank god, but he's all fucked up now. He's gonna be in a wheelchair for a long time."

"Oh, man." I didn't know what to say. Round-faced, funny Felipe, who just wanted to smoke some dust and get zooted. "Doug . . . I'm so sorry."

"Yeah." He let out a gasp, like a whimper, then pulled it back together. "Anyway, so, the situation is that, um, my responsibility, you know . . . I can't really be with you . . . in the same way anymore."

My heart was breaking, but not for me. "Oh, yeah. I mean, I understand. I'm sad, but . . ."

"I gotta do what I gotta do," he explained.

"Yeah, I understand."

"Well, all right. You stay good."

"Okay. You too, Dougie. Bye."

I put down the phone. It was over. No more Dougie Paradise – I'd see him around school sometimes, his blue eyes haunted and dim, but he wouldn't speak to me again, or even look my way. No more dust, no more squatting for me. I was home now: Janice Erlbaum, white homegirl. I hauled upstairs to my room, fell on my futon, put my thumb in my mouth, and closed my eyes.

12

BOYSES AND GIRLSES DRINKING CLUB

You might think I'd turn over a new leaf, it being spring and all. Other juniors in my class were sending away for college applications and studying for their SATs; I was busy stuffing twenties from the snack stand into my bra and trying to sleep with Leland Banks. College was just not as much of a priority to me as sex and cash were. I had a hard time explaining this to Mr. Sheldon.

"I'm pretty busy these days," I hedged, cornered in the fourth-floor hallway between classes. "I'm working after school again, and I have to help take care of my baby brother. And you know, I'm still adjusting to being back home."

Sheldon nodded, eyebrows climbing toward his precise hairline. He knew exactly how busy I was, how well-adjusted. From under his high eyebrows, Sheldon saw everything. "Well, notwithstanding, Janice, you still need to think about college. You're a very bright student, when you deign to attend class, and you've got a real future ahead of you, if you apply yourself now."

"Uh-huh." I ducked my head. Praise made me feel weird, especially when it was conditional.

"And you know, extracurricular activities are very attractive to colleges. We're having auditions for the spring play next week – it's *Oklahoma!* this year. Don't you want to think about rejoining the Drama Club?"

"Uh, well . . ."

In truth, I never meant to quit Drama Club. It just happened – I cut school on a whim the first Thursday of the new semester, and then the next Thursday I wanted to go smoke pot with Alice and Hope at

Alice's place after school, so I blew off Drama Club again. I kept thinking I could just pick it back up, show up one Thursday in the auditorium after eighth period and take my usual place at the center of the attention, maybe charm Sheldon into giving me the lead in the spring play again this year. But then something happened the next Thursday that distracted me – I think I was going out with Dougie Paradise by then – and then I kind of lost the months of February and March, so now here we were, almost April, and I'd never rejoined.

"I mean, I *want* to, I'm just so busy . . ."

I *did* want to rejoin Drama Club, and I desperately wanted to do the spring play – to hear the applause swelling like waves around me, to look out this time and see my mother in the crowd. I just didn't know if I could afford to do the play this year – the time it took from my social life, the training that interfered with my drug use. The risk that this year some other girl might be better than me – maybe that adorable sophomore Jenny Scharf, whose penchant for displaying her tightly packed cleavage led people to compare her to "a younger version of Janice." What if Sheldon gave her the lead soprano role instead of me? How would I look, deposed as the school's drama queen, relegated to the bit part of Granny Whatsername, as Jenny Scharf's breasts belted out "Surrey with the Fringe on Top"?

"Mm *hmm*," said Sheldon. His smile went flat. "Well, I'm sure you'll let us all know when you've made up your mind."

"Yeah, I mean . . ." I wanted to apologize, but I knew what he'd say: *What are you sorry about, Janice? You're the one who's suffering.* "Okay. See you."

I spent the rest of the day in a funk, smoking and moping in the bathroom after every class. Jimmy Wilson was doing the spring play – he was probably glad I'd dropped out. I shouldn't have cut that first Thursday – I was busy chasing Leland, like a ninny.

"Don't be bummed out about Drama Club," said Alice, like it was the stupidest thing ever, like I was getting upset over the Smurfs.

"Yeah," consoled Hope. "We're gonna have Drinking Club instead."

"That sounds good," I admitted.

"It's going to be awesome," Alice gloated. "Me, you, Hope, and the Boyses. Tomorrow night, my place. I already got, like, five bottles of booze."

"Is that going to be enough?" Hope fretted. The Boyses were legendary drinkers – Leland, we knew, could down a fifth of vodka straight and still get it up to have sex in the bathroom of a party with Leila Ariano from the Bronx High School of Science. His buddy Sam King had once finished an entire bottle of Jägermeister by himself before passing out on the floor.

"It better be enough," sniffed Alice. "It cost a fucking fortune."

"I'll bring a bottle of something, too," I offered. This was a historic night in the making, one we'd been waiting for since sophomore year, and I was grateful to be a part of it. "What time does it start?"

Alice, our exultant social director, laid out the schedule for the evening. "So, you guys will get there early, around eight, and we'll get dressed and you can help me set up. Hope, you're bringing the herb, right?"

"Yup. Got it."

"And Janice, you said you're bringing booze. Why don't you make it either vodka or tequila? I know Ollie likes tequila."

"Okay."

She whipped her head back to Hope, smacking me with her hair. "So we'll get set up, we'll run to the store if we need to, we'll smoke a joint – the Boyses are showing up around nine or ten, I don't know what they're bringing. It'll probably be just Ollie, Sam, and Leland, unless they bring Mike Shanahan or someone – I don't know." She raised her hand, cigarette aloft. "I call Ollie. It's my house, so I get first dibs."

Of course Alice would choose Ollie Wythe, the hands-down handsomest of the Boyses, our school's most notorious seduction machine. One blink of his thick, brown lashes made girls want to stop in their tracks and step out of their panties; when they did, they'd rarely get a second date. Alice tossed her head and smirked – things would be different with her.

"Awww," Hope mock-complained. "I kind of wanted Ollie."

"Too bad," said Alice firmly. "Maybe you can have him when I'm done with him. And you can invite whoever you want to the next one.

As long as my mom keeps staying at her boyfriend's, I'm going to keep having parties. And you two get to be the guests."

She put one arm around each of us, and I flushed with warmth, heating like an electric coil. I didn't deserve friends like these. Somehow, they'd managed to forgive me for the gaffes of the past few months – the nefarious Jay Finster affair, my distasteful association with Dougie Paradise – I didn't know how. Maybe they kept me around because I tried so hard to please them, or because three hot chicks running around together was somehow better than only two. Maybe I was there for comic relief – it certainly entertained Alice when I'd get drunk at a party and take my shirt off, insisting I was hot.

"You're *hilarious*," she told me all the time. "You really are."

Whatever it was, it didn't matter. I was back under Alice's arm, one of the Girlses again.

I got home around seven, and my mother sat knitting in front of the TV, Jake upstairs in his crib for the night. I put down my stuff and joined her on the couch, picking grapes out of the old ceramic bowl between us, chipped from an ancient fight with Dave.

"How was school?" she asked, staring at the screen.

"Eh. All right."

"Just all right?" Mom glanced sideways at me for a second, needles clicking. She'd been watching me more closely these days, when she had the energy. I wondered sometimes how much she knew about my extracurricular activities. If she had a clue, she wasn't letting on. "Everything okay?"

"Yeah, just . . . Mr. Sheldon's on my case about college."

She nodded, glancing at the screen again. My mother had said it a number of times – she didn't care if I went to college or not. She never went to college – she started working full-time right out of high school so she could get away from her own crazy parents. Now, twenty years later, she was successfully self-employed, with a business card that read BARB ROSEN, INC., *CORPORATE EVENTS*. She used to be just BARB ROSEN, *FREELANCE PLANNER*, but recently she'd become INC., and

CORPORATE EVENTS. Apparently, it meant she got paid more for the same job. Even on meds, my mom was pretty shrewd.

Commercials. She put down her needles and her navy blue yarn – sweater for Jake in progress – and muted the TV. "Well, you know how I feel about it, Jan. You need to choose something to do. If you want to go to college, I support that decision. And if you want to get a real job and go to work, I support that, too."

"Thanks, Mom."

She switched into Lecture Mode, her voice dropping sternly. "But I am concerned that you do *something*, whatever it is. If you really want to be independent and support yourself, you're going to have to make a living, and that means hard work. You can't just keep running all over town with your friends, you know. It's a tough world out there."

Yeah, thanks for the tip, Mom. "I'm working hard," I argued. "My grades are good."

"Not as good as they could be. You got a B minus in French last quarter. And you failed gym."

I rolled my eyes in frustration. Was this "mothering" I was now receiving? I thought we'd moved past all that. In my mind, she'd forfeited the right to tell me how I should live sometime around, oh, the night I left home. "It's first-period gym, Mom. I have enough credits without it."

"Well . . ." The commercial was over. She unmuted the TV and picked up her needles again. "It wouldn't kill you to attend class anyway."

I sat with her for a minute or two, watching the TV, letting the argument dissipate. "Hey, I'm gonna stay at Alice's tomorrow, all right?"

She sighed. "All right. But be back by ten A.M. Saturday, we have a lot to do."

"Yup." I hoisted myself off the sofa, grabbed my stuff, and started heading upstairs.

She called back at me, still staring ahead at the screen. "And don't be so hungover that you can't move."

"I won't," I muttered, stomping away.

. . .

Eleven P.M. Friday, and we were down one bottle of vodka, one bottle of tequila, and a bunch of beers and joints between the six of us – me, Hope, and Alice; Leland, Ollie, and Sam – the Boyses and Girlses Drinking Club. It was a splendid idea of Alice's, I had to admit, we were having a tremendous time, and I was currently perched on the arm of the chair of one Mr. Leland Banks, pestering him for a swig of his whiskey as he held it out of reach with his far arm, keep-away style.

"No more for you, little girl. You're gonna get sick."

"So are you!" I cried, delirious. "Give it to me, you big pig!"

Alice sat on Ollie Wythe's lap, flipping her hair in his face and smirking proudly as Ollie idly massaged her back with one hand. "Seriously, J, don't drink any more," she said. "I don't want to have to clean up after you."

"I know!" Okay! So sometimes I threw up; Alice didn't have to remind everyone. It wasn't like I was the only one who ever threw up – Alice herself had overdone it on occasion and wound up puking in the bathrooms of various East Village dive bars, and there was the time Hope ate a big handful of mushrooms and vomited all over Washington Square. Still, I was the one who did it most often. I hopped off the arm of the chair and appealed to Sam King on the couch.

Sam King was a nice Jewish boy with a vicious drinking habit, one of the best-liked guys at school – always friendly, always funny, always adorable, with his jug ears and marble-hard body. Always drunk. Lots of girls at school had tried their luck with Sam, but it generally seemed like he'd rather drink and quote lines from the movie *Caddyshack* than hook up. He nursed a bottle of rum, a dazed look on his face. "Sam, they're telling me I can't have any more to drink." I squeezed my cleavage together and leaned over, reaching for his bottle. He passed it to me, and I slugged from it, victorious.

I flopped down next to Sam. Maybe he would pay attention to me, and Leland would get jealous. I didn't know why I was wasting my time on Leland, he never made a move on me no matter how hard I flirted – what was he, gay? What kind of idiot turned down free sex? Sam was much cuter than Leland anyway. Leland was funny-looking, with an uneven Afro. He wasn't the nicest, or the handsomest of the Boyses, but he was the smartest, and the angriest, and he was the de facto leader of the group, and that made him the most desirable to me.

I snuggled up to Sam and looked over at Leland, but he wasn't paying attention. He was looking at Hope. I looked at Hope too. Her lips made a pink bow as she sucked in smoke from the joint, her cheekbones prominent, her green eyes nearly closed, like a cat's. She was beautiful. Leland stared at her, and there was no mistaking that look; I wore it for him. He was in love with her. My heart fell like a drunk down the stairs.

Of course Leland wanted Hope. Hope was incandescent, her brilliant red-gold hair crowning her heart-shaped face, peachy fuzz glowing on her ripe limbs. Hope hadn't devalued her own stock by throwing up at parties, or smoking angel dust at the Squat. Relative to all the other Boyses' groupies – and there were a bunch of us, not just the Girlses, tailing the guys from pool hall to park to kegger – Hope was the least compromised, the most pure. If I was Leland, I would have gone for Hope, too.

Ollie and Alice slipped away to the other room. "We're just gonna . . . change the music . . ." Leland barely noticed, mooning at Hope like an orbiting mass. I rested my head on Sam's lap, nestling my cheek against his warm, denim-covered thigh. I wished Sam would reach down and pet my hair, or indicate in some way that he wanted to fool around with me, so we could leave the room together and I wouldn't have to see this.

Leland reached his hand out to Hope. "Come sit with me," he demanded.

"Nuunh," demurred Hope, legs pouring languidly out of her skirt. "I'm comfortable. There's no room in that chair."

"Come on, get over here, woman," Leland insisted. He tried to sound like he was joking. "I'm all lonely and alone."

"Except for that bottle of whiskey," noted Sam. "She's a fine girl, that one is."

I laughed and patted Sam's knee, cheek still resting on his thigh. I left my hand on his knee. He didn't budge.

Hope didn't budge either. She pouted in her easy chair, watching the public-access porn ads on the silent TV. She didn't want to sleep with Leland, she wasn't into him like that. Leland was too short and bossy for her, and his face wasn't cute enough. She kind of wanted to make out with Sam. Or she could just sit around drinking and watching TV, laughing and smoking pot – that was fine with Hope. She didn't need to have sex with everybody all the time just because it was the weekend, and she could.

Leland's face hardened into a grimace. He picked up his bottle and sucked at it, big gulps of fiery solvent. "*Be* that way," he said, and he turned to Sam. "Bitches."

Sam reached over my head to clink fifths with Leland.

I sat up to say something bright, too fast, and felt a little swimmy. The room was so hot and close. "Anybody want something from the kitchen?" I woozed off of Sam's lap and toward the fridge. "Ice?"

I stood in front of the sink, balancing against the counter, and poured myself a glass of water. I needed to lie down, I knew, or I was probably going to throw up. If I sat in that room watching Leland pine over Hope, I was definitely going to throw up. I swung my woozy ass back into the living room, aiming at Leland's chair. "I think I'm going to go lay down," I said, and sailed by him into Alice's bedroom.

I collapsed onto the bed in the dark, tilting room. I could hear Alice and Ollie in the next room, his grunting, her whining. *Congratulations, Alice.* The room spun around me, rocking me into an unsteady daze.

I don't know how long I lay there, in and out of my stupor. At some point, I opened my eyes, and Leland was standing in the door of the bedroom.

"What the hell," he grumbled, and climbed into bed with me.

I was in love with him. It was hopeless, I knew it as soon as he hopped out of bed that magic night without an extra word, not even a kiss on the head, so he could go back and chafe his eyeballs staring at Hope some more. He didn't give a shit about me. It didn't stop me. I knew he was in love with Hope, everyone knew it – you could see him, over the course of any given Friday night at Drinking Club, getting drunker and gloomier, watching her talk to the other Boyses. I didn't care. I sat, biding my time, watching him simmer, always looking for my shot. At any time he might decide to grab me again, and use me to make a point.

Hope was apologetic. "Dude, I told Leland I'm not into him, he should just get with you. I don't know what his deal is."

I nodded gratefully. "What'd he say?"

"He got mad at me, of course. He told me I was full of shit, and he didn't give a shit about me anyway."

"Oh." I tried to make myself believe this was true. "Did he say anything about me?"

She shook her head. "No. I don't know, dude. You should find someone else. Leland's all fucked up. He's got, like, a fucked up family life."

"I know." I swooned, picturing his scowl, the tendons in his thick hands. "I feel like . . . that's part of why we connect, because we both know what it's like – "

"I guess," she interrupted, wrinkling her nose. "I don't know. I mean, I love Leland, I love all the Boyses, they're like our brothers, you know? I just don't think it's necessarily a good idea to *date* any of them."

Alice could attest to that. Ollie Wythe had moved on from their brief affair to a fling with a sophomore named Irene, then a freshman named Jeanette – a *freshman* – then some chick in, like, her twenties, who he met at a bar. The other Boyses sat around Alice's and toasted him in absentia, whooping about his many sexual accomplishments. "That chick had tits out to *here*, man!" "No, out to *here*!"

Alice kept a frozen smirk on her face. What did she care about Ollie? She could have anybody she wanted. Last Friday at Drinking Club, she tore Sam away from his precious bottle and fucked him in her mom's bedroom. He'd been dazed and smitten ever since. Tonight, Sam showed up at Alice's right at 9 P.M., freshly showered, with Leland and Mike from the Squat trailing behind him. No Ollie. "He's out banging that old elderly bitch!" High fives.

I sidled up to Mike from the Squat, hoping Leland would notice, hoping Leland would care. I sat on Mike's knee with my back arched as he rolled a joint. "Where you been at?" Mike asked, and I noticed his speech was slow, his eyes dull, the grin I remembered not so wide.

"Running around," I bragged. "How about you?"

He lit the joint and passed it to me, his faded grin obscured through a mouthful of smoke. His tan pants were covered in building dust, and he smelled like PCP. "Nowhere, man."

I got up and ferried the joint to Hope and Sam.

Every week at Drinking Club was a new puzzle, like one of those logic games they give you on standardized tests, where you take all the variables and you make a grid and you fill in the boxes based on the clues. Across the top of tonight's grid, you'd write LELAND, SAM, and MIKE FROM THE SQUAT. Then down the left side, you'd put ALICE, HOPE, and JANICE.

Then you'd look at the clues:

JANICE was in love with LELAND.
LELAND was in love with HOPE.
SAM was in love with ALICE.
NOBODY wanted to fool around with MIKE FROM THE SQUAT.

Et cetera. You could work it out, eventually, if you had the patience and you weren't drunk. We couldn't work it out. The night wore on, and no couples emerged. We got drunker and drunker; Mike went to throw up in the bathroom.

I tried cozying up to Leland, over talking to Alice by the stereo. "Hey, sailor," I said, like I was Mae West.

"Hey, shipwreck," he replied, laughing out a big lungful of smoke. Alice cracked up, grabbing his arm in mirth. I acted like this was all hilarious and floated back to the couch, where Sam sat glowering at Alice, her hand still resting on Leland's arm.

"Sammy," I tried. "Hey, Shammy."

He didn't respond. I followed his gaze. Now Leland's hand was on Alice's back, and she hitched back her curtain of hair so he could whisper something in her ear. I could feel Sam's breath quickening next to me, saw the blood rushing to his face. Alice looked at us on the couch and nudged Leland.

Leland turned for half a second, then turned back.

"Fuck it," he said, audible over the music and the TV, and the sound of Mike from the Squat puking in the other room.

Alice pouted in my direction, a combination of *sorry* and *too bad*, as Leland steered her away. The door closed.

Sam lifted his near-empty bottle of tequila, his eyes shut like a nursing baby. He drained the last inch and threw it across the room. It didn't break.

"Well, I'm finished," he said. "You wanna suck my dick?"

13
ACCIDENTS

It really wasn't that bad. That was what I kept telling myself. At least I was having fun. At least my life wasn't boring. Just think, I could be married to lame, pasty Jimmy Wilson from the Drama Club by now, I could be Mrs. Milk and Cookies. I could be back at the group home, bickering with Genie the JAP, getting whipped by Becky the Baby at hearts. Instead, I was leaning over to sniff some coke off Hope's marble notebook in a bathroom stall in Washington Square Park. *Shazzam.* How you like me now?

So what if Leland didn't love me the way I loved him – his reckless soul, his evil laugh. The summer was about to begin; I'd meet somebody new. Leland would come around. And we were getting out of school soon – the Boyses graduating, starting at nearby colleges in the fall; me and Alice and Hope turning seventeen and going into our senior year. "*Seniors*, baby," we kept saying to one another, like it was the password to the VIP room at Palladium. "We're gonna be *seniors*."

Everything was great. My mom switched to knitting with acrylic yarn for the summer and made Jake a new blanket. She made me a cropped sweater that showed my stomach. It was too itchy to wear, but I appreciated it. My mom seemed to be doing okay – she was stressed and crabby when she came home from work; then the pill would kick in, and she'd relax. She'd make her business calls early in the evening, her voice smooth as fondue – no longer did she threaten caterers with disembowelment if they fluffed a job. She still nibbled the side of her thumbnail when she got anxious, and her involuntary sigh persisted, but she was holding strong. Her lawyer was still fighting Dave in court; I got the update every week: "Dave fired his lawyer – he's acting as his own attorney now. He's trying for weekend visitation, but the judge is on our side."

"That's good." Neither of us wanted to think about Dave taking Jake for the weekend; it was upsetting enough just remembering the way he'd pick up Jake and swing him until he cried, the way he tucked him under his arm that night and ran out into the street. His squinty, creepy face, tongue poked sardonically in the side of his cheek – *The boys must be on you like dogs, Janice.* I suppressed a shudder.

"You may still be called to testify," she warned me. "So be ready."

"Oh, I'm ready," I said.

My mom smiled, wan. "I know you must be."

My mom and I were getting along just swell these days. I figured out exactly what her limits were – I could spend one night per weekend "sleeping at Alice's" (which meant "crashing somewhere, sometimes at Alice's"), and I'd better be home by 1 A.M. on the other night to turn off her alarm before going to puke as quietly as I could. And I could stay out for a while after school on weeknights, but not too often – at least twice a week I should get home before 7:00 or 8:00. But basically, as long as I helped bathe, feed, and entertain Jake, as long as I did my share of laundry and dusting, she was content to leave me alone and watch TV – no lectures, no hassles, no peeing in a cup. It was less like having a mom and more like having a thirty-nine-year-old roommate.

Five months later, I was still grateful to be home. Every day, I appreciated the food in the fridge, the privacy in my bedroom, the bathtub, where I could linger. If I wanted to smoke, I lit a cigarette and smoked it; I didn't have to lean halfway out a window in all kinds of weather, always expecting that tap on my shoulder – *you're busted.* It never got old, reveling in the fact that I wasn't at the group home anymore, that I wasn't at the shelter, eating Cream of Wheat. I sometimes wondered what happened to my old roommates – Vondell, wobbling around the men's room of Port Authority; Shirley the Nympho, hairless in lockup. And sometimes I didn't care a bit.

It didn't matter if I was a joke to my friends, if Leland Banks fucked everybody but me, if my name was permanently engraved in a stall in the boys' room at school. At least I *had* friends; at least I was famous. Everything was fine, and it was only going to get better.

. . .

Then the close calls started.

I don't know what it was about this particular hangover on this particular Saturday morning – I'd grown fairly accustomed to waking up queasy on weekend mornings, the tang of vodka and vomit in my nose, deep fissures of pain in my temples. Usually, I'd fight past it – I'd just throw myself in the shower as soon as the alarm rang, grab a scalding cup of coffee before the train, and get to work with my hair wet and my hickeys fresh in time for my morning shift.

But not this day. This particular Saturday, I chose to shut off the alarm and go back to an uneasy sleep. *I should at least call in sick,* I thought, before drifting off again. *Alfredo's gonna freak out if I just don't show.*

Jake fussed in his room, and my mom poked her head in my door on her way to tend to him. "Jan? You working today?"

"Day off." I yawned. "Maybe I'll sleep another hour."

"All right." She closed the door again, and I slept.

When I woke up, I felt much more refreshed. I glided downstairs to the sunny kitchen, where Jake sat with his picture book, my mom making muffins and coffee. I squinted at the clock – noon. I was supposed to be at work two hours ago. I loved that job; I was hooked on the social prominence it gave me, not to mention the dual incomes. I definitely needed to call and make up an excuse.

But I didn't. I spent the day with my mom and Jake, going to the library and the playground, picking up the dry cleaning. *I should call the girls,* I thought as the sun swung into late afternoon light. *I bet they're up in the park. I really should call Alfredo and tell him I'm okay, I just got sick, sorry I didn't call before . . .*

And that was the day everybody got arrested. Star, Rodney, and Darius – all three of the cashiers that shift – at closing they got called into the office, where the police were waiting to search them for the marked bills they'd planted in the register. As it turned out, Star was wrong about the police not searching your bra. They had a female cop for that.

Star, Rodney, and Darius were led away in handcuffs, and if I had not been too hungover to go to work that morning, I surely would have been right there with them, hiding my face under my sweatshirt, the female cop's hand hot on the top of my head as she ducked me into the backseat of the squad car. My former colleagues faced up to six months in jail, said Emil, one of the kitchen guys, when I ran into him the next day in Sheep Meadow.

"I think they were looking for more people," he said, one hand shading his eyes from the sun. "But now that everybody's heard about it, nobody's gonna be stealing."

"Wow," I said. All my blood drained out through my fingers and the soles of my feet. I looked over at the snack stand, fifty yards away, and moved slightly to the left so a tree blocked me from view. "That's fucked up."

It was a warm day in early May, lots of bikinied girls shimmering with tanning lotion on their towels in the grass, but I was shivering as I walked briskly away from the Meadow, looking for a faraway rock where I could sit down and catch my breath. *Six months in jail . . . looking for more people . . .* I could practically feel the cold, heavy bite of the cuffs on my wrists, hear the back door of the cop car slamming shut like a vault. I'd been planning on showing up for my shift on Monday, acting like I hadn't known I'd missed my Saturday shift, playing it off like a scheduling mistake – *Come on, Alfredo, you know I'd never miss work without calling!* That was what an innocent person would do. An innocent person would show up for work on Monday.

I never went back to my job at the snack stand. And when me and the girls went to hang out in Sheep Meadow, I stayed a good fifty yards away, behind the sight line of a tree. I waited for Alfredo to call and ask me what had happened, when I was coming back; or maybe to tell me that he knew I'd been stealing, that they had some other kind of proof, and that the cops were on their way. Neither call came.

I was unemployed for a few weeks, then I got a job at a bakery near my mom's house, where I sometimes dropped croissants on the floor so they couldn't be sold and I could eat them. But that wasn't stealing; I was done with stealing. After I lost my job at the snack stand, I never stole another dime.

. . .

Then Mike Shanahan from the Squat got his head bashed in.

It was the second catastrophe I'd barely missed that summer. I heard about it from Alice and Hope after school the next day, Hope's teeth chattering in the warm sun as she described the scene. "Dude, it was awful. We were coming back from Coney Island, you know, and everybody was tripping, and like running around, and Mike kept sticking his head out the subway window . . ."

Alice rushed in, nodding her pale head back and forth, yes and no, hugging herself around the sternum. "And I was just about to say to him, *Hey, stop fucking around,* you know? And then this *pole* rushed up, and smacked him right in the head, and all of a sudden, he falls backwards and hits the floor . . ."

"His head was *cracked open*, dude, there was so much blood, we were all screaming! Leland ran and got the conductor; Sam was, like, holding Mike's head wrapped in a T-shirt, but it wouldn't stop *bleeding* . . ."

Hope sobbed a little, and Alice hugged her. "Jesus," I said, still unwilling to believe this wasn't all a prank, starting with the part where they all went to Coney Island without inviting me. "I can't even believe it."

"Believe it," said Alice firmly. "They had to send a *helicopter* to get him to the hospital. He's still in a coma – they don't even know if he's going to live."

Hope's eyes filled again, her voice quavering. "Dude, you're *so* glad you weren't there. It was the worst thing I've ever seen in my life."

"Like, his *head* was *open* on the subway floor."

I was still bizarrely stuck on not being invited, couldn't even begin to comprehend the rest. "I can't even . . ." I tried to think about Mike. How pasty and fried he'd looked just a few weeks ago at Drinking Club, that night I sat on his lap; how fresh and sexy he used to look, before he dropped out of school and started living at the Squat. Mike Shanahan used to be hot shit around the circuit. I remembered him entering a party back in sophomore year, hearing all the Boyses shout his name, thinking how slick and unattainable he was.

I had to concentrate on Mike, on the tragedy. I had to cry like the other girls cried, otherwise I wouldn't get any of the sympathy. A groupie wailed down the block: "God, I was just talking to him the other night in the park . . . I can't believe I won't see him there later!" Everybody was running around, dramatically manifesting their grief, like it was a talent show, a contest for the most bereaved.

"I used to have history with him last year! I can't even eat, I'm so upset!"

"I know, I used to see him all the time in Sheep Meadow! I don't even want to ride the subway anymore!"

Leland and Sam and Ollie stood in a cluster on the corner, their stunned faces ashen, fists hanging limp at their sides. Ollie's eyes were red and swollen; Sam's were half-shut, and he swayed like he was on the deck of a listing ship. Leland glared down the block like a man out for vengeance, like he was waiting for the pole that had brained Mike to show up on the corner, so he could beat that fucking pole's ass.

Seeing them, it hit me, a cannonball to the chest – Mike, as we knew him, was gone. He wasn't showing up at the park later; he wouldn't be there for the next episode of Drinking Club, opening beers with his teeth and telling that joke with the punch line "Budweiser makes my pussy hurt!" Mike was missing, he was nowhere. His carcass lay in a hospital bed with a note pinned to his frontal lobe that said, *Out – be back later.* Maybe.

I approached them, chest hitching in rising panic. "Leland . . ." *Please tell me it isn't true.* Now I was getting hysterical – this wasn't a prank, or a misunderstanding, or an excuse to show off, this horrible thing had *happened*, did anybody really understand that? People were streaming past us, murmuring, "I don't know, some guy who used to go here." "Wow, that sucks." I turned to Leland, aghast, and pressed myself against his unyielding chest.

"Leland," I begged him. If anybody could make it not be true, if anybody could go back and make this not happen, it was Leland Banks, leader of the Boyses, most powerful man on the planet, and my one true love. *Please go back and fix this. Invite me to the beach with you this time; I'll sit next to Mike on the subway home. I'll make sure he doesn't stick his head out the window. And we'll all go home okay, and we'll see Mike in the park tonight, and everybody will be happy. And everything will be okay.*

He held me for a second, his arms deadweight around me, then released me. "It's gonna be all right," he said, gruff and unconvinced.

I stepped backward and nodded, tried to fix my face. Sunglasses, tissues, lipstick, a cigarette. Some girl who barely knew Mike Shanahan came running up, bawling, and threw herself against Leland.

"Oh my god, Leland," she cried. "Tell me it isn't true!"

There was a memorial party that weekend at a club called Blackbirds, a brick-walled speakeasy in an alley off Canal Street. It wasn't meant to be a memorial party – it was just another party we'd all been planning to attend. And Mike was supposed to be there, goddamn it, just like he always was, telling his jokes, rolling his joints, getting girls to sit on his lap. Instead, the party turned into a shiva. We sat there and did shots in Mike's honor, grim as a game of Russian roulette, as what seemed like every scenester in the city stopped by to pay their respects.

The club filled up fast – people from school, from the Squat, from the Meadow. *Would it be this way for me?* I wondered. *Would I get a crowd, if I died?* I recognized some of Dougie Paradise's boys in the crowd; they turned their backs on me. *Would Leland be sitting there in the corner, a shaky pyramid of empty shot glasses on the table, weeping for me?*

Alice and Hope tapped me – "It's too crowded in here. Let's go smoke one." I nodded and followed them out of the club, repairing to a nearby loading dock, where Alice pulled a joint out of her cigarette pack. Some girls we knew from another school passed by, their bangs teased like Bananarama's. "Hey," they said sympathetically, moving along.

"Hate them," muttered Hope under her breath.

"Look how they're dressed," Alice hissed. "Like they came here to get laid."

I looked down at my own outfit – like all my outfits, it was tight, black, and low-cut, with white whiskers of deodorant on the underarms of my shirt, and my bra strap showing. I adjusted my neckline demurely.

"Bimbos," I said, rolling my eyes.

Alice and Hope didn't even have to exchange looks anymore to communicate their disgust with me. Their telepathy was strong enough to transmit a radiant field of scorn covering the entire loading dock. I was an embarrassment, a pain in the ass, always needing a place to crash on weekends, forever wearing the wrong thing. I was another person who wasn't there on the train with Mike that day, who didn't witness it like they did. Mike's accident bonded Alice and Hope even tighter than before; I could have bonded with them too, but I was once again excluded.

Goddamn it, I tried not to let myself think. *I wish to hell I'd been there.*

I kept my chin up anyway, making my brave face. Hey, I was legiti-mately friends with Mike, I deserved to mourn. To get shit-faced, stinking drunk, and make whatever kind of idiot I wanted out of myself. Alice stubbed out the half joint and put it back in her cigarette pack; Hope fluffed her hair, smoothing the front with her fingers. "Ready?" she asked. We dusted off our butts and went back into the club.

The grieving had kicked into high gear. Leland and Sam were going to get thrown out of the club any second – they were bellowing at two kids from Stuyvesant High who had made the mistake of saying "Mike was a great guy." *Was.*

"He's not dead!" Sam roared. "He's not fucking dead!" Sam's face was brick red; he smashed his glass down on the table. "I'll fucking kick your ass!"

Leland was right behind him, Ollie grabbing his arm. "Don't do it, man. They're not worth it. They don't even know Mike. Just forget it." Leland let Ollie restrain him for a minute as Sam raged, spit thick in the corners of his spastically gaping mouth.

"You motherfuckers, you fucking motherfuckers!" Sam broke at the waist, doubled over, knees buckling, grabbing the table for support. "Auughhhh!" he cried, bent like he'd been knifed in the gut. He held on to the table and shrieked. "Auughhhh!"

The music kept pumping, strobe lights flashing, and Leland launched himself at one of the Stuyvesant guys, and Sam flipped the edge of the table, sending glasses and bottles flying. And the last thing

I saw, before I ran, was the club's big, bald bouncer, barreling at the Boyses like a train, like a subway coming back from Coney Island, the trip you could never untake.

A half hour later, Leland's eye was swollen shut. He yelled pirate songs as we staggered up Sullivan Street – "Yo *ho*! Yo *ho*! Yo! Fucking! HO!" There were maybe ten of us in a loose pack – girls, Boyses, and groupies – weaving our way toward Washington Square, the Boyses stopping here and there to piss on shuttered store windows or hurl their empty bottles against walls. It was almost two in the morning, and the park was unusually dead. We fell onto a stoop across the street from the park, Leland singing at the top of his lungs.

"Yo *ho*! Yo *ho*! Yo, I'm talking to you, you fucking ho." Leland made himself laugh – a miserable croak of a laugh, but a laugh nonetheless. Sam couldn't even sit up straight; he sprawled in a mess of limbs all over Alice. "I love you, Al," he kept repeating. "You know I love you, right?"

Alice's eyes were nearly closed; she swayed as she rubbed her hand in a circle on his shoulder. "I love you too, Sam."

"Not like I love you." His voice was muffled by her lap. "Not like that."

"Shhh," she said, swaying in a barely perceptible clockwise circle. "It's okay."

There was no more pot, no more money for beer, no more parties or wakes left to crash. This was the time of night when things always started to get flaky, when the frustration peaked – another night wasted, unless something desperate were to be done. "What the fuck are we doing?" bellowed Leland. "You fucking pansy bunch of landlubbers!"

Ollie picked up his skateboard and took the hand of one of the groupies, a sweet, dumpling-faced girl named Beth who wore nonironic pigtails. *Why didn't the girls get groupies?* I wondered. We were fabulous; we deserved to have a bunch of lowerclassmen following us around like interns, like assistants. We should at least have been able to borrow the Boyses' groupies, to find willing subjects we could take home for a night of sex and adulation.

"I think we're going home, man," Ollie told Leland. "I think we're done for the night." Ollie climbed down the steps, Beth trailing silently behind him, and put his fist out for Leland to pound.

"We're not fucking done!" Leland roared.

Beth let out a little *eep*, and I felt for her, a weird mix of pity, jealousy, and disgust. She just wanted to go home with Ollie Wythe and lick his wounds, get a piece of the drama inside her; then she could go to school on Monday and tell all of her sophomore friends how she comforted him in his hour of need, how he poured his heart out and wept on her bosom. Maybe that would make it easier when he blew her off in a week.

Ollie leaned in and bear-hugged Leland, who continued to protest. "Sit your ass back down there, you scurvy prick! You're not fucking going anywhere."

"No, it's late," said Hope, barely intelligible through her moaning yawn. "I'm so fucked up." She turned to Alice, her other half. "You wanna go?"

Alice kept swaying in her stately circle as she continued to rub Sam's shoulder. "Yeah, I guess we better . . . soon . . ." She tried to lift Sam's head, his mouth agape. It appeared that Sam was either asleep or unconscious. She tried pushing and shaking him, but he remained inert. "Hey, Sammy, you gotta get up."

"Get up!" Leland hollered at him. "Get the fuck up, Pirate Sam!"

Sam's brown eyes stretched partway open and then closed again. "I love you, Al," he slurred.

Everybody was making leaving noises. What time was it, three? I'd told my mom I was "sleeping at Alice's," so I wasn't expected until tomorrow morning. I certainly couldn't go home now, at 3:00 A.M., a flaky hour indeed. I could walk over to the Squat, see if anybody'd be willing to let me crash there. Or I could actually hit up Alice for a place to stay.

"Hey . . . can I crash at your place?"

I winced, waiting for the answer. She wrinkled her nose and swayed. I could tell she didn't want to say yes, but she didn't have a handy reason for saying no. "Well . . . do you have to?"

I dropped my head. "Well . . . I don't really have anyplace else to go."

"Well . . ." She looked super put out. I didn't understand what the issue was. Alice's place had plenty of room, and I was always happy to sleep on the floor if the beds were full. But she had a snoot on, like a giant third wheel had just run over and crushed her foot. "If you can pay for a cab . . ."

My head dropped even lower, my chest caving in. "I don't have any money." I *knew* losing that job was going to come back to bite me in the ass.

Ucchhh . . . I was *so* annoying. Alice bugged her eyes at Hope, who shrugged in return, making a face like a confused duck, like *what do you want* me *to do about it?*

"It's okay," I said, smiling furiously. "I can figure something else out."

"Yo ho!" Leland staggered up behind me, grabbing my shoulders, pressing himself roughly into me. He smelled like a week-old cigarette butt floating in the dregs of a beer can. "Yo ho! You're not deserting the fucking ship, are ye?" He threw one arm around my neck in a wrestling hold, his horrible breath crawling in my ear like a salamander. "You're coming home with me tonight."

My heart soared drunkenly in my chest – Leland wanted me; he needed me. I *knew* all I had to do was wait for him, just stand there hoping I was on the corner of the right place and the right time . . .

Alice and Hope looked at me, telepathing their disgust. "Whatever," said Alice, wobbling as she climbed down the stoop. "See you guys later."

Leland continued to hold me by the neck like a hostage, flipping me around in front of him to watch Hope and Alice walk away. We stood there, swaying together, as the rest of the crew disbanded around us, leaving us alone on the quiet street.

He let me go. I looked at him, his swollen-shut eye, the bruise on his cheek, his teeth-bared snarl of pain.

"Well, come on," he said, defeated. He turned. And I followed him home.

A few weeks later, in August 1986, a girl I didn't know named Jennifer Levin was killed in Central Park.

Jennifer Levin was a year older than me. She'd recently graduated high school, just as I'd graduated my junior year, and she was going off to college right after Labor Day. She was out drinking with her girl-friends at a bar on the Upper East Side called Dorrian's Red Hand – Alice and Hope and I went there once, but it was full of horse-faced, intolerably clad preppies, so we left. Jennifer Levin liked Dorrian's; she and her two best girlfriends drank there all the time. They took a picture there on the night of her death, pouting with their sunglasses on, cigarettes dangling rakishly from their pursed lips. It was printed in the paper a bunch of times after her killing.

That picture looked just like the picture in my wallet, the one of me, Alice, and Hope at a Woolworth's photo booth, pressing our faces in tight, looking like a bunch of incredibly sexy bitches. The story was familiar, too. Jennifer Levin was a teenage party girl from a middle-class New York Jewish background, being raised by her divorced mom. That summer she slept with a hot, popular guy named Robert Chambers, who then blew her off. On the night she died, she saw Robert Chambers at Dorrian's Red Hand, and she said to him, "Sex with you was the best sex I ever had."

I knew this, because they brought it up at Robert Chambers's murder trial, to prove what a slut Jennifer Levin was. And I remembered it, because it is exactly what I said to Leland one night at Alice's when I was trying to get him to sleep with me again. "I don't even care about you," I purred in his ear, "but sex with you was the best sex I ever had."

Leland didn't buy it. Maybe Robert Chambers bought it. Or something else Jennifer Levin said to him worked, because they left the bar together, and they went to Central Park. They had sex on the ground under a tree behind the museum, and then Robert Chambers, the "Preppy Killer," strangled Jennifer Levin with her bra as she clawed at his face and arms, fighting for her life.

I saw the pictures of Robert Chambers in the papers. He was tall and well-built, with chiseled features set in a bored look. He was gorgeous. There was no question in my mind – I would have gone after him, too, if I'd seen him around. I studied his remorseless blue eyes in the TV footage; watched him lie to the police, telling them it was all Jennifer's fault, she was raping him. He was on the cover of the papers every other day, and even after he pleaded guilty to first-degree manslaughter, he got bags of fan letters in jail.

They subpoenaed Jennifer's diary in court for evidence. Jennifer Levin was promiscuous, said the defense. She had sex and drank illegally as a minor in bars. And why was Jennifer running around like that anyway, forcing herself on Robert Chambers? Wasn't this tragic, accidental strangling really her own fault?

I couldn't pass a newsstand without seeing her. That picture of her with her friends, that sexy, badass look she was working. I bet she hated her chubby cheeks the way I hated mine; bet she spent twenty minutes that night picking out that exact T-shirt, while her friends sat there alternately smoking Marlboro Lights and reapplying their lipstick. They no doubt told her to *hurry the fuck up, Jen!* And *You look great, just wear that!* She appraised herself in the mirror, sucking in her cheeks. She tugged her T-shirt hem and thought, *If Robert Chambers sees me tonight, he's gonna die.*

I don't think people understood why I took her killing so hard, why Jennifer Levin meant so much to me. "It's fucked up," agreed Alice. "But it's not like somebody you knew."

It was a lot like somebody I knew. But it wasn't. In the summer of 1986, I wasn't arrested for stealing, I didn't bash my head in on the subway, and I wasn't strangled to death by a guy who despised me under a tree in Central Park. My life went on. Everything was fine.

14

SOMETHING HAS TO HAPPEN

It was an eternal August that year. It felt like it lasted forty days and forty nights, like a biblical punishment, like the planets just refused to move. All the hippies and the Wiccans and the girls who read their horoscopes in the *Post* were running around in the parks insisting, "Mercury's in retrograde! Mercury's in retrograde!" This was supposed to explain why everybody's vibes were so fucked up.

Whatever it was, the bad energy was palpable. Fistfights all over the place, people smoking crack. Ollie Wythe had his skateboard stolen; somebody tried to knife Sam King coming out of a bar on East Fifth Street. Washington Square was a shitty place to be. The Girlses and Boyses staked out permanent territory on the stoops across the street from the north side of the park – close enough to catch the foot traffic, easy enough to dash in and procure some drugs, but without the hassle of sitting there all night watching the local hoods shake down baby skater boys for their beer money. I drifted back and forth between the stoop and the park, never comfortable, never happy.

I was doing a lot of acid. It wasn't helping. My sensors were too acute. I couldn't sit there tripping on the stoop with the Boyses and the Girlses anymore, watching Sam watch Alice flirt with Leland, who watched Hope. I couldn't ignore Alice's funny put-downs anymore – "I can't believe you don't carry rubbers in your bag, Janice; that's like me not carrying lipstick" – or Leland's barely masked contempt. My leg jiggled compulsively. I kept getting up and going into the park to bum a cigarette, or to talk to this skater kid from school, or to the deli for another beer.

"Get me one too," someone ordered. I shuffled off with my hands in my pockets, pretended I was too high to hear.

I walked around the fluorescent deli on Eighth Street. I didn't want beer. I'd been drinking beer since I was twelve years old, and I'd always hated the taste of it. I didn't know what I wanted, but all the colors were phenomenal, the words on the packages so optimistic. A grapefruit – if I noticed it and didn't select it, would the grapefruit feel bad? I picked the grapefruit up to soothe it, then put it down. I was just making it feel worse.

There was a security mirror on the wall, a flash of silver reflecting a beaming orange face. I was sucked over, entranced by the vision of this beautiful girl, her reckless smile, her bright green eyes, her heaving, pink cleavage. My breath stopped short in my chest.

Oh my god, I recognized. *That's me.*

Supernatural, like seeing someone you thought was dead. I reached out and touched my finger to the finger of the girl in the mirror. She touched back, and our eyes locked, our pupils a solid beam of black between us. Instant understanding.

She smiled. *About time you showed up.*

She was visibly relieved to see me, and I was moved almost to tears. I'd been neglecting this beautiful girl, my best friend, keeping her like a forgotten doll in a shoe box, waiting to be played with. The secret me, the one I thought only I could see. Here she was.

Listen. I drew closer, marveling at the tenderness in her gaze as she drew closer to me. *I . . . I miss you. I'm sorry things are so hard.*

Her lips were slightly parted, as mine must have been, her head bobbing in sympathy. *I know. We have to stop meeting like this.*

We sighed in unison.

I didn't want to move. I wanted to stay all night in the deli on Eighth Street, finger to finger with the mirror, talking to myself. I mean, I knew I was tripping, but I also knew that this was real, that it *was* really me in the mirror, that I actually existed, if I knew where to look. This was why I took acid, to find myself in strange mirrors, to let myself know I was alive and not alone.

I love you, I told my glowing reflection.

I love you too, she said.

But people were noticing, the woman at the counter leaning over to frown in my direction – another bratty, drunk teenager, trying to knock things over, or steal them. Two girls snickered at me from over by the soda. Other fucking people, they were always in my way. Trying to make me act the way they wanted me to act. Telling me it was time to go back into my box.

The girl in the mirror creased her brow, started to fade, our electric fingers parting as I retreated from her. *I'm sorry*, I said again, and I knew she was sorry for me, too. She got to hide in reflections; I had to go out there and live in the ugly world.

I'll see you soon, I promised.

I tore myself away.

The next day was Sunday, and by noon the thunderclouds were gathering over the city like the black undersoles of giant shoes waiting to drop. I fussed around the house as it threatened to rain, anxious for no good reason I could discern. Weather like that always made me feel swollen, ready to burst.

"Are you going out later today?" my mom asked, casually.

"I don't know," I moped. "Probably not."

Just another Sunday, spent stuck at home – my mom eating cottage cheese from the container, making her phone calls for work, Jake running from room to room with his He-Man shield and sword set, yelling *"Rragh!"* I cracked a Stephen King novel, put it down; got up and started organizing the clothes in my closet, abandoned the project. I was out of sorts. I lay back down on my bed. I wished I had a joint. I always wished I had a joint. Even when I had one in my hand, I wished for another one ready to go right after it. Right then, I'd have settled for a roach, if one had been available, wrapped in a crutch fashioned from the cardboard cover of a matchbook and smoked out the window of my bedroom.

Maybe, if I'd been counting, I might have noticed that I'd been home for over six months, the magic number of months it usually took my mother to change her mind. But even if I had been counting, I probably wouldn't have worried. Things were stable at home, there was no mention of Dave, except in the context of court – the ongoing custody case, the civil suit he'd recently filed against my mother for having him arrested last year. He wanted six million dollars, my mom told me – "And where he thinks I'm supposed to get six million dollars, I'd like to know." She raised her eyes to the ceiling and sighed. "What a lunatic."

I was long past worrying about Dave returning; her only feelings about him were loathing and regret, which she still expressed to me sometimes – "When I think of what I put you through, Jan, what I put us all through . . ." I sidestepped it every time. "I know, Mom. It's okay."

I wasn't worried about Dave; I was more worried about my mom revoking my curfew, or busting me while I was tripping. Sometimes I came home on the tail end of an acid trip, and I *knew* she knew something was going on, she had to know. The way she looked at me, her wry comments – "Don't *you* look bright-eyed and bushy-tailed?"

It's a trick, don't confess, don't confess. "Yeah? Actually, I'm kind of tired. Maybe I'll go lay down and read awhile."

A skeptical look passed over her melting, skull-shaped face. *Mm hmm.* I slunk out of the room, a narrow escape.

So of course I'd be jittery the next day, my brain chemicals fizzing like soda, the taste of exploding bubbles in my nose. It wasn't a premonition, this unshakable feeling that something was amiss. It was an acid hangover. It was the weather.

My mom's voice drifted up from the downstairs phone, along with her cigarette smoke – ". . . make it a little later, more like three. Well, I'm sorry. Look, I tried . . ." Her voice trailed off as she paced back to the kitchen. Jake appeared at my bedroom door, a pink patch of belly showing from between his undershirt and pajama pants.

"You Skeletor!" he told me, brandishing his plastic sword. "Chase me!"

"Oh no!" I cried, hoisting myself feebly off the bed. "Quick, he's getting away!"

Jake squealed and darted off, giggling as I chased him down the stairs and through the living room. He headed for my mom in the kitchen, who put her hand over the phone. "Jake, not now, honey."

I stopped and looked at her. Something about her tone of voice – too low in her throat. Jake tore out of the kitchen, giggling some more. I stayed and waited for her to go on with her call.

"Excuse me," she said, hand still covering the receiver.

"Who is it," I asked.

"It's a business call," she said, irritated. "If you have to know."

"Okay." I turned to leave the kitchen. She did not resume speaking until I was well clear.

I chased Jake around, waiting for her to emerge from the kitchen. Her voice rose and fell, rose and fell, but I couldn't hear any of the words. I didn't have to. The cadence was enough, the tone of her voice, muffled as it was by her hand.

It wasn't a fucking *business call*. She was talking to Dave.

Jake reprimanded me for my lackluster chasing efforts as their conversation continued. "You Skeletor!" he admonished, sword and shield dragging on the rug. "He-Man getting away!" "Okay, Jakey." Only one hemisphere of my brain was paying attention. One ear heard Jake running and yelping ahead of me, the other ear was trained on the kitchen. Were they still talking? I couldn't hear anything at all. Then my mother, exasperated. "Well, that's the best I can do, you can take it or leave it! We'll see you at three!" The phone hit the cradle hard. I let Jake run away from me and went to the kitchen.

She stood at the sink smoking, didn't turn in my direction. "Jan," she said. "It's not what you think."

"Okay," I agreed reasonably, ready to hear an alternate explanation. *Please*, I thought. *Let there be an alternate explanation.*

"He won't leave me alone," she said, exasperated. "He keeps fighting me in court. I'm getting worn out here, Jan, I don't want to go broke. I don't know what to do anymore."

"Okay, so . . ." *Go on*, said my hand gesture. I understood the theory, but what did all this mean in practical terms?

She faced me and exhaled, a harsh cloud of billowing smoke. "I told him, if he drops the case, I'd let him see Jake. I'm meeting him today at three at the diner down the block, just for an hour and a half. That's it, Jan. I promise, he's not setting foot in here."

The look on my face must have said what I could not muster in words. Her own face hardened in reply.

"Janice, listen to me. I am not taking him back. This is about getting rid of him. I swear to you. The only reason I didn't tell you was because I didn't want to upset you."

She didn't want to upset me, so she lied to me? Incredible. I laughed, a gasp. Her chin shook as her voice rose.

"You know, I'm trying my goddamn hardest to protect you, the two of you, working six days a week so I can put food on the table, while *you're* out running around, and I have to be on the phone with my lawyer every three hours . . ."

"That's not my fault!" I cried. "*I* didn't bring him around!"

She slammed her hand on the counter. "You'll never stop blaming me, will you! Not for a single second!"

"Mom, I'm not blaming you! I'm just in shock! I can't believe you're letting him – "

"Jan, there was nothing else I could do! All right? I'm doing my best!"

Jake ran into the kitchen, swordless, his round face worried and red, and grabbed my mother's leg. "No yelling! No yelling!"

"Jake, Mommy and Janice are talking right now! Go to your room! Go to your room!"

He plunked down on the floor and started bawling. "Noooo! No yelling!"

"Look what you're doing!" she snapped at me. "It's okay, Jake. It's okay." She threw her cigarette in the sink and picked Jake up in her arms as he squalled. "I'm taking him up to his room; we can talk about this later. I have enough to deal with today without you making it harder for me."

Kaaa-choom! The thunder struck, the clouds burst. The rain started to pour. I stared at my mother; she stared back, unbowed. She turned, Jake in her arms, and started upstairs.

I put my shoes on, and my sweatshirt, and walked out into the rain.

I could have taken a train to Midtown, I supposed. I could have read-mitted myself to the shelter – why not? Lots of girls went back. They ran away from foster care, or their families again, and showed up at the shelter, where the nuns pulled their files. *Reunification failed. Subject reports continued abuse. Stepfather has returned.*

Well, Dave hadn't returned. I sat at the Bagel Buffet near Washington

Square, watching the black clouds hurl rain against the streets, clearing my head over a cup of coffee. He hadn't returned, she was just letting him visit Jake. My mother was letting Dave say good-bye so that he would drop the lawsuits, so we could get rid of him for good. She wasn't taking him back. I was overreacting, again.

I tried to relax, tried to picture them right now, sitting at the diner in our neighborhood, my mom cold and noble, sacrificing herself on this ugly errand for the good of her children. Jake, driving the salt-shaker around the table like a car. And Dave – skinny, itchy, balding, smirking, evil-eyed Dave, sitting across the table from my mother, reaching out to manhandle his three-year-old son. I felt like throwing up my coffee, like calling the cops. *Officers, something bad is happening right now, and I don't know how to stop it.*

The clock on the wall said 3:45. What were they talking about now? Were they talking about the divorce? Was it civil? Were they fighting? She was smart to meet him in a public place, where he couldn't go berserk. I wondered if her lawyer had recommended it. Maybe all of this was Steinman's idea. Maybe it was legal strategy. She was probably recording everything, the way she used to record his calls. Maybe she even brought papers ready for him to sign, whereby he swore to fuck off and disappear forever.

I should have gone with them, I realized. Rather than give my mom a hard time, I should have been helping her. *I should go right now,* I thought, already starting to collect my matches and change off the table, *I have to make sure everything's okay. What if he's . . . ?*

I stopped. I pictured them chatting calmly, drinking coffee, the way they used to when I was twelve, thirteen. Talking about painting the bathroom, talking about Mayor Koch. He'd say something wry, she'd offer an arch assent, and they'd both smirk. Maybe they were just talking. Or maybe he was apologizing. Sometimes after a breakup, if bullying wasn't working, he'd go so far as to apologize for some of the things he'd said, or how he'd acted. "I know I was wrong," he'd tell her, wheedly, "but I want you to understand what made me act that way." Then he'd go back to berating her, under the guise of apology.

She could even be falling for it. Couldn't she? So what if they'd been apart for almost a year. It didn't matter. She was still Barb Rosen, the much-married star of the *I Changed My Mind* show. All the anti-anxiety pills in the world weren't going to stop Dave from getting back in. All he needed was a foot in the door.

I was frozen, half in and half out of my chair, hand on my matches, unable to move. I should go. I should stay away. I had to protect Jake. Everything was fine. My mother had lied to me. She was trying to protect me. I hated her. I loved her.

There was no decision to be made. It was all true. I forced myself to sit back in my chair and finish my coffee, hands shaking, watching the sky thicken and fall like bullets on the sidewalk. I gathered my things with my shaking hands and started home.

My mother was already upstairs in Jake's room, toweling him off and slipping him into dry jammies. I could hear him yelling as I came in – "No! Udder ones! I wan' dose!" Jake almost never threw tantrums; it was a rough day for him. I waited in the doorway of his room for my mother to acknowledge me, my hair dripping rain into the hood of my sweatshirt, down my neck, and over my collarbone.

"Jake, those are dirty, you have to wear these." She struggled to pull an undershirt over his head, his face purple as a raisin. Her face was drawn tight and turned away from me.

"Hi," I said.

She didn't turn. "You're back," she noted, sour. "Give me a hand."

I took the wet towel, grabbed the pajama bottoms with the trucks on them. "Hey, Jakey-boo, it's your trucks! You wanna wear your trucks?"

"No, wan' udder ones!"

Jake sat on his dressing table and cried for all of us, a long, strangled yell of frustration, as my mother jammed the pajama bottoms over his kicking legs. She picked him up and placed him heavily in his crib. "That's it! Now you calm down and be quiet, mister. And don't you climb out this time, or Mommy will be very angry with you!"

Jake sat in the middle of his crib, screaming bloody murder. I tried shushing and petting him, but he batted my arm away – payback for all those times I'd swatted him – *god*, I was a failure at taking care of him. "Aw, Jake. It's okay, Jakey. Calm down, Jakey-boo." My mother stalked out of the room. I went to follow her. "Okay, Jakey, I'll check on you in a few. I love you, Jakey."

She went into the bathroom and took her pill, her face exhausted in the harsh light. I lurked in the open doorway. She rinsed her hands, looked at herself in the mirror.

"What happened?" I asked, sympathetic.

She brushed past me, headed downstairs to the kitchen.

"Mom," I said. I followed her.

She sat at the table with her smokes and ashtray. I sat down across from her. "How did it go?" I asked.

"It went fine," she clipped. She wasn't looking directly at me. I noticed that the sides of her thumbs were freshly gnawed. She picked at one thumb absently with her index finger. Maybe not so fine.

"That's good," I suggested humbly. I faked a smile. "So . . . what's the deal?"

She sighed, annoyed. "The *deal* is that we're working something out."

"Okay." *Working something out.* My heart sped up; I tried to ignore it. Too much coffee at Bagel Buffet. Too much acid. *Don't be paranoid*, I scolded myself. "What . . . what does that mean?"

"Well, it doesn't mean I'm taking him back, Jan, so you can stop worrying. He's not hiding in the linen closet." Her voice dripped with sarcasm. "I know you don't trust me, but you can trust me on this. I had quite enough of him today, I don't need any more of him, thank you."

"Okay." I shrank back in my chair a little. "I'm sorry, I just . . ."

"Oh, I know. You just had to run away. Right out the door. Isn't that right?" She grabbed a smoke from her pack and lit it, clicking her lighter impatiently. "I could have really used your support, you know. It was a miserable afternoon."

"I'm sorry," I said again. "I was just surprised. You didn't tell me . . ."

"I was trying to tell you, Jan, but I knew you wouldn't listen. You always react the same way. The minute things get rough, you're out the door, and the rest of us can just go to hell."

"That's . . . totally unfair." I could barely get the words out, I was so stunned. *She* lied to me, *she* arranged a meeting with Dave, why was *I* the one defending myself? That was one of her favorite shirts she was wearing. "He . . . you . . . you always . . ."

She set her jaw and looked right at me. "I am *trying* to get a divorce, Jan. It is taking me longer than expected, but I am trying. I'd love to run away from the situation, believe me, but I can't. I am doing the best I can."

"I know," I protested.

"Do you?" she snapped. "I don't think you do. I don't think you appreciate all that I have been going through. Everything I do for you and for Jake . . ."

Like what – house us? Feed us? That wasn't so heroic, in my book; that was the bare minimum required of parents under the law. I was supposed to be grateful, after she'd dragged me like luggage through her first two marriages, then dumped me like a busted Samsonite for the third? My voice got louder to match hers. "I *do* appreciate it, Mom."

"You could still be living in that home, you know. *I* got you out of there."

Yeah, after she put me there. "I know, Mom, I appreciate that . . ."

"And I expect you to act like a member of this family!"

"I do!"

We stared at each other, smoke pluming from my mother's nostrils. She broke the stare and sagged a little bit. The pill was kicking in. She'd had a long day, she was tired. She ran her hand over her eyes, pinched the bridge of her nose.

"All right," she said. "I just . . . I need your support, Jan."

I sat back and looked at her, her shoulders shaking slightly as she crumbled, crying a brief, dry cry under the hand shielding her eyes. It wasn't like I didn't want to support her, I'd always wanted to support her, to act like a member of her family. But then suddenly I had to support myself. I didn't want to have to choose anymore, her or me – I just wanted it to be the two of us. It was all I'd ever wanted, really.

My mother pulled herself together, eyes still shaded, and sighed.

"I know, Mom," I told her, my voice gentle again. "I'm sorry."

She nodded from behind her hand. "Thanks, Jan," she said. *I'm sorry, too.*

I got up and stood there for a second. I would have hugged her, but my mother and I hadn't hugged in years.

"Okay," I said. I left the room and went to check on Jake.

Some people will tell you that LSD makes you paranoid. Paranoid, hah! – aware is more like it. Acid elucidates all those things you would ordinarily take for granted: the color of the clouds, the frailty of the social contract, the disgusting miracle of the human body. The fact that people are deliberately cruel to other people, and to animals; that sadism always trumps innocence, paper/scissors/rock. The fact that we're all going to die, and all the TV in the world is not enough to distract us from our dreadful wait . . .

Such were my thoughts as I lay back on the concrete bench in Washington Square, shadows and figures moving without meaning around me. The summer was finally down to its dregs; soon I'd turn seventeen and start my senior year – ten months after that, I'd graduate, and be free. Where was the rest of the clique tonight? Nearby, no doubt. I didn't know. It didn't matter. I was content to stay inside my psychic bubble, alone in a crowded park, contemplating things too intense and profound for lesser men to ponder.

Some tendril of a notion appealed to me. *Someone's looking at you. Get up.* Like a finger hooked under my ribs, pulling me upright. *See?*

Zing. There he was, on an opposite bench, this insanely beautiful platinum-haired guy. He stared at me frankly, and I stared back, taking in his fine cheekbones and strong nose, the phoenix tattooed on his wiry bicep. Who could this be? He sat near the rest of the skateboarders, toting a board of his own, but I'd never seen him before. I had an unerring eye for cataloging hot guys; I certainly would have remembered him.

Our eyes met, and he raised his eyebrows slightly. I blushed.

Someone hailed him – "Yo, Sebastian!" – and he turned away. I ducked my red face to my chest, tried to slow my pounding heart.

Sebastian.

Tripping or no, I had to meet him. He was like a unicorn, a fairytale creature, right there in front of me – if I didn't seize this impossible moment, I'd never see the likes of him again. I rose from my bench like a sleepwalker drawn to a dream, floated up to the outskirts of his group. My tongue was clenched like a fist in my mouth. "Hey," I said to this kid Alexi, who I sort of knew from around.

"Hey," said Alexi, spacey. "What's up."

Alexi's pupils were as big and black as mine. It was like everyone in the southeast quadrant of the park that night had taken the same acid. Sebastian shined next to him like a diamond.

"Hi," I breathed.

Sebastian turned his big, black pupils to mine, reading my naked mind. *You're the most beautiful person I've ever . . .*

"Sit down," he suggested, just in time, as I sank to the bench beside him.

I don't know what anybody else said after that. All I heard was Sebastian, his breath, his heart beating next to me. People around us "hung out" – that is, they complained about their boredom, boasted about fun they once had, and disparaged one another's moms. Sebastian and I sat close and quiet, our upper arms almost grazing. The air between us crackled with static.

At what point did he turn to me? It felt like we'd been sitting there for years. My muscles had locked from maintaining this perfect posture, this so-close-but-not-quite stance. "Do you want a beer?" he asked. His voice was close and warm. I flushed again, fat-tongued.

"Oh . . . no. Thanks. I'm okay."

He shifted a bit, and his bicep touched mine in passing. *Zzzzt.* I looked down, noticed the thick scar on the inside of his right arm; looked up and noticed the crow's-feet next to his dazzling eyes, the color of mint. They were staring into mine. He was amused, smiling a goofy off-kilter smile.

"What do you want, then?"

I want to go home with you, and I never want to leave.

"I . . . don't know," I said.

He rose and extended his hand. "Come take a walk with me."

. . .

I walked around the West Village with Sebastian for hours. The acid waxed and waned, but the glow between us only grew. "Where have you been?" I finally asked. It was like meeting the girl in the mirror, like I'd been expecting him forever. "Why haven't I seen you before tonight?"

"I don't know," he answered, perplexed. Washington Square isn't that big a park. It was ridiculous that it had taken us so long to meet.

We walked to the end of the Christopher Street pier, sat on the edge and looked at the river, the lights sparkling orange across the river from New Jersey like fireflies. I told him about the last few years of my life. ". . . So my mom met this crazy guy named Dave, and she got pregnant, so they got married, and he was this total abusive asshole, so I left home and went to this shelter, and everybody there wanted to kill me . . ."

Sebastian reached out and took my hand, so hot in his I thought it would melt like wax. He understood completely. He had a story of his own. ". . . So we're all living in Mom's camper outside of Reno, and she can't afford to keep the five of us, so me and my brother Max take off to San Francisco, and we're living in this abandoned house . . ."

Sebastian DelFranco was twenty-three years old. He was born in New Mexico. Now he lived on the Lower East Side, and worked as a bar-back at a nightclub called Area. He'd never known his father. His older brother was in jail. His mom was a crazy hippie with a string of boyfriends and too many kids. She used to hit them with a belt, or put them in the closet, when she couldn't take them anymore.

"Oh my god." I ached with empathy, pained with his remembered pain, like he was my separated twin. I felt him, rocking on his heels in the dark closet, the pungent smell of spilled booze and dirty clothes; I knew it like I knew the back of my old bedroom door. I was him, he was me, and the acid was in full agreement. "I wish I could have . . . made it stop."

He felt the same. Everything I was feeling. He leaned over and kissed me. It was the softest kiss, closed-mouth and on the lips – not a sex kiss but a love kiss. He drew back, eyes shining into mine, and I drew forward. He kissed my forehead, stroked my hair, and I sighed at his touch – had anyone ever stroked my hair before? We sat undisturbed at the end of the pier as he petted me like a cat. I watched the minute hand of his watch edge closer and closer to my curfew.

"I have to go soon," I said, rueful. I was already going to be late, but it was worth it.

Sebastian got to his feet and helped me up, retaining my hand as we walked to the subway station. The uptown train rumbled under our feet as we tried to say our good-byes.

"So . . ." I said.

"I'll call you tomorrow," he promised. Of course he would, and every day after. We were together now, and we'd never really be apart again.

"Okay." I raised my face to meet his.

He kissed me, one hand on my cheek, and I turned to walk down the subway stairs. When I turned around, he was still there at the top, smiling at me.

If I had died right then, I would have died happy.

15
ECSTASY

I love you.

I lay in Sebastian's bed in his little apartment, tripping on Ecstasy, marveling at his sinewy back, the trail of tiny platinum hairs on the nape of his neck, the tattooed dragon on his shoulder blade. God, I loved him. I wanted him to wake up so I could tell him again. I curled around him from behind, pressed my nose into his musky neck, kissed and bit him behind the ear. He stirred and pulled my arm around him like a blanket.

"I love you," I said in his ear.

"Muh muh moo," he agreed, sleepy.

I petted him and kissed him, and his breathing leveled off again as he went back to dozing, so painfully exquisite that I could barely stand to look at him. I had to uncoil my limbs from his and sit up. I reached over for my book bag, digging quietly for various items until I had things just the way I liked them – datebook on my lap, cigarette in one hand, pen in the other.

Friday, Sept. 27, 1986 – One month anniversary! Saw the
Boyses after school but didn't stop and say hi, went right to
the park and Sebastian was waiting for me on our bench
with a rose, love him <u>so much</u>. He bought two hits of X for
anniversary, I got wine. Called Mom, told her I'm sleeping at
Alice's, then went to his place, took X. First time I ever tried it
– <u>so</u> amazing. Went dancing at Area, saw Andy Warhol, came
home and ★ ★ ★. Still tripping, he's asleep. I am so happy I
am crying. Thank you god for giving me Sebastian
DelFranco. He saved my entire fucking life.

My heart was a ricocheting rubber ball, I could barely keep it in my chest. I stubbed out my cigarette, closed my datebook, and capped my pen, but I couldn't sit back and fall asleep. I was still too high, my jaw stiff, my eyes vibrating like a fly's wings; still too happy. This was, quite possibly, the best night of my life.

First, just the fact of the anniversary – the great and glorious fact that some generous force of the universe had seen fit to unite us, a fact I celebrated every night before I went to bed, and every morning when I awoke, as well as most of the moments in between; not to mention the thirty-one days of bliss since we'd met, the afternoons he picked me up from school and took me home to this very bed, where we shared a sweaty pillow, our eyes locked, beaming. "It's our anniversary," I kept saying to Hope and Alice all day long. "I can't hang out after school today, I'm going straight to the park, it's our anniversary. Did I tell you guys what we're doing for our anniversary?"

"Yeah, taking X and going to Area, you mentioned it." Alice smirked, smoking on the corner after school. "Have fun."

Alice and Hope were probably hanging out with the Boyses, as usual, at the same old dive bar on First Street, or maybe going to another three-dollar keg party on Broadway and Houston. In fact, it looked like Ollie Wythe was coming down the block right now, flanked by Leland and Sam. Part of me wanted to stop and gloat – that is, say hello – to the Boyses, the returning alumni, who'd graduated three months ago and were still hanging around here, hawking high school chicks. I hoped Leland would catch a glimpse of me, my hair flying as I took off down the street, in a hurry to get to the park. Because it was *our anniversary*.

I rushed down to Washington Square, spotting Sebastian as soon as I passed under the arch – a bright platinum light shining at me from the bench where we first met, a red rose in his hand. He leaned forward and caught me as I threw myself gratefully into his arms and kissed him, eyes closed, for about a minute and a half.

"I missed you," he said, when he could speak. "Happy anniversary."

He handed me the stem of the rose, the petals soft as skin against my nose, thick with musty scent. "It's so beautiful."

His cracked smile spread across the left side of his face. "Well, that's not all." He put his hand over mine and a capsule fell into my palm. "Are you ready for this?"

Was I ever. "Yep." We locked eyes, and he withdrew his hand. He passed me a bottle of water. "Okay then, let's do it."

We threw down the capsules right there on our bench, making impish faces at each other, sticking out our tongues. "Now what," I asked, excited, then before he could answer: "Let's go back to your place, and I can give you your present."

He waggled his eyebrows at me. "Perfect."

I laughed and hit him, right on the bicep tattoo. "You're a dirty old man."

I had a real present to give Sebastian, a bottle of expensive Beaujolais my mom had gotten from a client and stashed in the cabinet. We ran back to his place, tumbled up the stairs to his apartment, and he practically pushed me from the door to the bed, but I grabbed my bag and managed to fend him off long enough to present him with the bottle. "Here," I told him, "this is for us."

He took the bottle carefully in his arms, regarding it at arm's length like a newborn baby. "Wow, that's great, babe." His voice was hushed. "That's perfect. That's amazing."

Beautiful, perfect, amazing. Exactly. The light from the ceiling started to twinkle, and my chest was rising and falling faster now, deeper. The Ecstasy must have been kicking in, though it was hard to distinguish from the everyday ecstatic joy I was feeling. There was a swirly sheen over everything, like an oily film on my eyeballs; the sensation of disks moving under my feet, gears turning in my head. *I love everything,* I thought, breathing like an ox through my nose. *Everything is perfect. I'm so happy and lucky to be alive.*

"Are you . . ." Sebastian turned to me with wonder, like a child seeing his first snow.

"Yeah, I'm . . ." Floating. Thrumming with sensation, with feelings, with joy in every fingertip and follicle. In love with you.

We fell together onto the bed, and stayed there for hours.

The rest of the night had some kind of strobe effect working on it; I could only see it in flashes – the streaking red taillights of the other cars as we cabbed over to Area, the throng of people crowded around the velvet rope, their eager, upturned faces. The gilded mass of bodies on the dance floor, Sebastian's hands around my waist; looking up at his flushed face, his beatific smile. *Are you having a good time? Amazing.* I gulped. Drinking a delicious pink drink; dancing like a dervish. Men without shirts, women without pants, a muumuued queen wearing a lipstick mouth painted on the side of his cheek, like Picasso. Sebastian's breath on my neck. *Do you want to go soon? I'm having the best time ever. I love you. Let's go.*

Now I checked the clock – 3:00 A.M. I should have been down from the X by now, sacked out like Sebastian was, a look of peaceful contentment on his angelic face. I slipped out of bed and paced around the small apartment. Maybe I'd smoke some pot to bring me down. Sebastian always got the best stuff, from working at nightclubs. I uncapped the pot-filled film canister on the coffee table and tapped out a healthy bud.

God, I loved this relationship.

I twisted myself a mangled joint on a book of comics and lay back on the couch, surveying the concert posters, the ripped-off subway ads on the walls, Sebastian's sketchbooks and pens and ink everywhere, the shelf of his totems and figurines. A dismembered skateboard in the corner, surrounded by loose parts. Books all over the table, the floor – *The Anarchist Cookbook,* some Carlos Castaneda. A letter from his brother Max in prison, the handwriting slanted strangely to the left. *Got a letter from Mom today, first in a long Time, tell that Bitch if she's gonna write send Stamps. Stay Strong Always, Love your Bro Max.*

Sebastian stirred in bed. I slid Max's letter under a magazine, wiggled my toes, bounced my legs. Salsa music floated by in the cool night; I got up and pressed my hand to the window, my heat leaving a silver-purple fog on the cool pane. The kids slinging dope on the corner below all knew me now, they knew I was with Sebastian; they nodded briefly when I passed them on the street. Everywhere I went, I was under his charmed protection.

My reflection smiled wild-eyed at me in the window, her hand pressed to mine. Here we were again, tripping again, me and me. *Can you even fucking believe it?* I asked myself. We could see Sebastian sleeping, like a white-hot coal in the reflection over my shoulder.

The me in the window beamed. *I know, it's so great. We totally deserve it, too.*

We grew somber and dipped our heads, had a moment of silence for the girl we were back in the shelter, so desperate; the girl who lay under ugly, zit-faced Andrew Winkler, who lay under all those worthless fucks, begging to be noticed, to be seen.

I looked up again, and there were tears in my eyes. A hard, scared look on her face, a mix of fright and pride. *We'll never have to do that again*, I promised.

She stared back at me, just as determined as I was. *I know*, she swore.

Sebastian stirred behind me in the half-empty bed, and I turned to rejoin him, the silver-purple fog fading as I pulled my hand away.

"Well, look who showed up," said Alice, smirking as ever, as I came down the block before school.

"Oh my god, you're actually *here*," said Hope. She leaned over and pecked my cheek. "I haven't seen you in, like, a million years."

"Hey." Alice leaned in for her peck. I should've cut school more often; the attention was flattering. I adjusted my sunglasses and sipped my coffee, duly ignoring the underclassmen swarming around our ankles like squirrels. "What's going on?"

"Nothing," Hope moaned. "Not a single fucking thing. This fucking place is so boring. I thought senior year was supposed to be so great."

"I know," Alice pounced. "It's like, 'These are the best years of your life.' Bull*shit*. I can't wait to get out of here."

I nodded to no one – Alice and Hope were busy lighting each other's cigarettes, comparing the heels on their boots. The two of them were talking about going to college together out on the West Coast after graduation. Alice wanted to move to Los Angeles, where her aunt was a minor TV actress; maybe she'd go to UCLA or something, and her aunt would help her get into "the business." Hope just wanted to move out of her mom's house. They didn't ask me if I wanted to go to L.A. with them, which I didn't – imagine, me leaving New York! – especially now that I had Sebastian. Still, it would have been nice if they'd asked.

"Are you sticking around all day?" asked Hope, offering me a light off her smoke.

"Or are you going to cut out and see Se*bas*tian." Alice cooed and fluttered her lashes, imitating my girlish, fan-club crush.

"Hang out," Hope insisted. "Come to fifth-period lunch. We'll go to the park after school. We never hang out anymore."

"Yeah," said Alice, more sincere. "We miss you. All the Boyses ask about you, too. Even *L*eland." Coo. Flutter.

Bullshit. The Boyses didn't even notice I was gone; they never wanted me there in the first place. Alice just wanted to keep me around for my connections. Now that I was with Sebastian, I knew all the club doormen and the X dealers and the hot guys on skateboards. Suddenly, I was useful again.

"I don't know," I hedged. "It's Friday – I was just gonna come in for homeroom, then cut out. I have to get marked present or they're gonna call my mom."

Hope rolled her eyes. "Ugh, they called my mom last week because I got busted cutting Spanish. Look where she kicked me!" She lifted her pant leg and showed off the blue patch on her shin.

Hope's mom: still going strong. "Sucks," I sympathized.

Alice peered nervously down the block. "I better go in soon. I have to give an *oral report* during first. Is that bullshit, or what?"

"Sucks," said Hope. "I think maybe I want to get breakfast."

"I'll get coffee with you," I offered. "I need at least another cup before I go in."

Alice looked stricken, her eyebrows bunching together for comfort. "You guys!" she whined. "Don't go without me."

I tried not to smile. "It's just *coffee*," Hope told her. "I'll see you in the bathroom before homeroom."

Any separation between them now required kissing. Alice kissed me too for good measure.

"What's up with that?" I asked Hope, as we walked toward the Cuban place on Eighth Avenue.

Hope shook her head. "I don't know, dude, she's freaking out. Her mom said she wants to move in with her boyfriend and give up the apartment. And Alice is like, 'Um, where am I supposed to live? Can you maybe wait one year while I graduate high school, and, like, maybe go to college?' "

"Holy shit."

"Yup. And her mom's all like, 'I won't have any money to give you for college, because I'm spending it all on rent, blah blah blah.' So Alice is basically just waiting for her mom to kick her out. Thank god we're moving to L.A. Alice's mom sucks."

"Wow. Sucks." I actually felt bad for Alice, which I'd never even considered possible before. I'd always thought how great it would be to have a mom who was never around; I'd never really considered the downside.

"Yeah." Hope laughed at herself. "Sucks for me too. I'm over there, like, all the time."

"I know."

We ducked inside the Cuban place, got our coffee at the counter, and sat at a table.

"What's up with your mom?" she asked. "Is she taking whatsis-name back again?"

"No," I said. "I mean, I don't think so. She's just trying to get him to work out a custody deal, something about the divorce papers . . ." I realized how naïve I sounded, defending her, like a complete sucker. "I have no idea," I confessed. "I try not to think about it. I'm thinking of moving in with Sebastian, anyway . . ."

"Oh shit," hissed Hope, slouching in her chair. "There's Mr. Sheldon."

I peeked over as Mr. Sheldon stepped up to the counter, meticulously specifying his order – "One level teaspoon of sugar, please, and just a splash of half-and-half. And I'd like the eggs firm, please, not runny."

"He's such a fag," muttered Hope. "I bet he has AIDS."

"Shhh, don't let him see you."

I hunched over my coffee, hiding under my shoulders and hair. I really didn't want to be busted cutting by Sheldon; I knew he'd drag us into the dean's office and give me an extra lecture. *I had high hopes for you, Janice, I wanted to see you succeed, but you've got to be responsible, blah blah blah . . .*

"Hello, ladies," said Sheldon brightly, whisking past us with his tray. He took a booth in the far corner of the restaurant and shook out his *New York Times*. Hope and I sat like statues, frozen in our guilty poses.

"Dude," she whispered out of the corner of her mouth. "I don't think he's gonna bust us."

I peeked over. His face was entirely obscured by the *Times*; behind it, I knew, he was humming a show tune.

"He's just sitting there," I reported. We relaxed a little bit. "He's not going to bust us."

"It's because we're seniors," she posited. "They know we're leaving soon, and they can't tell us shit."

"Yeah, probably," I agreed, stealing another look at Sheldon and his paper. Or maybe it was because Sheldon liked me.

Or maybe because he'd given up on me, and he didn't give a shit anymore.

Hope and I finished our coffee. Moaning and bitching, we walked down the block toward school. We paused at the front door, then opened it. *Okay. Here goes nothing.*

By midnight, I never wanted to leave Sebastian's place. It was so comfy and snug in his bed, the crisp October air slipping in through the cracked windows, his hot leg slung over mine as we lazed and schmoozed with the TV on in the background. I was still drunk from the bottle of wine we'd enjoyed with our take-out rice and beans, and high on a variety of fun substances, and totally happy, except that I had to tear my ass out of bed now, and run run run to the cold cold bathroom and make myself presentable to go home to my mother's house.

"Ucch!" I complained, throwing off the covers. Freezing! Annoying! Laborious! I dashed naked into the bathroom, washed and splashed and flushed. I could hear Sebastian sigh, get out of bed, turn off the TV. I came out of the bathroom, and he was sitting in his boxers on the couch, relighting a joint.

"Why don't you just stay here with me?" he asked, put out. His hair was all pointy and bed-shaped, and I could smell his delicious skin from paces away. I went over and put my arms around him from behind.

"Baby, I can't. My mom will freak out on me if I'm not home by one. She's been a total bitch lately. 'You're never here anymore, blah blah blah . . .' I don't want to piss her off any more."

"Your mom," he scoffed. Sometimes he thought it was cute and hot that his girlfriend was only seventeen and still in high school. Other times it was a big, bogus drag. He hit the joint and passed it to me. "Why does she get to run your life?"

"She doesn't." I hit the joint and passed it back, turned to look for my bra and stockings. "Please, baby, you know I don't want to go, don't make it harder . . ."

"So if you don't want to go, don't go! *I* don't want you to go, I want you to stay."

I pulled on my sweater and my skirt, tucking and fussing, cursing at the jammed zipper on my boots. I wanted to stay so badly, wanted to rip off my itchy hand-knit sweater and say "Okay!" and jump back into bed with him – wouldn't we both be delighted? Sebastian always gave me everything I wanted, couldn't I do this one thing for him? I whirred through a Rolodex of possible scenarios and excuses, searching for some way to explain not going home tonight. Nothing would do.

"I can't," I said, frustrated. "I have to go."

He was frustrated too, but he didn't want to fight, and neither did I. "Hey," he said, extending the joint. I came over and hit it, and he reached out for my waist. He pulled me down, and I sat next to him. "I'm sorry. I just hate this part."

"I know." I kissed his lips. "Me too."

He kissed me back, and there was kissing, and things threatened to devolve from there. I had to push myself off the couch and start packing my bag. He lay back and regarded me, his arms behind his head, feet crossed in an attitude of self-satisfied repose.

"You should move in here. Then you wouldn't always have to run home for curfew."

"God, I wish," I said. Wallet, cigarettes, keys . . . now where was my datebook? . . . "My mom would never let me."

"What do you mean, let you? What is she going to say? After the way she treated you . . ."

"Honey . . ."

"She doesn't have the right to tell you shit, as far as I'm concerned."

"I know, babe." I spied my datebook next to the bed and nabbed it. I had about three minutes to run downstairs and hurl myself into a taxi and beg the driver to drive quickly so I could make it home in time to shut off my mom's alarm clock. I loved that Sebastian was my hero, that he stuck up for me in every instance, that he'd never even had to meet my mom to be categorically certain that she was wrong about everything and I was right. But I couldn't stay and agree with him that I was right because I had to go.

I threw on my jacket and leaned down for one last kiss. He grabbed me by the wrist. "I mean it," he said. "You should move in with me."

I studied his beautiful face, his mint green eyes intently focused on mine. He was serious, I realized. He actually wanted me here with him all the time. Here, in this little walk-up apartment, these two rooms on Rivington Street, the place I longed to be all day and all night when I was away.

I kissed him again. "I'll be back as soon as I can."

He let go of my wrist slowly, unwillingly. "I love you, baby."

"I love you too. So much."

I slipped away, out the door, down the stairs, onto the sidewalk, and then I turned and looked up. Sebastian hung his head out the window, ready to watch me until I got in a cab.

"Get home safe," he called quietly.

"I will." I smiled back, and walked away.

PART FOUR

Best Years Of Your Life

16
HIGH LIFE

Sometimes it was like I was dreaming. Like I was back at the group home, lying in my old bed across from Genie the JAP, imagining how great things were going to be when I turned seventeen and met the love of my life. *And I'll move into an apartment with him, and I'll do whatever I want, whenever I want. And there'll be nobody there to tell me I can't.* I half-expected to wake up and see Sister Thomas Rita at the foot of my bed, or Mavis, or my mom – somebody yelling at me to get my ass up and moving, or else. Instead, I woke up next to Sebastian, in our charmed little apartment on Rivington Street, pigeons stuttering on the fire escape, the smell of strong, spicy coffee wafting over from our neighbors' apartment. The rumble of cars over the manhole down the block. All real.

Sometimes I thought I must be hallucinating. And then sometimes I really *was* hallucinating, which made it even more confusing. I thought I had to be imagining all this – Sebastian, with his weathered tattoos, the joint smoldering in the ashtray on the table, my old, beat-up book bag at my feet. Maybe it was all a fantasy. Or maybe we lived in a multitude of universes at one time, and somewhere in other dimensions, other versions of me lived other versions of my life, versions in which I'd never met Sebastian. I shivered, thinking of all those loveless Janices toiling away on hostile planets, fearing that I might fuck up somehow, fall through space and time, undo the miraculous coincidence of our first meeting, and wind up stuck back in my old life, in the dark ages, B.S., Before Sebastian.

What a gruesome time. Was it only four months ago? I could see myself back then, like watching a girl in a horror movie, as I shambled around the park, trying to shake the notion of another year at home, with my incredible mood-changing mom, always dodging Dave's boogeyman shadow. And now here I was, post–dinner and sex on a Monday night, watching Sebastian change the wheels of his skateboard, clad only in his boxer shorts, humming along to the Psychedelic Furs. I had my notebook out on the couch, and some Shakespeare play I was supposed to be reading, but instead of working I was looking around the room, marveling that this was where I lived. This was who I lived with. This was my life.

Sebastian was right, of course – my mom couldn't stop me from moving out. I was seventeen, above the age of consent. All I had to do was walk into the living room one night and say, "Mom, I need to talk to you about something. I'm moving in with Sebastian." She could say whatever she wanted after that – it didn't make a damn bit of difference.

She put down her needles and muted the TV. "Well, I knew *this* was coming," she said, wry.

I was prepared, too. "Listen, Mom, I love you and Jake a lot, and I still want to come and see you on weekends and help out on Saturdays. But I'm seventeen now, and I'm probably going to college next year, and I want to be independent. And you know, I've thought about it, and it's my life, and this is what I want to do."

The words came out faster than I'd rehearsed, and there was a big, loud silence at the end, an illegitimately pregnant pause. I shifted my weight from foot to foot, trying not to clear the buildup in my throat, waiting for her to say something. She stared at me – my ripped neckline, my caked eyeliner, my high-heeled boots – the look on her face half-sympathetic and half-sad. Had I learned nothing from watching her?

She sighed and picked up her needles again, turning away. "What do you want me to say, Jan? Good luck? I think it's a mistake, but . . . you're going to do what you want anyway." She sighed again, and the needles started clacking. "You always have."

Well, it wasn't a mistake. It wasn't a mistake, and it wasn't a hallucination, and it wasn't a dream. Sebastian was right there across the room, frowning with happy concentration as he applied grease to the ball bearings of his wheels, and I was here too, on the couch in my leggings and a T-shirt, with my notebook in front of me, exactly where I was supposed to be. I reached out and scratched my leg. I was real. It was true. Here I was – home. Finally, I was home free.

"You are *so* fucking lucky," said Hope.

She bent over our coffee table, a rolled-up dollar bill to her nose, and did a thin, sparkly line of coke off the mirror. She threw her head back and pinched her nostrils, flashing an involuntary look of wide-eyed surprise as the coke landed in the back of her throat. She shook it out and beamed.

I was higher than a helium balloon, scraping and bumping along the underside of the ceiling. "I'm psyched, right?"

"It's pretty sweet," agreed Alice. She gathered her hair into a ponytail with one hand as she leaned over for a line. Everything Alice did was graceful and with purpose, like she was on camera – I always admired her completely seamless performance. Too often, I forgot how I was coming off to my invisible audience, and the reviews later were scathing. I straightened up, stretched my spine, and unkinked my legs, totally agitated by my excitement.

"Yeah. We should have *a lot* of fun tonight."

Alice tapped her nostrils daintily, swabbed the mirror with her wet finger, and smeared it on her gums. "Hell yeah, girlfriend."

I tried to lean back in my chair and enjoy the sight of them, gawking at Sebastian's drawings, the neon Miller High Life sign, the three-foot bong next to the couch. There was a quarter gram of coke on the mirror and the promise of more later, when we'd hook up with a broker named Evan in the back room of this brand-new, superexclusive club called Nell's, where Sebastian was now employed.

This wasn't a couple bottles of off-brand booze and a bunch of high school boys in your mom's empty apartment. *This* was how you hosted a motherfucking *party.*

Hell yeah, girlfriend.

I was so fucking lucky. I prowled the halls at school, slapping hands with the other seniors, bragging, "I was out *so* late last night, I haven't slept since yesterday." People didn't whisper about me anymore, or not to my face at least, and what were they going to say, anyway? "I heard that girl Janice is living with her boyfriend, and they have sex twice a day!" I didn't care if I ran into my exes in Washington Square – bring 'em on, I said. Let's get a look at old Domenic Burns, at that swaggering asshole Jay Finster. Let's see Leland Banks and the Boyses now.

Maybe Alice and Hope and I would swing through the park on the way to the club tonight, take a victory lap in our skimpy Lycra outfits. Or maybe we'd hang out here for a while longer, swigging our screwdrivers and sucking up some more coke. We could put on some Prince and dance around, take gargantuan hits of pot from the three-foot bong, trash a bunch of girls we knew through the scene – "Tina Morena? Total prostitute. She will give anybody a blow job. So pathetic." "That girl Heather, the one who fucked Leland? Took too many mushrooms and shit her pants in Sheep Meadow."

God, it felt great to have friends, people that you'd shared so much with over the years – the men, the memories . . . I wanted to launch into a long speech about how lucky we were to have found one another, how deeply connected I felt to both of them in every way, how vitally important they were in my life, and how much I loved them, but my jaw was chattering for some reason and I felt a little ill.

"Let's go soon," I said, swallowing hard. "Do you guys want another line? Maybe we should save it. Do you want to smoke a joint? Wow, I'm thirsty."

"You guys," announced Hope, breathing through her clenched teeth. "I totally love you both. Seriously, you guys are my best friends. I totally want to smoke a joint, and then let's go."

"Totally," agreed Alice. Each of her eyes was about three inches in diameter. "Let's each do one more line and then smoke a joint and then let's go."

"Okay."

Three hours later, we made it out of the apartment. "Should we take a cab? Let's take a cab. Do you want to walk? I love you guys." We took a cab over to Nell's and pushed our way into the throng, ten deep around the velvet ropes. The crowd was mostly what they called "yuppies," this recent plague of people in their twenties and thirties who took cabs down from the Upper East Side, got drunk on over-priced drinks, and then left at three in the morning with a recent acquaintance and a half gram of cocaine. They looked hopefully at the two doormen, who scanned right over their scalps in a bored, profes-sional manner, looking for freaks and hip-hop kids and male models.

"Damn," said Alice, elbowing her way to the front, seeking the doorman's eye. "People are pushy."

"Ladies," said the doorman, waving us forward.

This was the golden moment, the pinnacle of all we'd achieved in our years of clubbing. The flashbulbs of invisible paparazzi popped in my head as everyone turned to scowl at us – who were *we*? Why, we were the *hot, underage girls*, thank you. You couldn't have a party without us. We nodded regally to the door guy, mutually cool, and glided inside.

Alice's smirk threatened to eat her entire face as we parted the velvet curtains and made our entrance into the first floor.

"Dude," said Hope, sniffling like a rabbit. "This is awesome."

Nell's look was part library, part bordello, with lots of overstuffed seating, and red banquettes in the dining area. We wended our way through the crowd – and, all right, some of those yuppies were pretty hot, in their square-shouldered suits, cocky grins on their scrubbed faces – downstairs, to the dance floor and the lounge beyond. Alice and Hope wanted to cruise the room, I went to the bar to look for Sebastian. Soon enough, he came swinging out of the kitchen, hoist-ing a tub full of glasses. I planted myself at the end of the bar and waited for him to see me.

"Hey, baby." He dashed over and gave me a sweaty kiss, started unloading glasses at top speed. "Place is fucking mobbed tonight. You don't have any more of that stuff left, do you? I need to keep moving."

I dug in my bag for the little packet of coke and swiped it to him over the bar, as people craned over me in piles, trying to shout in their drink orders like it was the stock exchange. "Thanks, baby. I'll be back in a few." Sebastian scurried off with the empty tub.

Alice and Hope were in the back lounge, twittering to each other on a plush divan.

"The Beastie Boys are here," Alice informed me. "We just said what's up to them."

I always missed the important stuff. "Cool."

I scanned the room for Evan, the craggy-faced, sandy blond yuppie who always had a bunch of coke on him, or near him. He wasn't a dealer, exactly – he was just a thirtysomething guy in a suit who did a lot of coke and knew how to purchase it cheaply and in bulk. Evan was supposed to be worth a lot of money, he owned his own 3-D computer animation company, and Sebastian and I had already spent a good number of hours at Evan's spartan, all-white apartment in Battery Park City, watching video footage of a red ball bouncing in slow motion on a black-and-white checkerboard floor as we did lines off the glass coffee table through the empty chassis of a ballpoint pen. "It looks so *real*." *Sniiifffff.* "I know, we're going to make a fortune off this shit."

Evan didn't seem to be at the club yet, which sucked – I really wanted more coke. Me and Sebastian were getting used to doing it a few times a week, hanging out with our new best friend, Evan, after the club closed, watching the sun rise from Battery Park City, listening to him rave, "That's the great thing about you two, you're so *real*! You guys are *real*!" Going home with a little goody bag, maybe a quarter gram, which we'd stretch as long as we could, two or three days sometimes, until I was licking the empty paper package, jonesing for more. Cocaine was the most useful thing in the world. It helped me get through school, helped me get up in the morning and cram for tests, speed-reading over my Cuban coffee. It helped me clean the house, and write in my notebook, and exercise. It made me feel successful. Without it, I noticed, I felt crabby and thick.

Or like right now, itchy, like I had fleas. I kept swiveling my head around the room, waiting for Evan the coke broker to show up, catching glimpses of Sebastian flying back and forth across the crowded room to the bar. My leg started jiggling. It was almost 2:00 A.M. If Evan wasn't showing up, who else could we pester for some coke? Just a tiny bit more, just one more line?

. . .

"One more line," said Sebastian, back at our apartment. It was nine-thirty in the morning, the sun dazzling through the unshaded window. We had only a tiny bit of coke left over from our 5:00 A.M. trip downtown to Evan's, where we'd left Alice and Hope, still partying with Evan and a few other hangers-on he'd acquired at the club.

"One more," I agreed, teeth gnashing, seething. Why did Sebastian always get to dole out the coke? He acted like he had more control over it than me, which was ridiculous, and insulting – he was always warning me about doing it too often, how we had to let a few days go by between binges. I thought he was just being cheap – he'd rather spend our limited drug budget on pot than coke – and paranoid. I wasn't *addicted* to coke, I was simply *choosing to do it all the time*, because it had recently become much more available to me. And what the fuck did he mean by *addicted* anyway? That was a matter of opinion. In my opinion, Sebastian did too much acid.

I ducked my head and sniffed up the line. Sebastian fixed the rest of the powder into a line for himself – a slightly thicker line than mine, I noticed – and snorted it. We sat back, and I let the tingle cascade down my throat, burning toward my heart like a gunpowder fuse. Then it hit, and I rode the crest of a wave so high I felt like I could see the whole ocean at once, the refracting curvature of the earth.

This was what made it all worth it, all the scrambling and the scheming, the anxious waiting and the miserable headaches – this feeling of manifest destiny, of unstoppable rightness. I was a genius, the most sensitive being on the planet; ideas and impressions rushing into my head faster than I could record them, whole novels, symphonies, shades of violet-gray. *Try to remember, write it down . . .* It was all I could do to stay upright, to keep my head from lolling back, as Sebastian's did, his eyelids fluttering as he dealt with his own super-human powers.

I gripped the arm of the couch like a life buoy and hung on.

It was frightening to be so high but scarier to be low, as we were a few hours later – sick to our stomachs, banned from sleep, muscles twitching and sore. My throat was raw, my eyes stinging. Sebastian tried rolling a joint, which only made me cough and heave a little, slick snot bubbling up in my esophagus.

"I can't fucking take this," I begged him. "We gotta get some more. I can't . . ."

He shook his head, his face pale and thin. We'd been through this and through this. There was no money, there was nowhere to get it, not at noon on a Saturday. "Baby, we can't . . ."

"Yes, we can! Call Evan! Call Steve-O! Call somebody! I'll go up to Tompkins Square Park! There's always someone around Tompkins." I jumped up and started rifling through Sebastian's pants for a twenty.

"Babe, that Tompkins shit is mixed with gasoline! It's yellow! That shit is crack, don't you *ever* snort shit off the street. You gotta calm down, baby."

"Don't tell me to calm down!"

I threw his pants at the wall, picked up a book and threw it too. My breath came out heavy; my chest was aching as I spun around, whipping myself into a tornado as I looked for more things to throw. My hands flexed, balled into fists, flexed again, my breath practically steaming now, a strangled yell rising. "Baby!" Sebastian tried to get his arms around me, but I wrested free. He knew the signs by now – I was launching into a full-on tantrum.

The tantrums had started – I don't know when. I don't know how. One minute I'd be lying in bed, and the next minute I'd be in a hysterical rage, screaming myself hoarse and beating myself with my fists. There was nothing I could do to stop a tantrum once it began. It was like I was becoming a werewolf, going feral against my will. The only thing to do was restrain me so I didn't tear myself to shreds with my nails, beat my head against the walls. Sebastian grabbed me, wrapping his arms around me as I struggled, gasping against his chest. The harder I fought, the tighter he held.

"No!" I cried. My pitch rose into a shriek. "Nooooooo!"

"Baby, baby, come on! You gotta stop it! Cut it out! The neighbors are gonna – "

"*I don't give a fucking shit! You let me go!*"

I started clawing and kicking, flailing as hard as I could in his tight grip. He pulled me in even tighter. "Goddamn it, cut it out!"

How often did he have to do this with me? Once a week? His arms strained to keep me contained, his shins taking a beating as I wrestled with his legs.

"Nooooooo!"

He tackled me backward and pinned me onto the bed, muffling me against his chest. I was suffocated under him, sobbing, thrashing in anguish. I was suffering, couldn't he see that? How could he deny me what I needed? He must hate me, he must want me to die. He was so sick of me and my fucking tantrums that he wanted me dead!

"You hate me," I sobbed, hysterical. "You wish I was dead."

"Baby, I don't hate you. You have to calm down. Calm down, now."

I could hear the frustration in his voice, feel the strain of his muscles keeping me pinned, and my frenzy broke. I was consumed with shame. He hated me, it was audible. He was sick of me. I stopped wrestling against him, sagged into the bed, and wept from the depth of my ruined gut. I'd destroyed everything – our relationship, his love for me. It was irreparable. He hated me.

"Oh god, you hate me, you hate me . . ."

He kept his warm weight on top of me. "Calm down, baby. Calm down."

"No," I whimpered, my chest hitching. "You hate me. You wish I was dead." I didn't blame him. I wished I was dead, too. The hissing voice in my head said it over and over: *I wish I was dead, I wish I was dead. Just kill me, I wish I was dead.*

"Stop it, baby. You know I love you."

"Nooooo . . ."

I could feel Sebastian's heart working way too hard, as mine was, its tinny echo reverberating in my throat, my mouth, my fingertips while I gasped for breath. I was really wearing him out with this shit. He slumped on top of me, tucking me in his arms again. I clung to him, limp, still snuffling into his wet chest.

"I'm sorry," I whispered. "I'm sorry, honey, I'm so sorry. I'm sorry. I'm sorry."

"Shhhh, it's okay." He tried to keep his tone soothing. In the wake of a tantrum, I required lots of soothing or another one flared up again right away. "It's okay, baby, it's okay."

"I'm sorry," I begged him. "I am, honey, I'm so sorry. I won't ever . . ."

He was so heavy. He just wanted to sleep, his hardworking heart to rest. "I know, baby. Try to calm down. Try to shut your eyes . . ."

Sebastian's breathing slowed. His hold on me loosened, and he rolled to the side, spent. I tried closing my swollen eyes and saw only a heavy blackness, like I was buried alive. I pressed against Sebastian's chest and shivered, aching in my empty bones, digging in against the howling torment the next few hours would bring.

The blizzard hadn't passed. It was just starting.

17

AULD LANG SYNE

New Year's, 1987. I called Alice from the pay phone downstairs on Rivington Street.

"Yeah, I got it," I told her, covering the mouthpiece with my hand like a spy as a lone junkie lurched past me down the block. "I'm on my way now."

"*Finally,*" she groaned. "Thank god."

I heard the radio on in the background, Hope pacing around Alice's living room, crunching the ice in her drink. "Is that Janice? Oh my god, finally!"

I gritted my teeth, which were already gritted – Alice and Hope knew perfectly well that buying cocaine was a lengthy, unpredictable process. First Sebastian and I had to wait hours for his friend Steve-O to show up; then we had to do a couple of lines with Steve-O, bullshit, laugh at his jokes. You couldn't ever rush the deal, you always had to act like it was a social call – like we all got together to hang out and exchange ideas about society and philosophy and music, and incidentally, while he was there, did Steve-O happen to have any extra drugs he'd be willing to exchange for money? – otherwise he got pissed and ignored your number on his pager. Then, once Steve-O's appetite for conversation was sated and he finally left, Sebastian and I had to divvy it up – our stash versus the stuff we were going to sell.

It wasn't like Sebastian and I were actually dealing cocaine or anything – we were just trying to cover our own expenses. Evan, the 3-D yuppie, had abruptly disappeared, his stark white apartment abandoned, no answer at his various numbers. I hesitated to speculate on what might have happened to him. In any case, we found ourselves without a coke patron, somebody to lay down lines for us and hook us up with doggie bags at seven in the morning, so Sebastian and I had it figured out – for every hundred dollars' worth of coke we snorted, we had to sell two hundred dollars' worth to break even. Less, if we cut it with baby laxative.

"What the hell," I justified. "Half of it's for Alice and Hope – it's not like they'll even notice."

So it took an extra half hour to cut the coke and package it, taking little hits of it here and there, and by that time it was almost ten, and Sebastian had to go to work. He splashed some water on his face, threw on his all-black work wear and his down coat, and grabbed his skateboard.

"How do I look?" he asked, manic.

His eyes were bulging like a frog's, the veins in his temples wriggling like worms after a rain. "You look great," I said. "I'll see you at the club around one."

"Bring the rest of the quarter grams, I bet we sell out." He patted himself down three times in rapid succession, like a superstition, like the sign of the cross. "Got everything. All right. I love you."

We kissed. "I love you too, babe. Happy New Year. Now go make money."

He was out the door like a white-blond comet, dashing down the stairs; I heard his skateboard hit the street and pick up speed. I wiggled into my tights, my little black dress, and my pointy boots; packed my bag: money, keys, datebook, pen, paperback copy of *The Women's Room*, cigarettes, lighter, matches, canister of pot, rolling papers, and cocaine kit – an empty mints tin containing multiple folded envelopes of cocaine, a cut-off drinking straw, a razor blade, and a pocket mirror, reflecting just a shard of my wicked eye as I closed the lid of the tin.

I ran a wet finger over the mirror on our coffee table, smearing my twinkly reflection, and swiped my gums with the residue, then shimmied out the door and over to the F train to Alice's.

"Thank god you're here!"

The party at Alice's was in full swing – the Boyses, the groupies, some other seniors from school – maybe twenty-five people packed into the apartment, drinking some kind of red punch, smoking some pungent weed. A chubby, drunk groupie named Elaine was dancing in the living room, lifting up her shirt to show her enormous bra; I smirked in her direction. Hope and Alice grabbed me at the door, attacked me with air kisses, and dragged me straight into the bathroom.

"Is it good? Did you try some?"

I dug out my kit and presented them each with an envelope. "It's good. They're fifty apiece. I made them extra fat for you guys."

"Awesome." Someone banged on the bathroom door. Alice yelled, "Go away!"

Hope was already slicing a line from the small pile she'd dumped on the back of a magazine, dipping her head. Alice gave me a bunch of bills and gathered her hair back, impatient. She did her line, and they cut a courtesy line for me, the dealer.

"Thanks," I said. I sniffed it up. Delicious, as always, the minty numbness.

"No, thank *you*," said Hope. "Seriously. We were going to be totally bumming if we couldn't get coke for New Year's."

"I know." Alice shivered a little. "God, that tastes good. Ungh."

Someone banged on the door. Leland's rowdy growl: "Come on, bitches, open up, I gotta take a piss!"

Alice and Hope and I rolled our eyes. Our little Leland. We put away our drugs and money, checked our faces and tugged our hems.

"Ready?" Alice opened the door with a flourish, and we made our grand entrance into her living room. "All right!"

I felt like I hadn't seen these people in years, even the ones I'd seen at school just before the holidays. I almost never saw the Boyses anymore, though all of them were exactly where we'd left them, still going to the same dive bars, drinking themselves senseless over Mike from the Squat, whose body still clung to life in a coma ward out in Queens, the tubes in his head leaking fluid the color of apple juice into a bag. How far I'd come since all that happened, how fast everything changed. Disorienting, sometimes.

Leland bumped against me as I sashayed past. "Hey, woman! Happy New Year! Where the hell have you been?"

I leaned in for a social kiss, and he grabbed me in a full-body embrace, hands pressing into my ass, nuzzling against my neck. "Uh, Leland!" I pushed at his chest, and he laughed at me like a cartoon lecher.

"Ah ha ha ha." He groped me indiscriminately, because he could. Same big, strong hands as I remembered, same thick, wide chest and bulging arms. The smell of whiskey and sweat. "What the hell happened to you! You're all skin and bones!"

"Leland . . ."

Leland's hands ran up my sides, his tongue up the side of my neck. I got warm without meaning to. "What?" he said wetly in my ear. "You don't love me anymore?"

I pushed him off me. "You're obnoxious."

He laughed and let me go, and I pressed past him toward the kitchen, where Hope was ladling punch into a coffee mug. Her eyes were gleaming and her tongue swished compulsively over her gums. Alice's pucker was drawn as tight as a knot. Both of them kept wrinkling their noses like they were Samantha on *Bewitched*. I was no doubt doing the same.

"Ugh, Leland just *molested* me in the living room."

"I know, he's totally in love with you," reported Hope. "He's such an idiot."

"He's not in love with me," I scoffed. "He hasn't seen me in forever. And he knows I'm with Sebastian." I looked out into the living room, where Leland was now grinding on chubby, drunk, shirtless Elaine. "See? He's all over her now."

"No," said Alice, staring intently over my head at the scene. "It's true. He's all, like, 'I blew my chance with Janice, wah wah wah.' He knows you're with Sebastian, and he hates it."

I didn't believe my ears, which were ringing from the massive line of cocaine and baby laxative I'd just snorted in the bathroom. Leland couldn't have said all that; he'd never have reciprocated my feelings for him; I was happy I'd moved on. "Are you kidding me? He said that?" I gulped and wrinkled my nose. "You're kidding, right?"

"Yeah, no, it's true," Hope assured me. "Now that he can't have you, he's all fucked up over you."

I grabbed a mug of punch and drained it. Leland was dancing with Elaine, but he was definitely staring my way, just the way he used to stare at Hope. Fucking ridiculous. I was in love with him for months, and he could barely stand me. Then I finally found real, true love with someone else, and now he loved me back?

"Bullshit," I said, turning my back on the living room. "He doesn't love me. He just wanted to grab my tits."

I didn't plan to stay at the party too long, but then some chick who was with Ollie Wythe wanted to buy some coke from me, and I went into the bedroom to set them up, and of course they cut me a courtesy line, after which I kind of needed to clear my head, because I was *zooted*. I slipped out of my shoes and lay back gingerly against the pillow, my body stiff as a tin man's, my heart beating ominously fast. Ollie and his chick started babbling to each other, oblivious; then they started dry-humping next to me on the bed. I would have taken the hint and left the room, but I didn't really feel like I was able.

I'd done it again, goddamn it, I did too much coke. And it wasn't like drinking too much, where you could throw up and feel better – when you did too much coke, you just had to deal with it, had to control your galloping terror, had to paste yourself to a flat surface and try not to freak out while your body did its best to cope. I felt my chest tightening, my heart working way too hard, my throat starting to close. *Don't panic. Don't panic.*

I lay there stiff as a mummy as Ollie and his chick thrashed next to me. Maybe they thought I'd suddenly fallen asleep, maybe they were politely ignoring me. Maybe they forgot I was there. Maybe I was having a heart attack right there on the bed next to them, and they wouldn't even fucking notice.

I really need to get to a hospital, I thought, a thought I was entertaining more and more these days. *I am going to die right here of a heart attack because I'm too ashamed to ask for help.*

If only I could ever say no to a line of cocaine. I never, ever turned it down. It didn't matter how wired I was already, how sick and speedy and afraid – if you put down another line, I had to take it. Even as I prayed for it to leave my system, I craved more, the bitter, icy drip down my throat. Most nights, I just had to ride out the bad feeling. Then I'd be ready to do more.

Ollie and his chick left the room, and I was alone with my deafening pulse, with the argument in my head.

I'm going to die.

You're not going to die.

I'm going to die.

You're not going to fucking die.

I'm going to die.

Shut up! Stop freaking out! Do you hear me?

I'm going to die. I'm going to DIE!

STOP FREAKING OUT! STOP FREAKING OUT! STOP FREAKING OUT!

I clutched the bedcovers, moaned out loud. I tried to slow my breath. People kept opening the door, seeing me on the bed, and backing away. Nobody was supposed to see me like this anymore; I was supposed to be better than all this now, I was supposed to be untouchable, a queen. "Is she all right in there?" someone asked just outside the room. I didn't hear the answer.

I had to try to stop freaking out and pull it together. If I concentrated on my breath, I'd be all right. *I'm all right, I'm all right, I'm all right.*

The door opened again, and a shadow stood in the jamb. Leland.

"Hey, you all right in here?" His voice was husky, tentative.

I didn't want to lift my head and nod. "I'm all right," I slurred with effort, hoping he'd go away.

He came in and sat down on the bed next to me, squinting in the dark room. I could just about make out his dark brown eyes, muddy pools of light. "Yeah? You don't look all right. Look at you, Jesus! You're sweating like crazy."

"I'm hot," I mumbled. "I'm all right."

He pressed his hand to my forehead. "No you're not. Jesus! What the fuck did you do to yourself?"

"I'm fine." I tried to focus my fluttering eyes. "I just need a glass of water."

Leland looked me over like an amateur paramedic, feeling my neck, my heart, the side of my face. He pulled back and frowned at me.

"You're all fucked up on coke," he declared, bitter. "That's all you chicks do these days, do coke and go to clubs. That's why we never see you anymore. You think you're too good for us. And look at you."

I sat up, wobbly, and batted his hand away. "I'm fine, I just drank too much. *You* drink too much alla time." I tried to rise from the bed, but I didn't make it on the first shot. I could taste metal in my mouth, my nostrils. I was going to be sick.

"Yeah, well, I don't look as bad as you. You look like death warmed over."

"Thanks," I said, as haughty as I could manage. This time I was able to rise to my feet, but my knees threatened to buckle. *Damn*, I was fucked up. Leland reached out to steady me.

"Jesus, Janice."

Was that disgust, or concern? I'd historically had trouble telling the difference. I let him hold me up a little as I got my bearings. Here I was, in Alice's mom's bedroom, which was spinning, as this room was wont to do. I'd been here a million times and it was always spinning; it was just a peculiar feature of the room. I'd lain down in this very bed with Leland once, and I'd recreated this room in my head over and over, fantasizing about that time. Now here I was again, in the spinning room, in Leland's arms, his face inches away, his eyes staring hard into mine.

My heart was so loud. I had to get away from him before it burst.

"I'm fine," I said. I pushed off his chest and lurched out of the room.

I shot like a pinball through the crowd and out the door; made it almost a block and a half before I stopped and threw up in an empty lot. I was wrong about cocaine before – puking actually helped quite a bit. I crouched against the wall and caught my breath in the cold air, then dipped a finger into my coke kit and put a little sprinkle on my tongue. I felt much stronger already.

By the time I got to Nell's, it was 3:00 A.M., January 1, 1987. Sebastian was pissed. He didn't stop and grab a kiss at the crowded bar; he just nodded his chin at me and gestured with his head, *Go stand over there. I'll send you the customers.* I tried to pantomime, *I'm sorry, I got hung up,* but he was already on his way back to the kitchen.

I fixed myself up in the ladies' room, washed my face in the sink, redid my hair and lipstick in the mirror. I scowled at my dead-eyed reflection – *Yeah, you're tough, what about it.* Went into a stall and did a tiny, tiny line, a very intelligent, responsible line, because I was not going to do too much coke, ever again. I was going to *learn* from my mistakes.

The tiny line hit me, and I felt brilliant. Perfect. I left the stall, breezed past my stunning profile, and took up my position near Sebastian's bar, where I was suddenly, briefly, the most popular girl in the room.

"What the fuck were you doing at Alice's until two in the morning? You were there for four fucking hours!"

It was 6:00 A.M., and Sebastian was insane, pacing like a panther, his hair standing on end, bar grime staining his contorted face. He might have taken some acid at work around 1:00 or 2:00 A.M., and I knew for sure that he'd been doing lines of coke on and off for the past twelve hours. As had I. I'd actually reached a point where I didn't want any more cocaine, where all I wanted was to sleep, but Sebastian was wide awake and on a tear.

"Baby, I wasn't feeling well! I told you, I got sick! I threw up for almost an hour! It wasn't my fault!"

Sebastian glared at me with the red, bulging eyes of an alien. "I swear to god, if you were fucking somebody else . . ."

"I wasn't fucking somebody else!"

He whipped around to face me, slammed his hand against the wall. "Then why won't you tell me who was there!"

"I *told* you who was there! Honey, you're being paranoid. Smoke a joint with me, honey, calm down . . ."

"Don't tell me to calm down!"

I leapt back from him, frightened. The tantrum was on the other foot tonight. I'd seen Sebastian get plenty fucked up before, but he was really starting to go berserk. It was probably the weeklong coke binge we'd been on – what we called "celebrating the holidays" – neither of us had been fully down from our high since Christmas Eve. Thanksgiving, maybe. Maybe Halloween.

"Baby," I begged him. "You're scaring me, please. Please, baby. I didn't do anything wrong. I swear to you."

Every vein and tendon stuck out in his neck; his eyes were disturbingly wide. "Tell me who was there tonight. Tell me. It was Alice, and Hope, and the *Boyses* . . ."

He sneered their names. Sebastian didn't think much of Alice and Hope – as little as he thought of my mom, he thought even less of my girlfriends. And he *hated* the Boyses. The first time he met them, he refused to shake hands with any of them. He just stood at the bottom of the stoop with one foot on his skateboard, arms crossed, ready to jet. He ranted about them every time I mentioned their names, disgusted that these were actually my friends.

"Asshole, conformist, beer-drinking jocks, arrogant pricks, *exactly* the type of guys who fucked with you in junior high . . ."

I could not defend them. Especially Leland. It was like Sebastian knew the history between us without ever being told. He was so psychically sensitive, he could read my mind right through my eyes. I denied that Leland and I had even been anything but friends – "And I don't even like him that much as a friend," I swore, which was even honest – but Sebastian knew better. I couldn't hide anything from him. Tonight he could tell just from looking at me that I'd stood alone in an empty room with Leland, that I'd let him hold me up in his thick arms. I was guilty, and Sebastian could smell it on me.

I broke down and wept. "Honey, I'm sorry, they were there, you're right. But I promise, I didn't do anything, I promise, honey! I would never do anything with anybody but you!"

His face gathered into a tight knot, and he stared steel-eyed at me. "I knew it."

"Sebastian . . ." I reached for him, and he pushed past me.

"I knew it! I fucking knew it! I *knew* you were with them tonight!" He started pulling on his clothes, jerking spastically around the room like a toy car gone haywire. I grabbed his arm, and he flicked me off.

"Please, honey!" I grabbed him again, and he twisted to get away.

"You're such a fucking liar!"

"I didn't do anything, I swear! Look at me, look! Yes, they were there tonight, and I *didn't do anything*! I never would! I swear!"

He turned to me and glared, his eyes trained on mine. "You swear."

"Honey, I swear, I swear. I would never. I swear."

He breathed furiously, considering me, reading my mind. *It's true. You have to believe me. It's true.* The confusion on his face, the slope of his brow as he searched my eyes – he wanted to believe me, but he knew better, he *knew* . . .

I could see him relenting, crumpling, his eyes welling up. I wanted to sink to my knees with relief. "I don't know," he moaned, sagging against me, face still agonizingly twisted. Limply, he let me lead him to the couch and sit him down, swearing again and again: "I love you, honey, I only love you. I won't see them anymore. I promise. I won't see them ever again. I'm done with them. I promise, I promise . . ."

It took hours to convince Sebastian that I had been faithful to him, that I still loved him, that I wasn't lying. By the time he finally succumbed to exhaustion around 11:00 A.M., I wasn't even sure anymore that it was so.

Our post–New Year's resolution: *Quit doing coke. Just quit it. Right after the stash runs out. Or maybe we should do the rest of the stash right now so we'll run out of it sooner, and then we won't buy any more, because we quit. Yeah! That sounds good. Let's start quitting right away!*

I think it might have been late January, but it could just as easily have been early February. I don't know what day or night or time it was. I don't know when we'd last slept. We hadn't eaten in a while – I knew, because I was only vomiting water, and dry heaving over the toilet, as Sebastian searched and scraped for remnants of the coke in the other room, periodically calling in to check on me.

"Babe? Babe!"

I'm all right. I'm all right. I'm going to be all right.

My heart fluttered like a plastic bag in the wind. I rested my head on the cool tile floor and swore for the millionth trillionth time this was never going to happen again.

This fucking sickness, this addiction – it was all my fault. Everything had been so heavenly perfect, and I'd ruined it, because I couldn't stick to the three-days-between-binges rule. Sebastian had warned me, begged me, tried to stop me, but I had to scream and throw tantrums and bully him into spending the rent money on yet another eightball. And now everything was right here in the toilet with me – our health, our futures, our finances. Our legendary and eternal love, gasping and blue on the cold floor.

I'm all right. I just gotta quit this shit. I'll be all right. I'll quit, and I'll never do it again.

If only I were believable anymore. If only I had any credibility with myself, with anybody. Alice and Hope stopped buying cocaine from me – they knew I was cutting the stuff and shortchanging them, and that was disgusting enough to make them want to do less of it. "I don't know, dude," Hope hedged when I ran into her at school, not meeting my bloodshot eyes. "I guess I'm just not that into doing coke right now."

I didn't dare face my mom – I'd been blowing her off for weeks now, lying about how busy I was applying to college. The last time she saw me, she frowned right away.

"I don't like how skinny you are, Jan. Are you eating enough? I hope you're not running around, making yourself sick . . ."

I'm fine, Mom. Everything's fine.

I lifted my head off the bathroom floor for another round of heaving. *Hlllllll.* Throat stuck out like a strangling goose, a stabbing strain between my ribs. *Hlllllll.* Nothing in my stomach, which contracted so hard I couldn't catch my breath between waves. Spiraling circles blocking my sight.

I heaved and heaved, regret spinning into fear, the same old fear. *I'm going to die. This time it's serious. I'm really going to die. Hlllllll.* My eyes popping from their sockets, lungs shriveled in the fiery cage of my chest. *Can't breathe! I'm going to die. I'm going to die.*

It wasn't my life flashing exactly; it was more like events that would happen after I died. Jake. My mom explaining to Jake that I was dead. *Janice isn't coming over anymore, Jakey.* Jake crying and crying. A weird flash of Jake at my age, seventeen, saying, *I had a sister, but she died from coke*. People hooking up at my memorial – Leland and Alice, Sam and Hope. Everybody from school smirking. *She was such a waste*.

"Babe?" called Sebastian. He was still thrashing around the apartment, hunting for little grains of coke, residue, anything.

"Unh," I cried weakly.

He appeared in the doorway of the bathroom, eyes bugging. "How you doing, baby? You need anything?"

My heart shivered in my chest, a bird shaking in the rain. *Hllllll.* I retched futilely some more as Sebastian patted my back. "You want some water, baby? You gonna be okay?"

I couldn't speak, could only choke on bile, snot running down my face mixed with spit and tears. Surely the deafening thump of my heart was loud enough to answer. *I'm going to die.* I shivered and sweated, heaved again, and sobbed, and Sebastian grabbed me by both shoulders.

"Baby, talk to me. You okay?"

I shook my head no, inasmuch as I was able. My bursting chest, the stabbing pain under my rib, my whole body splitting asunder – *I'm going to die. My heart is going to explode.* I heaved and heaved, hysterical. Sebastian held me by the shoulders and slapped my face.

"Come on, baby. Come on."

He jerked me up to my feet, corralled me backward into the tub. *Hllllll.*

"Hang on. You're gonna be all right! You're gonna be fine."

He pulled off my nightshirt, covered in spume and sweat, and turned on the shower, shocking cold. I writhed, fighting it, frantic to catch my breath, and he slapped me again.

"Come on, baby. Come on."

I could barely make out his desperate face, still as beautiful and magic to me as the day we met. *Sebastian.* I wanted to stay with him, wanted to go back in time to September, when I cut school and we made love all day, warm and safe. When he traced the outline of my face with his finger, and gathered me in his taut arms, and I rested against his chest to the sound of his slow, sure heart, knowing that *Sebastian DelFranco saved my entire fucking life.*

It was around here that my eyes completely slipped out of focus, and a cold, calm numbness spread from my very core. It was around here, Sebastian says, that I lolled back in the tub, and my head went limp on my neck. It was around here that he screamed, pounded on my chest, pinched my nose, and blew in my mouth, as the freezing rain of the shower beat down on us both.

It was around here, I'm pretty sure, that I died.

18

THE AWAKENING

Okay, *obviously*, I didn't die. Obviously, I don't really know most of what happened that morning. I had to go by Sebastian's eyewitness account.

"You scared the hell out of me, baby. I was ready to call an ambulance. Thank god you came around. We're *never* doing that shit again."

Sebastian looked like he'd aged about ten years overnight, deep lines cut into his brow, his face gray. I gratefully agreed. "Never."

I lay in bed, ribs aching like I'd been wrung, a searing pain between my eyes, like the inside of my face had been scrubbed with sandpaper. Sebastian stripped the apartment of anything cocaine-related – the mirror, the blades, the straws, the baby laxative. The grinder, the scale. My cocaine tin. They all went in the garbage bag. Then he went out and bought a bunch of groceries and got an ounce of pot on credit. He called his friend Pepe and had him cover his shift at the club. He propped me up in bed so I could see the TV, fed me sips of water and soup, and surrounded us both with a puffy, comforting cloud of pot smoke.

And that was it – we quit cocaine. We smoked joint after joint after joint, but we quit cocaine. We just stopped. We didn't have any, we didn't buy any, we didn't do any. We talked about it all the time – "God, just think if we were wired right now, we'd be so twitchy and freaked out" – but we never did it again. We were done. After a few days of bed rest, I was ready to walk around again, to call my mom and tell her I was recovering from my weeks-long flu. I went back to school. Everything felt fresh and tender, my skin prickling in the February air, my appetite back with a vengeance.

"You're looking *a lot* better," said Alice, double-edged as always, on the corner after school.

"Seriously," Hope agreed.

"Thanks," I said. I didn't stop to hang out with them. I had work to do if I wanted to graduate in June and get into one of the city colleges. I went straight home to Sebastian, smoked the joint he had rolled for me, wolfed down a bacon-lettuce-tomato sandwich, and cracked open my college applications.

Write about a significant experience in your life. What happened? Why was it significant? What did you discover about yourself?

Huh.

How about "The Time I Got Stabbed in the Face by a Pregnant Girl." Or "My Recent Cocaine Overdose," by Janice Erlbaum. I didn't know what to tell them. The last few years of my life had been one long Significant Experience, ever since I first walked out of my mother's apartment. All I'd discovered was that I was lucky to be alive.

Thank god for Sebastian. I'd said it since the night we met, but never more so than now. My savior, my sanctuary – he was the reason I was still here tonight, toasty and overfed in the cozy apartment. I watched him sitting next to me on the couch, poring over an issue of *Thrasher*, one hand resting absentmindedly on my foot.

He felt me looking at him, patted the foot. "Hey, baby."

"Hey, baby. I love you."

He leaned over and gave me a kiss. "I love you too. So much."

It was like a second honeymoon. A slightly sadder and wiser honeymoon than the first, like we'd been married and divorced, and remarried again; we'd seen what failure looked like, and we were taking a vacation inside our apartment to forget. Like tourists, we stopped to appreciate every little detail of our post-coke landscape: "I love the way the light comes through the windows in the morning." "I know, I can smell the coffee from next door again."

We were so delicate around each other, tiptoeing and baby-talking, both of us still so fragile. As badly as I was shaken, I felt like Sebastian was shaken even worse, his lean body wrecked, his balance unsteady. His skateboard shot out from underneath him at odd moments; he stumbled. He didn't trust himself anymore. He hated going to work and being around cocaine – he felt, as I did, that the only safe place was inside the apartment, protected by a thick layer of pot smoke. He blew off shifts at the club, which meant less money, but I could hardly complain. What did I contribute? I hadn't worked in six months. Any money I had was mooched off my mom. Otherwise, I was dependent on Sebastian.

Dependent. What a weird way to wind up, after fighting so hard to be free. It chafed a little – more and more as winter melted into spring, and I got itchy to go outside. I wanted excitement, I complained, I wanted to have fun like we used to. So Sebastian went out and got us some X. But it wasn't very strong X, and we spent most of the trip bemoaning how much happier we should have been.

We didn't even have sex. That's how old and married we were.

I retreated into my datebook.

March 12, 1987 – Sitting here at home alone, Sebastian
working tonight thank god. I miss him when he's not here but
then when he's here I feel trapped. I don't know. Went to
every class today, including double gym. Ten more weeks and
I graduate. Then college I guess. Maybe I could be a banker. I
want to be rich. I want to be able to take care of myself. I want
to stop sucking my thumb and having tantrums. I want better
friends. I want to write every day. I love Sebastian and I want
to be able to still do what I want. Whatever that is.

I started cutting lunch. It was the only period I could still afford to cut. I attended all of my classes, from first period to eighth, but instead of going to fifth-period lunch, I went to the empty typing room, and I wrote. I wrote a story about a houseful of teenage prostitutes in L.A. I wrote a story about a teenage girl having an affair with her father's bisexual male lover. I wrote a story about a pregnant teenage girl hustling a bunch of different guys for money by telling each one he was the dad. These were comedies.

I started a screenplay. It was about three teenage girlfriends and their romantic relationships. One of the main characters was named JP; she was this insanely cool chick who lived with her fabulous older boyfriend on the Lower East Side. At one point in the script, JP is counseling her friend Paige on men, and she says:

> You know deep in your heart that all guys are assholes.
> Then you meet one you like, and he likes you, and you say,
> this one's different, this one isn't like other guys, this one
> isn't an asshole. He's an exception, and all. Then later you
> find out he's an asshole just like all the rest. He just hid
> it better.

At the end of the second act, JP cheats on her fabulous older boyfriend at a party. I don't know why. I never got to the third act. A lot of my projects went unfinished.

The typing room was an excellent place to write. I sat in the back with the light off and the door closed, and nobody disturbed me. The electric typewriter hummed patiently, *ommmmm*, waiting for me to tell it what to do, and my thoughts came out loud and decisive with each key strike – *clack clack clack, and that's that*. I rocked to the rhythm of the carriage return, the *tzzzing!* of finishing another line, fingers eager for the next.

I was totally startled when the door opened and Mr. Sheldon popped his head inside.

He seemed surprised as well. "Oh! Hello, Janice. I heard the noise, and I wondered who was in here . . ."

"Hey, Mr. Sheldon."

He hesitated a moment, then entered the room. I took my hands off the keys and put them in my lap.

"What are you doing in here? Do you have a project for Ms. Gerber's class?"

"No, I'm just . . . typing." I had the urge to turn over the finished pages on my desk – *Jane was sick of fucking Richard, but Richard was part of her master plan* – but I resisted.

"Well." He smiled at me, eyebrows raised. "How industrious."

I smiled back. I missed Mr. Sheldon. I always felt a little twinge of regret when I saw the Drama Club's posters in the hallways, or the notice about auditions for the spring play; I could still hear the echo of that long-ago applause. Sometimes I thought maybe I should have stayed a drama geek.

"How's the play coming?" I asked him.

He rolled his eyes heavenward. "Oh, it's going well enough. We've got some hard workers this year. Nobody as talented as you, but we can't ask for everything, can we?"

I ducked my head, guilty and pleased at the same time. "Naw, I'm sure it's great, it's always great."

He bowed his head slightly at the compliment. "Well, we do our best."

There was a weird pause, and I felt suddenly shy. Almost like a romantic thing, but not a sexual one – not at all. Hard to describe. I reached a finger over and tapped the space key a few times. Sheldon cleared his throat.

"So have you heard from any colleges?" he asked. "Did you apply?"

"Yeah, I applied to Hunter, I should get in. I mean, I want to stay in the city, so . . . that's cool."

He nodded, and the eyebrows went up again. "Well, that's wonderful. You can come back and see us as an alumnus."

What a funny idea. I'd always planned to get the hell out of this place and never return. But . . . yeah, definitely. When I was rich and famous, I'd definitely swing by and say what's up to Mr. Sheldon.

"Yeah," I said. "That would be nice."

I rifled my stack of pages. Sheldon looked at his watch. "All right," he said, brisk. "Off to class, then."

"All right." And I didn't know why, but I added, "Thanks, Sheldon."

He bowed again, smoothed his tie, and stepped gracefully out of the room.

Roxanne was perplexed. On the one hand, there was the Duke, her handsome, valiant husband-to-be. He would give her anything her heart desired, she would never feel fear or want again. On the other hand, there was Hugo, who she both feared and wanted. What if her heart desired him?

I kept the pages of my current romance tucked in my history book, and my datebook stayed with me at all times. There was too much personal stuff in there – all my crushes and my grudges, my grandiose fantasies and my naked self-hate. Plus all my comings and goings – drugs done, people encountered, places attended, money spent. Evidence that could be used against me later. I didn't leave the house without it.

I didn't suspect Sebastian of snooping, though I myself snooped all the time, peeking at letters from his brother Max, postcards from his crazy mom: *Don't forget the equinox, it never forgets you.* I kept my datebook close to my person, especially as I started to hang out more often after school, taking a walk through the park on the way home, going drinking with Alice and Hope. Sebastian had relented somewhat on the topic of Alice and Hope – he was even marginally civil to them if they called or dropped by.

"It's your little friend *Hopey*," he said, passing me the phone. I scowled at him and grabbed it.

"Hey, what's up."

"Hey," she said, tough and efficient, like an old-school secretary, cigarette no doubt hanging off her lower lip. "We're meeting at Zodiac Bar at ten. I don't know what we're doing from there. I think Ollie knows a party uptown."

"Cool. See you there."

"All right."

I passed the receiver back to Sebastian and went back to painting my toenails.

"That was fast," Sebastian noted.

I kept my eyes on my toenails. "Yeah. I'm just gonna meet them at Zodiac. I probably won't stay long."

"Uh-huh."

"I just figure, since you're working . . . I'd get out of the house . . . get a drink . . ."

I could tell, he was working as hard as I was to keep his face neutral, his tone light. It was almost working. "Uh-huh," he said, somewhat less than casually.

I clammed up. I wasn't doing anything wrong. I wasn't going out to meet the Boyses – I was going to meet the girls. And if me and the girls ran into the Boyses somewhere in our travels, I could hardly be blamed for that. Sebastian was probing me with those lie-detector eyes. I didn't look up.

"Well, have fun," he groused. "I'm gonna be working my ass off."

I bit my lip. "I hope it's not too bad tonight," I said sympathetically to my toenails. "I love you, honey."

Alice and Hope were sitting at a table in the dingy bar, smoking over their vodka and tonics as the Boyses played pool at the three-quarter-sized table. The place was typical of the bars we frequented – a dark, smoky dive in the East Village where old Ukrainian men played polka and Sinatra on the jukebox and the vodka came from a jug. Tonight, as usual, we were the only patrons under the age of fifty.

"Hey, girlfriend." Alice gave me her welcome pout, the invitation to lean down and air kiss. I bussed her and Hope hello.

"What up, J."

"What up."

I pulled up a chair, tossed my hair, and peeked over at Leland, who was leaning across the pool table, cue sliding back and forth between his bridged fingers, assessing a tricky shot. Sam stood behind him, nodding at the setup. It looked like Sam and Leland were wiping the table with their opponents, Ollie Wythe and his latest chick.

"Ugh, Leland's here. I haven't seen him since New Year's."

Hope knocked back the rest of her drink and started crunching the ice. "God, I feel like I see the Boyses all the time."

"That's because we *do*," Alice bitched. "Ucch, I can't wait to graduate and get the hell out of here."

"Word," agreed Hope.

I had nothing to add. I was graduating, but I wasn't getting the hell out of anywhere. Alice and Hope were moving to L.A. together in the fall, and I was staying right here on Rivington Street. Forever. Till death do I move. "I'm gonna go get a drink."

I stood up and moved toward the bar, pointedly ignoring the pool table. My posture was excellent; I carried myself with Alice-level poise and conviction. "A vodka tonic, please." The bartender, a stout woman in a stained apron, poured it and accepted my money without looking at me. If she looked at me, she'd have to ask me for ID, and neither of us wanted that. She grunted and slid the glass to me.

"Thank you," I said, ever charming. My drink smelled like turpentine. Why did I even bother with alcohol anymore? I was a terrible drinker, always had been, and the taste of booze just made me remember all those nights on my knees in various bathrooms, practically puking out of my ears. I carried the drink in front of me like a prop and waltzed over to the pool table, where Ollie's chick was lining up for a shot. I presented myself to Ollie for a kiss. "Hey, handsome!"

"Hey! There she is." He gave me a hug and a smooch.

I waved across the table at Sam and ignored Leland. Leland gave me a hard glare, which only made my big fake smile wider.

Sam waved back. I blew him a kiss and a wink.

Ollie left his hand on my shoulder, dropping his voice as he ducked down to my ear. "Hey, you don't have any . . . with you, do you?" He pantomimed a sniff.

I shook my head. "Nah, man, sorry. I'm out of the biz."

He looked at me skeptically. "Yeah? Not even a little?" He made a cute pleading face, like I might be hiding something that he could persuade me to give up, and I completely understood how he got laid all the time.

"No, seriously, I haven't even seen any in months. We're done with it. I'm a full-time pothead now."

He laughed and pounded his fist over mine. "*Irie,*" he said, like he was Jamaican, instead of a white boy from the Upper East Side.

"*Irie,*" I replied.

I strolled back to Alice and Hope at the table. I could feel Leland's eyes on me, burning like beams of light from across the room as I slung myself into my chair.

"*Now* what?" I complained, languorous. "Don't we have someplace better to go?"

There was noplace better to go that night – we never left the bar. I kept thinking I would go home soon, maybe get some writing done, or reread the stuff I'd already written, which was always gratifying. But

I was enjoying Leland's simmering rage, feeling him stalk around behind me, hearing his forced jocularity fall flat. It became clearer and clearer that I was ignoring him as the night wore on and I still hadn't looked his way.

Hope leaned in and lowered her voice. "What's going on with you two?"

"With who?" I asked, straight-faced. Alice leaned over the table, trying to hear better.

"Why are you ignoring Leland? Duh."

I straightened up. "I'm not ignoring him. I just don't want to deal with him."

"Right, I get that, but why? I mean, it just seems weird and totally obvious that you're not talking to him."

I flushed. It wasn't like I'd planned to show up tonight and ignore Leland – I wasn't *planning* on seeing Leland at all. I was just going out for a drink with the girls, and if the Boyses were there, oh well. Then I walked in the door, and I saw him right away, playing pool in the back, and he saw me too, and my mouth went dry. And I didn't know what to say.

"Well, you know . . . last time I saw him was at Alice's on New Year's, and . . ." What was it about that night? *He grabbed me, and he smelled good, and then later in the bedroom he was holding me . . .* "And he completely molested me! He was practically begging me to have sex with him. And I was like, 'Ewww, I'm not even going to deal with you on that level.' You know?"

"Mm *hmm*," agreed Alice. "You're so right. He should *not* have been grabbing you like that. You're a married woman!"

Hope was still puzzled. "So . . . what, you're not talking to him ever again?"

"Well . . ." Good question. I'd sort of dug myself a hole without thinking about it. Now that I'd taken this radical anti-Leland stance, I was going to have to justify it somehow. "I think Leland owes me an apology," I decided. "He was really disrespectful of me on New Year's."

There – a platform. A position I could stick to. Leland had groped me, which was wrong. I was right. Alice nodded. Hope's nose stayed wrinkled, unsatisfied.

"Well, whatever, dude. He's coming over here, so . . ."

Alice's eyes widened, and Hope shrank back in her chair. I didn't have time to turn around before Leland was standing in front of us, seething.

"What's up," he said, directly to me.

My leg started to bounce under the table. "Excuse me?"

"I said, what's up." His dark eyes were focused on mine, his temples pulsing.

Hope and Alice shot each other a look and spoke almost in unison. "We're gonna . . ." "Um, we're gonna go to the ladies' . . . yeah."

They picked up their purses and squeezed past Leland toward the bathroom. Alice flashed me an *eek!* look as she passed and showed me her crossed fingers for good luck.

Leland stood in front of me. I kept my face neutral, despite the shaking leg and distinct dampness flooding my armpits. "Nothing's up," I said, coolly. "What do you want?"

"I want you to fucking talk to me."

His jaw was tight, his breath hard. He was above-average mad. I'd seen Leland angry, plenty of times, but never over me – it was really quite a becoming look for him. An evil smile threatened to break across my face. I turned my head slightly so he wouldn't see it.

"All right," I said, hair covering my half smirk. "We're talking."

He grabbed my forearm, and I jerked with surprise. "What the fuck are you doing? Is this some kind of a game?"

I wrested my arm away and rubbed it, sullen. "Ow! Jesus. What the fuck do you want from me, Leland?"

Sam looked over from the pool table, concerned; the bartender frowned in our direction. Leland dropped his voice to a growl. "I want you to come outside and talk to me. Right now."

My heart started pounding, and my hands were pooled with sweat, my fists clenched like I was ready for a street fight. I felt like I was on coke. I couldn't get away from his blistering stare, I was burning up, I was going to explode.

"Fine," I said, hopping out of my seat. "Let's go."

I followed Leland out of the bar and onto the sidewalk, his hands stuffed hard in his pockets, his back hunched. He turned the corner onto First Street, and I turned too. He stopped in front of a stoop on the near-deserted street, a woman in rags picking through the garbage cans on the corner, and he turned to me. His eyes were softer than I'd ever seen them, tear-shaped. He actually looked pained. *Good*.

"So what?" I challenged, arms across my chest. "What did you want to say to me, *Leland?*"

He didn't speak. He stared at me, eyes narrowed, brow lined, and shook his head, incredulous. It was gratifying to see him struck so dumb. I felt a surge of energy run through me – so *this* was what it felt like to render people powerless. I felt like I was Alice. I imitated her trademark kissyface sneer.

"Huh, *Leland?* What is it? You practically dragged me out of the bar, what's so fucking important?"

His eyes bulged with frustration, narrowed again. "I'm trying to . . ." He stopped and shook his head, started fresh. "Listen . . ."

My hands gripped my hips, almost pinching myself, like a dream. There he was, *Leland Banks*, squirming in front of me, twisting like a fish. It was delirious, delicious. "I'm listening, but you're not saying anything, you're just – you know. I'm about to walk away and go back to my friends . . ."

I turned to illustrate how I'd walk away, and he grabbed me by the shoulder and spun me around.

"I fucking love you!" he yelled. "All right?"

I swear to god, I wasn't expecting it.

He searched my eyes for some reply. I gaped in shock, recoiled. He dropped my shoulder and paced backward a few feet, opened his arms, palms up – *you win*.

"Okay? I'm in love with you. I can't think about anything else. I can't sleep at night. It's been driving me crazy for weeks now. All right? Are you happy?"

"I . . ."

And I was the one struck dumb. This was *true*, this was *happening* – Leland, confessing his love for me. A *year too late*. So much to try to understand, so fast. Like good news, bad news: The good news is, you finally got what you always wanted. The bad news is, you can't have it.

Fear, and wanting. Leland stood in front of me, begging an answer. I shook my head in disbelief. "Leland . . ." I said, gasping a little, or laughing. Unable to catch my breath. "I mean, I wasn't expecting this, I . . . I don't know what to say . . ."

He advanced toward me, urgent, lips slightly parted, eyes sincere. "I know, I know it's crazy . . ."

I put my hand out, still shaking my head. "I mean, I'm with Sebastian, he's . . ." Just the thought of Sebastian made me shudder, what he'd say if he saw me right now.

"I know." Leland's features hardened. "Trust me, I know."

I kept my hand out, my head shaking. "I . . . I don't know what you want me to say. I mean, I . . . I care about you . . ."

He drew closer, my hand against his thumping chest. "I know you do. I know you do. You did for a long time, and I was an idiot, but I'm telling you now . . ."

"Wait . . . Leland . . ."

He didn't wait. He leaned in and brought his lips to mine.

"I can't," I cried.

And then I did.

19

MY VICE

I love you.

I sat at a table at the Zodiac Bar, watching Leland and Sam work the pool table. Leland took a tough shot, banking a ball off the side of the table before it rolled dutifully into the pocket; he turned and blew the chalk on the tip of his cue, that show-off. He knew I was watching him out of the corner of my eye, but he didn't look over, and neither did I. I kept my attention fixed on Alice and Hope.

". . . *think* I totally have the perfect dress for the prom, but I don't have any money left over for shoes. . . ."

". . . I know, it's so fucking expensive, plus the limo, and the X . . ."

Alice put her hand on my wrist. "You're getting the X for us, right?"

"I'm on it," I assured her. "Definitely. It's set."

"Thank god." She tossed her hair over her shoulder. "I don't think I could handle the whole prom thing without the appropriate drugs."

"Seriously," Hope agreed. "How corny would that be?"

As much as Hope and Alice and I frowned on stupid school-related ceremony, we were getting soft in our old age – the closer to graduation we got, the more sentimental we became. We bought yearbook boosters ("A&H&J, homies for life. Never forget: B&GDC, tripping in Trig, 'follow your nose!' Girlses '87 forever!"), and we'd decided, as a group, to attend the prom.

Alice's hand fluttered over my wrist again. "So, Janice, who are you taking as your date?"

She was smirking at me, as always, the old wives' tale come true – her face was frozen like that, and it would stay that way forever. I kept my smile fixed and my tone light. "Um, Sebastian, of course."

"Of course," she repeated, looking slyly over at Leland. "Who else would you take?"

I dropped the smile. Alice resettled her ass on its chair, pleased with her hit. *She knew.*

Nobody knew about me and Leland. At least, nobody was supposed to know. Nobody knew that we'd been meeting on Friday nights after Sebastian went to work, thrashing around in his bedroom in his mom's apartment, then splitting up and arriving separately to meet the rest of the crew at the bar. Nobody knew how he held my face in his hands, crushing me to his chest; how his eyes got glassy when he looked at me, and his breath came out like a moan. How, afterward, we lay in his bed and stared at the ceiling, and he started thinking out loud, talking to me like he forgot I was there – talking about dropping out of college and becoming a paramedic; about his best friend, Sam King, and how Sam drank too much. I soaked in every word, every confidence, head spinning at all I was entrusted with. How he kissed my forehead and whispered something I couldn't hear.

Nobody knew.

At least, nobody would be able to tell by looking at us. Leland stayed over on his side of the bar with the Boyses, and I sat nursing my vodka tonic with Alice and Hope, talking about prom dresses. Nobody could find out about me and Leland; that we'd agreed. "Don't go telling those loudmouth bitches," he'd admonished me. "They'll fuck this thing up so fast . . ."

"I won't," I swore. "And don't you tell the Boyses. They already think I'm . . ." I shook my head, ashamed.

He set his square jaw. He knew what they thought.

I understood that we couldn't let anybody know – of course I did, I had more to lose than anyone else. I could barely admit it to myself sometimes. *I'm having an affair with Leland*, I whispered to myself, and didn't believe it. Couldn't allow myself to think it. Had to evade Sebastian's lie-detector eyes, keep Leland buried in a vault, stashed like stolen jewels in a safe-deposit box, admiring them only when I was alone. Otherwise, just pretend it wasn't happening. What's not happening? Nothing's not happening. See?

Still, I wished that Leland could at least be affectionate toward me, that he didn't feel it necessary to flirt with other women, loudly announcing to the rest of the Boyses how stacked that one was, or how willing. I sat in my chair with the girls and prayed for him to brush past me, to give me an undercover look or caress. I understood why he had to ignore me in public, but it made me nervous and depressed. It reminded me of the old days, watching him out of the corner of my eye, yearning for him to look over and realize that he loved me.

He loved me. I told myself over and over. I replayed the scene of our first real kiss, his tortured speech on the sidewalk around the corner from this very bar – *I love you. I can't sleep at night.* It never failed to thrill and inspire me. It was enough reason to keep going, keep lying, keep hoping for a repeat. Leland hadn't said he loved me since that night; the most he ever said was, "Get over here as soon as you can." Or, "Where were you? Why didn't you call me sooner?" I took that as proof of his love – the edge of urgency in his voice, his proud face twisted with frustration.

"I'm sorry," I'd say, dipping my head. "I got here as soon as I could."

It was starting to make me a little cranky, I realized, observing Leland as he high-fived Sam over some boorish remark or other. After all I was risking to be with him, he couldn't throw me a tiny bone? Say something romantic, like he did that first night, maybe buy me a rose? Sebastian still bought me a rose now and then – more and more, recently, since he'd begun to detect some distance between us, which I explained away as the product of "pressure."

"About what?" he asked, doubtful. "From who?"

"You know, school," I lied, making sincere eyes to meet his. *It's TRUE,* I instructed myself. *I really am stressed out about school. SCHOOL.* "Graduation, college – all that stuff."

Sebastian nodded, trying to understand. He'd never finished high school, never applied to college. Maybe it was really as stressful as I said it was. Maybe my testiness, my outbreak of bad skin, my loudly roiling stomach pains were really the results of school pressure. He had to accept my story, for now.

Pressure. Here in the bar, it was practically barometric. The cold front coming from the pool table clashed with the sweltering heat underneath; I felt like I was breathing in a thick fog. I tried to keep my head straight, my eyes focused, my breath steady. Leland circled the pool table like a cyclone, shooting, gloating, clinking beers. Calling everybody's name but mine. Alice observed me, flicked her eyes at Hope, and turned to me with a smile.

"Hey, do you guys want to go outside?"

It was better outside the bar. Wasn't it? Hard to tell. We sat on a stoop around the corner, Alice and Hope on the top step, me one step below, and I waited for one of them to bust out a joint – maybe that would help settle my stomach. They just sat there and looked at me.

"So," said Alice coyly. "When were you planning to tell us?"

"Tell you what," I said, as my stomach plummeted. "Why. What's up."

Hope exhaled, annoyed. I was failing the polygraph, I could tell. What was it? My bouncing leg, my thin sheen of sweat? My utter and incontrovertible guilt? "Dude, we're not stupid. We're your best friends. It's totally obvious something's up with you and Leland."

"And it's kind of insulting that you didn't tell us about it." Alice folded her arms.

"I mean . . ."

They stared at me, miffed. I felt like I'd swallowed something pointy and it was stabbing me in the throat. "What . . . what . . ."

"Just talk to us," Alice demanded. "We're not mad at you, we just want to know what's going on. We're worried about you."

"Yeah, dude. You can't keep, just . . . doing things, you know?"

Hope sounded almost motherly, which considering both our moms, was not really a good thing. I went on the defensive.

"Um, I'm not sure what you guys want me to say, but . . ."

Alice put out her arm, like, *Stop.* "Just . . . tell us the truth. We're not going to tell anybody. We just want to help. I mean, if there's something going on between you and Leland, that's pretty big, you know? You guys should at least be honest about it with the rest of us." She cocked her head at me, as though her point could not be denied. "I mean, we're all, like, a family."

"Yeah, really." Hope nodded.

I looked at the two of them on the top step of the stoop, frowning down at me with concern. They looked like actual vultures, perching with their hands wrapped around their knees, arms bent at their sides like wings. But they were my family, my sisters. Girlses forever.

"Okay," I said, deflating with a huge sigh. "Me and Leland are . . ."

And god, I wanted to tell them the truth, but I didn't know what to say. What were we? In love? Secretly boyfriend-and-girlfriend? Doomed?

". . . sleeping together," I concluded.

Alice and Hope shared a triumphant look.

"I knew it," said Alice.

Hope shook her head. "Oh my god, dude. That's so crazy."

"I know. I know." I shook my own head, thinking about it. Running down to the pay phone while Sebastian was in the shower – "Oh, I'm just going out for rolling paper, I'll be right back." Dialing, my heart pounding. Getting Leland's mom, wincing through my rehearsed speech – "Hi, Mizzes Banks, it's Leland's friend Janice, is Leland there, please?" Then Leland, gruff as always – "Ten-thirty. All right. Yup. All right." Tonight I'd been so flustered, I almost went back upstairs without the rolling paper.

"So what are you going to do about it?" Alice pressed. "Are you going to leave Sebastian?"

I grimaced at the very words. "God, no. No. I can't. I could never . . ."

Ugh. I pressed my fist into my surging stomach, holding in the pain. I could never leave Sebastian. The thought was petrifying. Where would I live? Who would take care of me? Sebastian was my entire life – well, except for the one tiny part that was Leland. I would not survive a separation from Sebastian, I'd lose too much blood and tissue, I'd die on the operating table, heartless.

"I don't know what I'm going to do," I confessed.

"I bet," said Alice, not quite sympathetic.

"Well, what do you want to do?" asked Hope.

"I want to . . ."

Run away. Run far away from both of them, from everybody. Find a place that was all mine, and go hide. I almost laughed as it occurred to me – what a weird impulse. Wasn't the problem that I loved both of them, didn't I really want to be with both of them? Here I was, scampering all over town, frantically changing my underwear, lying like a psychopath, so I could be with both of them. And really, now that Hope asked me, all I wanted was to be alone.

"I don't know," I repeated. I put my face in my hands and doubled over. "I'm totally fucked."

Alice reached over and patted me on my turtled back. She didn't disagree.

"Well, if you want *my* opinion . . ." she offered.

I groaned quietly into my own lap. *Alone.* It sounded better and better with every passing second.

". . . I think you should break up with Sebastian. I mean, if you don't love him anymore, you should tell him."

"I agree," said Hope, like, *sheesh.* "You really should."

Yeah. And if I didn't love him anymore, that would be easy. But I still loved Sebastian, deeply, undeniably. Even as I turned away from him in bed at night, even as I nagged and sulked and picked on him constantly, trying to compile a list of plausible reasons I could use to rationalize leaving, I still cared for him. I still loved him. I still needed him. How terribly selfish of me, to continue to take pleasure in his company, to let him cook for me and quell my tantrums, when I was lying to him the entire time, sleeping with a man he abhorred. But I loved him. To tell him the truth would kill him, and I loved him too much for that.

"I can't," I whispered into my knees. "I can't."

"Well . . ." Alice clicked her tongue, annoyed. Why couldn't I just do what was most convenient for the rest of the clique? "Then you have to break it off with Leland. And he is *not* going to be happy about that."

Alone. Away. I pressed my face tighter into my lap, breathing in the warm gray-blackness, praying for some kind of hyperspace function to just whisk me off the stoop, out of my current situation completely. I breathed and prayed. Nothing happened. I did not magically find myself transported to a desert island, or back in time, before the night this whole fucked-up affair started. I was still here on the stoop, Alice and Hope talking over my bent back.

"... *have* to be honest with Leland, he *totally* thinks you're leaving Sebastian ..."

"... *have* to be honest with *one* of them, at *least*, I mean ..."

Oh god. "All right," I said into my lap. I lifted my head and looked straight ahead. I could stay calm, nobody had to help me. "I get what you're saying."

"Good," snotted Alice. "Because it's really gotten to be, like, ridiculous with the two of you ..."

"I get it," I repeated, teeth clenched.

"We're just worried about you," Hope said again. She tucked a hank of strawberry hair behind her ear. "Because we care."

"I know."

"Exactly. If one of us was doing something stupid, you'd tell us, right?"

Alice gave me a pitying look, and I reddened, a sound like rushing water in my ears.

"I'm not stupid," I said, overloud.

"Oh, I know," Alice clarified hastily. "That's why we're so, like ..."

"... freaked out," finished Hope.

"*Okay*," I said, fully flush. "*I hear you.*"

I heard them loud and clear, even over the furious torrent in my head; I could *hear* them, googling their eyes at each other behind my back – *She's so crazy. She's so fucked up.* Yeah, I was fucking crazy, no doubt about it, or I was having an aneurysm, bloody waterfalls gushing from my brain. *Just shut up, shut up!*

Alice made an affronted noise. "Um, don't yell at *us*, okay? *We're* not the ones who got you into this whole thing."

"Yeah," agreed Hope, because that was what Hope always did. "I mean, don't turn on *us*. We're, like, your only friends right now."

Hope didn't sound like anyone's mom anymore, she sounded exactly like Alice. Was there a difference, really? One had darker hair, the other had bigger breasts – otherwise, with their identical spoiled-milk faces, they could have been twins. *They* were the sisters, I realized; I was just the wacky neighbor. They weren't my family; they were the people who lived near me. I wasn't related to either of them at all.

I rose from the stoop.

"Where are you going?" asked Alice, imperious.

"We're trying to help you out here," noted Hope.

"You have to make a decision about the situation," Alice decreed. "What are you going to do?"

I was going to do what I did best, the one thing that'd always served me so well. I turned my back to them and started down the steps.

"Janice . . ." warned Alice.

"I'll see you later," I said. I walked away.

I got back to the apartment on Rivington Street and paced. I didn't feel right at home anymore, looking at the dent I'd kicked in the closet door during one of my tantrums, the tub where I'd nearly croaked, the blown-up picture of me and Sebastian from Coney Island last year, so happy and in love. The sofa where I sometimes sat when Sebastian was at work, fantasizing about Leland. All the damage I'd done, packed into two small rooms – it made me restless.

Friday, 2:00 A.M. There was a time when I would have gone straight to Nell's and downstairs to Sebastian's bar, to hang around and be near him and catch smooches on his break. Those heady, hilarious nights, when I'd stay until the end of his shift, dancing on the near-empty dance floor, and we'd go get steak and eggs and Bloody Marys at the place on Sixth and Avenue A, then roll ourselves home and fall into bed, that giddy, sated feeling of being well-fed and well-loved. I didn't like going to Nell's anymore; Nell's was too crowded, and it reminded me too much of cocaine. And I didn't like bugging Sebastian at work, watching him bust his ass to pay our rent while I sat around on a velvet settee, earning nothing. Waiting for my mother to hand me a check so I could enroll in college for the fall. Which was the least of the things that made me feel guilty with respect to Sebastian.

I couldn't go see Sebastian; he wasn't there anymore. My best friend, my confidant, my partner in all manners of crime. The hero of my story. And I'd killed him, replaced him with a burnt-out, paranoid shell of himself. He knew something was wrong – Why didn't I want to buy plane tickets to go see his mother next month? Why did I start crying whenever he touched me in bed? – but I wouldn't tell him what it was. I denied everything outright, every time he brought it up. "It's not somebody else! I'm not trying to leave you, honey! I'm just so confused . . ."

The cognitive dissonance was killing him. "What is it?" he begged me again and again, pressing me tight to his chest. "Just tell me, baby. Tell me what it is. Whatever it is, it's okay. I love you."

Leland. I couldn't say it. *I'm in love with Leland, and I promised him I'd leave you. And I don't know what to do.*

I paced the small apartment, packed a bowl and smoked it. Couldn't sit on the couch. Kept pacing. The situation was untenable. I had to do something. I'd promised Leland I'd leave Sebastian. I'd promised Sebastian I'd be with him forever.

I paced over to the window, put my hand on the glass. There she was – mussed red hair, smudged eye makeup, cleavage hanging out of her black Lycra shirt. My twin. She looked miserable; she looked like she blamed me for it. I could barely meet my own eyes.

What are we doing? she asked, anguished.

I couldn't answer. I tried thinking of Leland, that night on the side-walk outside the bar. *I love you. I can't live without you.* It still thrilled, but not enough; I pressed the mental button to play it again. *I love you. I can't live without you.* And again. *I can't live without you.* I wanted to shoot it straight into my arm, feel it slam into my heart the way it did the first time. I needed to hear Leland say it again. I'd do anything to get that feeling back.

My reflection hung her head as I hung mine. She knew that she was going back in her box, that I was leaving her again to chase after some guy. I didn't want to look at her anymore, the reproach of her frightened face. I set my jaw, hell-bent.

We're doing what we have to do, I told myself, and turned away.

Like trying to slip the tablecloth out from under the dishes, without the dishes catching on. That was what it was like, trying to break up with Sebastian without actually breaking up with him.

"A dorm room?" he asked, incredulous. "Why would you get a dorm room?"

"Well, I probably couldn't get one," I hedged. We sat on the cursed couch in front of the muted TV, his hand on my foot, my foot cringing at his touch. "I mean, Hunter's a commuter school, so they only have a few dorms, and they're probably all full by now . . ."

Sebastian shook his head. "But . . . but why would you even think about it? Doesn't it cost money?"

It was a bad idea, the dorm room gambit. I shouldn't have brought it up; I'd have to backpedal fast. "Well, I have that college fund my grandma left me, and my mom's helping out, but . . . you're right, it's stupid. Never mind. I just thought . . ."

Sebastian's face looked like the tragedy mask, his forehead creased with pain, his mouth contorted into a gaping frown. "What? I don't understand. Why are you even thinking about moving out into a dorm room?"

"I'm not, I said I'm not! I just thought about it, but I decided not to!"

"But *why* would you even think about it?"

His voice rose to a whine, and I jerked my foot away, thwarted and sick inside. "I don't know, because it's part of going to college! I mean, I could be going someplace out of state, but I'm staying here to be with you, and it's . . . I don't want to miss the experience of school, you know?"

"*What?*" He stared at me like I was a pod person, like I'd been kidnapped by aliens and replaced with a robot. The Janice he knew *hated* the experience of school, she was only going to college until she could get a real job. None of this had ever been in any plan we'd discussed – there were no dorm rooms, no talk of me "maybe crashing at Alice's for a few days" so I could hang out with the girls before they moved to L.A., no "just a few days apart" so I could "figure things out." There was nothing to figure out! We were going to visit his mom in New Mexico this summer, we were going to take mushrooms and hike in the desert, we were going to come back to our apartment where we lived together, and we were going to keep living together until we got married and had kids and died. That was our plan!

All plans – his, mine, ours – were currently failing. I felt a stab of guilt between my ribs, tried to suppress the rising hysteria that wanted to seize me by the solar plexus. "Listen, I'm not getting a dorm room,

okay? I'm not! I'm sorry I even mentioned it! I just wish you understood what I'm dealing with!"

I broke down and started to cry.

He sat and stared at me, his own eyes filling. "I'm trying!" he
shouted, anguished. "Goddamn it, I'm trying to understand you! I
don't know what the fuck is going on!"

"Nothing's going on! I'm just . . ."

It was safer just to cry, not to put it in words. Just keep pushing him
away with tantrums and black moods and no sex, praying that he'd
leave me – praying for it, dreading it, knowing I deserved it. I cried
harder and harder, whipping myself with the truth, which was that I
deserved to lose Sebastian. I'd never deserved him in the first place. I'd
cheated on him. And even if I could break it off with Leland, I could
never take back what I'd done.

"I know something is going on," he cried. "Something's changed.
You don't want to be with me anymore." He collapsed into deep gut
sobs of his own, folding like a jackknife. "You don't want to be with me,
oh god . . ."

I couldn't stand to see what I was doing. Desperately I reached for
him, wrapped my arms around his heaving chest, pressed my face into
his neck, tasted the salt of his sweat and tears. "No, honey, it's not true!
I do love you, I do want to be with you! I swear, I swear, I promise. I've
just been so . . . I'm sorry! I'm so sorry, honey. I love you. I love you. I
swear. I don't want to go anywhere, I never want to leave you. I never
want to leave you, honey!"

I kissed his neck, his head behind the ears, pressed my breasts
against him as he sobbed and sobbed. "I love you, I love you so much,
honey. I'm so sorry. I . . . it'll get better soon, I promise, honey. I love
you, I love you, honey. I'm so sorry."

Our tears mixed as I slid my face over his, kissing his lips, seeking
his tongue with mine. He resisted, then embraced me back, harder
than he'd ever held me before. Our bodies fell back together on the
couch, his over mine, his hands pulling my clothes away.

Leland. A craven whisper from the stem of my brain.

My stomach twisted, my heart shrank. There was no withdrawing
now. I buried my face in Sebastian's neck and squeezed tight. We were
doing what we had to do.

20

THE END

And then, just like that, it was over.

"Thank fucking god," moaned Alice, busting out of the auditorium in her blue robe and mortarboard, cigarette already to her lips. "I didn't think I could stand another second of that place."

"Hallelujah," agreed Hope, her rolled-up diploma squeezed tight in her fist. "Free at last!"

I laughed, giddy, as we stepped out into a frothing sea of blue-robed graduates, everyone hugging and cheering and posing for pictures on the sunny June sidewalk. My mother hurried over with her camera, waving at me.

"Jan!"

My mom looked good, in her work suit and heels, her face bright and relaxed. She looked almost happy. It was a happy day. She'd taken the afternoon off to see me graduate, left Jake with his babysitter so we could have a celebratory lunch – "Just the two of us, like adults," she'd said. "It's been too long since we've really had a chance to talk."

Now she approached, and I kissed her cheek. "Hi, Mom."

She held me by the upper arm and beamed at me. "Congratulations, honey. This is really terrific."

"It's all right," I demurred. "I mean, everybody graduates, it's no big deal."

"It's a very big deal," she assured me. "And I'm very proud of you."

I couldn't stifle my stupid grin. "Thanks, Mom."

She held up her camera to me and the girls. "Okay, girls, let's get one with the three of you."

"Oh, yay!" Alice and Hope flanked me on both sides, an angel and a devil, one for each shoulder.

"Terrific," said my mom. "One more."

We made horns behind one another's heads and stuck out our tongues.

"Very nice," commented my mom. *Click.*

"Thanks, Mizzes Erlbaum!"

Well, actually, it was Rosen. Barb Rosen. Barbara Jean Rosen Erlbaum Sidleman Malley Rosen. But Alice and Hope had already scooted away to get more pictures taken elsewhere.

I scanned the crowd one last time for people I wanted to say good-bye to. There was my long-ago ex, Jimmy Wilson, puffing in front of his doting parents' camera with his girlfriend, Karen Newfield – I heard they were getting engaged. I didn't need to say good-bye to him. Or to any of the party clique; I'd see them around, and if I didn't, it wasn't any big loss. No Dougie Paradise – he wasn't around anymore. He'd dropped out of school last semester. I think he was doing a lot of dust.

I saw Mr. Sheldon, taking a picture with the cast of this year's spring play, his posture stick-straight, his smile as proud as any parent's. I wanted to go over and say something, but he was surrounded by his actors, and I didn't want to butt in. I don't know if he even saw me wave. *Bye, Sheldon.*

"Okay," I told her, tucking my mortarboard under my arm. "I think we're done here."

"Great," she said. She patted me on the shoulder, so brief. "Let's go get some lunch."

My mother and I sat across from each other at a restaurant in the Village. It had been a few weeks since I'd last seen her, for brunch with Jake; I scanned her as she glanced over the menu. Her brow was lined a little deeper each time, her jaw more severe, but she didn't look forty – she never looked her age. We could have been sisters, me and my mom, lunching together in the Village. We could have been pals.

She shut her menu and clapped her hands together, pleased. "So. How about a glass of champagne?"

I laughed out loud. "You don't drink," I reminded her.

"Well, you should have one, at least," she protested. "It's a special day. We have a lot to celebrate." She reached into her briefcase and pulled out a long, thick sheaf of paper. It hit the table with an audible *thump*. "Look what I got, Jan."

I had to look at it for a minute to see what it was. The divorce. I'd been waiting for it since I was twelve years old, and there it was, all sixty pages of it, held together with a black binder clip and a rubber band, corners dented from the inside of her briefcase. My flimsy diploma barely compared to this momentous document. It was like looking at the stone tablets of Moses.

"It's done," she told me. "Dave's gone for good this time. He surrendered full custody of Jake, no visitation, nothing. It's taken me a few years, Jan, but I finally did it."

There was a lump in my throat, a stone I couldn't swallow. "I'm really happy for you, Mom."

She smiled her ironic smile, a mix of relief and regret. "Thanks, Jan. I'm pretty happy about it, too."

We ordered our food, and my glass of champagne.

"But enough about me," she said. "How are you? How's everything with Sebastian?"

"I'm good," I lied, fiddling with my silverware. "Everything's . . ."

She waited, eyebrows poised. Ordinarily I would have told her how great everything was, how happy Sebastian was that I was starting college, how we were planning to visit his mother this summer and go hiking. I always had to brag to her over brunch how well we were doing – "Yeah, I think they're going to promote Sebastian to bartender soon, he's the hardest working one there. And I think we're going to start investing in art, Sebastian really wants to start his own gallery." Who knows how much of it she believed, watching the weight drop off my body all winter, looking at my chewed-up bottom lip. She never called me on anything, if she knew; she never asked me if maybe I'd made a mistake, as she'd predicted long ago. She'd actually been pretty supportive – helping me with money, promising money for college. Maybe, after all this time, with the divorce on the table between us, my diploma resting on top, I could even trust her.

I mean, if anyone would understand bad decision-making, it would be my mom.

"Everything's terrible," I admitted. "I don't know what to do."

Her forehead furrowed. "I'm sorry to hear that, Jan. What's going on?"

I couldn't give her the specifics. I couldn't say it out loud. "I . . . I need to move out," I told her. "I still love him, but I think I need to get my own place."

The concern on her face deepened, her voice lowered. "Are you breaking up? Are you all right? He's not hurting you, is he, Jan?"

I shook my head no, shamefaced. *Kind of the opposite, actually.* She nodded, she believed me. She'd met Sebastian, she knew he wasn't an abusive guy – kooky and half-cocked, maybe, but not violent. She thought a second, then put on her business face, her taking-on-a-task look.

"Well, okay. The fact remains, you still want to leave."

My turn to nod, eyes cast down at the napkin on my lap. *Please don't gloat, Mom, please don't say you told me so.*

"I don't suppose you want to come back home," she said, matter-of-fact. "I know you're probably used to your freedom by this point." She didn't even sound like she begrudged me. She sounded like she understood.

I started to chew the left side of my lower lip, dragging it under my canine. "Yeah, well . . . I'm going to try to get a dorm room, but I won't be eligible until next semester, and I don't think I can wait that long. Maybe I can go to the Y . . ."

My mother shook her head, and I could see her mind working, her eyes squinty and faraway, her fingers drumming the table, then stopping abruptly. "No, you won't go to the Y," she said, decisive. "You went to enough places like that already. It's enough. Here's what I think, Jan. I think you should let me pay for school, and you should take your grandma's college money and use it for an apartment. That's what I think."

I stared at her, my mouth unhinged at the jaw, astonished. "Really?"

"Yep." She nodded, agreeing with her own plan. "Absolutely. I always told you I'd help you with school. And you barely knew your grandmother before she died; it would be nice for you to get *something* out of that relationship." She smiled wryly. "Remember when you were five, and we left your father, and we moved to Grandma's in the Bronx? It was one of the first helpful things my mother ever did for me, ever since I'd moved out of her house, back when I was your age." Her face grew serious. "I think it's only fitting that she – and I – should help you out now."

"Mom, that's . . ." I groped for words. "That's so *awesome* of you."

She waved it off, but she was pleased – pleased with her plan, pleased with my reaction. "It's the least I can do, after what we've been through."

Well, I wasn't going to mention it, but . . . okay. "Thanks, Mom," I said, my throat sticky.

My mother was looking into my eyes, the same hazel-green as her own, a tender smile on her face. Then her face got serious, and she reached for my hand across the table. "Jan, I love you."

I reached my hand toward hers, and said what I hadn't said in six years.

"I love you too, Mom."

I sat on the subway, paging through the real estate listings in *The Village Voice*, the F train rocking as it sped through the tunnel toward the party at Alice's. I was looking at places in Brooklyn, near my mom and Jake. It was cheap, it was familiar, and it wasn't anywhere near Sebastian's apartment on Rivington Street.

Studio apt., $600/month, sunny, good block. Studio, $650/month, wood floors, close to subway. I circled the ads with my red pen. *Call Delores, 718 . . .*

The subway deposited me on Alice's block, full of brownstones and bodegas, sparrow-stuffed trees lining the sidewalk. *Maybe I'll find a place around here*, I thought. Or maybe not. No point, really. Alice and Hope were leaving for L.A. soon – we planned to spend the summer partying, then we'd say good-bye. After that, I'd probably never see this block again.

From yards away, I could hear the Fine Young Cannibals blasting through the vivid window, the sounds of boys shouting and girls laughing. A little graduation soiree, just twenty or thirty of our closest friends. The Boyses would be there, of course, spreading the wisdom they'd accrued since their graduation last year – "College chicks are sluts, yo! They're worse than you little high school biddies!" And Leland, his back turned to me, giving no hint of last night's assignation.

My feet slowed as I looked up at the bright window, pulsing with noise and shadows. I almost wished Leland wasn't there; almost didn't want to see him tonight. Last night at his house, things had not gone well – I'd arrived late again, after walking Sebastian to work, and Leland had immediately jumped on me.

"Where were you? It's almost eleven already. What the hell's going on?"

My head dropped in defeat. *I got here as fast as I could, goddamn it. I'm working as hard as I can.* I'd already spent two hours placating Sebastian, prevaricating, walking him to work so I could prove how much I wanted to be with him every second; then I had to sprint across town, and for what – this? I didn't need a cross-examination right now. I needed a hug, and a glass of water, and a joint.

"I'm sorry," I said, reaching out for Leland. He shook his head, hands on his hips, and stared at the floor.

"I don't know if I can do this much longer," he said, head shaking. "It's driving me crazy. I gotta know what's happening. Are you leaving him, or what?"

"I am," I stressed. "I'm trying. It's just taking me longer than I hoped." I reached out for him again. "Please, Leland, just . . ." *Just give me a break. Just be nice to me. Just let me have one second of the day when I feel like all this might be worth it.*

Nothing. Nothing but angry sex, and then ultimatums: *You have to; you can't.* Leland's face was stony as Rushmore, his body turned away from me in his bed.

"We can't do this anymore. Not until you leave Sebastian."

I reached out again and was rebuffed. I retracted my wounded hand. "I *am* leaving him," I swore.

Leland didn't believe me. He swung his legs over the side of the bed, didn't look at me. "Well, either you will or you won't. But I can't do this anymore."

I pressed my lips together, flat and tight. *Neither can I.* I couldn't do it anymore, and I couldn't stop.

I paused on Alice's stoop for a minute to gird myself. Bits of conversation wafted down from the window, along with the sweet, hamster-cage smell of pot. I lumbered up the stairs and pushed open the door.

"*There* you are," hissed Hope, grabbing my wrist, urgent. "I tried to call you. Leland's been . . ."

Leland came thundering toward me through the hot, crowded room, his bulldog face livid. "*There* she is!" He stopped just short of slamming into me, bellowing, spit flying. "*You fucking slut!*"

"What?" The music was loud, but Leland was louder. The fifteen people in Alice's living room stopped, plastic cups of punch halfway to their mouths, to stare at us.

"YOU HEARD ME." His breath steamed out of his nose, his fists clenched at his sides. "YOU'RE A FUCKING LIAR, AND A SLUT!"

Trouble, big trouble. Cataclysmic trouble. My field of vision narrowed, and my entire body beat with my loud, pounding heart. "What the fuck did I do?"

Alice hurried over. "Calm down, you guys. Leland, calm down . . ."

"No, FUCK THAT." He slapped her hand away. Sam King stepped up behind him and put his hand on Leland's shoulder. Leland shook it off and glared at me.

I couldn't get the words out, like I was being choked. "W-what the f-fuck is going on?"

He leaned into me. His whiskey breath was wet on my face, his voice menacing. "I SPOKE to him, Janice. I CALLED him, and I SPOKE to him."

All the blood left my head in a sickening plunge, and I felt like I was rushing down a rabbit hole, swirling down a drain. "You . . . called . . . Sebastian?"

Leland narrowed his eyes, smug. "That's goddamn right, I did. And you've been lying to me. You told me you were leaving him. You're a fucking *liar!*"

He roared, and I jumped back, tears sharp in my eyes, in the back of my throat. Sam grabbed Leland by the arm – "Cool out, man, she's not worth it. Calm down. Calm down."

"I didn't lie to you, Leland!"

"I SPOKE TO HIM!" Leland struggled against Sam's restraining grasp, and the girls all ducked and jumped behind the guys a little, an excited murmur rippling around the room.

"Well WHAT THE FUCK DID YOU DO THAT FOR?" I burst out, just as loud as he was, just as furious – no, more. He called Sebastian? Why? Did he *want* to ruin my life, did he want to kill me? That fucking prick! *Sebastian.* I could picture him, ripping my clothes out of the drawers, throwing them into the street, tears of rage streaming down his beautiful face. Taking a belt, wrapping it around his neck . . . *Oh, god, Sebastian, my baby, my love.* I had to get home to him, had to tell him – what could I tell him? – that Leland was a liar! And whatever Leland said was untrue! I wasn't in love with him, we weren't having an affair, I would never see Leland again! And I really meant it this time!

Leland raged at me, "You fucking *lied* to me! You fucking *whore!*"

"FUCK YOU!" I cried. "I didn't fucking lie! I can't believe you called him, you fucking . . ."

The circle of faces seemed to close in around me: Hope, looking disgusted, moving quickly to Alice's side; Alice, smirking, permanently smirking, her nose forever in love with her upper lip; Sam King, glowering at me, his hand on Leland's bicep – "She's not worth it, man, she's just a slut . . ." Ollie Wythe, some idiot groupie stuck to his side like a sparkly barnacle. Leland, continuing to bellow in my face, "You *whore*, you FUCKING LIAR!"

I could barely make myself heard through his shouting, throat hoarse with held-back tears. "Fuck you! No, fuck *you*, Leland! I did everything I could to be with you . . ."

"YOU FUCKING LIED TO ME!"

He stabbed his finger in my face, and a bubble burst. "FUCK YOU!"

"You guys!" Alice tried to push between us. "Stop it, this is crazy! Stop it! Both of you!"

"FUCK YOU!" raged Leland, full in my face.

"NO, FUCK YOU!" I screamed back. "*ALL OF YOU!*"

And all of them – all the Boyses and the Girlses and the groupies and the hangers-on, and the people who used me for drugs, and fucked me over, and didn't invite me to move to L.A. with them – all of them looked at me, shocked, like the music had come to a screeching halt. Leland spun on his heel and turned away from me, Sam and Ollie close behind. Hope stood with her praying hands over her mouth and nose, *Oh my god, oh my god, oh my god.* Alice looked at me reprovingly, her hands on her hips.

"You know what, Janice, you *really* shouldn't . . ."

I didn't hear the rest of the sentence. I was gone.

It was the longest subway ride I ever took. I shook and shook, rocked back and forth, prayed, swallowed my own vomit, and prayed some more. *Sebastian.* He was home alone tonight – rare for a Saturday night. I must have just left for Alice's when the phone rang. He picked it up. It was Leland. What did he say? *I'm fucking your girlfriend, man, just thought you should know.* Could I lie my way out of this? I could lie, I could always lie, it was what I did for a living. Or I could tell him the truth, though the idea made me so queasy I thought I'd hurl all over myself – still, maybe, since he already knew, maybe I could be honest with Sebastian. Maybe I could throw myself upon his mercy, beg for his forgiveness, tell him he could fuck anybody he wanted to make it even.

I just had to get home.

The subway made interminable stops, each stop a different memory. Coming back from Coney Island, one of our first excursions, clutching the stuffed armadillo he won for me, our kisses sticky from cotton candy, the dizzy Tilt-A-Whirl feeling still with me as I lay my head on his shoulder. A late afternoon with Sebastian last fall, after walking through Prospect Park, the smell of smoke and horses in the air, holding an orange leaf he'd presented to me like a flower, like a wish.

Then: Riding this train back from Alice's last New Year's Eve, coked up to my eyeballs, the sweat from Leland's hands still stinging my upper arms.

I ran from the subway to our building and raced up the narrow stairs, chest bursting. There was Sebastian, on the couch, his face as pale as his white-blond hair, his eyes bright pink and shining. He was holding the two halves of a ripped photo, the frame smashed in the corner. "Honey." I fell panting to my knees in front of him. "Honey."

He looked down at me like I was a blood-covered murderer – horrified, revulsed, defiant.

"I knew it," he said, his voice shaking. "I *knew*."

I reached out, trembling, to touch the leg of his camouflage pants, and he moved away from me, further back on the couch. "Please, Sebastian, I don't know what happened, but you have to believe me . . ."

"You don't know what happened?" He laughed a crazy, high-pitched laugh, his pure green eyes flashing. "You don't know what happened? You were the one *fucking Leland*! Didn't anybody tell you?"

"I . . . I wasn't! It was a mistake!" The lies spurted out of me like arterial blood, unbidden. "I didn't! Honey, you have to believe me, I didn't! He was mad, because I was *going* to, but I didn't, because I love you! Honey, please . . ."

"*Please*," he spat, disgust all over his beautiful face. "Please fucking spare me."

I slumped, my head dropped, my shaking hand fell short. I was losing him; I'd already lost. There was no hope. The nausea rose in my throat, and the room started to lose meaning around me – I could see the loose threads in the worn rug, the grain of the table leg, the toe of his thick-soled sneaker, but none of it made any sense. "Honey," I heard myself say, faraway and high. "Honey, I'm sorry, I'm so . . ."

"Why?" His voice came from deep in his stomach, low and sick. "Why?"

I shook my head, disoriented from the shock. *Why?* I asked my knees, the rug. *Why* did I fuck everything up all the time? *Why* couldn't I be happy with what I had; why did I always have to have *more*? I couldn't keep blaming Leland – *Well, he started it! Leland made me do it!* – it wasn't about Leland. Leland was Mount Everest; I climbed him because he was there.

"I don't know," I whispered. "I . . ."

"Goddamn it!" Sebastian jumped off the sofa, and scraps of our ripped-up photos fell to the ground around me – a field of my red hair, the elbow of his black winter jacket, lips pressed to an eyeless cheek. Written on the back in pen – *mber 86. ever.* "You don't even have a fucking reason, do you!"

"Please, honey . . . I'm sorry, I'm so sorry . . ."

I crawled toward him on the floor, barely aware of the pain in my knees, the sobs escaping from the prison of my ribs, and he backed away, his eyes darting around as if for a weapon. "Get away from me! I don't want to look at you!"

"Honey . . ."

I reached out for him blindly, for the glowing light of his hair, the wiry arms that used to embrace me, as he stared at me with hate. *Hate.* He hated me. It was like being plunged into an ice bath, my body seized and freezing.

"Get," he said coldly. "Out."

I couldn't. I couldn't leave. I had to stay, had to stay here in our little apartment, the only place I'd ever felt safe. He couldn't throw me out, I'd die out there. "Honey," I blubbered, "please, I'm so sorry, I'm so sorry, honey . . ."

"I want you to *get out!*"

"Honey, wait, please, I . . . Wait, Sebastian!"

Sebastian grabbed his skateboard with one hand and the doorknob with the other. "I can't fucking look at you. I want you to get out. Pack, and leave."

"Honey . . ."

He ripped open the door, turned to look at me one last time. There was no recognition in his steely eyes. "I *never* want to see you again."

The door slammed behind him, and I was alone.

A Significant Experience
BY JANICE ERLBAUM

When I was fifteen years old, I walked out of my mother's house and went to a shelter for homeless teens. It was the most important decision I ever made – a decision that both saved and risked my life. I'd hoped that leaving home would get me away from the chaos and violence of my mother's most recent marriage; I thought I could do a better job of taking care of myself than she could. But under my own supervision, I almost killed myself, both accidentally and on purpose, a few too many times. I've often wondered in the years since that night, did I make the right choice?

It's a question I started debating with myself from the first night I walked out. On one hand, I was very happy I'd left – I was finally free of my fucked-up family (or so I thought at the time), and I was deciding my own future. I had wanted to become self-reliant, and for the most part, I was. On the other hand, I was deprived of a lot: normalcy, privacy, security. I bore the stigma of being "homeless" (though I never spent a single night without a place to sleep, for which I'm supremely grateful); then I bore the stigma of being a "bad girl" in a group home. I have tried to wear it as a badge of honor, but I don't know if that's always been a success.

As it happened, the shelter and the group home were both chaotic and sometimes violent places. The group home was especially hostile and punitive – if I left home seeking more autonomy, I wound up with significantly less. Ironically, a year and a few months after the night I left, I wound up going home to my mom's, where I lived for a few months. But even though she'd dumped her husband and made the house more stable, the instability remained in my life. It was almost like it had become a part of me, something I could never really run away from.

I know a lot of the other girls at the shelter felt they'd made the right choice in leaving home – not that it was always really their choice. "No regrets," they'd say. "Wouldn't change a thing." That's what you're supposed to say, when you've survived something shitty: That which does not kill you makes you stronger. And it's true – leaving home showed me a strength I didn't know I had, it taught me skills I'd never had before, and it introduced me to people I never would have met otherwise. It made me appreciate my life so much more, from the little things – clean sheets on a warm bed, a crisp apple from the fridge – to the big things – the love of my family, the promise of a great life ahead of me. My experience raised my tolerance for pain, and reduced my willingness to invite it. It taught me to fight for my life, and to be reckless in the pursuit of my own survival.

But it would be easy for *me* to say it was worth it; I'm still here. I lived through it mostly intact, and a lot of people I knew didn't. Would *they* say it was worth it, if they could say? I don't think they would. I have a lot of survivor's guilt, wondering why I didn't suffer the same consequences some of my peers did. I never thought of myself as "lucky" before, but now I do.

So was it worth it, after all? I don't know. I don't know if I'll ever know. Maybe in twenty years, I'll look back and say, *Look where I wound up, that was the worst mistake of my life.* Or maybe I'll be happy; maybe I'll be doing really well, and I'll say, *I'm glad I was there, it made me who I am, and I wouldn't have missed it for anything.* I know I'll always be grateful for the people I lived with, and loved; that memories of them will always inspire me. I hope I will see them all again, somehow.

One question I *can* answer is this: Would I do it again?

Yes. Without a doubt. If I ever find myself in a place that's too chaotic, or violent, or feels life-threatening to me in any way, I will leave. Sometimes I may have to leave behind people I love in order to get out – I pray that never happens again. But if it does, I will do what I have to do, what I've always done: I'll go, and I'll find a new home. And I know, wherever that home is, being there will be the most significant experience of my life.

Nothing, of course, is ever as over as it seems.

I mean, I'd love to say that that was the end of everything, that I made a "clean break," as if that's ever possible; I'd love to pretend that once I walked away, I never came crawling back. I would have loved to have said that about leaving home, too, "Yeah, I walked out on my mom when I was fifteen, never looked back," but obviously, it didn't happen like that. Maybe I walked away, but I did it in circles.

I sat on the floor of the near-empty bedroom at my mom's, leaning back on a bag of clothes propped against the wall. There was nobody else in the apartment – my mom was at work, Jake at his new pre-school daycare – and the place was humming with the silence. I stared at the phone, still plugged into its jack, sitting unringing on the blue carpet. I didn't want to pick it up.

I should call Alice. She'd called a few times over the last few days – she probably tried Sebastian's first and got no answer, so she was trying me here. "Just want to see if you're okay," she sang into the answering machine in her soupiest, most matronizing way. "We miss you. Let us know what's up. Love you, girl." Hope echoed in the background: "Love you! Call us!"

I'd call them – not today, but tomorrow. They'd insist that I come right over to Alice's, where they'd coo over me, get me high, and pass me wads of toilet paper to sop up the snot and tears. Hope would get all whipped up on my behalf – "Leland's such an asshole! He's the one who started the whole thing with you, it's not like he didn't know you had a boyfriend! You were always *way* too good for him. You're lucky you guys are through."

And Alice would agree. "Leland's a *total* asshole. He's like, 'I'm never speaking to Janice again.' Like you care if he ever speaks to you!"

Like I cared.

I would never call Leland again, though I'd see him over the next few months – at a bar with the rest of the clique, at Hope and Alice's going-away party – and he would turn away from me, stiff, his solid back like a locked door, and I'd turn away as well, two magnets back-to-back, repelling each other in a circle. It would take years for us to be able to say a civil word to each other, to look anywhere near the other's face, to sit in the same section of the room without finding an excuse to leave.

I'd stay in love with him for a long time. And then one day, years later, I'd realize that I wasn't anymore.

But I still loved Sebastian – still do, in my own fond way. I would call him that day from my old empty room, but he wouldn't answer. I'd leave the same message I'd been leaving for three days straight: "I'm sorry, I'm so, so sorry. I know you can never forgive me, but I want you to know how much I wish I'd never hurt you." I'd call him like this for almost a week, always repeating the same words, "I'm sorry, I'm sorry, I'm sorry," until I was hoarse from just that phrase.

And then, one afternoon, he'd pick up. "Okay," he'd tell me, his raggedy, smoked-out voice deeper and sadder than I'd ever heard it before. "Let's talk."

We would talk. I would walk heavy-legged up the familiar stairs to Sebastian's apartment, where we'd talk, cry, fight, make love, and cry some more – this would go on for weeks. We'd try to reconcile, and for a little while there, we'd even fool ourselves into thinking it could work again, but it would be hopeless, a desperate dance to the music of a death rattle.

A year later, Sebastian would move back to the West Coast, where he remains to this day, skateboarding and selling his artwork. I will still hear from him sometimes, with news of his exploits – two weeks ago, he sent me a picture of his newborn baby girl. Her name is Phoenix. He included some old pictures of me, smirking at him from the backseat of a cab, sitting in the butterfly chair in our old apartment. Making the kiss lips, radiant with first love.

What a beautiful, amazing time, he wrote.

But first:

My new apartment was on Vanderbilt Avenue in Brooklyn, on the first floor of a six-floor walk-up, just a few blocks from my mom and Jake's. I picked up the spare key from the superintendent's wife, who eyeballed me from under her head wrap, crossing her arms over her broad chest.

"You sure you old enough to rent? You a responsible tenant? You not gonna make a lot of noise and trouble, right? You a good girl?"

In her West Indian accent, it sounded like "gull." I smiled.

"I'm good," I promised her.

She nodded skeptically and handed over the key. "Okay, then."

The place was nearly empty, except for the new futon on the floor, a present from my mom. I'd get my old dresser and desk from her place this week, maybe buy a sofa from the thrift store nearby – that would fill up most of the room. I could stretch out both arms and practically touch the walls of the apartment. My apartment.

Mine. And mine alone. No Big Perla, no pregnant Sherri, no nuns. No Genie the JAP, no Julie the Snitch. No Mom, though she was only five minutes away, Jake in his short pants and lace-up shoes racing downstairs to greet me when I rang the bell. No boyfriends, no girlfriends, no lovers. Just me. Alone.

I walked the six paces to the kitchen area, lined in an old gray-and-white checkerboard tile. The kitchen window was swollen with years of paint – I heaved it open and the chips rained on the sill. The window looked out over a narrow alley, and a calico stray paced underneath, her scraggly tail crooked, sussing me out.

You the new tenant, lady? Cat lover, maybe? Awfully hungry out here . . .

She could count on me. I would go to the bodega that afternoon, come home with a bag of kibble, and see if she wouldn't maybe take to living indoors. I'd unpack my bags, put my sole toothbrush by the bathroom sink. Make some soup. Roll a joint. Take a bath. Double-check the locked door, keeping me safe inside. Then I'd lie down on my new futon, and open my datebook.

August 1, 1987

Home.

In loving memory of Mr. Alan Fleisig

THANKS

This book is in your hands right now thanks to acquiring angel Arielle Zibrak; Bruce Tracy, the editor of my dreams; Alice Martell, my spectacularly cool agent; and Eric Nelson, the mensch who made it all happen. Great gratitude to Claire Kingston of Ebury UK, and Katie Stackhouse at Random House Australia. Thanks to Tia Schellestede and Emilie Blythe McDonald, who helped me with every single chapter of the book, more than once; thanks also to early readers Sarah Fisch, Lori Mocha, and luckydave, late readers Edward Clapp and Anne Elliott, and spiritual consorts Kat Fasano, Dana Piccoli, and Rachel L. Most humble thanks to Deb Stoller, Anne Larsen, Bob Holman, Francis "Faceboy" Hall, Amanda Stern, Stefan Kelly, Mona Simpson, Molly Peacock, John Strausbaugh, Penny Arcade, Eileen Myles, Sapphire, and Janeane Garofalo. Much love and gratitude to my father, Larry, and my beloved stepmom, Sylvia. Love and thanks also to my outstandingly awesome brother, and to my mom, whose support has always been a great gift. And lastly but mostly, so much gratitude for Bill Scurry – my love, my heart, my home.

ABOUT THE AUTHOR

JANICE ERLBAUM is a longtime columnist for *BUST* magazine and a volunteer at a shelter for homeless teens. She lives in New York City with her husband and three cats, and you can find her at www.girlbomb.com.

ABOUT THE TYPE

This book was set in Electra, a typeface designed for Linotype by W. A. Dwiggins, the renowned type designer (1880–1956). Electra is a fluid typeface, avoiding the contrasts of thick and thin strokes that are prevalent in most modern typefaces.

Preface

One can say that operations research consists of the application of scientific methods to the complex problems encountered in the management of large systems. These systems arise, for example, in industry, administration and defense. The goal is to aid management in the determination of policy via the use of tractable models.

A model can be defined as a schematic description of the system under consideration (which may be a company, a market, a battle, or a transportation network, for example). To be useful, the model must include a representation of the interaction between the system elements. An example could be the model of perfect gases. Perfect gases do not exist, but the concept helps us to understand the behavior of real gases. Similarly, the atomic model helps us to understand the structure of material. One of the non-trivial problems of operations research is the choice of an appropriate model. For example, sub-atomic particles help in the understanding of superconductivity, but they could result in an unnecessarily complex model for the behavior of gases if we were interested only in the relationship between volume, temperature and pressure. In fact, all scientific disciplines use models and one could even argue that all conscious activity of the human mind is performed through modelling.

Problems of decision making are as old as the proverbial apple. In contrast, the serious use of specific quantitative techniques in decision processes has emerged only recently (since World War II). There are two major reasons for this:

Organizational problems are increasing in size and complexity. As a result, systematic methods for analyzing such problems are becoming more and more essential.

The second reason is the development of computers. Computers are not only necessary to solve operations research models, but they have influenced directly our ways of thinking about complex systems. In many instances one can observe a parallel development of operations research and computer science.

It is convenient to consider operations research as consisting of two intimately related parts:

"Model building"   i.e., the extraction from a complex reality of a
                      scheme that represents it adequately for the
                      purposes under consideration.

"Model solving"   i.e., the development of techniques to resolve
                      models of decision procedures (for example:
                      in a given context under certain assumptions,
                      what is the course of action most likely to
                      succeed).

Since operations research models are most often mathematical models solved
with the help of computer algorithms, one might be led to believe that one can
consider the field totally as an abstraction. However, this is not the case.
What makes operations research a fascinating subject for study and research is
that there is a dialectic relationship between the two parts. The mathematical
techniques should be considered in the context of the concrete problems that
they are intended to solve. On the other hand, operations research is much more
than a common-sense approach to real-life problems.

In this book we are concerned with the "model-solving" aspects of operations
research. In fact, the examples given make no pretense to be realistic models.
They are proposed as an overly simplified version in order to enable the reader,
as easily as possible, to acquaint himself with the type of problems that can be
tackled and to exemplify the mathematical techniques used. However, we would
like to emphasize that model building is both important and difficult. Being
able to define the system, choose the variables and decide what can reasonably
be neglected, requires as much intelligence and creativity as solving the models.

In this text we intend to be, in fact, more specific, insofar as we limit
ourselves to solution techniques for a particular class of models that are defined in the first chapter and are called linear programs. Thus we explore only
a fraction of the model-solving section of operations research. However, it is
also true that linear programming is the best known of the mathematical techniques of operations research (and, some say, the most used mathematical technique). This may well be due to the fact that it has proven to be a very effec-
tive and efficient tool for solving practical problems. It also has given rise
to a deep and beautiful mathematical theory. In fact, the discovery of the simplex method for solving linear programs, in 1947, by G.B. Dantzig was in many
ways the birth of operations research.

Springer Texts in
Electrical Engineering

1 C

Michel Sakarovitch

Linear Programming

Consulting Editor: John B. Thomas

With 12 Illustrations

Springer-Verlag
New York Heidelberg Berlin

A Dowden &
Culver Book

Michel Sakarovitch
Université Scientifique
  et Medicale de Grenoble
Laboratoire I.M.A.G.
BP 53X
38041 Grenoble Cedex
France

Library of Congress Cataloging in Publication Data
Sakarovitch, Michel
  Linear programming.
  (Springer texts in electrical engineering)
  Includes bibliographical references and index.
  1. Linear programming. I. Title. II. Series.
T57.74.S24   1983   519.7'2   83-362

Printed and bound by R.R. Donnelley & Sons, Harrisonburg, VA.
Printed in the United States of America.

9 8 7 6 5 4 3 2 1

ISBN 0-387-90829-3 Springer-Verlag New York Heidelberg Berlin
ISBN 3-540-90829-3 Springer-Verlag Berlin Heidelberg New York

The material presented here has been developed for an undergraduate course first at the University of California (Berkeley) and then at the University of Grenoble (France). The book is largely self contained, the only prerequisite being a year of calculus. Notions of linear algebra that are useful are presented in some detail. In particular, I have discussed the solution of linear systems of equations to the extent which I think necessary for the understanding of linear programming theory. Depending on how much of the final two chapters is included and on the initial level of the students in linear algebra, the topics in this book can be covered in a quarter or a semester.

This course is "computer oriented" in the sense that the algorithms (which are first depicted on simple examples) are given in a very intuitive algorithmic language, which makes their coding on a computer rather simple.

We are most grateful to Betty Kaminski for her efforts and perseverance in preparing the camera copy from which this book was produced.

Grenoble, February 1982

Contents

List of Figures

Chapter I. Introduction to Linear Programming

The goal of this chapter is to introduce those optimization problems which, just after World War II, G. B. Dantzig named "linear programs." The great success of linear programming (i.e., the study of linear programs) led authors who became interested in various optimization problems to link the term "programming" with that of a more or less fitted adjective, thus calling these problems convex programming, dynamic programming, integer programming, and so on. The result is that in operations research the term "program" has acquired the very precise meaning "optimization problem." It is not possible, however, to use the word "programming" for the study of general problems of optimization (hence, we say "mathematical programming"), because more or less simultaneously the term "program" was taking on another meaning -- much more in harmony with the original one -- that of a sequence of instructions in the context of computer science. This nice example of the development of scientific language does not make things clear for the beginner. To avoid confusion in this book we therefore use the term "program" as equivalent to an optimization problem and "code" or "computer code" for what is called a program in computer science.

The notion of duality, which is central to the understanding of linear programming, is introduced in Chapter II. Necessary notions of linear algebra are reviewed in Chapter III, and the concept of basic solutions is defined in Chapter IV. Chapter V is devoted to the presentation of the simplex algorithm. The two phases of the simplex method are presented in Chapter VI together with some theoretical results. In Chapter VII we present computational aspects of the simplex and the revised simplex algorithm. The geometrical interpretation of the simplex algorithm is given in Chapter VIII. Chapter IX contains some complements on duality, and parametric linear programming is presented in Chapter X. Finally, Chapter XI is devoted to the presentation of a very important special linear program: the transportation problem.

1. Examples and Definition of Linear Programs

a. A production planning problem: A firm can produce two products, product 1 and 2, using raw materials I, II, and III. The way the factory works can be depicted schematically by the following table:

Product

		1	2
Raw Material	I	2	1
	II	1	2
	III	0	1

As the table indicates, to produce 1 unit of product 1, requires 2 units of raw material I and 1 unit of raw material II; and to produce 1 unit of product 2, requires 1 unit of product I, 2 units of raw material II, and 1 unit of raw material III. Moreover, we know that for each unit of product 1, the firm gets a reward of 4 units (say $4,000); for each unit of product 2, a reward of 5 units; and that the production technology is linear, e.g., to produce x units of product 1, 2x units of raw material I and x units of raw material II must be used. There are 8, 7, and 3 units of raw materials I, II, and III, respectively, available for production. Any unused material has no salvage value. The problem is to find a production plan that will be feasible (i.e, which will not use more raw materials than are on hand) and which will bring the maximum possible reward.

Letting x_i denote the quantity of product i produced, the problem can be set up in the following way:

$$(P_1) \begin{cases} z = 4x_1 + 5x_2 & \text{be maximum subject to} \\ x_1 , \ x_2 \geq 0 \\ 2x_1 + x_2 \leq 8 & \text{(I)} \\ x_1 + 2x_2 \leq 7 & \text{(II)} \\ x_2 \leq 3 & \text{(III)} \end{cases}$$

This problem has the immediate geometric solution shown in Figure I-1 (next page).

Figure I.1: Geometric Solution for (P_1)

b. __A transportation problem__: A special imported product S is needed in three factories located at Denver, Phoenix, and Chicago. The weekly consumptions of this product are, respectively, 400, 300, and 200 tons. Product S is delivered into the country through the harbors of New York and Seattle, the quantities available being 550 tons a week in New York and 350 in Seattle. Transportation costs are supposed to vary in proportion to the transported quantities, the unit costs being:

	Denver	Phoenix	Chicago
New York	5	6	3
Seattle	3	5	4

This table shows that to convey x tons from New York to Phoenix, for instance, the cost is $6x. And the problem consists in determining an optimal "transportation plan," i.e., in finding what are the quantities of product S to send from each harbor to each factory in such a way that:

(α) Demands are satisfied (each factory receives at least what is needed).

(β) Quantities sent from each harbor do not exceed availability.

(γ) Quantities sent are non-negative.

(δ) The total transportation cost is minimum subject to the preceding constraints.

Let us assign to New York harbor index 1, to Seattle harbor index 2, and indices 1, 2, and 3, respectively, to the factories of Denver, Phoenix, and Chicago. x_{ij} will denote the quantity of product S sent from harbor i (i=1 or 2) to factory j (j=1,2, or 3) each week. The linear program is then

$$(P_2) \begin{cases} \begin{array}{lr} x_{11}+x_{21} & \geq 400 \\[6pt] x_{12}+x_{22} & \geq 300 \\[6pt] x_{13}+x_{23} & \geq 200 \end{array} \left.\right\} (\alpha) \\[18pt] \begin{array}{lr} x_{11}+x_{12}+x_{13} & \leq 550 \\[6pt] x_{21}+x_{22}+x_{23} & \leq 350 \end{array} \left.\right\} (\beta) \\[12pt] x_{11},x_{12},x_{13},x_{21},x_{22},x_{23} \quad \geq 0 \qquad\qquad (\gamma) \\[12pt] \text{Under these constraints, let} \\[6pt] z = 5x_{11} + 6x_{12} + 3x_{13} + 3x_{21} + 5x_{22} + 4x_{23} \quad \left.\right\} (\delta) \\[6pt] \text{be minimum} \end{cases}$$

A set of x_{ij} satisfying (α), (β), (γ) would give a "feasible" transportation schedule. We say that it is a feasible solution. The problem consists in finding, among all feasible solutions, one that gives z its minimum value. Here the number of variables (which is equal to 6) forbids the utilization of a geometric approach to solve (P_2).

Remark 1:   One may be tempted to believe that what has been done here is "model building" since we started with an apparently "real-world problem." However, one must appreciate the fact that the problem, as we stated it, is in a very academic form. It seldom occurs that real problems are so schematic and simple. For instance, it is not obvious, in reality, that costs of shipping are unique, are linear, or that the quantity needed each week is precisely known, constant, and so on. As was indicated in the preface, this example (as well as others given in this book) must not be considered as anything other than an aid to the understanding of the theory.

Definition 1:   A linear program is an optimization problem in which:

(a)   The variables of the problem are constrained by a set of linear equations and/or inequalities.

(b)   Subject to these constraints, a function (called the objective function) is to be maximized (or minimized). This function depends linearly on the variables.

Remark 2:   Very often, as is true in the examples depicted above, the variables may be interpreted as the level of activity at which some processes will operate. The objective function may be a reward one tries to maximize or a cost one tries to minimize.

2. Definitions and Notations

Definition 2: If I is a set, $|I|$ denotes the "cardinality of set I," i.e., the number of elements in I. This notation will be used for finite sets.

Definition 3: "$m \times n$-matrix" A is (for us) nothing more than a rectangular (m rows and n columns) array of (real) numbers satisfying the rules of addition and multiplication recalled in Definition 4.

The element of row i $(1 \leq i \leq m)$ and column j $(1 \leq j \leq n)$ of matrix A will be denoted A_i^j.

Definition 4: Given a $m \times n$-matrix A and a $p \times q$-matrix B: The sum C of A and B exists only if

$$m = p \quad \text{and} \quad n = q$$

It is denoted $C = A + B$ and is defined by

$$C_i^j = A_i^j + B_i^j \qquad i \leq i \leq m; \quad 1 \leq j \leq n .$$

The product D of A by B (in this order) or "the product of B by A on its left" exists only if

$$n = p$$

It is denoted $C = A \times B$ or $C = AB$ and defined by

$$C_i^j = \sum_{k=1}^{n} A_i^k B_k^j \quad 1 \leq i \leq m; \qquad 1 \leq j \leq q$$

(C is an $m \times q$-matrix). Exercise 11 provides an intuitive background for this definition.

Definition 5: An n-column vector[†] $x \in R^n$ may be considered as an $n \times 1$-matrix. Components of x are real numbers denoted $x_1, x_2, \ldots, x_n$.

Definition 6: If $x \in R^n$ and if $J \subset \{1,2,\ldots,n\}$ (read "J is a subset of the set of indices $1,2,\ldots,n$"), x_J will denote the $|J|$-column vector, the elements of which are x_j for $j \in J$.

Definition 7: An n-row vector[†] c may be considered as a $1 \times n$-matrix. The components of c will be denoted $c^1, c^2, \ldots, c^n$. If $J \subset \{1,2,\ldots,n\}$, c^J denotes the $|J|$-row vector, the elements of which are c^j for $j \in J$.

Definition 8: We call "scalar product of an n-row vector c by an n-column vector x" the scalar (i.e, the 1×1-matrix) obtained according to Definition 3 in multiplying the $1 \times n$-matrix c by the $n \times 1$-matrix x :

$$cx = \sum_{j=1}^{n} c^j x_j$$

[†] The introduction of concepts of column vector and row vector may seem an exaggerated concern of formalism in a treatise that is aimed at practical and computational applications. However, this light complication in the beginning gives in the sequel a very useful consistency of notations.

Definition 9: If $J \subset \{1,2,\ldots,n\}$ vectors c^J and x_J are defined as stated in Definitions 5 and 6, the scalar product of c^J by x_J is

$$(1) \qquad c^J x_J = \sum_{j \in J} c^j x_j$$

Definition 10: Let A be an $m \times n$-matrix, $J \subset \{1,2,\ldots,n\}$, and $I \subset \{1,2,\ldots m\}$; let $k \in \{1,2,\ldots,m\}$, $\ell \varepsilon \{1, 2,\ldots,n\}$, x be an n-column vector and y an m-row vector. Then:

(a) A^ℓ denotes the m-column vector made out by the ℓth column of A.

(b) A_k denotes the n-row vector made out by the kth row of A.

(c) A^J is the $m \times |J|$-matrix made out by the union of column A^j for $j \in J$. The product of A^J by x_J is the m-column vector defined by

$$(1') \qquad A^J x_J = \sum_{j \in J} A^j x_j$$

(d) A_I is the $|I| \times n$-matrix made out by the union of rows A_i for $i \in I$. The product of y^I by A_I is the n-row vector defined by

$$(1'') \qquad y^I A_I = \sum_{i \in I} y^i A_i$$

(e) A_I^J denotes the submatrix of A, the elements of which are A_i^j for $i \in I$, $j \in J$. Note that if $I = \{i\}$ and $J = \{j\}$, A_I^J is written A_i^j.

(f) Depending on the circumstances, we will thus write matrix A in one of the following forms:

$$A; \quad \begin{bmatrix} A_1^1 & A_1^2 & \cdots & A_1^n \\ A_2^1 & A_2^2 & \cdots & A_2^n \\ \vdots & \vdots & & \vdots \\ A_m^1 & A_m^2 & \cdots & A_m^n \end{bmatrix}; \quad \begin{bmatrix} A_1 \\ A_2 \\ \vdots \\ A_m \end{bmatrix}; \quad [A^1, A^2, \ldots, A^n]$$

or more generally:

$$\begin{bmatrix} A_{J_1}^{I_1} & A_{J_1}^{I_2} & \cdots & A_{J_1}^{I_p} \\ A_{J_2}^{I_1} & A_{J_2}^{I_2} & \cdots & A_{J_2}^{I_p} \\ \vdots & \vdots & & \vdots \\ A_{J_q}^{I_1} & A_{J_q}^{I_2} & \cdots & A_{J_q}^{I_p} \end{bmatrix}$$

where $I_1 + I_2 + \ldots + I_p = \{1,2,\ldots,n\}$

$\qquad J_1 + J_2 + \ldots + J_q = \{1,2,\ldots,m\}.$

Definition 11:   Comparison of matrices: Let A be an $m \times n$-matrix and B an $m' \times n'$-matrix. It will be meaningful to compare matrix A and matrix B if and only if $m' = m$ and $n' = n$. By definition, in this case, we will say that $A = B$ (resp. $A \leqslant B$) if

$$A_i^j = B_i^j \quad \text{for all } i = 1,2,\ldots,m; \; j = 1,2,\ldots,n$$

(resp. $A_i^j \leqslant B_i^j$ for all $i = 1,2,\ldots,m; \; j = 1,2,\ldots,n$)

Moreover, $A \geqslant 0$ (resp. $x \geqslant 0$)   means

$$A_i^j \geqslant 0 \text{ for all } i = 1,2,\ldots,m; \quad j=1,2,\ldots,n$$

(resp. $x_j \geqslant 0$ for all $j = 1,2,\ldots,n$)

Definition 12: Matrix transposition: Let A be an $m \times n$-matrix. The "transpose of A" will be denoted A^T; it is the <u>$n \times m$-matrix</u>, the elements of which are

$$(A^T)_j^i = A_i^j \quad \text{for } i = 1,2,\ldots,m; \; j = 1,2,\ldots,n$$

Note that:

(a) The transpose of a column vector is a row vector

(b) $(A^T)^T = A$

(c) $(Ax)^T = x^T A^T$

Definition 13: U_m (or U when no ambiguity exists) denotes the $m \times m$-unit matrix, i.e.,

$$(U_m)_i^j = \begin{cases} 1 & \text{if } j = i \\ 0 & \text{otherwise} \end{cases}$$

Examples: 1.   Let

$$A = \begin{bmatrix} 2 & 1 & 1 & 0 & 0 \\ 1 & 2 & 0 & 1 & 0 \\ 0 & 1 & 0 & 0 & 1 \end{bmatrix} \quad b = \begin{bmatrix} 8 \\ 7 \\ 3 \end{bmatrix} \quad \bar{x} = \begin{bmatrix} 3 \\ 2 \\ 0 \\ 0 \\ 1 \end{bmatrix}$$

$c = [4,5,0,0,0]$

$\bar{y} = [1,2,0]$

$J = \{1,2,5\}$

Then we have

$$A^T = \begin{bmatrix} 2 & 1 & 0 \\ 1 & 2 & 1 \\ 1 & 0 & 0 \\ 0 & 1 & 0 \\ 0 & 0 & 1 \end{bmatrix} \qquad c^T = \begin{bmatrix} 4 \\ 5 \\ 0 \\ 0 \\ 0 \end{bmatrix} \qquad b^T = [8,7,3]$$

$$A^J = \begin{bmatrix} 2 & 1 & 0 \\ 1 & 2 & 0 \\ 0 & 1 & 1 \end{bmatrix} \qquad A^J \bar{x}_J = \begin{bmatrix} 8 \\ 7 \\ 3 \end{bmatrix} = b$$

$$\bar{y}A = [4,5,1,2,0] \geqslant c$$

$$c^J \bar{x}_J = 22$$

2. We can write linear program (P_1) in a compact matrix form. The activity of the firm is defined by the 2-column vector

$$x = \begin{bmatrix} x_1 \\ x_2 \end{bmatrix}$$

The way the firm is working is depicted by the matrix

$$A = \begin{bmatrix} 2 & 1 \\ 1 & 2 \\ 0 & 1 \end{bmatrix}$$

The supply in raw material and the unit reward are defined respectively by

$$b = \begin{bmatrix} 8 \\ 7 \\ 3 \end{bmatrix} \qquad c = [4,5]$$

so that (P_1) can be written

$$(P_1) \begin{cases} \text{maximize} \quad z = cx \quad \text{subject to} \\ \\ Ax \leqslant b; \ x \geqslant o \end{cases}$$

3.   Linear Programs in Canonical Form

Definition 14:   A linear program is in "canonical form" if it is written
in the following way

(2) $\left\{\begin{array}{l}\text{Find vector x such that} \\[8pt] cx = z \text{ is maximized} \\[6pt] \text{subject to the constraints} \\[6pt] Ax \leqslant b, \quad x \geqslant 0\end{array}\right.$

where

$$A \text{ is a given } m \times n\text{-matrix}$$
$$b \text{ is a given } m\text{-column vector}$$
$$c \text{ is a given } n\text{-row vector}$$
$$x \text{ is an (unknown) } n\text{-column vector}$$

Traditionally, (2) is usually written in the form

(P) $\left\{\begin{array}{l} Ax \leqslant b, \quad x \geqslant 0 \\[10pt] cx = z \text{ (Max)} \end{array}\right.$

where the notation

$$cx = z \text{ (Max)}$$

must be read "z denotes the value of the scalar product cx and we will try and
make z maximum." z is the "objective function."

Remark 3:   Equivalently, linear program (P) can be written in detached coefficient form

(P) $\left\{\begin{array}{l} A_1^1 x_1 + A_1^2 x_2 + \ldots + A_1^n x_n \leqslant b_1 \\[8pt] A_2^1 x_1 + A_2^2 x_2 + \ldots + A_2^n x_n \leqslant b_2 \\[8pt] \begin{array}{ccc} \cdot & \cdot & \cdot \\ \cdot & \cdot & \cdot \\ \cdot & \cdot & \cdot \end{array} \qquad \begin{array}{l} x_j \geqslant 0 \\[6pt] j = 1, \ldots, n \end{array} \\[8pt] A_m^1 x_1 + A_m^2 x_2 + \ldots + A_m^n x_n \leqslant b_m \\[8pt] c^1 x_1 + c^2 x_2 + \ldots + c^n x_n = z \text{ (Max)} \end{array}\right.$

Remark 4:   Constraints $x \geqslant 0$ (which mean, see Definition 11, $x_j \geqslant 0$ for j = 1,
2,...,n, could have been included in the set $Ax \leqslant b$. To do this, it would
suffice to define the $(m + n) \times n$-matrix A' and the $(m + n)$-column vector b' by

$$A' = \begin{bmatrix} A \\ -U_m \end{bmatrix} \qquad\qquad b' = \begin{bmatrix} b \\ 0 \end{bmatrix}$$

and (P) would become

$$(P') \quad \begin{cases} A'x \leqslant b' \\[2mm] cx = z \ (\text{Max}) \end{cases}$$

This procedure might seem very natural since nothing in the definition of a linear program forces variables to be non-negative and we will in fact meet linear programs with nonconstrained variables. However, the usage is to separate non-negativity constraints on the variables from the other constraints and we will see that this is well justified:

(a) Non-negativity constraints have, in general, a very specific physical origin (activities that cannot conceivably work at a negative level, for instance).

(b) These constraints play a particular role in the process of solution.

Definition 15: Let us come back to the linear program in canonical form:

$$(P) \quad \begin{cases} Ax \leqslant b, \quad x \geqslant 0 \\[2mm] cx = z \ (\text{Max}) \end{cases}$$

Each vector x that satisfies the constraints

$$Ax \leqslant b, \quad x \geqslant 0$$

is called a "feasible solution." The set of such x's is the set of feasible solutions. For the sake of compactness, we pose

$$(3) \qquad D = \{x \in R^n \mid Ax \leqslant b, \quad x \geqslant 0\}$$

D is also called the "domain of feasible solutions." Problem (P) can be stated:

Find $\bar{x} \in D$ such that

$$c\bar{x} \geqslant cx \text{ for all } x \in D$$

Such an $\bar{x}$, if it exists, is called an "optimal solution."

Example: Let us go back to linear program (P_1) and Figure I.1. The set of
(x_1, x_2) that correspond to points inside the polygon A B C D E are feasible
solutions of (P_1). $x_1=3$, $x_2=2$ is, as we shall prove later, an optimal solution.
We notice that this optimal solution corresponds to a vertex of the polygon.
We will see in Chapter VIII that this fact is not due to chance.

Remark 5: Given the linear program

$$(P) \quad \begin{cases} Ax \leqslant b, \quad x \geqslant 0 \\ cx = z \ (\text{Max}) \end{cases}$$

Three cases may occur:

(a) The set of feasible solutions $D = \{x \in R^n \mid Ax \leqslant b, \ x \geqslant 0\}$ is nonempty
and there exists (at least) one optimal solution; example:

$$(4) \quad \begin{cases} x_1 \leq 1 \quad x_1 \geq 0 \\ x_1 = z \ (\text{Max}) \end{cases}$$

(b) The set of feasible solutions D is empty; example:

$$(5) \quad \begin{cases} x_1 \leqslant -1 \quad x_1 \geqslant 0 \\ x_1 = z \ (\text{Max}) \end{cases}$$

(c) The set of feasible solutions D is nonempty, but there does not exist
any optimal solution; example:

$$(6) \quad \begin{cases} -x_1 \leqslant 1 \quad x_1 \geqslant 0 \\ x_1 = z \ (\text{Max}) \end{cases}$$

The value of the objective function z is not bounded in the set D.

Remark 6: What is said in Remark 5 is just pure logic: Either D is empty or
not. If D is nonempty, an optimal solution may or may not exist. We will
prove later that in the third case, i.e., if there exist feasible solutions but
no optimal solution, we always are in the unboundedness type of situation.

This fact is not obvious. Let us consider the very simple optimization
problem (which is not a linear program; why?).

$$(7) \quad \begin{cases} x_1 < 1 \quad x_1 \geq 0 \\ x_1 = z \ (\text{Max}) \end{cases}$$

The set of feasible solutions is the segment [0,1) (open on the right side)
but there is no optimal solution.

It is to prevent situations of that type (and also because strict inequalities never have physical significance in a model) that strict inequalities are
forbidden in linear programming.

4. Equivalent Formulations of Linear Programs

Definition 16: Recall Definition 14, where we defined a linear program in
canonical form. The linear program

$$(PS) \quad \begin{cases} Ax = b \quad x \geqslant 0 \\ cx = z \ (Max) \end{cases}$$

is said to be in "standard form." If some constraints are equations and others
are inequalities, we say that we have a "mixed form."

Remark 7: Note that linear program (PS) can easily be written in canonical
form. The ith constraint of (PS) is

$$A_i x = b_i$$

and we have

$$(8) \qquad A_i x = b_i \longleftrightarrow \begin{cases} A_i x \leqslant b_i \\ A_i x \geqslant b_i \longleftrightarrow -A_i x \leqslant -b_i \end{cases}$$

so that (PS) can be written

$$(\hat{PS}) \quad \begin{cases} \hat{A}x \leq \hat{b}, \ \hat{x} \geqslant 0 \\ cx = z \ (Max) \end{cases}$$

with

$$\hat{A} = \begin{bmatrix} A \\ -A \end{bmatrix} \qquad \hat{b} = \begin{bmatrix} b \\ -b \end{bmatrix}$$

(i.e., $\hat{A}$ is a 2m × n-matrix and $\hat{b}$ is a 2m-column vector).

Definition 17: Although optimization problems (PS) and $(\hat{PS})$ are formally
different, we see that they are, in fact, "the same."

In general, we will say that two optimization problems (0) and (0') are
"equivalent" if to each feasible solution of one of these problems, one can
find a corresponding solution to the other in such a way that for a pair of
homologous solutions, the values of the objective functions are equal.
(Note that in the example above the correspondence was simply identity.)

<u>Theorem 1</u>:   Any linear program can be written in canonical or in standard form.

   <u>Proof</u>:   To prove this theorem we will show five points:

         1. An inequality $A_i x \geqslant b_i$ can be transformed into an inequality with a "$\leqslant$" sign.

         2. An equality constraint can be replaced by a set of two inequalities.

         3. An inequality can be replaced by an equation.

         4. Minimization and maximization problems are equivalent.

         5. If some variables are not constrained to be positive or zero, it is, however, possible to go back to canonical or standard form.

   <u>Proof of 1</u> is trivial: it suffices to multiply by -1. <u>Proof of 2</u> has been given in Remark 7.

   <u>Proof of 3</u>. We have

$$(9) \qquad A_i x \leq b_i \quad \longleftrightarrow \quad \begin{cases} A_i x + \xi_i = b_i \\[2mm] \xi_i \geqslant o \end{cases}$$

The new variable we added to go from the inequality to the equation is called a "slack variable." The value of this slack variable measures by how much $A_i x$ is less than b_i. ($A_i x$ cannot be greater than b_i since ξ_i is constrained to be non-negative.)

   <u>Proof of 4</u>. Let D be the domain of feasible solutions of a linear program. We have

$$\underset{x \in D}{\text{Min}} \; [cx] = -\underset{x \in D}{\text{Max}} \; [-cx]$$

Assume that $\overline{\overline{x}}$ is a solution of $\underset{x \in D}{\text{Max}} [-cx]$ and let $\overline{x} \in D$ with

$$c\overline{x} < c\overline{\overline{x}}$$

Multiplying by -1, we get

$$-c\overline{x} > -c\overline{\overline{x}}$$

which contradicts the fact that $\overline{\overline{x}}$ is an optimal solution of the maximization problem. So if one of these problems has an optimal solution, so does the other, and optimal solutions of one of these problems are solutions of the other.

Proof of 5. We will just show that the linear program

(10)
$$
\begin{cases}
Ax \leqslant b & x_2, x_3, \ldots, x_n \geqslant 0 \qquad x_1 \text{ unrestricted} \\
cx = z \text{ (Max)}
\end{cases}
$$

can be written in canonical form. Extension to the general case is straightforward. We let

(11) $x_1 = x_1' - x_1'$; $x_1', x_1'' \geqslant 0$

And we show that

(12)
$$
\begin{cases}
A^1 x_1' - A^1 x_1'' + A^J x_J \leqslant b \qquad x_1', x_1'', x_J \geqslant o \\
c^1 x_1' - c^1 x_1'' + c^J x_J = z \text{ (Max)}
\end{cases}
$$

(where $J = \{2, 3, \ldots, n\}$) is equivalent to (10) according to Definition 17:

(i) If x_1', x_1'', x_J is a feasible solution of (12), then $x_1 = x_1' - x_1''$, x_J is a feasible solution of (10) with equality of objective functions.

(ii) If x_1, x_J is a feasible solution of (10), then x_1', x_1'', x_J with

$$x_1' = \text{Max } [0, x_1]$$

$$x_1'' = -\text{Min } [0, x_1]$$

is a feasible solution of (12) and the values of the objective functions are equal.

Remark 8: The method used in the proof of point 5 allows us to "reduce" unconstrained variables to constrained ones and to show how general the canonical or standard form is. But, in practice, if we have linear programs with unconstrained variables, it would be very inefficient to use the procedure just described. We will show, in Chapter V, how advantage can be taken of the fact that some (or all) variables are unconstrained.

Example: Linear program (P_1) can be written in standard form after adding slack variables (which we call here x_3, x_4, x_5):

$$
(P_1) \quad
\begin{cases}
2x_1 + x_2 + x_3 & = 8 \\
x_1 + 2x_2 \qquad + x_4 & = 7 \\
x_2 \qquad\qquad + x_5 & = 3 \\
4x_1 + 5x_2 & = z \text{ (Max)}
\end{cases}
\qquad x_j \geqslant 0 \text{ for } j = 1, 2, \ldots, 5
$$

Remark 9:   An expression of Theorem 1 in matrix notations is given in Exercise 12.

5. Elements of Geometry of Linear Programs

This short section, which is a preview of Chapter VIII, is aimed at giving an intuitive background to linear programming theory and to the method of solution that will be presented later: the simplex algorithm. Let us consider the linear program

$$(P) \quad \begin{cases} Ax \leqslant b \qquad x \geqslant 0 \\ \\ cx = z \text{ (Max)} \end{cases}$$

The set of points in R^n which satisfy, for a given $i \in \{1,2,\ldots m\}$,

$$(13) \qquad A_i x = b_i$$

constitute a "hyperplane." This hyperplane separates R^n in two regions, two "half spaces," such that two points are in the same half space if and only if the segment joining them does not intersect the hyperplane (13).

The set of points satisfying

$$Ax \leqslant b$$

is the intersection of half spaces

$$A_i x \leqslant b_i \quad \text{for } i = 1,2,\ldots,m$$

This intersection (itself intersected with the "non-negative orthant" $x \geqslant 0$) is a "convex polyhedron." A tetrahedron, a cube, and a diamond are examples of convex polyhedra in R^3. A convex polygon is a convex polyhedron in R^2 (see Figure I.1).

The points of the polyhedron of feasible solutions to (P) which satisfy for an $i \in \{1,2,\ldots,m\}$ or a $j \in \{1,2,\ldots,n\}$

$$A_i x = b_i \qquad \text{or } x_j = 0$$

belong to a "face" of the polyhedron. Intersection of n faces determines (in general) a "vertex" of the polyhedron. Intersection of n - 1 faces determines (in general) an "edge" of the polyhedron. Linear program (P) consists in finding an $\bar{x}$ and a $\bar{z}$ such that the hyperplane

$$cx = \bar{z}$$

cuts the domain of feasible solutions "as far as possible" in the direction of increasing z (this is the procedure we used in solving example (P_1) in section 1). In general, the intersection is reduced to a point $\bar{x}$ which is a vertex of the polyhedron.

The simplex algorithm proposes a journey from a starting (nonoptimal) vertex to an optimal vertex through a series of visits of a chain of adjacent vertices of the polyhedron.

EXERCISES

1. Consider the linear program

$$(P) \begin{cases} x_1 + 2x_2 - 3x_3 = 1 \\ 2x_1 + x_2 - 5x_3 \leqslant 2 \\ x_1 + 3x_2 - x_3 \geqslant 1 \\ x_1 + 2x_2 + 3x_3 = z \text{ (Max)} \end{cases} \qquad x_1 \leqslant 0, \; x_2 \geqslant 0$$

(a) Write this linear program (1) in canonical form; (2) in standard form.

(b) (P) being written in standard form, we have m = 3, n = 6. Write A^2, A_3, A^4. Let $I = \{1,3\}$, $J = \{2,4,5\}$ and write b_I, c^J, A_I, A^J, A^J_I.

2. A manufacturer wishes to produce 100 lbs. of an alloy that is 30 percent lead, 30 percent zinc, and 40 percent tin. Suppose that there are on the market alloys 1,2,3,4,5,6,7,8,9 with compositions and prices as follows:

Alloy	1	2	3	4	5	6	7	8	9	Desired
% lead	10	10	40	60	30	30	30	50	20	30
% zinc	10	30	50	30	30	40	20	40	30	30
% tin	80	60	10	10	40	30	50	10	50	40
Cost per lb.	4.1	4.3	5.8	6.0	7.6	7.5	7.3	6.9	7.3	Min

Obviously, the manufacturer can purchase alloy 5 alone, but this will cost $760. If he buys 25 lbs. of 1, 25 lbs. of 2, and 50 lbs. of 8, he gets 100 lbs. of mixture with the required proportion, which costs only $555. The number of combinations that will give the desired blend seems to be infinite (is it?)

and the manufacturer would like to find a systematic way of getting a result. Write this problem as a linear program (the cost of blending is assumed to be 0).

3. A farm has two lots, A and B (200 and 400 acres, respectively). Six kinds of cereals, I, II, III, IV, V, and VI, can be grown on lots A and B. The profit for each 100 lbs. of cereal is:

	I	II	III	IV	V	VI
Profit/100 lbs.	24	31	14	18	61	47

To grow 100 lbs. of cereal we need some area (in acres) and quantities of water (in cubic meters):

	I	II	III	IV	V	VI
Area on lot A	0.01	0.015	0.01	0.008	0.025	0.02
Area on lot B	0.01	0.017	0.012	0.01	0.03	0.017
Water (in m^3)	60	80	50	70	107	90

The total volume of water that is available is 400,000 m^3. We try to make a maximum profit while respecting various constraints. Write this problem as a linear program.

4. After n experiments a physicist is sure that a certain quantity Q varies with variable t. He has good reasons to believe that the law of variation of Q is of the form

(*) $Q(t) = a \sin t + b \tan t + c$

and he wants to determine "as well as possible" the values of parameters a, b, and c from the n experiments made. These experiments have given him for t_1, t_2, ..., t_n values Q_1, Q_2, ..., Q_n.

His experiments were not error free and the law (*) of variation may be just an approximation. Thus the linear system

$$a \sin t_i + b \tan t_i + c = Q_i \qquad i = 1, 2, \ldots, n \qquad (n > 3)$$

with three unknowns a, b, c has no solution. The physicist has two different ideas of what a good adjustment may mean:

(a) Find the values of a, b, c that minimize

$$\sum_{i=1}^{n} |a \sin t_i + b \tan t_i + c - Q_i|$$

(b)   Find the values of a, b, c that minimize

$$\underset{i=1,2,\ldots,n}{\text{Max}} \qquad (a \sin t_i + b \tan t_i + c - Q_i)$$

In either case, and for physical reasons, coefficients a, b, and c must be non-negative. Show that each of these adjustments can be written as a linear program.

5.   To feed a given animal we need four nutrients, A, B, C, and D. The minimal quantity each animal needs per day is

0.4 kg of A; 0.61 kg of B; 2 kg of C; 1.7 kg of D

To obtain the food we mix two flours, M and N:

1 kg of M contains 100 g of A, no B, 100 g of C, 200 g of D

1 kg of N contains no A, 100 g of B, 200 g of C, 100 g of D

With $1 we can buy

4 kg of M   and   8 kg of N

Write as a linear program the problem of finding the daily quantity of flours M and N that must be bought to feed one animal at minimum cost. Solve graphically.

6.   The cost matrix of a transportation problem (analogous to problem (P_2) of Section 1) with 3 plants (corresponding to harbors) and 4 markets (corresponding to factories) is

	M_1	M_2	M_3	M_4
P_1	4	4	9	3
P_2	3	5	8	8
P_3	2	6	5	7

Supplies are 3, 5, 7 in plants P_1, P_2, P_3, respectively. Consumptions are 2, 5, 4, 4 in M_1, M_2, M_3, M_4, respectively. Write this transportation problem as a linear program and check that the following shipping matrix corresponds to a feasible solution:

	M_1	M_2	M_3	M_4
P_1	0	0	0	3
P_2	0	5	0	0
P_3	2	0	4	1

7. Show that the problem

$$(P) \quad \begin{cases} Ax = b \qquad \alpha_j \leqslant x_j \leqslant \beta_j \qquad j = 1,2,\ldots, n \\ \\ cx = z \ (\text{Max}) \end{cases}$$

(where α_j and β_j are given reals) is a linear program. Write (P) in standard form.

8. Show that the problem

$$(P) \quad \begin{cases} Ax + Uv = b \qquad x, v \geqslant o \\ \\ cx - \sum_{i=1}^{n} |v_i| = z \ (\text{Max}) \end{cases}$$

(where U is the $m \times m$ unit matrix) is a linear program.

9. We consider the two linear programs

$$(P) \begin{cases} Ax \leqslant b \quad x \geqslant 0 \\ cx = z \ (\text{Max}) \end{cases} (P_1) \begin{cases} Ax \leqslant b \quad x_j \geqslant 0 \quad j = 2,3,\ldots,n \\ cx = z \ (\text{Max}) \end{cases}$$

Show that if $\overline{x}$ is an optimal solution of (P_1) with $\overline{x}_1 \geqslant 0$, then $\overline{x}$ is an optimal solution of (P).

10. Show that linear program (P_2) can be written in standard form without adding slack variables.

11. Let A be an $m \times n$-matrix and B be an $n \times q$-matrix. Matrix B can be viewed as a device that transforms q-column vectors x into n-column vectors y by

$$y = Bx$$

Matrix A can be viewed as a device that transforms n-column vectors y into m-column vectors z by

$$z = Ay$$

(a) For the numerical example

$$A = \begin{bmatrix} 1 & 0 & 2 \\ 3 & 2 & 1 \\ 0 & 1 & 1 \end{bmatrix} \qquad B = \begin{bmatrix} 2 & 1 \\ 0 & 1 \\ 1 & 2 \end{bmatrix}$$

show that the concatenation of the two devices is the device C, which transforms x into z by

$$x = Cz$$

where C = AB

(b) Prove the property in general.

12. A is a $m \times n$-matrix. Let I, J, K be a partition of $\{1,2,\ldots, n\}$ (i.e., I, J, $K \subset \{1,2,\ldots, n\}$; $I \cap J = J \cap K = K \cap I = \phi$; $I \cup J \cup K = \{1,2,\ldots,n\}$) and L, M, N be a partition of $\{1, 2,\ldots,m\}$. Consider the linear program

$$(P) \quad \begin{cases} A_L x \leqslant b_L & x_I \geqslant 0 \\ A_M x \geqslant b_M & x_J \leqslant 0 \\ A_N x = b_N & x_K \text{ unconstrained} \\ cx = z \text{ (Max)} \end{cases}$$

Give the structure of $\hat{A}, \hat{b}, \hat{c}$ and $\tilde{A}, \tilde{b}, \tilde{c}$ if

$$(\hat{P}) \quad \begin{cases} \hat{A}x \geqslant \hat{b} & x \geqslant 0 \\ \hat{c}x = z \text{ (Max)} \end{cases} \qquad (\tilde{P}) \quad \begin{cases} \tilde{A}x = b & x \geqslant 0 \\ \tilde{c}x = z \text{ (Max)} \end{cases}$$

are equivalent to (P).

Chapter II. Dual Linear Programs

In this chapter we show that it is possible to associate to any linear program another linear program (which we call "dual"). Using different types of arguments we prove how close the relationship is between a linear program and its dual. In fact, these two programs must be considered as two facets of the same problem rather than as two different problems. And we will see in subsequent chapters that when one solves a linear program, its dual is solved at the same time. Thus the concept of duality is very central to linear programming and this is why it is introduced so early in the book.

1. Formal Definition of the Dual Linear Program

<u>Definition 1</u>: Given a linear program in canonical form

$$(P) \begin{cases} Ax \leq b \qquad x \geq 0 \\ \\ cx = z \ (\text{Max}) \end{cases}$$

(where A is a (given) $m \times n$-matrix, b is a (given) m-column vector, c is a (given) n-row vector, and x is an (unknown) n-column vector), we call the "dual" of linear program (P)

$$(D) \begin{cases} yA \geq c \qquad y \geq 0 \\ \\ yb = w \ (\text{Min}) \end{cases}$$

(where A, b, and c are the same as in (P) and y is an (unknown) m-row vector).

This definition is due to Dantzig and von Neumann.

<u>Remark 1</u>: In detached coefficient form (P) is written

$$(P) \begin{cases} A_1^1 x_1 + A_1^2 x_2 + \ldots + A_1^n x_n \leq b_1 \\ A_2^1 x_1 + A_2^2 x_2 + \ldots + A_2^n x_n \leq b_2 \\ \quad \vdots \qquad \vdots \qquad\qquad\quad \vdots \\ A_m^1 x_1 + A_m^2 x_2 + \ldots + A_m^n x_n \leq b_m \\ c^1 x_1 + c^2 x_2 + \ldots + c^n x_n = z \ (\text{Max}) \end{cases} \qquad \begin{array}{l} x_j \geq 0 \\ j = 1, 2, \ldots, n \end{array}$$

and (D) is written

$$(D) \begin{cases} A_1^1 y^1 + A_2^1 y^2 + \ldots + A_m^1 y^m \geq c^1 \\ A_1^2 y^1 + A_2^2 y^2 + \ldots + A_m^2 y^m \geq c^2 \\ \quad \cdot \qquad \qquad \qquad \cdot \qquad \cdot \\ \quad \cdot \qquad \qquad \qquad \cdot \qquad \cdot \\ \quad \cdot \qquad \qquad \qquad \cdot \qquad \cdot \\ A_1^n y^1 + A_2^n y^2 + \ldots + A_m^n y^m \geq c^n \end{cases} \qquad \begin{array}{l} y^i \geq 0 \\[4pt] i=1,2,\ldots,m \end{array}$$

Remark 2:   We note that the variables of the dual are in a one-to-one correspondence with the constraints of the linear program we started with (for convenience this linear program is called the "primal"), while the constraints of
the dual are in one-to-one correspondence with the variables of the primal.
This is shown in the following diagram:

Reading this table "horizontally" gives problem (P); a "vertical" reading
gives its dual.

Example: The dual of problem (P_1) of section I.1 (a) is

$$(D_1) \begin{cases} 2y_1 + y_2 \qquad \geq 4 \\ y_1 + 2y_2 + y_3 \geq 5 \\ 8y_1 + 7y_2 + 3y_3 = w \ (\text{Min}) \end{cases} \qquad y_1, y_2, y_3 \geq 0$$

Note that, for convenience, we have written the components of vector y as if it were a column vector. The reader must convince himself that it makes no difference.

Note that $y_1 = 1$, $y_2 = 2$, is a feasible solution of (D_1). The corresponding value of the objective function w is 22.

Remark 3: We have spent some time in Chapter I showing that any linear program can be written in canonical form. Thus any linear program has a dual. We will now answer the questions:

    (a) What is the dual of the dual?

    (b) What is the dual of a linear program written in standard form? Under mixed form?

Theorem 1:   The dual of the dual is the primal.

    Proof: Linear program (D) can be written

$$(D) \begin{cases} -A^T y^T \leqslant -c^T & y^T \geq 0 \\ -b^T y^T = w' \ (\text{Max}) \end{cases}$$

(D) being in canonical form, we can take its dual in following the process of Definition 1. The dual of (D) is

$$(DD) \begin{cases} -uA^T \geqslant -b^T & u \geqslant 0 \\ -uc^T = w'' \ (\text{Min}) \end{cases}$$

where u is an (unknown) n-row vector. Let

$$x = u^T$$

(DD) can be written equivalently (by taking the transpose and multiplying constraints by -1)

$$(P) \begin{cases} Ax \leqslant b & x \geqslant 0 \\ cx = z' \ (\text{Max}) \end{cases}$$

                                                     q.e.d.

Remark 4:   This property is a justification of the term "dual."

Remark 5:   The dual of the linear program in standard form,

$$(PS) \begin{cases} Ax = b & x \geqslant 0 \\ cx = z \ (\text{Max}) \end{cases}$$

is

$$(DS) \begin{cases} yA \geqslant c \\ yb = w \text{ (Min)} \end{cases} \qquad y \text{ unrestricted in sign}^\dagger$$

To prove this we write (PS) in canonical form (as we learned to do in Section I.4):

$$(PS') \begin{cases} A_i x \leqslant b_i & i = 1,2,\ldots,m \\ -A_i x \leqslant -b_i & i = 1,2,\ldots,m \qquad x \geqslant 0 \\ cx = z \text{ (Max)} \end{cases}$$

And we can apply to (PS') the process of Definition 1 to find its dual. The constraints of (PS') (other than $x \geq 0$) are in one of two groups. Let us associate dual variable y'^i to the ith constraint of the first group and y''^i to the ith constraint of the second group. Let y' (resp. y") be the m-row vector the ith component of which is y'^i (resp. y''^i). Then the dual of (PS') is

$$(DS') \begin{cases} y'A - y''A \geq c \\ y'b - y''b = w \text{ (Min)} \end{cases} \qquad y', y'' \geq 0$$

By posing $y = y' - y''$, we see that (DS') is equivalent to (DS) (Section 1.4).

Remark 6: More generally, it is convenient to be able to write the dual of a linear program without passing through the canonical form (however, for exercise and for checking, we recommend that the beginners always follow this process).

    Let us assume that the objective function is to be maximized and that the ith constraint is

    (a) $A_i x \leqslant b_i$

In this case, when we go to the equivalent canonical form, the constraint will not be changed and the dual variable y^i must be $\geqslant 0$.

    (b) $A_i x \geqslant b_i$

In this case, when we go to the equivalent canonical form, the constraint will be multiplied by -1 and the corresponding dual variable y^i must be $\leqslant 0$ ($-y^i \geq 0$.

---

†This is also denoted $y \gtrless 0$.

(c) $A_i x = b_i$

In this case, when we go to the equivalent canonical form, we have two constraints

$$A_i x \leqslant b_i$$

$$-A_i x \leqslant -b_i$$

If we call y'^i and y''^i the corresponding dual variables we note that each time one of these variables is written in an expression with a coefficient, the other one is there with the opposite coefficient. So that we can pose

$$y^i = y'^i - y''^i$$

this variable of the dual (we say "dual variable") being not constrained.

Go on assuming that the objective function is to be maximized and that the constraint on primal variable x_j is

(a) $x_j \geqslant 0$

When we go to the equivalent canonical form we do not change variables and the corresponding constraint of the dual is

$$\sum_{i=1}^{m} A_i^j y^i \geqslant c^j$$

(b) $x_j \leqslant 0$

To go to the equivalent canonical form we pose $x'_j = -x_j$ and the corresponding constraint of the dual will be

$$-\sum_{i=1}^{m} A_i^j y^i \geqslant -c^j$$

i.e.

$$\sum_{i=1}^{m} A_i^j y^i \leqslant c^j$$

(c) x_j not constrained $(x_j \overset{<}{>} 0)$

In this case, to go to the equivalent canonical form we pose (see Remark I.10)

$$x_j = x'_j - x''_j \qquad x'_j, \ x''_j \geqslant 0$$

To variable x_j will correspond the constraints

$$\begin{aligned} \sum_{i=1}^{m} A_i^j y^i &\geqslant c^i \\ -\sum_{i=1}^{m} A_i^j y^i &\geqslant -c^j \end{aligned} \quad \to \quad \sum_{i=1}^{m} A_i^j y^i = c^j$$

These remarks can be put together as in Table II.1.

TABLE II.1: Duality Rules

Primal-Maximization		Dual-Minimization	
ith constraint	$\leqslant$	ith variable	$\geqslant 0$
ith constraint	$\geqslant$	ith variable	$\leqslant 0$
ith constraint	$=$	ith variable unrestricted	
jth variable	$\geqslant 0$	jth constraint	$\geqslant$
jth variable	$\leqslant 0$	jth constraint	$\leqslant$
jth variable unrestricted		jth constraint	$=$
Primal-Minimization		Dual-Maximization	
ith constraint	$\geqslant$	ith variable	$\geqslant 0$
ith constraint	$\leqslant$	ith variable	$\leqslant 0$
ith constraint	$=$	ith variable unrestricted	
jth variable	$\geqslant 0$	jth constraint	$\leqslant$
jth variable	$\leqslant 0$	jth constraint	$\geqslant$
jth variable unrestricted		jth constaint	$=$

The proof of the lower part of the table (which is equivalent to the first part read from right to left) is left to the reader as an exercise.

2.   The Objective Function Values of Dual Linear Programs

Theorem 2: Let (P) and (D) be a couple of dual linear programs

$$(P) \begin{cases} Ax \leq b, \quad x \geqslant 0 \\ \\ cx = z \ (Max) \end{cases} \qquad (D) \begin{cases} yA \geq c, \quad y \geqslant 0 \\ \\ yb = w \ (Min) \end{cases}$$

For every couple of feasible solutions $\overline{x}, \overline{y}$ of (P) and (D), respectively, we have

(1) $\overline{z} = c\overline{x} \leqslant \overline{y}b = \overline{w}$

<u>Proof:</u>   Let us write down, in detached coefficient form, that $\bar{x}$ is a feasible solution to (P):

$$A_1^1\bar{x}_1 + A_1^2\bar{x}_2 + \ldots + A_1^n\bar{x}_n \leqslant b_1 \qquad \bar{x}_j \geqslant 0$$

$$\vdots \qquad\qquad \vdots \qquad\quad j = 1, \ldots, n$$

$$A_m^1\bar{x}_1 + A_m^2\bar{x}_2 + \ldots + A_m^n\bar{x}_n \leqslant b_m$$

Multiply each of these inequalities by the corresponding $\bar{y}^i$. Since $\bar{y}^i \geqslant 0$ by assumption, this operation does not change the sign of the inequality:

$$\bar{y}^1 A_1^1\bar{x}_1 + \bar{y}^1 A_1^2\bar{x}_2 + \ldots + \bar{y}^1 A_1^n\bar{x}_n \leqslant \bar{y}^1 b_1$$

$$\vdots \qquad\qquad \vdots \qquad\qquad \vdots$$

$$\bar{y}^m A_m^1\bar{x}_1 + \bar{y}^m A_m^2\bar{x}_2 + \ldots + \bar{y}^m A_m^n\bar{x}_n \leqslant \bar{y}^m b_m$$

Now adding all these inequalities, we get

$$(2) \qquad \sum_{i=1}^{m} \sum_{j=1}^{n} \bar{y}^i A_i^j \bar{x}_j \leq \sum_{i=1}^{m} \bar{y}^i b_i$$

Starting from the set of inequalities

$$\bar{y}^1 A_1^1 + \ldots + \bar{y}^m A_m^1 \geqslant c^1$$

$$\vdots \qquad\qquad \vdots$$

$$\bar{y}^1 A_1^n + \ldots + \bar{y}^m A_m^n \geqslant c^n$$

which states that $\bar{y}$ is a feasible solution of (D), and multiplying each inequality by the corresponding non-negative $\bar{x}_j$ and adding, we get

$$\sum_{j=1}^{n} \sum_{i=1}^{m} \bar{y}^i A_i^j \bar{x}_j \geq \sum_{j=1}^{n} c^j \bar{x}_j$$

which together with (2) gives the result.

This proof can be formulated more briefly by using matrix notation:

Since $\bar{x}$ is a feasible solution to (P), we have

$$A\bar{x} \leqslant b$$

Since $\bar{y} \geqslant 0$, this gives

(2') $\qquad \bar{y}A\bar{x} \leqslant \bar{y}b$

In the same way, since $\bar{y}$ is a feasible solution to (D), we have

$$\bar{y}A \geqslant c$$

Since $\bar{x} \geqslant 0$, this gives

$$\bar{y}A\bar{x} \geqslant c\bar{x}$$

which together with (2') gives the desired result. q.e.d.

Corollary: Let $\bar{x}$ be a feasible solution to (P) and $\bar{y}$ be a feasible solution to (D); then if $c\bar{x} = \bar{y}b$, $\bar{x}$ and $\bar{y}$ are optimal solutions of (P) and (D), respectively.

Proof: Suppose that there exists $\bar{x}'$, a feasible solution of (P) such that $c\bar{x}' > c\bar{x}$. Since $c\bar{x} = \bar{y}b$ we have $c\bar{x}' > \bar{y}b$, which contradicts Theorem 2.

Example: We have seen in the example following Remark 2 that $y_1 = 1$, $y_2 = 2$, $w = 22$ is a feasible solution to the dual of (P_1). This shows that the solution $x_1 = 3$, $x_2 = 2$, $z = 22$ we obtained in Section I.1(a) by geometric arguments is in fact an optimal one.

Remark 7: The importance of the corollary of Theorem 2 lies in the fact that it provides a "certificate of optimality." Assume that you have found an optimal solution of a linear program (either by solving it with the simplex algorithm or by a good guess or by any other way) and that you want to convince a "supervisor" that your solution is in fact optimal. It will then suffice to exhibit a dual feasible solution giving the same value to the objective function. We will see later that if the solution has been obtained through the simplex algorithm, you will have at hand, together with your optimal solution of the primal, an optimal solution of the dual.

Remark 8: From Theorem 2 we thus conclude that for every $\bar{x}$, $c\bar{x}$ belongs to some interval $[\alpha, z_{max}]$ and that, in the same way, for every feasible $\bar{y}, \bar{y}b \in [w_{min}, \beta]$. α may be $-\infty$ or finite and β may be $+\infty$ or finite. Moreover, these two intervals have at most one point in common (their end points), in which case this common point corresponds to an optimal solution for both primal and dual problems. What is left unsolved at this point is under which conditions the two intervals might have a common point, or when there might be a gap between two intervals. (See Figure II.1.)

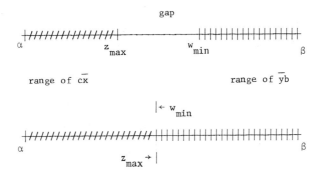

Figure II.2: Possible Ranges of $c\bar{x}$ and $\bar{y}b$

We will see in Chapter VI that there is, in fact, no gap. Moreover, if one
of the intervals is empty(i.e., if one of the problems does not have a feasible
solution), while the other has a feasible solution, the latter problem does not
have an optimal solution.

3.   Economic Interpretation of Duality (An Example)

Up to this point duality has been introduced in a completely abstract
fashion. With any linear program we have associated another one called its
dual. Developments of preceding sections show the strong mathematical connec-
tion between a pair of dual programs. Moreover, we will see (as announced
above) in Chapter IV that when we solve a linear program, solutions for both
primal and dual problems are found simultaneously. Duality is an intrinsic
basic property of linear programming.

In Chapter IX we will give further results of duality. We will show that
for linear programs that are models of real systems, dual variables have practical (in general economic) interpretations. We now just give an example (in-
spired from [3]) of practical interpretation of the pair of dual problems.

Let us go back to transportation problem (P_2) of Section I.1(b)

$$(P_2)\begin{cases} x_{11} + x_{12} + x_{13} & \leq 550 \\ & x_{21} + x_{22} + x_{23} \leq 350 \\ -x_{11} & - x_{21} & \leq -400 \\ - x_{12} & - x_{22} & \leq -300 \\ - x_{13} & + x_{23} \leq -200 \\ -5x_{11} - 6x_{12} - 3x_{13} - 3x_{21} - 5x_{22} - 4x_{23} &= z\,(\text{Max}) \end{cases}$$

$$\begin{aligned} & x_{ij} \geq 0 \\ & i=1,2 \\ & j=1,2,3 \end{aligned}$$

the dual of which is

$$(D_2)\begin{cases} y_1 & - y_3 & \geq -5 \\ y_1 & - y_4 & \geq -6 \\ y_1 & - y_5 & \geq -3 \\ y_2 - y_3 & & \geq -3 \\ y_2 & - y_4 & \geq -5 \\ y_2 & - y_5 & \geq -4 \\ 550y_1 + 350y_2 - 400y_3 - 300y_4 - 200y_5 &= w(\text{Min}) \end{cases}$$

$$\begin{aligned} & y_i \geq 0 \\ & i=1,2,\ldots,5 \end{aligned}$$

Now suppose that a transportation specialist comes to the firm that needs product S in the factories of Denver, Phoenix, and Chicago and proposes the following deal: I shall buy product S in harbors 1 and 2 and pay $\$\pi_1$ for each ton of S in New York and $\$\pi_2$ for each ton in Seattle. I guarantee to deliver 400, 300, and 200 tons, respectively, to factories 1, 2, and 3 and charge you $\$\eta_1$, $\$\eta_2$, $\$\eta_3$ for a ton in each of these places (respectively). I will set up my prices in such a way that

$$(3)\begin{cases} \eta_1 - \pi_1 \leq 5 \\ \eta_2 - \pi_1 \leq 6 \\ \eta_3 - \pi_1 \leq 3 \\ \eta_1 - \pi_2 \leq 3 \\ \eta_2 - \pi_2 \leq 5 \\ \eta_3 - \pi_2 \leq 4 \end{cases} \qquad \eta_i,\ \pi_j \geq 0$$

The manager of the firm that needs product S is then forced to agree that given the transportation costs he will be better off if he lets the transportation specialist take care of transportation. The deal is therefore closed to

the satisfaction of the transportation specialist. But the latter has some
freedom in choosing his prices (he promised only that constraints (3) will be
satisfied). Since he wants to maximize his return, he wants

$$400 \; \eta_1 + 300 \; \eta_2 + 200 \; \eta_3 - 550 \; \pi_1 - 350 \; \pi_2 \; = w' \; (\text{Max})$$

Then we see (after defining $y_1 = \pi_1$, $y_2 = \pi_2$, $y_3 = \eta_1$, $y_4 = \eta_2$, $y_5 = \eta_3$)
that the transportation specialist's problem is precisely (D_2), the dual of
(P_2).

EXERCISES

1. Write the dual of the linear program

$$(P) \quad \begin{cases} 3x_1 + x_2 - 2x_3 = 4 \\ x_1 - 2x_2 + 3x_3 \leqslant 1 \\ 2x_1 + x_2 - x_3 \geqslant 2 \\ 3x_1 + 4x_2 + 2x_3 = z \; (\text{Min}) \end{cases} \qquad \begin{array}{l} x_1, x_2 \geqslant 0 \\ x_3 \lessgtr 0 \end{array}$$

2. <u>Show</u> (using the example following Remark 2) that graphical solution of
    (P_1) found in Section I.1(a) is in fact optimal. <u>Hint</u>: Use the
    corollary of Theorem 2.

3. We consider the linear program

$$(P) \quad \begin{cases} Ax \leqslant b, & x \geqslant 0 \\ cx = z \; (\text{Max}) \end{cases}$$

(P) is said to be "primal feasible" if $b \geqslant 0$ and "dual feasible" if $c \leqslant 0$.

   (a) Show that if (P) is primal feasible, (P) has an obvious feasible
solution.

   (b) Show that if (P) is dual feasible, (D) the dual of (P) has an obvious
feasible solution.

   (c) Show that if (P) is both primal and dual feasible, (P) has an obvious
optimal solution.

   (d) Show that if for an index i, we have

$$b_i < 0 \quad \text{and} \quad A_i \geqslant 0$$

(P) has no feasible solution.

(e)   Show that if for an index j we have

$$c^j > 0 \qquad \text{and} \qquad A^j \leqslant 0$$

(P) has no optimal solution.

4.   Consider the linear program

$$(P) \begin{cases} 2x_1 & + & x_2 & \leqslant & 6 \\ x_1 & - & x_2 & \leqslant & 1 \\ x_1 & + & x_2 & \leqslant & 3 \\ 3x_1 & + & 2x_2 & = & z \ (\text{Max}) \end{cases} \qquad x_1, \ x_2 \geqslant 0$$

(a)   Write (D), the dual of (P).

(b)   Check that $x_1 = 2$, $x_2 = 1$, $y_1 = 0$, $y_2 = \frac{1}{2}$, $y_3 = \frac{5}{2}$
are feasible solutions to (P) and (D), respectively. Conclusion?

5.   Write the dual of linear program of Exercise 1.5.   A competitor Y of
the firm X that sells flours M and N decides to sell nutrients A, B, C, and
D directly. Y will sell A, B, C, and D in the proportions indicated in
Exercise 1.5.   He wants to be competitive with X and maximize his profit.

(a)   Show that the problem of Y is a linear program. Write down this
linear program.

(b)   Show that the best price system for Y is to sell D at some price
(what price?) and to give away A, B, and C (recall that the proportions of A,
B, C, and D sold are given).

(c)   Deduce from the preceding that the graphical solution of the linear
program of Exercise 1.5 is in fact optimal.

6.   We consider the following "game" problem:

Minimize δ under the following constraints:

$$(P) \begin{cases} x \geq 0 \\ \sum\limits_{j=1}^{n} x_j = 1 \\ A_i x \leqslant \delta \qquad\qquad i = 1, 2, \ldots, m \end{cases}$$

Show that (P) is a linear program, the dual of which can be written

$$\text{(D)} \begin{cases} \text{Maximize} \quad \lambda \quad \text{under the following constraints:} \\ y \geq 0 \\ y \ A^j \geq \lambda \qquad\qquad j = 1,2,\ldots,n \\ \sum_{i=1}^{m} y^i = 1 \end{cases}$$

(where A is a given $m \times n$-matrix).

7. A function $f: E \to R$ is said to be "superadditive" (resp. "subadditive") if

$$f(x_1 + x_2) \geq f(x_2) + f(x_2) \quad (\text{resp. } f(x_1 + x_2) \leq f(x_1) + f(x_2))$$

$$x_1, \ x_2 \ \varepsilon E$$

Show that the value of the objective at the optimum of

$$\text{(P)} \begin{cases} Ax \leq b \qquad x \geq 0 \\ cx = z \ (\text{Max}) \end{cases}$$

is a superadditive function of b and a subadditive function of c.

8. Write the dual of linear program of Exercise I.7.

9. Show that the feasible solution proposed for the transportation problem of Exercise I.6 is in fact an optimal one.
(Hint: Try a solution to the dual given by $\pi_j - \eta_i = c_{ij}$ whenever $x_{ij} > 0$.)

10. Let A be an $m \times m$-matrix "symmetric" (i.e., $A^T = A$). The following linear program is said to be symmetric:

$$\text{(P)} \begin{cases} Ax \leq b \qquad\qquad x \geq 0 \\ (b^T)x = z \ (\text{Max}) \end{cases}$$

Show that if the linear system

$$Ax = b$$

has a solution with $x \geq 0$, this solution is an optimal solution to (P).

11. Let $P_1, P_2, \ldots, P_n$ be n points of a network. A commodity is produced in P_1 and consumed in P_n. To each couple (P_i, P_j) we associate a nonnegative number c_{ij}: the maximum quantity of commodity that can be shipped from i to j in one day.

(a) Write, as a linear program, the problem that consists of sending a maximum amount of commodity from P_1 to P_n (the flow is conservative, i.e., there is no accumulation of commodity at any node). What is the number of constraints, the number of variables?

(b) Write the dual of this problem.

12. Show that in linear program (P_2) inequalities can be replaced by equations without adding slack variables. Prove that if $(\eta_1, \eta_2, \eta_3, \pi_1, \pi_2)$ is a feasible solution to the dual of (P_2), so is

$$(\eta_1 + a, \eta_2 + a, \eta_3 + a, \pi_1 + a, \pi_2 + a) \qquad a \in \mathbb{R}$$

and give an economic interpretation.

Chapter III. Elements of the Theory of Linear Systems

If we look at a linear program in standard form,

$$(P) \quad \begin{cases} Ax=b & x \geqslant 0 \\ \\ cx = z \ (Max) \end{cases}$$

we can see it is made of:

1. A system of linear equations $Ax = b$ (we also say a "linear system").

2. A set of nonnegativity constraints on the variables $x \geqslant 0$.

3. An objective function $cx = z$, which we try to make maximum.

Thus one must not be surprised in finding that the theory of linear systems plays a central role in linear programming. The goal of this chapter is to recall elements of this theory that will be needed in the sequel. In the first section we define the concept of "solution" of a (general) linear system (which may contain a number of equations smaller than, greater than, or equal to the number of unknowns) and of redundancy. In Sections 2 and 3 we show how manipulations on the equations of a linear system can be viewed as matrix multiplication of the matrix of coefficients $[A,b]$ of the system. Finally, in Section 4 we introduce the very important "pivot operation" and describe (without proof) how a linear system can be solved through a sequence of pivot operations.

In this chapter (as in the preceding ones) A is an $m \times n$-matrix, b is an m-column vector, and c is an n-row vector. Consider the linear system

$$(1) \ Ax = b$$

In detached coefficient form, (1) is written

$$(1') \quad \begin{cases} A_1^1 x_1 + A_1^2 x_2 + \ldots + A_1^n x_n = b_1 \\ A_2^1 x_1 + A_2^2 x_2 + \ldots + A_2^n x_n = b_2 \\ \quad \vdots \qquad \vdots \qquad \qquad \vdots \qquad \vdots \\ A_m^1 x_1 + A_m^2 x_2 + \ldots + A_m^n x_n = b_m \end{cases}$$

(1) can also be written

$$(1'') \ A_i x = b_i \qquad i = 1,2,\ldots,m$$

1.   Solution of Linear Systems (Definition); Redundancy

It is obvious to anyone that the two (systems of) equations

$$\text{(S)} \quad x_1 + x_2 - 1 = 0$$

$$\text{(S')} \quad 2x_1 + 2x_2 - 2 = 0$$

are, in fact, identical. We now define more rigorously the equivalence of
linear systems.

Definition 1: Let $\hat{A}$ be an $\hat{m} \times n$-matrix and $\hat{b}$ be an $\hat{m}$-column vector. We say
that linear system (1) is "equivalent to" the linear system

$$\hat{A}x = \hat{b}$$

if and only if these two systems have the same solution set, i.e.,

$$\{x \mid \hat{A}x = \hat{b}\} = \{x \mid Ax = b\}$$

Theorem 1:   Let y be an m-row vector. (1) is equivalent to

$$\text{(}\hat{1}\text{)} \quad \begin{cases} Ax = b \\ (yA)x = yb \end{cases}$$

(Note that yA is an n-row vector and yb is a scalar; $(\hat{1})$ is a system with m + 1
equations.)

Proof: Let $\bar{x}$ be a solution of (1). We have

$$A_i \bar{x} = b_i \quad \text{for } i = 1, 2, \ldots, m$$

Multiplying the ith equality by y^i and adding, we get

$$yA\bar{x} = yb$$

Thus $\bar{x}$ is a solution of $(\hat{1})$. Conversely if $\bar{x}$ is a solution of $(\hat{1})$, it is a
solution of (1).

Definition 2:   An equation that belongs to a linear system is said to be
"redundant" if it is a linear combination of the other equations of the system.
If a system contains a redundant equation, the system itself is said to be
redundant.

Remark 1: $(m + 1)^{st}$ equation of $(\hat{1})$ is, by construction, a redundant one. In
general, linear system (1) will contain a redundant equation if there exists an
m-row vector y such that

$$\text{(2)} \quad yA = 0, \quad yb = 0, \quad y \neq 0$$

The ith equation of (1) is then redundant if $y^i \neq 0$.

Theorem 2:   Assume that an equation of system (1) is redundant and denote by
$(\tilde{1})$ the linear system obtained in deleting this redundant equation.   Then (1)
and $(\tilde{1})$ are equivalent.

Proof: Is the same as the proof of Theorem 1.   If $\overline{x}$ is a solution of $(\tilde{1})$, it
satisfies the redundant equation and thus (1).   If $\overline{x}$ is a solution of (1), it
is also a solution of $(\tilde{1})$.

Remark 2:   A redundant equation can thus be deleted from a linear system without changing the solution set: it "adds no information" about the system.
This is why it is called redundant.

    Great care must be taken of the following fact: Redundancy is a property
of an equation in relation to a whole system.   A system may contain several
redundant equations but after deletion of a single one of these, the system
might become nonredundant.

Definition 3:   A linear system (1) is said to be "inconsistent" if there
exists an m-row vector y such that

     (2*) $yA = 0, \quad yb \neq 0$

Remark 3:   From Theorem 1 it is apparent that if (2*) holds, then (1) has no
solution.   The $(m + 1)^{st}$ equation of $(\hat{1})$ would read

         $0x = \alpha \neq 0$

which is clearly infeasible.   In fact, we will see in Section 4 that if (1) has
no solution, then one can find y such that (2*) holds, so that a system is
inconsistent if and only if it has no solution.

    A linear system that is neither inconsistent nor redundant is said to be
of "full rank."   In this case, from (2) and (2*) we have

     (2') $yA = 0 \rightarrow y = 0$

Examples: 1.   Consider the linear systems

$$(E_1) \quad \begin{cases} x_1 & + 2x_2 & + x_3 & = 5 \\ 2x_1 & + 3x_2 & + x_3 & = 7 \\ x_1 & + 3x_2 & + 2x_3 & = 8 \end{cases}$$

$$(E_2) \quad \begin{cases} x_1 & & - x_3 & = -1 \\ & x_2 & + x_3 & = 3 \end{cases}$$

$$(E_3) \quad \begin{cases} x_1 + x_2 = 2 \\ x_2 + x_3 = 3 \end{cases}$$

$$(E_4) \quad \begin{cases} x_2 + x_3 = 3 \\ x_1 + x_2 = 2 \end{cases}$$

(E_1) is redundant, as can be seen by taking $y = (3, -1, -1)$. Deleting the first equation, we get the equivalent system

$$(E_1') \quad \begin{cases} 2x_1 + 3x_2 + x_3 = 7 \\ x_1 + 3x_2 + 2x_3 = 8 \end{cases}$$

Taking $y = (1, -1)$, we get the first equation of (E_2). Taking $y = (-\frac{1}{3}, \frac{2}{3})$, we get the second equation of (E_2). Similarly, it can be shown that equations of (E_1') can be generated by linear combination of those of (E_2). Thus, from Theorem 1, (E_1') and (E_2) are equivalent. We leave it to the reader to prove that (E_2) and (E_3) are equivalent.

By looking at (E_1'), we cannot say much about its solution set, whereas (E_2), (E_3), and (E_4) are written in a way that gives directly an explicit formulation of the solution set. In (E_2), we can consider that x_3 is a parameter (or a "free variable"; we will also say a "nonbasic variable") that can be given arbitrary values, corresponding values of x_1 and x_2 being $x_1 = -1 + x_3$, $x_2 = 3 - x_3$.

$$\mathcal{D}(E_2) = \{x_1, x_2, x_3 |\ x_1 = -1 + x_3, \ x_2 = 3 - x_3\}$$

Similarly, in (E_3), x_2 is the nonbasic variable

$$\mathcal{D}(E_3) = \{x_1, x_2, x_3 |\ x_1 = 2 - x_2, \ x_3 = 3 - x_2\}$$

2. Consider the linear system

$$(E_1^*) \quad \begin{cases} x_1 + 2x_2 + x_3 = 5 \\ 2x_1 + 3x_2 + x_3 = 7 \\ x_1 + 3x_2 + 2x_3 = 7 \end{cases}$$

Taking $y = (3, -1, -1)$, we get (2*), which shows that (E_1^*) is inconsistent.

These examples should help the reader to understand what we mean by "solving linear system (1)."

Definition 4:   Solving system (1) is either:

      (a) Proving that (1) does not have any solution, or

      (b) Finding an *equivalent system*

$$(3) \qquad \hat{A}x = \hat{b}$$

such that there exists $J \subset \{1,2,\ldots,n\}$ for which $\hat{A}^J$ is, up to a permutation of rows or columns, the unit matrix.

In this case, we say that (1) has been solved with respect to the set J of indices (or variables). Set J is called "basic." The complementary set

$$\bar{J} = \{1,2,\ldots,n\}\backslash J$$

is the "nonbasic" one.

Remark 4: (E_2), (E_3), (E_4) may be considered, according to Definition 4, as solutions of (E_1) with respect to basic sets $\{1,2\}, \{1,3\}, \{1,3\}$, respectively.

(E_3) and (E_4) are obviously the "same" system. Since we want to say that (E_4) is a solution of (E_1) as well as (E_3), we introduced the fact that $\hat{A}^J$ is "up to a permutation of rows or columns" the unit matrix.

Remark 5:   Suppose that (3) is a solution of (1) with respect to basic set J. (3) can be written, by separating basic columns from nonbasic ones,

$$(3') \qquad \hat{A}^J x_J + \hat{A}^{\bar{J}} x_{\bar{J}} = b$$

Since $\hat{A}^J$ is by assumption, up to a permutation of rows, the $m \times m$-unit matrix, one is tempted to write (3') in the following way:

$$(3'') \qquad x_J + \hat{A}^{\bar{J}} x_{\bar{J}} = b$$

which makes it appear clearly that the system has been solved with respect to the basic set J of variables (give arbitrary values to the nonbasic variables and deduce, by a few multiplications and additions, the corresponding values of basic variables).

But this formalism assumes that we know which basic variable appears in which equation, i.e., that there is a (perfect) order on the indices in J. So when one reads (3"), one must take J as an ordered set or a "list." For instance, (E_3) is the solution of (E_1) with respect to $(1,3)$, whereas (E_4) is the solution with respect to $(3,1)$.

Form (3") is very convenient and will be used in the sequel. The reader is warned that especially when we actually compute solutions of systems, this formalism contains a slight ambiguity that necessitates some care (see, for example, Remark V.1).

Remark 6: Recall that we defined "solving" system (1) with respect to the (ordered) set of indices J as finding an equivalent system

$$(3) \qquad \hat{A}x = \hat{b}$$

for which $\hat{A}$ is the unit matrix.   (3) cannot contain a redundant equation. This can be seen either by going back to Remark 1 or by noting that no equation of (3) can be obtained as a linear combination of the other equations of the system, since each equation of (3) contains a variable that is not contained in the other equations.

2. Solving Linear Systems Using Matrix Multiplication

Remark 7: Recall that we defined (Definition I.3) the product of $m \times n$-matrix A by $n \times q$-matrix B (or the product of B by A on its left) as being the $m \times q$-matrix C defined by

$$(4) \qquad c_i^j = \sum_{k=1}^{n} A_i^k B_k^j$$

Note that (4) can also be written

$$(4') \qquad c^j = AB^j$$

which means that to obtain the jth column of the product, we just have to multiply matrix A by the n-column vector B^j. In other words, the jth column of C just depends on A and on the jth column of B.

Remark 8: We leave it as an exercise (Exercise 5) to show that the matrix product is associative, i.e.,

$$A \times (B \times C) \;=\; (A \times B) \times C$$

if the product exists.

Definition 5: Let B be an $m \times m$-matrix and U be the $m \times m$-unit matrix (Definition I.12). If there exists an $m \times m$-matrix C such that

$$C \times B \;=\; U$$

then

      (a) B is said to be "regular."

      (b) C is said to be the inverse of B and is denoted B^{-1}.

If no such C exists, B is nonregular or "singular."

Remark 9: We leave it as an exercise to show the following properties:

      (i) $B \times B^{-1} = B^{-1} \times B = U$; $(B^{-1})^{-1} = B$; for a given B, B^{-1}, if it exists, is unique.

      (ii) Let B and C be two $m \times m$ nonsingular matrices. Then

$$(B \times C)^{-1} \;=\; C^{-1} \times B^{-1}$$

and thus $B \times C$ is nonsingular if B and C are nonsingular.

Theorem 3: Let B be a regular $m \times m$-matrix. Linear system (1) is equivalent to

    (5) $(BA) x \;=\; Bb$

(The property is true whether or not (1) is redundant).

Proof: Let $\bar{x}$ be a solution of (1). We have

$$A_i \bar{x} \;=\; b_i \qquad\qquad i = 1, 2, \ldots, m$$

multiplying the ith equality by B_k^i and adding, we get

$$\sum_{i=1}^{m} B_k^i A_i \bar{x} = \sum_{i-1}^{m} B_k^i b_i$$

which shows that $\bar{x}$ is a solution of (6).

Conversely, the same proof would show that if $\bar{x}$ is a solution of (5), it is also a solution of

$$(B^{-1}(BA))x = B^{-1}(Bb)$$

and thus of (1), since matrix products are associative.

Remark 10: As a consequence of Theorem 3, we see that to solve the full-rank linear system (1) with respect to the basic set J, "it suffices" to multiply both matrix A and vector b on their left by $B = (A^J)^{-1}$.

Thus, full-rank system (1) can be solved with respect to basic set J (in other words, J is a basic set with respect to which (1) can be solved) if A^J is square nonsingular.

We will see in the sequel how to solve (1) without explicitly computing $(A^J)^{-1}$.

Examples: 1. For system (E_1'), we have

$$A = \begin{bmatrix} 2 & 3 & 1 \\ 1 & 3 & 2 \end{bmatrix} \qquad \begin{bmatrix} 7 \\ 8 \end{bmatrix}$$

Take $J = 1,2$:

$$(A^J)^{-1} = \begin{bmatrix} 1 & -1 \\ -1/3 & 2/3 \end{bmatrix}$$

The reader will check that

$$(A^J)^{-1} A = \begin{bmatrix} 1 & 0 & -1 \\ 0 & 1 & 1 \end{bmatrix} \qquad (A^J)^{-1} b = \begin{bmatrix} -1 \\ 3 \end{bmatrix}$$

and we have the coefficients of (E_2).

2. Consider the system

$$
(6) \quad \begin{cases} 2x_1 - 3x_1 + 7x_3 - 2x_4 = 5 \\ 3x_1 + 4x_2 + 2x_3 - 3x_4 = 33 \end{cases}
$$

This system is nonredundant but $J = \{1,4\}$ is not a basic set. In effect, $A^{\{1,4\}}$ is singular. But $J = \{1,2\}$ is a basic set, as we will see later.

Remark 11: To keep this text as compact as possible, the following properties will be stated without proof:

1. Given any full-rank linear system

$$
(3) \quad \hat{A}x = \hat{b}
$$

   equivalent to the full-rank system (1), there exists a nonsingular matrix B such that

$$
\hat{A} = BA, \ \hat{b} = Bb
$$

2. A corollary of the preceding is that all full-rank equivalent systems have the same number of equations.

3. Thus, if (3) is equivalent to (1), and if (3) is full rank, $\hat{m} \le m$.

4. If (1) is a full-rank linear system, there exists J such that A^J is square nonsingular. Thus, if (1) is full rank, $m \le n$.

Definition 6: An "eta-matrix" is a unit matrix except for one of its columns. An eta-matrix of order m is thus completely specified when we are given:

   (a) The rank of its nontrivial column.
   (b) The m-column vector constituting this nontrivial column.

The eta-matrix with vector d being the rth column will be denoted

$$
D(r;d)
$$

Examples: The following are eta-matrices of order 4:

$$D_1 = D\left(3; \begin{bmatrix} 4 \\ 3 \\ 2 \\ 2 \end{bmatrix}\right) = \begin{bmatrix} 1 & 0 & 4 & 0 \\ 0 & 1 & 3 & 0 \\ 0 & 0 & 2 & 0 \\ 0 & 0 & 2 & 1 \end{bmatrix}$$

$$D_2 = D\left(1; \begin{bmatrix} 0 \\ 1 \\ 0 \\ 1 \end{bmatrix}\right) = \begin{bmatrix} 0 & 0 & 0 & 0 \\ 1 & 1 & 0 & 0 \\ 0 & 0 & 1 & 0 \\ 1 & 0 & 0 & 1 \end{bmatrix}$$

$$D_3 = D\left(1; \begin{bmatrix} 1 \\ 3 \\ 2 \\ 3 \end{bmatrix}\right) = \begin{bmatrix} 1 & 0 & 0 & 0 \\ 3 & 1 & 0 & 0 \\ 2 & 0 & 1 & 0 \\ 3 & 0 & 0 & 1 \end{bmatrix}$$

Remark 12:   We leave it as an exercise to prove the following properties:

(i)   The product of two eta-matrices $D(r;d)$ and $D'(r;d')$
(same r) is an eta-matrix $D(r,d'') = D(r;d) \times D'(r;d')$ with

$$d_i'' = \begin{cases} d_i' + d_i d_r' & \text{for } i \neq r \\ d_r d_r' & \text{for } i = r \end{cases}$$

(ii)   An eta-matrix $D(r;d)$ is nonsingular if and only if

$$d_r \neq 0$$

when this is the case, $D'(r;d') = (D(r;d))^{-1}$ is given by

$$d_i' = \begin{cases} -d_i/d_r & \text{for } i \neq r \\ 1/d_r & \text{for } i = r \end{cases}$$

Example: Let us go back to the preceding example. We see that D_2 is
singular, whereas

$$D_1^{-1} = \begin{bmatrix} 1 & 0 & -2 & 0 \\ 0 & 1 & -3/2 & 0 \\ 0 & 0 & 1/2 & 0 \\ 0 & 0 & -1 & 0 \end{bmatrix} \qquad D_3^{-1} = \begin{bmatrix} 1 & 0 & 0 & 0 \\ -3 & 1 & 0 & 0 \\ -2 & 0 & 1 & 0 \\ -3 & 0 & 0 & 1 \end{bmatrix}$$

3. Finding Equivalent Systems of Linear Equations: Elementary Row Operations

As announced in Remark 10, we will see how to solve (1) without computing $(A^J)^{-1}$.

Definition 7: Given the linear system

(1) $Ax = b$

we introduce two transformations:

(a) ER01(r,α): "Elementary row operation of the first kind," which
is specified by parameters $r \in \{1,2,\ldots,m\}$ and α (nonzero scalar),
consists in replacing the rth equation of (1),

$$A_r x = b_r$$

by

$$\alpha A_r x = \alpha b_r$$

leaving the other equations of the system as they are.

(b) ER02(r,k,β): "Elementary row operation of the second kind," which
is specified by parameters $r, k \in \{1,2,\ldots,m\}$, $r \neq k$, and
scalar β , consists in adding to the kth equation of (1) the
r^{th} equation multiplied by β . In other words, after ER02(r,k,β)
the kth equation of the linear system has become

$$A_k x + \beta A_r x = b_k + \beta b_r$$

the other equations being left unchanged.

Example: Consider the linear system

(6) $\begin{cases} 2x_1 - 3x_2 + 7x_3 - 2x_4 = 5 \\ 3x_1 + 4x_2 + 2x_3 - 3x_4 = 33 \end{cases}$

Apply ER01(1,1/2):

$$\begin{cases} x_1 - \dfrac{3}{2} x_2 + \dfrac{7}{2} x_3 - x_4 = \dfrac{5}{2} \\[2mm] 3 x_1 + 4 x_2 + 2 x_3 - 3x_4 = 33 \end{cases}$$

ER02(1,2,-3) gives

$$\begin{cases} x_1 - \dfrac{3}{2} x_2 + \dfrac{7}{2} x_3 - x_4 = \dfrac{5}{2} \\[2mm] \dfrac{17}{2} x_2 - \dfrac{17}{2} x_3 = \dfrac{51}{2} \end{cases}$$

ER01(2,2/17) gives

$$\begin{cases} x_1 - \dfrac{3}{2} x_2 + \dfrac{7}{2} x_3 - x_4 = \dfrac{5}{2} \\[2mm] x_2 - x_3 = 3 \end{cases}$$

ER01(2,1,3/2) gives

$$\begin{cases} x_1 + 2 x_3 - x_4 = 7 \\[2mm] x_2 - x_3 = 3 \end{cases}$$

We see in this example that a sequence of well-chosen elementary row operations have "solved" the linear system. We will now recall the proof that such
manipulations are valid.

Note that system (6) has been solved with respect to basic variables
{1,2}. If we wanted to solve it with respect to {1,4}, after applying
ER02(1,2,-3), we would have been blocked: the coefficient of x_4 is zero in
the second equation.

Theorem 4: Elementary row operations introduced in Definition 6 do not change
the solution set of (1).

Proof: Since $\alpha \neq 0$, $\alpha A_r x = \alpha_b r$ has the same solution set as $A_r x = b_r$.

Now, by ERO2(r,k,β), the system

(1") $A_i x = b_i$ $i = 1, \ldots, m$

is transformed into the system

(1*) $\begin{cases} A_i x = b_i & i \neq k \\ A_k x + \beta A_r x = b_k + \beta b_r \end{cases}$

Let $\bar{x}$ be a solution of (1"); we have

$$A_i \bar{x} = b_i \qquad \text{for} \quad i = 1, \ldots, m$$

and, in particular,

$$A_k \bar{x} = b_k$$

$$A_r \bar{x} = b_r$$

which implies that

$$\beta A_r \bar{x} = \beta b_r$$

and thus

$$A_k \bar{x} + \beta A_r \bar{x} = b_k + \beta b_r$$

so that $\bar{x}$ is a solution of (1*).

Conversely, if $\bar{x}$ is a solution of (1*),

$$A_i \bar{x} = b_i \qquad \text{for} \quad i = 1, \ldots, m, \quad i \neq j$$

so that

$$A_k \bar{x} = b_r$$

and

(*) $\beta A_r \bar{x} = \beta b_r$

But we also have

$$A_k \bar{x} + \beta A_r \bar{x} = b_k + \beta b_r$$

which by subtraction of (*) gives

$$A_k \bar{x} = b_k$$

so that $\bar{x}$ is also a solution of (1'').

Remark 13: An elementary row operation changes the matrix [A,b] of coefficients of system (1), providing -- from Theorem 1 -- an equivalent system. The
same change would have been obtained through matrix multiplication.

ER01(r,α) consists, in fact, in multiplying matrix [A,b] on its left by
the eta-matrix

$$T(ER01(r,\alpha)) = D(r;d) \quad \text{(see Definition 6)}$$
with
$$d_i = \begin{cases} 0 & \text{if } i \neq r \\ \alpha & \text{if } i = r \end{cases}$$

Similarly, ER02(r,k,β) consists of multiplying [A,b] on its left by the
eta-matrix:

$$T(ER02(r,k,\beta)) = D(r;d)$$
with
$$d_i = \begin{cases} \beta & \text{if } i = k \\ 0 & \text{if } i \neq k, i \neq r \\ 1 & \text{if } i = r \end{cases}$$

Verification of these facts is straightforward calculus.

Example: Let us go back to the solution of system (6):

$$A = \begin{bmatrix} 2 & -3 & 7 & -2 \\ 3 & 4 & 2 & -3 \end{bmatrix} \qquad b = \begin{bmatrix} 5 \\ 33 \end{bmatrix}$$

$$T(ER01(1, 1/2)) = \begin{bmatrix} 1/2 & 0 \\ 0 & 1 \end{bmatrix}, \qquad T(ER02(1,2,-3)) = \begin{bmatrix} 1 & 0 \\ -3 & 1 \end{bmatrix}$$

$$T(ER01(2, 2/17)) = \begin{bmatrix} 1 & 0 \\ 0 & 2/17 \end{bmatrix}, \qquad T(ER02(2,1,3/2)) = \begin{bmatrix} 1 & 3/2 \\ 0 & 1 \end{bmatrix}$$

and the product

$$B = T(ER02(2,1,\tfrac{3}{2})) \times T(ER01(2,\tfrac{2}{17})) \times T(ER02(1,2,-3)) \times T(ER01(1,\tfrac{1}{2}))$$

is equal to

$$B = \begin{bmatrix} 4/17 & 3/17 \\ -3/17 & 2/17 \end{bmatrix}$$

The reader is invited to check that

$$B \times A = \begin{bmatrix} 1 & 0 & 2 & -1 \\ 0 & 1 & -1 & 0 \end{bmatrix} \quad ; \quad B \times b = \begin{bmatrix} 7 \\ 3 \end{bmatrix}$$

or, in other words that

$$B = \begin{bmatrix} 2 & -3 \\ 3 & 4 \end{bmatrix}^{-1} = (A^J)^{-1} \qquad J = \{1,2\}$$

4. Pivot Operation

Definition 8: Let $[A,b]$ be the $m \times (n+1)$-matrix called the "augmented matrix" of system (1). The following sequence of elementary row operations is called a "pivot operation on the element A_r^s" $(1 \le r \le m; \; 1 \le s \le n; \; A_r^s \ne 0)$:

> Perform $ER01(r, 1/A_r^s)$
>
> for all $i = 1,2,\ldots,m$ except $i = r$ do
> | $ER02(r,i, -A_i^s)$
> end for all

Remark 14: In the pivot operation, $ER01(r, 1/A_r^s)$ is performed before entering the loop. Thus when performing elementary row operations of the second kind (in the loop) matrix A has been changed in such a way that $A_r^s = 1$.

Theorem 5: The pivot operation on A_r^s is possible if and only if $A_r^s \ne 0$. In this case, the solution of (1) is not changed by the pivot operation.

Proof: If $A_r^s = 0$, $1/A_r^s$ is not defined and the pivot operation cannot be performed. If $A_r^s \neq 0$, the pivot operation is a sequence of valid elementary row operations. The property is then a consequence of Theorem 4.

Example: Linear system (6) has been solved, in the example following Definition 6, by the succession of two pivot operations:

(a) The first pivot operation on $A_1^1 = 2$ gives the new linear system (characterized by matrix $\hat{A}$ and vector $\hat{b}$)

$$\hat{A} = \begin{bmatrix} 1 & -3/2 & 7/2 & -1 \\ 0 & 17/2 & -17/2 & 0 \end{bmatrix} \qquad \hat{b} = \begin{bmatrix} 5/2 \\ 51/2 \end{bmatrix}$$

(b) The second pivot operation on $A_2^2 = 17/2$ gives

$$\hat{\hat{A}} = \begin{bmatrix} 1 & 0 & 2 & -1 \\ 0 & 1 & -1 & 0 \end{bmatrix} \qquad \hat{\hat{b}} = \begin{bmatrix} 7 \\ 3 \end{bmatrix}$$

the "solution" of (5).

We note that

$$\hat{A} = DA \qquad \hat{b} = Db$$

with

$$D = \begin{bmatrix} 1/2 & 0 \\ -3/2 & 1 \end{bmatrix} = T(ERO2(1,2,-3)) \times T(ERO1(1,1/2))$$

and

$$\hat{\hat{A}} = \hat{D}\hat{A} \qquad \hat{\hat{b}} = \hat{D}\hat{A}$$

with

$$\hat{D} = \begin{bmatrix} 1 & 3/17 \\ 0 & 2/17 \end{bmatrix} = T(ERO2(2,1,3/2)) \times T(ERO1(2,2/17))$$

Remark 15: It is a direct consequence of the definition of pivot operation that it is defined uniquely in terms of the augmented matrix of the system. In fact, given a matrix and a nonzero element, A_r^s, we can define a pivot operation on this element without speaking of the linear system. Let $[\hat{A},\hat{b}]$ be the augmented matrix of (1) after a pivot operation on A_r^s has been performed. We have

$$(7) \quad \hat{A}_i^j = \begin{cases} A_i^j - A_r^j A_i^s / A_r^s & \text{if } i \neq r \\ A_r^j / A_r^s & \text{if } i = r \end{cases} \qquad \hat{b}_i = \begin{cases} b_i - b_r A_i^s / A_r^s & \text{if } i \neq r \\ b_r / A_r^s & \text{if } i = r \end{cases}$$

We note that for $j = s$, we have

$$\hat{A}_i^s = \begin{cases} 0 & \text{if } i \neq r \\ 1 & \text{if } i = r \end{cases}$$

Thus the pivot operation "creates" or "makes appear" a unit column in the sth column of A. Moreover, if $A_r^j = 0$ $(j \neq s)$ and $A_r^s = 1$, then

$$\hat{A}^j = A^j .$$

Remark 16: The pivot operation is a sequence of elementary row operations and each of these elementary row operations can be expressed as the multiplication of the augmented matrix of the system $[A,b]$ by a nonsingular matrix on its left (see Remark 13). Thus the pivot operation itself can be expressed as the multiplication of matrix $[A,b]$ on its left by a nonsingular matrix $P_i(r,s)$, which is the product of the matrices corresponding to elementary row operations composing the pivot operation. $Pi(r,s)$, called the "pivot matrix," is defined by

$$Pi(r,s) = T(ERO2(r, m, - A_m^s)) \times \ldots \times T(ERO2(r, r+1, - A_{r+1}^s))$$
$$\times \ T(ERO2(r,r-1, - A_{r-1}^s)) \times \ldots \times T(ERO2 (r,1,-A_1^s)) \times T(ERO1(r,1/A_r^s))$$

$Pi(r,s)$ is the product of m eta-matrices all with the nontrivial column in the rth position. Thus, from Remark 12, $Pi(r,s)$ is an eta-matrix

$$Pi(r,s) = D(r;d)$$

with

$$d_i = \begin{cases} -A_i^s / A_r^s & \text{for } i \neq r \\ 1/A_r^s & \text{for } i = r \end{cases}$$

In other words, we have

$$[\hat{A},\hat{b}] \; = \; \text{Pi}(r,s) \quad [A,b]$$

and

$$
\text{Pi}(r,s) =
\begin{array}{c}
\quad\quad\quad\quad\quad\quad r^{th}\ column \\
\left[
\begin{array}{ccccccccccc}
1 & 0 & 0 & \cdots & 0 & -A_1^s/A_r^s & 0 & \cdots & 0 & 0 & 0 \\
0 & 1 & 0 & \cdots & 0 & -A_2^s/A_r^s & 0 & \cdots & 0 & 0 & 0 \\
0 & 0 & 1 & \cdots & 0 & -A_3^s/A_r^s & 0 & \cdots & 0 & 0 & 0 \\
  &   &   & \ddots &   &   &   &   &   &   &   \\
  &   &   &   & 0 & -A_{r-2}^s/A_r^s & 0 &   &   &   &   \\
0 & 0 & 0 &   & 1 & -A_{r-1}^s/A_r^s & 0 &   & 0 & 0 & 0 \\
0 & 0 & 0 & \cdots & 0 & 1/A_r^s & 0 & \cdots & 0 & 0 & 0 \\
0 & 0 & 0 &   & 0 & -A_{r+1}^s/A_r^s & 1 &   & 0 & 0 & 0 \\
  &   &   &   & 0 & -A_{r+2}^s/A_r^s & 0 &   &   &   &   \\
0 & 0 & 0 &   & 0 & -A_{m-2}^s/A_r^s & 0 &   & 1 & 0 & 0 \\
0 & 0 & 0 & \cdots & 0 & -A_{m-1}^s/A_r^s & 0 & \cdots & 0 & 1 & 0 \\
0 & 0 & 0 & \cdots & 0 & -A_m^s/A_r^s & 0 & \cdots & 0 & 0 & 1
\end{array}
\right] & r^{th}\ row
\end{array}
$$

Remark 17: It is a direct consequence of what precedes (see, in particular, Remark 15), that the solution of a linear system (1) with respect to a basic set of indices J can be obtained through a sequence of pivot operations performed successively on the indices of columns $s \in J$ and indices of rows r, such that $A_r^s \neq 0$. We will not prove this fact, which is not used in the sequel. The corresponding method is known in the literature as the "Gauss-Jordan elimination method."

In this process, redundant equations will be automatically eliminated. At some time of the procedure, a redundant equation will read $0x = 0$. In the same way, if (1) has no solution, then at some time of the procedure an impossible equation $0x = \alpha \neq 0$ will appear.

If we start with a full-rank system (1) and if $D^{(1)}, D^{(2)}, \ldots, D^{(m)}$ denote the successive pivot matrices, we will have

(8) $$(A^J)^{-1} = D^{(m)} \times D^{(m-1)} \times \ldots \times D^{(2)} \times D^{(1)} .$$

Examples: 1. Let us solve the system

$$(E_1) \quad \begin{cases} x_1 + 2x_2 + x_3 = 5 \\ 2x_1 + 3x_2 + x_3 = 7 \\ x_1 + 3x_2 + 2x_3 = 8 \end{cases}$$

by the Gauss-Jordan elimination method. First, perform a pivot operation on $A_1^1 = 1$:

$$(\hat{E}_1) \quad \begin{cases} x_1 + 2x_2 + x_3 = 5 \\ - x_2 - x_3 = -3 \\ x_2 + x_3 = 3 \end{cases}$$

Now, perform a pivot operation on A_2^2:

$$(\hat{\hat{E}}_1) \quad \begin{cases} x_1 \quad - x_3 = -1 \\ x_2 + x_3 = 3 \\ 0x_2 + 0x_3 = 0 \end{cases}$$

The redundant equation is apparent and $(\hat{\hat{E}}_1)$ is identical to (E_2).

2. Let us now try to solve system (E_1^*). The same sequence of pivot operations as in the preceding example leads to

$$(\hat{\hat{E}}_1^*) \quad \begin{cases} x_1 \quad -x_3 = -1 \\ x_2 + x_3 = 3 \\ 0x_2 + 0x_3 = 1 \end{cases}$$

3. Solve

$$\begin{cases} x_1 + x_2 + x_3 - x_4 = 1 \\ x_1 - x_2 + x_3 - 3x_4 = 3 \\ x_1 + 2x_2 - x_3 + x_4 = 4 \end{cases}$$

with respect to the basic set $J = \{1,2,3\}$, the augmented matrix of this system being

$$[A,b] = \begin{bmatrix} 1 & 1 & 1 & -1 & 1 \\ 1 & -1 & 1 & -3 & 3 \\ 1 & 2 & -1 & 1 & 4 \end{bmatrix}$$

The system is solved through the sequence of pivot operations shown in the following tableau:

x_1	x_2	x_3	x_4	b
1	1	1	-1	1
1	-1	1	-3	3
1	2	-1	1	4
1	1	1	-1	1
0	-2	0	-2	2
0	1	-2	2	3
1	0	1	-2	2
0	1	0	1	-1
0	0	-2	1	4
1	0	0	3/2	4
0	1	0	1	-1
0	0	1	-1/2	-2

pivot operation
r=1, s=1
$$D^{(1)} = \begin{bmatrix} 1 & 0 & 0 \\ -1 & 1 & 0 \\ -1 & 0 & 1 \end{bmatrix}$$

pivot operation
r=2, s=2
$$D^{(2)} = \begin{bmatrix} 1 & 1/2 & 0 \\ 0 & -1/2 & 0 \\ 0 & 1/2 & 1 \end{bmatrix}$$

pivot operation
r=3, s=3
$$D^{(3)} = \begin{bmatrix} 1 & 0 & 1/2 \\ 0 & 1 & 0 \\ 0 & 0 & -1/2 \end{bmatrix}$$

and it is easy to check that

$$D^{(3)} \times D^{(2)} \times D^{(1)} \ = \ \begin{bmatrix} -1/4 & 3/4 & 1/2 \\ 1/2 & -1/2 & 0 \\ 3/4 & -1/4 & -1/2 \end{bmatrix} = \begin{bmatrix} 1 & 1 & 1 \\ 1 & -1 & 1 \\ 1 & 2 & -1 \end{bmatrix}^{-1} \ = \ (A^J)^{-1}$$

EXERCISES

1. Prove that the following two linear systems are equivalent:

$$\begin{cases} 2x_1 + 5x_2 + 3x_3 \ = \ 12 \\ x_1 + 2x_2 - x_3 \ = \ 5 \end{cases}$$

$$\begin{cases} x_1 \quad\quad - 11x_3 \ = \ 1 \\ \quad\quad x_2 + 5x_3 \ = \ 2 \end{cases}$$

2. Is the following linear system redundant?

$$\begin{cases} x_1 + x_2 - x_3 \ = \ 1 \\ 2x_1 + 3x_2 + x_3 \ = \ 2 \\ x_1 - x_2 - 7x_3 \ = \ 1 \end{cases}$$

3. Solve the system

$$\begin{cases} x_1 + x_2 + x_3 + 10x_4 + 2x_5 \ = \ 10 \\ x_1 + x_2 - x_3 + \quad\quad + 4x_5 \ = \ 6 \\ 2x_1 + 3x_2 - 2x_3 + 3x_4 + 10x_5 \ = \ 17 \end{cases}$$

with respect to the basis $J = \{1,2,3\}$.

4. Consider the system

$$\begin{cases} 2x_1 + 3x_2 + 4x_3 \ = \ 1 \\ x_1 - x_2 + x_3 \ = \ 2 \\ 4x_1 + 3x_2 + 2x_3 \ = \ -1 \\ 3x_1 - x_2 - x_3 \ = \ 0 \end{cases}$$

(a)   Try to solve this system by a succession of pivot operations. Clearly define these operations.

(b)   Show that any equation of this system is redundant. Discard the fourth equation.

(c)   Suppose that we want to know the values of x_1, x_2, x_3 for any right-hand side. System (1) can be written as

(2)
$$\begin{cases} 2x_1 + 3x_2 + 4x_3 = y_1 \\ x_1 - x_2 + x_3 = y_2 \\ 4x_1 + 3x_2 + 2x_3 = y_3 \end{cases}$$

Solve this system (i.e., give the expressions for x_1, x_2, x_3 as functions of y_1, y_2, y_3) by a succession of pivot operations and write the three pivot matrices D^1, D^2, D^3.

(d)   What is the inverse of

$$A = \begin{bmatrix} 2 & 3 & 4 \\ 1 & -1 & 1 \\ 4 & 3 & 2 \end{bmatrix} ?$$

(e)   Compute the product $D^3 \times D^2 \times D^1$ and explain your result.

5.   Prove that matrix product is associative.

6.   Prove Remark 9.

7.   Prove Remarks 12 and 13.

8.   Prove that if B and C are nonsingular $n \times m$-matrices, then $B \times C$ is nonsingular. Deduce that pivot matrix $Pi(r,s)$ introduced in Remark 16 is nonsingular. Can you prove this fact directly by finding $(Pi(r,s))^{-1}$?

9.   Let
$$(P) \begin{cases} Ax = b \qquad x \geq 0 \\ cx = z(max) \end{cases}$$

be a linear program in standard form and assume that any equation of the system
$$Ax = b$$

is redundant, but that after deletion of any equation, the system obtained is nonredundant. What can be said about the dual of (P) ?

Chapter IV. Bases and Basic Solutions of Linear Programs

In this brief chapter, we introduce some fundamental concepts in linear programming: bases, basic solutions, canonical form associated with a given basis, feasible basis, optimal basis. These notions are a key to the understanding of the simplex algorithm.

We start with a linear program in standard form:

$$(P) \quad \begin{cases} Ax &= b \qquad\qquad x \geq 0 \\ cx &= z \ (\text{Max}) \end{cases}$$

where A is, as before, an $m \times n$-matrix, b is an m-column vector, and c is an n-row rector. Moreover, we assume in this chapter that the linear system

$$(1) \qquad\qquad Ax = b$$

is full rank (i.e., not redundant and not inconsistent). This implies that $m \leq n$ (see Remarks III.3 and III.11).

1. Bases of a Linear Program

Definition 1: Given a linear program (P) in standard form such that (1) is full rank, we call the *"basis"* of (P) a set $J \in \{1,2,\ldots,n\}$ of indices such that A^J is square nonsingular.

In other words, J is a basis if and only if linear system (1) can be solved with respect to J (see Section III.1 and III.2).

If J is a basis of (P), A^J is the "basis matrix" corresponding to J.

Definition 2: To a basis J of linear program (P), we associate a particular solution of (1):

$$\begin{cases} x_J &= (A^J)^{-1} b \\ x_j &= 0 \qquad\qquad j \notin J \end{cases}$$

This solution is called the "basic solution," corresponding to basis J .

In other words, the basic solution corresponding to basis J is the solution of linear system (1), which we obtain in making all nonbasic variables equal to zero.

Example: By addition of slack variables x_3, x_4, x_5 , linear program (P_1) has been written in standard form in Section I.4.

$$(P_1) \quad \begin{cases} 2x_1 + x_3 + x_3 &= 8 \\ x_1 + 2x_2 + x_4 &= 7 \\ x_2 + x_5 &= 3 \\ 4x_1 + 5x_2 &= z \text{ (Max)} \end{cases} \qquad x_i \geq 0 \quad \text{for} \quad i=1,2,\ldots,5$$

$\{3,4,5\}$ is obviously a basis of (P_1) . The corresponding basic solution is

$$x_1 = x_2 = 0 , \quad x_3 = 8 , \quad x_4 = 7 , \quad x_5 = 3$$

We will see later that $\{1,2,5\}$ is also a basis. The corresponding basic solution is

$$x_1 = 3 , \quad x_2 = 2 , \quad x_3 = x_4 = 0 , \quad x_5 = 1$$

Remark 1: It is important to notice that the basic solution associated to a given basis is unique.

However, given $\bar{x}$, a solution of (1), there may exist several bases for which $\bar{x}$ is the corresponding basic solution. In this case, there is "degeneracy." We will come back to problems posed by degeneracy in Chapter V.

A trivial case of degeneracy is the case where b =0 . Then $\bar{x} = 0$ is the basic solution corresponding to every basis. In the case

$$\begin{cases} x_1 + 2x_2 + x_3 + 2x_4 &= 3 \\ 2x_1 + x_2 + 5x_3 + 3x_4 &= 3 \\ 3x_1 + 4x_2 + 5x_3 + 7x_4 &= 7 \end{cases}$$

the solution $x_1 = x_2 = 1$, $x_3 = x_4 = 0$ is the basic solution associated with both bases $\{1,2,3\}$ and $\{1,2,4\}$.

2. Writing a Linear Program in Canonical Form with Respect to a Basis

<u>Definition 3</u>: We consider the (very slight) generalization of (P):

$$(P_\zeta) \quad \begin{cases} Ax = b \qquad x \geq 0 \\ cx = z \text{ (Max)} - \zeta \qquad (\zeta \text{ given scalar}) \end{cases}$$

which must be understood in this way: "Find $x \in \{x \mid Ax = b, \ x \geq 0\}$, which gives to cx a maximum value, call it $\bar{x}$, and give to the objective function z the value $c\bar{x} + \zeta$."

<u>Remark 2</u>: (P_ζ) is a linear program nearly identical to (P) since when an optimal solution to (P) has been found, it is an optimal solution to (P_ζ) (the two linear programs have the same feasible and optimal solutions), the only difference being the corresponding value of the objective function, the difference of the objective functions being just ζ. In particular, $(P_0) \equiv (P)$.

Since (P_ζ) is quite the same as (P), it will sometimes be denoted (P) and it may seem that we do not gain much generality by writing (P_ζ) instead of (P). However, we will see in the sequel that this formalism is quite useful.

<u>Definition 4</u>: Given linear program (P_ζ), the $(m+1) \times (n+1)$-matrix

$$M = \begin{bmatrix} A & b \\ c & -\zeta \end{bmatrix}$$

is called the "matrix of coefficients" of this linear program.

<u>Remark 3</u>: Let M be the matrix of coefficients of linear program (P_ζ) and let $1 \leq r \leq m$, $1 \leq s \leq n$, such that $M_r^s = A_r^s \neq 0$. A pivot operation on A_r^s transforms the matrix M into the matrix $\hat{M}$ (see Remark III.15):

$$(2) \qquad \hat{A}_i^j = \begin{cases} A_i^j - A_r^j A_i^s / A_r^s & \text{if } i \neq r \\ A_r^j / A_r^s & \text{if } i = r \end{cases}$$

$$(2') \qquad \hat{b}_i = \begin{cases} b_i - b_r A_i^s / A_r^s & \text{if } i \neq r \\ b_r / A_r^s & \text{if } i = r \end{cases}$$

(3) $\hat{c}^j = c_j - c^s A_r^j / A_r^s$

(3') $\hat{\zeta} = \zeta + c^s b_r / A_r^s$

     Let $Pi(r,s)$ be the $m \times m$ pivot matrix defined in Remark III.16, and let η be the m-row vector defined by

(4) $\eta^i = \begin{cases} 0 & \text{if } i \neq r \\ c^s / A_r^s & \text{if } i = r \end{cases}$

Then it is easy to check that after a pivot operation on the element $M_r^s = A_r^s \neq 0$ of the matrix M, we obtain

(2*) $[\hat{A}, \hat{b}] = Pi(r,s) \times [A,b]$

(3*) $\hat{c} = c - \eta A ; \quad \hat{\zeta} = \zeta + \eta b$

Example: The matrix of coefficients of (P_1) is

$$M = \begin{bmatrix} 2 & 1 & 1 & 0 & 0 & 8 \\ 1 & 2 & 0 & 1 & 0 & 7 \\ 0 & 1 & 0 & 0 & 1 & 3 \\ 4 & 5 & 0 & 0 & 0 & 0 \end{bmatrix}$$

Perform a pivot operation on $M_3^2 = 1$. We obtain

$$\hat{M} = \begin{bmatrix} 2 & 0 & 1 & 0 & -1 & 5 \\ 1 & 0 & 0 & 1 & -2 & 1 \\ 0 & 1 & 0 & 0 & 1 & 3 \\ 4 & 0 & 0 & 0 & -5 & -15 \end{bmatrix}$$

the pivot matrix being

$$Pi(3,2) = \begin{bmatrix} 1 & 0 & -1 \\ 0 & 1 & -2 \\ 0 & 0 & 1 \end{bmatrix}$$

Theorem 1: Consider the linear program

$$(P_\zeta) = \begin{cases} Ax = b & x \geq 0 \\ cx = z(Max) - \zeta \end{cases}$$

and assume that linear system $Ax = b$ is full rank. Let B be a nonsingular $m \times m$-matrix and y an m-row vector of coefficients. Then (P_ζ) is equivalent (according to Definition I.15) to the linear program

$$(\hat{P_\zeta}) \quad \begin{cases} (BA)x = Bb & x \geq 0 \\ (c-yA)x = \hat{z}(Max) - \zeta - yb \end{cases}$$

Proof: (i) We have seen in Section III.2 that linear system (1) is equivalent to

$$(BA)x = Bb$$

provided that B is nonsingular. Thus (P_ζ) and $(\hat{P_\zeta})$ have the same solution sets.
     (ii) The value of the objective function of $(\hat{P_\zeta})$ is

$$\hat{z} = cx + \zeta - y(Ax - b)$$

Thus for all x solution of (1) (feasible solution of (P_ζ) and $(P_\zeta^{\wedge})$) we have

$$Ax - b = 0$$

and $\hat{z} = z$.

Corollary: Let M be the matrix of coefficients of linear program (P_ζ). Perform a pivot operation on a nonzero element M_r^s ($1 \leq r \leq m$, $1 \leq s \leq m$) of M. The matrix M thus obtained is the matrix of the coefficient of a linear program equivalent to (P_ζ).

Proof: This corollary is a direct consequence of Remark 3 and of the theorem.

Definition 5: Consider a linear program (P) where (1) is full rank and let J be a basis of (P). Apply the transformation described in Theorem 1 with

(a) $B = (A^J)^{-1}$

(b) $y = \pi$ solution of

(5) $\pi A^J = c^J$

(P) becomes

$$(Pc) \quad \begin{cases} x_J + (A^J)^{-1} A^{\bar{J}} x_{\bar{J}} = (A^J)^{-1} b \qquad x_J, \ x_{\bar{J}} \geq 0 \\ (c^{\bar{J}} - \pi A^{\bar{J}}) x_{\bar{J}} = z \ (Max) - \pi b \end{cases}$$

which is called the "canonical form with respect to basis J."

π is perfectly defined by (5) since A^J is nonsingular $(\pi = c^J (A^J)^{-1})$ and is called the "multiplier vector relative to basis J." The vector

(6) $$c(J) = c - \pi A$$

i.e.,

(6') $$(c(J))^j = \begin{cases} 0 & \text{if } j \in J \\ c^j - \pi A^j & \text{if } j \notin J \end{cases}$$

is called the "cost vector relative to basis J."

Remark 4: It may seem awkward to call (Pc) a "canonical form" while it is a standard form. But in (Pc) we can take basic variables x_j, $j \in J$, as slack variables (see Section I.4), and (Pc) is then written

$$(Pc') \quad \begin{cases} (A^J)^{-1} A^{\bar{J}} x_{\bar{J}} \leq (A^J)^{-1} b \qquad x_{\bar{J}} \geq 0 \\ (c^{\bar{J}} - \pi A^{\bar{J}}) x_{\bar{J}} = z(Max) - \pi b \end{cases}$$

Remark 5: Note that a linear program (P) is said to be written in canonical form with respect to basis J if the following two conditions are satisfied:

(a) A^J is, up to a permutation of rows or columns, the unit matrix.
(b) $c^J = 0$.

Theorem 2: Let M be the matrix of coefficients of the linear program

$$(P) \quad \begin{cases} Ax = b \qquad x \geq 0 \\ cx = z(Max) - \zeta \end{cases}$$

written in canonical form with respect to basis J. Let $r \in \{1, 2, \ldots, m\}$ and $s \notin J$, such that $A_r^s \neq 0$ and let t be the unique index in J such that $A_r^t = 1$.

Perform a pivot operation on the element A_r^s of M. The matrix $\hat{M}$ thus obtained is the matrix of coefficients of linear program (P) written in canonical form with respect to the basis

$$\hat{J} \;=\; J \cup \{s\} \backslash \{t\}^{\,\dagger}$$

Moreover, the value of ζ is increased by this operation by the quantity

$$c^s b_r / A_r^s$$

Proof: From the Corollary of Theorem 1, $\hat{M}$ is the matrix of coefficients of a linear program equivalent to (P) , i.e., of the same linear program written under a different form. From Remark III.15, matrix $A^{\hat{J}}$ is a unit matrix. From Remark 3, we have

$$\hat{c}^s \;=\; 0$$

$$\hat{\zeta} \;=\; \zeta + c^s b_r / A_r^s$$

Definition 6: To make references to pivot operations in the sequel light and precise, we will give the name

$$\text{PIVOT } (p,q,r,s;M)$$

to the pivot operation on the element M_r^s of the $p \times q$-matrix M, which transforms M into $\hat{M}$, i.e.,

$$\hat{M}_i^j \;=\; \begin{cases} M_i^j - M_r^j M_i^s / M_r^s & \text{if } i \neq r \\ M_r^j / M_r^s & \text{if } i = r \end{cases}$$

Example: In the example preceding Theorem 1, M is transformed into

$$M' = \hat{M} = \begin{bmatrix} 2 & 0 & 1 & 0 & -1 & 5 \\ 1 & 0 & 0 & 1 & -2 & 1 \\ 0 & 1 & 0 & 0 & 1 & 3 \\ 4 & 0 & 0 & 0 & -5 & -15 \end{bmatrix}$$

---

† If $I \subset J$, $J \backslash I$ denotes the set of elements of J not in I .

by PIVOT$(4,6,3,2;M)$. From Theorem 2, $\hat{M}$ is the matrix of coefficients of (P_1) written in canonical form with respect to

$$J' = \{3,4,2\} = \{3,4,5\}\cup\{2\}\backslash\{5\}$$

$$(P_1')\left\{\begin{array}{llll}
2x_1 & + x_3 & - x_5 & = 5 \\
x_1 & + x_4 & - 2x_5 & = 1 \\
x_2 & + x_5 & & = 3 \\
4x_1 & - 5x_5 & & = \hat{z}(\text{Max}) - 15
\end{array}\right.$$

(We see in this example how the fact that J' is the ordered set $(3,4,2)$ must be taken into account (see Remark III.5)).

Let us now perform PIVOT$(4,6,2,1;M')$. We get

$$M'' = \hat{M}' = \begin{bmatrix}
0 & 0 & 1 & -2 & 3 & 3 \\
1 & 0 & 0 & 1 & -2 & 1 \\
0 & 1 & 0 & 0 & 1 & 3 \\
0 & 0 & 0 & -4 & 3 & -19
\end{bmatrix}$$

the matrix of coefficients of linear program (P_1) written in canonical form with respect to $\{3,1,2\} = \{3,4,2\}\cup\{1\}\backslash\{4\}$. Let us now perform PIVOT $(4,6,1,5;M'')$. We get:

$$M''' = \hat{M}'' = \begin{bmatrix}
0 & 0 & 1/3 & -2/3 & 1 & 1 \\
1 & 0 & 2/3 & -1/3 & 0 & 3 \\
0 & 1 & -1/3 & 2/3 & 0 & 2 \\
0 & 0 & -1 & -2 & 0 & -22
\end{bmatrix}$$

the matrix of coefficients of linear program (P_1) written in canonical form with respect to $\{5,1,2\} = \{3,1,2\}\cup\{5\}\backslash\{3\}$:

$$(P_1''')\left\{\begin{array}{llll}
\frac{1}{3}x_3 & - \frac{2}{3}x_4 & + x_5 & = 1 \\
x_1 & + \frac{2}{3}x_3 & - \frac{1}{3}x_4 & = 3 \\
x_2 & - \frac{1}{3}x_3 & + \frac{2}{3}x_4 & = 2 \\
& - x_3 & - 2x_4 & = z - 22
\end{array}\right.$$

Note that the basic solution corresponding to basis $\{5,1,2\}$ is $x_1 = 3$, $x_2 = 2$, $x_3 = x_4 = 0$, $x_5 = 1$, $z = 22$; i.e., the solution that we proved to be optimal in Chapter II.

3. Feasible Bases, Optimal Bases

Definition 7: A basis J of a linear program (P) is feasible if the corresponding basic solution (see Definition 2) is feasible, i.e., if

$$x_J \;=\; (A^J)^{-1}\, b \;\geq\; 0$$

To say that a basis is feasible is an abuse of language. One ought to say "a basis such that the corresponding basic solution is feasible."

Theorem 3: If the cost vector relative to a feasible basis J is nonpositive, the basic solution corresponding to basis J is an optimal solution of (P).

Proof: Consider linear program (Pc) as introduced in Definition 5 and assume that

$$(7) \qquad\qquad c(J) \;=\; c - \pi A \;\leq\; 0$$

We have

$$(Pc) \quad \begin{cases} x_J \,+\, (A^J)^{-1} A^{\bar{J}} x_{\bar{J}} \;=\; (A^J)^{-1} b \qquad x_J, x_{\bar{J}} \geq 0 \\[2mm] (c^{\bar{J}} - \pi A^{\bar{J}}) x_{\bar{J}} \;=\; z\,(\text{Max}) - \pi b \end{cases}$$

Let $\bar{x}$ be the basic solution of (P) corresponding to basis J and let x be any feasible solution of (P); we have

$$z \;=\; cx \;=\; \sum_{j \notin J} (c^j - \pi A^j) x_j \,+\, \pi b$$

$$\bar{z} \;=\; c\bar{x} \;=\; \sum_{j \notin J} (c^j - \pi A^j)\bar{x}_j \,+\, \pi b \;=\; \pi b \quad \text{since } \bar{x}_j = 0 \text{ for } j \notin J$$

$$z - \bar{z} \;=\; \sum_{j \notin J} (c^j - \pi A^j) x_j \;\leq\; 0$$

since each term of this sum is the product of a nonpositive scalar $(c^j - \pi A^j)$ by a non-negative one (x_j).

Example: Basic solution associated to the basis $J = \{5,1,2\}$ of (P_1) is an optimal solution, as is apparent in the example ending Section 2.

Definition 8: A basis J such that the cost vector relative to J is negative or zero is said to be "optimal." The term "optimal basis" is also (as "feasible basis") an abuse of language.

Corollary of Theorem 3: The multiplier vector relative to an optimal basis of linear program (P) is an optimal solution of the dual of (P) :

$$(D) \quad \begin{cases} yA \geq c & \quad y \quad \text{unrestricted} \\ yb = w \text{ (Min)} \end{cases}$$

Moreover,

$$w_{min} = z_{max}$$

Proof: Let J be an optimal basis of (P), $\bar{x}$ be the basic solution of (P) relative to J, and π the multiplier vector relative to J. For $x = \bar{x}$, we have (see Definition 5)

$$\bar{z} = c\bar{x} = \pi b$$

By assumption, we have

$$c(J) = c - \pi A \leq 0$$

which means that $y = \pi$ is a feasible solution of (D), the corresponding value of the objective function being $w = \pi b$.

Thus we have a pair of feasible solutions $\bar{x}$ and π to linear programs (P) and (D), respectively, the corresponding values of the objective functions being equal. From the Corollary of Theorem II.2, $\bar{x}$ is an optimal solution of (P) and π an optimal solution of (D).

Remark 6: We wondered, at the end of Section II.2, whether it was true that when both a linear program (P) and its dual (D) have optimal solutions, we have $z_{max} = w_{min}$. The present corollary does not answer this question; we still do not know if it is true that whenever a linear program has an optimal solution, it has an optimal *basic* solution. We will prove this property in a constructive way in subsequent chapters.

We will also prove that basic solutions correspond to vertices of the polyhedron of feasible solutions.

Remark 7: We leave it as an exercise to show that for a linear program

$$(\breve{P}) \quad \begin{cases} Ax = b \qquad\quad x \geq 0 \\ cx = z(Min) \end{cases}$$

Theorem 2 becomes: "If the cost vector relative to a feasible basis J is non-negative, the basic solution corresponding to J is an optimal solution of (P)."

What would be the optimal solution of linear program $(\tilde{P}_1)$ obtained from (P_1) by changing "Max" into "Min" in the objective function?

EXERCISES

1. Consider the linear program

$$(P) \quad \begin{cases} x_1 + 5x_2 + 4x_3 \leq 23 \\ 2x_1 + 6x_2 + 5x_3 \geq 28 \\ 4x_1 + 7x_2 + 6x_3 = z(Min) \end{cases} \qquad x_1, x_2, x_3 \geq 0$$

(a) What is the dual (D) of (P)?

(b) Write (P) in standard form (name the slack variables x_4 and x_5).

(c) Is $\{1,4\}$ a basis? Why?

(d) Write (P) in canonical form with respect to the basis $\{1,4\}$.

(e) Is $\{1,4\}$ a feasible basis? Is it an optimal basis?

2. Prove that $\{1,2,3\}$ is an optimal basis of the linear program of Exercise II.4.

3. Prove that the multiplier vector relative to an optimal basis of

$$(P) \quad \begin{cases} Ax \leq b \qquad\quad x \geq 0 \\ cx = z(Max) \end{cases}$$

is an optimal solution of the dual (D) of (P).

4. Prove Remark 7.

5. Consider the linear program

$$(P) \quad \begin{cases} 4x_1 + 4x_2 + 4x_3 + x_4 \leq 24 \\ 8x_1 + 6x_2 + 4x_3 + 3x_4 \leq 36 \qquad x_i \geq 0 \qquad i = 1,2,3,4 \\ 5x_1 + x_2 + 6x_3 + 2x_4 = z \,(\text{Max}) \end{cases}$$

(a) Write (P) in standard form (the slack variables are named x_5 and x_6).

(b) Write (P) in canonical form with respect to the basis $\{3,4\}$.

(c) Is $\{3,4\}$ a feasible basis? Is it an optimal basis?

(d) Assume that the right-hand side of the first constraint is changed from 24 into 26. What is the new value of the solution? By how much has the objective function been increased?

(e) What can you say if the right-hand side of the first constraint is changed from 24 into 44?

6. Consider the linear program (P_2) as it is written in the example preceding Remark I.10.

(a) Show that in (P_2) the inequality signs can be changed into equality signs without using slack variables.

(b) Delete the redundant constraints of (P_2), if any.

(c) Prove that $\{3,4,5,6\}$ is a basis but that it is not a feasible basis. Check that $\{1,2,5,6\}$ is a feasible basis.

(d) Check that $\{1,2,3,4\}$ is an optimal basis. What is the optimal solution of (P_2) and of its dual (D_2)?

7. Consider the dual linear programs

$$(P) \quad \begin{cases} Ax \leq b \qquad x \geq 0 \\ cx = z \,(\text{Max}) \end{cases} \qquad\qquad (D) \quad \begin{cases} yA \geq c \qquad y \geq 0 \\ yb = w \,(\text{Min}) \end{cases}$$

Let

$$I \subset \{1,2,\ldots,m\} \,; \qquad \bar{I} = \{1,2,\ldots,m\}/I$$
$$J \subset \{1,2,\ldots,n\} \,; \qquad \bar{J} = \{1,2,\ldots,n\}/J$$

(a) Prove that (I,J) is a basis of (P) if

(i) $|I| + |J| = m$

(ii) $[A^J, (U_m)^I]$ is nonsingular.

Similarly, prove that $(\bar{I},\bar{J})$ is a basis of (D) if

(i) $|\bar{I}| + |\bar{J}| = n$

(ii) $\begin{bmatrix} A^-_I \\ \\ (U_n)^-_J \end{bmatrix}$ is nonsingular.

(b) Prove that a necessary and sufficient condition for (I,J) to be a basis of (P) is that $A^J_{\bar{I}}$ be square nonsingular.

(c) Prove that a necessary and sufficient condition for (I,J) to be a basis of (P) is that $(\bar{I},\bar{J})$ be a basis of (D).

(d) Prove that if (I,J) is a feasible basis of (P), $(\bar{I},\bar{J})$ a feasible basis of (D), then (I,J) is an optimal basis of (P) $(\bar{I},\bar{J})$ an optimal basis of (D).

Chapter V. The Simplex Algorithm

The simplex algorithm was discovered in 1947 by G. Dantzig as a tool to solve linear programs. Simplex algorithm is central to this course on linear programming because it exemplifies the process of operations research described in the preface: it is not only a very efficient way (its efficiency is not yet completely understood) of solving practical problems, used innumerable times by engineers, industrialists, and military people, but it is also the basis of a mathematical theory that can be used to prove various results.

We will try and keep these two points of view in this text, i.e., insist on the computational aspects (see, in particular, Chapter VII), of the simplex algorithm and show how it can be used as a mathematical tool.

The simplex algorithm can only be applied to linear programs that are written in canonical form with respect to a feasible basis. We show in Chapter VI how to accomplish this.

Here we assume that the linear program

$$(P) \quad \begin{cases} Ax = b \qquad x \geq 0 \\ cx = z \text{ (Max)} \end{cases}$$

is in fact written in canonical form with respect to the feasible basis J. Thus the three following conditions are satisfied:

(1) A^J is, up to a permutation of rows, the $m \times m$ unit matrix.

(2) $b \geq 0$ since J is a "feasible" basis.

(3) $c^J = 0$ (see Section IV.2).

(A is, as before, an $m \times n$-matrix, b is an m-column vector, and c is an n-row vector.)

Remark 1: We need to know the structure of A^J. We define the mapping

$$\text{col}: \{1, 2, \ldots, m\} \to J$$

such that

70

$$(4) \qquad A_i^j = \begin{cases} 1 & \text{if} \quad j = \text{col}(i) \\ 0 & \text{if} \quad j \in J \quad \text{and} \quad j \neq \text{col}(i) \end{cases}$$

In other words, this application defines the permutation of columns that allows us to find the unit matrix from A^J.

Example: Consider

$$(P_1) \quad \begin{cases} 2x_1 + x_2 + x_3 & = 8 \\ x_1 + 2x_2 \qquad\qquad + x_4 & = 7 \qquad x_i \geq 0 \quad i = 1,2,\dots,5 \\ x_2 \qquad\qquad\qquad + x_5 & = 3 \\ 4x_1 + 5x_2 & = z(\text{Max}) \end{cases}$$

(P_1) is written in canonical form with respect to basis $\{3,4,5\}$ and we have $\text{col}(1) = 3$, $\text{col}(2) = 4$, $\text{col}(3) = 5$.

The simplex algorithm is introduced for a particular case in Section 1, and for example (P_1) in Section 2. It is described in its generality in Section 3. Proof of finiteness is given in Section 4. It will remain to show how a general linear program can be written in canonical form with respect to a feasible basis, i.e., how to "initiate" the simplex algorithm. This is done in Chapter VI.

1. A Particular Case

The particular case we study here is the case where $n = m + 1$. Without loss of generality (by renaming the variables if necessary), we can assume that $J = \{2,3,\dots,m,m+1\}$. Thus, our particular program (which we call (PP)) can be written

$$(PP) \quad \begin{cases} A_1^1 x_1 + x_2 & = b_1 \\ A_2^1 x_1 \qquad + x_3 & = b_2 \qquad x_j \geq 0 \quad j = 1,2,\dots,m,m+1 \\ \vdots & \quad\ \vdots \\ A_m^1 x_1 \qquad\qquad + x_{m+1} & = b_m \\ c^1 x_1 & = z(\text{Max}) \end{cases}$$

We can also consider that $x_2, x_3, \dots, x_{m+1}$ are slack variables (cf. Remark IV.4):

$$\text{(PPC)} \begin{cases} A_1^1 x_1 \;\leq\; b_1 \\ A_2^1 x_1 \;\leq\; b_2 \qquad\qquad x_1 \geq 0 \\ \;\;\vdots \qquad\quad \vdots \\ A_m^1 x_1 \;\leq\; b_m \\ c'x_1 \;=\; z \text{ (Max)} \end{cases}$$

The domain of feasible solutions of (PPC) is a part of the half line $x_1 \geq 0$. Recall that, from (2), $b_i \geq 0$ for $i=1,2,\ldots,m$. Thus if $A_i^1 \leq 0$, the ith inequality does not play any role in the definition of the set of feasible x_1's (if $A_i^1 = 0$, i^{th} constraint is always satisfied; if $A_i^1 < 0$, the ith constraint is always satisfied for $x_1 \geq 0$) .

It is thus sufficient to determine $\mathcal{D}$, the domain of feasible solutions of (PPC), to restrict one's attention to constraints of

(5) $I = \{i \,|\, A_i^1 > 0\}$

When $I \neq \emptyset$, we have

$$\mathcal{D} = \bigcap_{i \varepsilon I} \;[0,\; b_i/A_i^1]$$

In summary, we have two cases:

(a) $I = \emptyset$: $\mathcal{D} = \{x_1 \,|\, 0 \leq x_1\}$

(b) $I \neq \emptyset$: $\mathcal{D} = \{x_1 \,|\, 0 \leq x_1 \leq \underset{i \varepsilon I}{\text{Min}}\; [b_i/A_i^1]\}$

Let us now go back to the solution of (PPC). If $c^1 \leq 0$, we know, by Theorem IV.3, that the basic solution associated with basis J , namely,

$$x_1 = 0, \quad x_2 = b_1, \quad x_3 = b_2,\ldots,x_{m+1} = b_m$$

is an optimal solution. (PPC) is solved.

If $c^1 > 0$, it is clear that it is in our interest (if we want to increase the objective function) to have x_1 as big as possible. Thus:

1. If we are in case (a), x_1 can increase without bound, z increases as $c^1 x_1$, and linear program (PP) does not have a bounded solution (no optimal solution, Remark I.5).

2. If we are in case (b) (i.e. $I \neq \emptyset$), we let x_1 be as large as possible. We pose

$$\bar{x}_1 = \underset{i \in I}{\text{Min}} \; [b_i / A_1]$$

Let r be an index of I for which this minimum is reached:

$$\bar{x}_1 = b_r / A_r^1 = \underset{i \in I}{\text{Min}} \; [b_i / A_i^1]$$

The values of the basic variables will be

$$\bar{x}_{i+1} = b_i - A_i^1 \bar{x}_i = b_i - A_i^1 b_r / A_r^1 \qquad i = 1, 2, \ldots, m$$

By construction, because of the definition of r, we have

$$\bar{x}_{i+1} \geq 0$$

Thus $\bar{x}$ is a feasible solution. We proceed now to show that $\bar{x}$ is an optimal solution.

We have just one way to show that a solution is optimal: it is to apply Theorem IV.3. We notice that

$$\bar{x}_{r+1} = b_r - A_r^1 b_r / A_r^1 = 0$$

Letting M denote the matrix of coefficients of (PP), we apply the pivot operation PIVOT$(m+1, m+2, r, 1; M)$ on the nonzero element A_r^1 of $\hat{M}$ (A_r^1 is nonzero since $r \in I$, by assumption). We obtain matrix M', which is the matrix of coefficients of linear program (PP) written in canonical form with respect to basis:

$$J' = J \cup \{1\} \setminus \{r + 1\}$$

(see Theorem IV.2). The reader will check that after the pivot operation (PP) writes

$$(PP') \begin{cases} x_2 \qquad\qquad -\dfrac{A_1^1}{A_r^1} x_{r+1} \qquad\qquad = b_1 - \dfrac{A_1^1 b_r}{A_r^1} \\[2mm] \ddots \qquad\qquad\qquad\qquad\qquad\qquad\qquad \vdots \\[2mm] \qquad\qquad x_r - \dfrac{A_{r-1}^1}{A_r^1} x_{r+1} \qquad = b_{r-1} - \dfrac{A_{r-1}^1 b_r}{A_r^1} \\[2mm] x_1 \qquad\qquad +\dfrac{1}{A_r^1} x_{r+1} \qquad\qquad = \dfrac{b_r}{A_r^1} \\[2mm] \qquad\qquad -\dfrac{A_{r+1}^1}{A_r^1} x_{r+1} + x_{r+2} \qquad = b_{r-1} - \dfrac{A_{r-1}^1 b_r}{A^1} \\[2mm] \qquad\qquad\qquad \vdots \qquad \ddots \qquad\qquad \vdots \\[2mm] \qquad\qquad -\dfrac{A_m^1}{A_r^1} x_{r+1} \qquad\quad + x_{m+1} = b_m - \dfrac{A_m^1 b_r}{A_r^1} \\[2mm] \qquad\qquad -\dfrac{c^1}{A_r^1} x_{r+1} \qquad\qquad = z(\text{Max}) - \dfrac{c^1 b_r}{A_r^1} \end{cases} \qquad x \geq 0$$

Since, by assumption, $c^1 > 0$ and $A_r^1 > 0$, we see that (PP') is written in canonical form with respect to the optimal basis J'. A single pivot operation has been sufficient to solve this particular linear program.

Geometric Interpretation: If we are in case (a), domain $\mathcal{D}$ is the half line $x_1 \geq 0$. The objective function monotonously increases with x_1 and thus is unbounded on $\mathcal{D}$.

If we are in case (b), domain $\mathcal{D}$ is the segment

$$\{x_1 \mid 0 \leq x_1 \leq b_r/A_r^1 = \text{Min}_{i \in I} [b_i/A_i^1]\}$$

and the objective function increases in proportion to x_1 in this segment. Thus, the optimum will be located at the extreme point of the segment for which

$$x_1 = b_r/A_r^1$$

Note that a segment or a half line are examples of convex polyedra. We check on this example that the optimal solution corresponds to a vertex of the polyedron.

Theorem 1: Consider the linear program

$$(PP) \qquad \begin{cases} Ax = b \qquad\quad x \geq 0 \\ cx = z(\text{Max}) \end{cases}$$

(where A is a $m \times (m+1)$ matrix) written in canonical form with respect to a feasible basis J , the application "col" being defined as in Remark 1. Let s be the unique column index not belonging to J .   If

(i) $c^s > 0$

(ii) $I = \{i \,|\, A_i^s > 0\} \neq \emptyset$

(iii)   r is defined by $b_r / A_r^s = \text{Min}_{i \in I} \, [b_i / A_i^s]$

then the application of $PIVOT(m+1, m+2, r, s; M)$ to the matrix

$$M = \begin{bmatrix} A & b \\ c & 0 \end{bmatrix}$$

of coefficients of (PP) transforms M into the matrix of coefficients of linear program (PP) written in canonical form with respect to the optimal basis

$$J' = J \cup \{s\} \setminus \{col(r)\}$$

Moreover, to update col, it suffices to write

$$col(r) = s$$

(i.e., matrix $M^{J \cap J'}$ is not modified by the operation).

Proof: This theorem is just a synthesis of what has been proved in this section.

2.   Solving an Example

Let us again consider

$$(P_1) \quad \begin{cases} 2x_1 + x_2 + x_3 & = 8 \\ x_1 + 2x_2 + x_4 & = 7 \qquad x_j \geq 0 \\ x_2 + x_5 & = 3 \qquad j = 1, 2, \ldots, 5 \\ 4x_1 + 5x_2 & = z \,(\text{Max}) \end{cases}$$

which is written in canonical form with respect to feasible basis $\{3, 4, 5\}$. This basis is not optimal since we have $c^1 = 4 > 0$, $c^2 = 5 > 0$.

It is in our interest (if we want to increase the objective function) to increase x_1 or x_2 .   The basic idea of simplex algorithm is to choose one of the indices $s \notin J$ such that $c^s > 0$ (if no such index exists, the present basic solution is optimal) and to increase x_s as much as possible.

Suppose that we decide to increase x_2 without being interested -- for the time being -- in x_1. We will even go one step further and forget about the existence of x_1. Then we will be able to use what we learned in Section 1; we consider

$$(PP_1(J,2)) \begin{cases} x_2 + x_3 & = 8 \\ 2x_2 \quad + x_4 & = 7 \\ x_2 \qquad + x_5 & = 3 \\ 5x_2 & = z(Max) \end{cases} \qquad x_2, x_3, x_4, x_5 \geq 0$$

The domain of variation of x_2 is

$$\{x_2 | 0 \leq x_2 \leq Min[8/1; 7/2; 3/1] = 3\}$$

Thus the optimal solution of $(PP_1(J,2))$ is obtained for $x_2 = 3$. We have

$$x_2 = 3, \quad x_3 = 5, \quad x_4 = 1, \quad x_5 = 0$$

We know that if we wanted to prove that this solution is optimal, we would have to perform a pivot operation on the element A_3^2 of the matrix of coefficients of $(PP_1(J,2))$. We decide to perform the very same pivot operation on the matrix of coefficients of (P_1) itself. This has been done in the example ending Section IV.2. We get

$$(P_1') \begin{cases} 2x_1 \quad + x_3 \qquad - x_5 & = 5 \\ x_1 \qquad + x_4 - 2x_5 & = 1 \\ x_2 \qquad + x_5 & = 3 \\ 4x_1 \qquad - 5x_5 & = z(Max) - 15 \end{cases} \qquad \begin{array}{l} x_j \geq 0 \\ j = 1,2,\ldots,5 \end{array}$$

Basis J' (with respect to which (P_1') is now written in canonical form) is not optimal (since $c^1 = 4 > 0$), but we can consider that we made some progress since, for the basic solution associated with J', the value of the objective function is 15.

Now we want to increase x_1, forgetting about the other nonbasic variables (i.e., leaving them at their zero value). Thus we will solve

$$(PP_1'(J',1)) \quad \begin{cases} 2x_1 & + x_3 & & = 5 \\ x_1 & & + x_4 & = 1 \\ & x_2 & & = 3 \\ 4x_1 & \cdot & & = z(\text{Max}) - 15 \end{cases} \qquad x_1, x_2, x_3, x_4 \geq 0$$

The domain of variation of x_1 is $\{x_1 \mid 0 \leq x_1 \leq 1\}$. For $x_1 = 1$ we have

$$x_2 = 3, \quad x_3 = 3, \quad x_4 = x_5 = 0, \qquad z = 15 + 4 = 4x_1 + 5x_2 = 19$$

We have been blocked by the second equation, so we perform a pivot operation on A_2^1. As we have seen in the example at the end of Section IV.2, linear program (P_1) will now be written in canonical form with respect to basis:

$$J'' = J' \cup \{1\} \setminus \{\text{col}(2)\} = \{1,2,3\}$$

$$(P_1'') \quad \begin{cases} x_3 - 2x_4 + 3x_5 & = 3 \\ x_1 & + x_4 - 2x_5 & = 1 \\ x_2 & + x_5 & = 3 \\ & - 4x_4 + 3x_5 & = z(\text{Max}) - 19 \end{cases} \qquad \begin{array}{l} x_j \geq 0 \\ \\ j = 1,2,\ldots,5 \end{array}$$

We still improved the value of the objective function but basis J'' is not yet optimal. We apply the same process to

$$(PP_1''(J'',5)) \quad \begin{cases} x_3 + 3x_5 & = 3 \\ x_1 & - 2x_5 & = 1 \\ x_2 & + x_5 & = 3 \\ & 3x_5 & = z(\text{Max}) - 19 \end{cases} \qquad \begin{array}{l} x_j \geq 0 \\ \\ j = 1,2,3,5 \end{array}$$

We see that pivot operation must be done on A_1^5 since

$$b_1/A_1^5 = 1 = \text{Min}[3/3,\ 3/1]$$

The new basis is

$$\mathbf{J}^{\prime\prime\prime} \;=\; \mathbf{J}^{\prime\prime}\cup\{5\}\setminus\{\mathrm{col}(1)\} \;=\; \{1,2,5\}$$

(P_1) written after this pivot operation on its matrix of coefficients is

$$(P_1^{\prime\prime\prime})\quad
\begin{cases}
\quad\qquad \dfrac{1}{3}x_3 - \dfrac{2}{3}x_4 + x_5 = 1\\[2mm]
x_1 \qquad + \dfrac{2}{3}x_3 - \dfrac{1}{3}x_4 \qquad = 3\\[2mm]
\quad x_2 - \dfrac{1}{3}x_3 + \dfrac{2}{3}x_4 \qquad = 2\\[2mm]
\quad\qquad - \; x_3 - 2x_4 \qquad = z(\mathrm{Max}) - 22
\end{cases}$$

$J^{\prime\prime\prime}$ is an optimal basis. The corresponding basic solution is

$$x_1 = 3, \quad x_2 = 2, \quad x_3 = x_4 = 0, \quad x_5 = 1$$

Geometric Interpretation: Let us draw in plane (x_1,x_2) the domain of feasible solutions of (P_1). It is the convex polygon ABCDE of Figure V.1.

Figure V.1: The Domain of Feasible Solutions of (P_1)

To start with, the problem was written in canonical form with respect to the basis $J = \{3,4,5\}$. The corresponding basic solution is $x_1 = x_2 = 0$: we are in A. Then, x_2 increases while x_1 remains equal to 0; the maximum value for x_2 is 3 (if we want to stay in $\mathcal{D}$): we have traveled along segment AB. On B, $x_5 = 0$ since we are limited by constraint III and since x_5 measures how far we are from the bound on this constraint. Point B corresponds to the basic solution associated with J'. We then let x_1 increase, leaving $x_5 = 0$. The maximum possible value for x_1 is 1: we describe segment BC. On C, $x_4 = 0$ (since we are limited by constraint II) and the solution is the basic solution associated with J''. We decide to increase x_5, taking from constraint III, but leaving $x_4 = 0$: we describe segment CD. D corresponds to the basic solution associated with J'', the optimal solution.

Remark 2: For such a simple example as the solution of (P_1), we see that an index (here, index 5), which at some time leaves the basis, has to enter again in some further step. Thus, the movement of an index into or out of the basis can never be considered as definitive.

Remark 3: At the beginning, we chose index 2 to enter the basis. This choice corresponds to the largest increase of the objective function by the unit of variation of the variable, since $c^2 > c^1$. However, the reader is invited to solve (P_1) again with the other choice (letting index 1 first enter the basis). He will then check that two basis changes are sufficient instead of three.

3. The Simplex Algorithm: General Case

This section will just be an extension of the two preceding ones.

Remark 4: Let us describe the main steps of the process that ended in the solution of (P_1) :

(a) (P) is written in canonical form with respect to feasible basis J.

(b) We associate with J its corresponding basic solution.

(c) If J is not optimal, we choose $s \notin J$ such that $c^s > 0$.

(d) Leaving all nonbasic variables (except x_s) at their 0 value, increase x_s as much as possible and adjust basic variables:

$$\begin{cases} x_k = b_i - A_i^s x_s & \text{for } k = \text{col}(i) \\ x_k = 0 & \text{for } k \notin J, \ k \neq s \end{cases}$$

This variation of the current solution induces an increase in the value of the objective function.

(e) If $A^s \leq 0$, the linear program does not have optimal solution (the objective function is unbounded).

(f) If $I = \{i \,|\, A_i^s > 0\} \neq \emptyset$, let r be an index such that

(6)
$$b_r/A_r^s = \min_{i \in I} [b_i/A_i^s]$$

(This minimum may be reached for more than one index; r is one of them.)

(g) x_s cannot be greater than $\bar{x}_s = b_r / A_r^s$.

(h)   For $x_s = \bar{x}_s$, one of the basic variables x_t with $t = \mathrm{col}(r)$ is equal to 0 .

(i) $\bar{J} = J \cup \{s\} \setminus \{\mathrm{col}(r)\}$ is a feasible basis.

(j)   The new solution

$$\begin{cases} x_s' = \bar{x}_s \\ x_k' = b_i - A_i^s \bar{x}_s \qquad \text{for} \quad k = \mathrm{col}(i) \\ x_j' = 0 \qquad\qquad\qquad j \notin \bar{J} \end{cases}$$

is the basic solution corresponding to basis $\bar{J}$.

(k)   In performing the operation PIVOT $(m+1, n+1, r,s;M)$ to the matrix M of coefficients of linear program (P), we obtain the matrix of coefficient of this linear program written in canonical form with respect to basis $\bar{J}$. Mapping "col" is updated in posing

$$\mathrm{col}(r) = s$$

This process is repeated until either:

(α)   The new basis is optimal (which can be seen in step (k)).

(β)   Linear program (P) does not have an optimal solution (step (e)).

Remark 5:   In view of Section 1, steps d to k of the preceding process can be formulated in the following way:

(d')   Let $(PP(J,s))$ be the linear program obtained from (P) by suppressing all nonbasic variables, except x_s (which is equivalent to fixing the values of these variables at 0). Solve $(PP(J,s))$ by the method of Section 1:

(i)   If $(PP(J,s))$ does not have an optimal solution, the same is true for (P) (see Exercise 1).

(ii)   If $(PP(J,s))$ has an optimal solution, the unique step for solving this linear program leads to a pivot operation, which we apply to the matrix of coefficients of (P) . We thus define a new feasible basis for (P) .

This process is repeated until either case (α) or (β) of Remark 4 occurs.

Remark 6:   If we closely examine the procedure of Remark 4, we see that:

   1. Step a is just an initialization (which is assumed to be done here).

   2. Steps c,e,f, and k correspond to operations.

   3. Steps b,d,g,h,i, and j can be considered as comments.

We can now repeat the procedure of Remark 4 in a more compact form.

Simplex Algorithm

Linear program (P) is written in canonical form with respect to a feasible basis J . The mapping "col" is defined as in Remark 1.

REPEAT the following procedure <u>until either an optimal basis</u> is obtained, **or** a set of feasible solutions for which z <u>is bounded,</u> is shown to **exist.**

   STEP 1: Choose an s such that $c^s > 0$. If such an s does not exist, basis J is optimal. STOP.

   STEP 2: If $A^s \leq 0$, no optimal solution exists (z is unbounded). **STOP.**

   STEP 3: Let $I = \{i \mid A_i^s > 0\}$ $(I \neq \emptyset$ because of STEP 2).
            Choose an r such that

   (6) $$b_r/A_r^s = \underset{i\varepsilon I}{\text{Min}} \; [b_i/A_i^s]$$

   STEP 4: Perform the pivot operation (defined by row r and column s) on the matrix of coefficients of linear program (P) . After this pivot operation, (P) is written in canonical form with respect to

   $$\bar{J} \; = \; J \cup \{s\} \setminus \{col(r)\}$$

            Let $J := \bar{J}$; $col(r) := s$.

END REPEAT

Remark 7: The validity of the operations of the simplex algorithm has been proved in preceding developments:

   Step 1: See Theorem IV.3.

   Step 2 and 3: See Remark 5 and Section 1.

   Step 4: See Theorem IV.2.

It remains to prove that the algorithm is finite. This will be done in Section 4.

Remark 8:   In the algorithm, we find two imprecise instructions:
   • In Step 3, we have to "choose" an $r \in K$ where

$$K = \{r \mid b_r/A_r^S = \underset{i \in I}{\text{Min}} \, [b_i/A_i^S]\}$$

If $|K| > 1$,   any $r \in \dot{K}$ can be taken and the pivot operation of Step 4 will be valid   ($\bar{J}$ is a feasible basis). The choice of r in K will be made more precise in Section 4, to guarantee finiteness of the algorithm.

   • In Step 1, we have to "choose" an s such that $c^S > 0$.

The correctness of the algorithm does not depend on which index s is chosen, as long as $c^S > 0$. Usually, one takes, as was done in Section 2,

(7) s such that $c^S = \underset{j}{\text{Max}} \, c^j$

This choice is not necessarily good (as program (P_1) exemplifies -- see Remark 3); its justification lies in the fact that it gives the greatest variation of the objective function by unit increase of the variable.

        Another argument consists of associating with each s such that $c^S > 0$ a line index $r(s)$,   the index on which we would perform the pivot operation in case index s would be chosen. The corresponding increase of the objective function would then be

(8) $c^S b_{r(s)}/A_{r(s)}^S$

and we choose the index s with which the largest increase of the objective function is associated. The reader is invited to check that applying this method on (P_1) would result in solving this linear program in two steps, instead of three. But a great number of experiments conducted over a large sample of linear programs have shown that in general, the gain[†]   brought by this method was not in relation with its cost (computation of $r(s)$ and of (8), for all s such that $c^S > 0$). In computer codes, neither criterion (7) nor the exploratory variant is used (see Chapter VII). For small academic examples, we will use criterion (7); in case of a tie, any choice of s among those will do.

[†]This gain is by no means systematic. The reader is invited to invent new coefficients for the objective function of (P_1) that would make the method fail.

Remark 9: Simplex algorithms (as any other algorithm) are composed of conditional instructions (Steps 1 and 2) and of operations (Steps 3 and 4). To perform any of those, we just need matrix M of coefficients of the linear program, which is transformed at each iteration by pivoting on element A_r^s. Thus, the solution of a linear program by the simplex algorithm can be presented in giving the sequence of tableaus of M. We present now, under this compact form, the solution of (P_1) as it has been obtained in Section 2:

x_1	x_2	x_3	x_4	x_5	b	
2	1	1	0	0	8	
1	2	0	1	0	7	
0	1	0	0	1	3 ←	J
4	5*	0	0	0	0	
2	0	1	0	-1	5	
1	0	0	1	-2	1 ←	
0	1	0	0	1	3	J'
4*	0	0	0	-5	-15	
0	0	1	-2	3	3 ←	
1	0	0	1	-2	1	
0	1	0	0	1	3	J"
0	0	0	-4	3*	-19	
0	0	1/3	-2/3	1	1	
1	0	2/3	-1/3	0	3	
0	1	-1/3	2/3	0	2	J'''
0	0	-1	-2	0	-22	

(P_1) is in canonical form with respect to:

[A * near a coefficent of the objective function indicates which column enters the basis; an ← indicates on which row we pivot.]

Remark 10: The reader is invited to verify that to solve the linear program

$$(P') \quad \begin{cases} Ax = b \qquad x \geq 0 \\ cx = z(Min) \end{cases}$$

the only point to change in simplex algorithm[+] is Step 1, which becomes:

Step 1': Choose an s such that $c^s < 0$. If such an s does not exist, basis J is optimal. STOP.

4. Finiteness of the Simplex Algorithm

Proof of the finiteness of the simplex algorithm is essential. Unless this proof is undertaken, we cannot be sure that a linear program (once it is written in canonical form with respect to a feasible basis) has either an optimal (basic) solution or a set of solutions for which z is unbounded (see Remark I.5).

Definition 1: The basic solution associated with the feasible basis J of the linear program

$$(P) \quad \begin{cases} Ax = b \qquad\quad x \geq 0 \\ cx = z(Max) \end{cases}$$

is said to be "degenerate" if at least one component of x_J is equal to 0, i.e., if vector $(A^J)^{-1} b$ is not strictly positive.

Remark 11: In Step 3 of the simplex algorithm, we define

$$K = \{k \mid b_k/A_k^S = \underset{i \in I}{Min} [b_i/A_i^S]\}$$

and we choose $r \in K$. If $|K| > 1$, consider $k \in K$, $k \neq r$. We will have, after pivoting,

$$\bar{b}_k = b_k - b_r A_k^S/A_r^S = 0$$

Conversely, if the starting solution is nondegenerate and if $|K| = 1$ at each iteration, it is easy to see that the solution will remain nondegenerate. Thus degeneracy is closely related to the fact that $|K| > 1$.

Theorem 2: If, at each step of the simplex algorithm, the basic solution associated with the current basis is nondegenerate, then the algorithm terminates (either in Step 1 or in Step 2), in a finite number of iterations.

Proof: From one iteration to the next, the value of ζ (which is the value of the objective function associated with the current basic solution) increases by

$$c^S b_r/A_r^S$$

[+] Note that unboundedness in this case means $z \to -\infty$.

(see Theorem IV.2). If no solution is degenerate, this increase will always be strictly positive. Since the basic solution is uniquely determined by the basis, value of ζ is uniquely determined by the basis.

Since ζ strictly increases from one iteration to the next, we cannot find, when applying the simplex algorithm, a basis that was previously met. Since the number of bases is finite (this number is bounded by $\binom{n}{m}$, the number of ways of choosing m basic columns out of n), the number of iterations of the algorithm is also finite.

Remark 12: Until 1951 (the simplex algorithm was found in 1947), it was not known whether it was possible that the algorithm (because of cycling among degenerate solutions) was nonterminating. In 1951, Hoffman proposed an example where the systematic choice of the first row in case of degeneracy would lead to cycling. Beale (1955) provided a simpler example. The following one is an adaptation by V. Chvatal of a case proposed by K.T. Marshall and J.W. Soorballe:

$$
\begin{cases}
0.5x_1 - 5.5x_2 - 2.5x_3 + 9x_4 + x_5 & = 0 \\
0.5x_1 - 1.5x_2 - 0.5x_3 + x_4 + x_6 & = 0 \qquad x_j \geq 0 \\
x_1 + x_7 & = 1 \qquad j = 1, 2, \ldots, 7 \\
10x_1 - 57x_2 - 9x_3 - 24x_4 & = z\,(\text{Max})
\end{cases}
$$

Most practical problems are degenerate. However, the occurrence of cycling in real problems is most exceptional (Ph. Wolfe reported in 1963 having come across such a case). This is why most computer codes presently used to solve linear programs do not include sophisticated routines such as the one that we are about to present to avoid cycling.

But from a theoretical standpoint, and especially because we use the simplex algorithm as a mathematical tool to prove theorems (see Chapter VI), we must make sure that some rule of choice for the pivot row in case of degeneracy will lead to a solution in a finite number of steps. The "perturbation technique" that we are about to present is due to Charnes [1952]. The following "smallest subscript" rule, proposed by R.G. Bland (1977), consists of:

1. Choosing the nonbasic variable for which $c^j > 0$ with the smallest subscript to enter the basis.

2. Choosing the candidate row for pivoting -- in case of a tie -- with the smallest subscript.

This rule is simpler to implement, but its proof is slightly more intricate. For didactic reasons, we prefer to present here the perturbation technique that enlightens the simplex algorithm itself. For a geometric interpretation, see Remark VIII.5.

Definition 2: Consider the linear program

$$(P) \quad \begin{cases} Ax = b \qquad\quad x \geq 0 \\ cx = z\,(Max) \end{cases}$$

written in canonical form with respect to some feasible basis J . We associate with (P) , the linear program

$$(P(\varepsilon)) \quad \begin{cases} A_i x = b_i + \varepsilon^i \qquad\quad i = 1,2,\ldots,m; \quad x \geq 0 \\ cx \;=\; z\,(Max) \end{cases}$$

called a "perturbed program," in which ε is a scalar and ε^i means "ε to the power i ". The basic solution associated with the feasible basis J of $(P(\varepsilon))$ is

$$\begin{cases} x_k = b_i + \varepsilon^i \qquad\quad \text{for} \quad k = col(i) \qquad i = 1,2,\ldots,m \\ x_k = 0 \qquad\qquad \text{for} \quad k \notin J \end{cases}$$

i.e., each component of x can be considered as a polynomial of degree m in ε :

$$\Lambda(\varepsilon) \;=\; \lambda^0 + \lambda^1 \varepsilon + \lambda^2 \varepsilon^2 + \ldots + \lambda^m \varepsilon^m$$

If not all coefficients of this polynomial are zero, $\Lambda(\varepsilon)$ keeps a constant sign in an open interval (0,h) for h > 0 small enough. This sign is that of the nonzero coefficients λ^k of lower index k . If this sign is + , we will say that polynomial $\Lambda(\varepsilon)$ is "positive" and we write

$$\Lambda(\varepsilon) \succ 0$$

Given polynomials $\Lambda'(\varepsilon)$ and $\Lambda''(\varepsilon)$, we will say that $\Lambda'(\varepsilon)$ is "greater than" $\Lambda''(\varepsilon)$ and we note that

$$\Lambda'(\varepsilon) \succ \Lambda''(\varepsilon)$$

if

$$\Lambda'(\varepsilon) - \Lambda''(\varepsilon) \succ 0$$

Remark 13:   Relation $\not{\succ}$ is a total order on polynoms (see Exercise 11).   Note that if $\Lambda(\varepsilon)$ is a positive polynomial, then

$$\Lambda(0) \geq 0$$

Remark 14: Consider an m-column vector $b(\varepsilon)$, each component of which being a polynomial $b_i(\varepsilon)$ of degree m in ε :

(9) $$b_i(\varepsilon) = b_i^0 + b_i^1\varepsilon + b_i^2\varepsilon^2 + \ldots + b_i^m\varepsilon^m$$

Let B be an $m \times m$-matrix. The product of matrix B by vector $b(\varepsilon)$ will naturally be

$$\bar{b}(\varepsilon) = B \cdot b(\varepsilon)$$

where $\bar{b}(\varepsilon)$ is an m-column vector, each component of which is a polynomial in ε :

$$\bar{b}_i(\varepsilon) = \bar{b}_i^0 + \bar{b}_i^1\varepsilon + \bar{b}_i^2\varepsilon^2 + \ldots + \bar{b}_i^m\varepsilon^m$$

with

$$\bar{b}_i^k = \sum_\ell B_i^\ell b_\ell^k$$

Note that $b(\varepsilon)$ can be represented by the $m \times (m+1)$-matrix

$$Q = \begin{bmatrix} b_1^0 & b_1^1 & b_1^2 & \ldots & b_1^m \\ b_2^0 & b_2^1 & b_2^2 & \ldots & b_2^m \\ \cdot & & & & \cdot \\ \cdot & & & & \cdot \\ b_m^0 & b_m^1 & b_m^2 & \ldots & b_m^m \end{bmatrix}$$

Then $\bar{Q}$, the matrix of coefficients of $\bar{b}(\varepsilon)$, is given by

$$\bar{Q} = BQ$$

Remark 15: We will apply simplex algorithm to the perturbed problem $(P(\varepsilon))$. We must specify how Steps 3 and 4 are performed (Steps 1 and 2 are unchanged).

Step 3: If $i \in I$, $A_i^s > 0$ and $b_i(\varepsilon)/A_i^s$ is a polynomial in ε that has the same sign as $b_i(\varepsilon)$:

$$b_i(\varepsilon)/A_i^S \;=\; b_i^0/A_i^S \;+\; b_i^1\varepsilon/A_i^S \;+\ldots+\; b_i^m\varepsilon^m/A_i^S$$

These polynomials can be compared in using the order relation of Definition 3. Thus, we can define the index set (corresponding to K):

(10) $L \;=\; \{k \,|\, b_k(\varepsilon)/A_k^S \;=\; \underset{i \in I}{\text{Min}} \;[b_i(\varepsilon)/A_i^S]\}$

and we will choose $r \varepsilon L$ (we will see later that $|L| = 1$).

Step 4: As we have seen in Chapter III, a pivot operation is equivalent to a matrix multiplication (by pivot matrix $Pi(r,s)$, see Section III.4). From Remark 14, we see that the pivot operation of step 4 will have to be performed on an $(m+1) \times (m+n+1)$-matrix:

$$\tilde{M} \;=\; \begin{bmatrix} A & Q \\ c & -\tilde{\zeta} \end{bmatrix}$$

instead of the matrix

$$M \;=\; \begin{bmatrix} A & b \\ c & -\zeta \end{bmatrix}$$

where $\tilde{\zeta}$ is the $(m+1)$-row vector, all coefficients of which are equal to 0 at the beginning.

Remark 16: At each iteration, $|L| = 1$. Suppose that this is not true and let k', $k'' \varepsilon L$. We have

$$b_{k'}(\varepsilon)/A_{k'}^S \;=\; b_{k''}(\varepsilon)/A_{k''}^S$$

i.e., matrix Q of coefficients of $b(\varepsilon)$ has two proportional rows. But this is impossible since, from Remark 15, Q is defined by

$$Q \;=\; (A^J)^{-1} \, Q_{init}$$

where

$$Q_{init} \;=\; [b, U_m]$$

is the value of Q at the beginning of the algorithm. Since Q_{init} is of

rank m (it contains the unit matrix) and since $(A^J)^{-1}$ is nonsingular, Q
is also of rank m and cannot have two proportional rows.

Remark 17: At each iteration of the simplex algorithm applied to the perturbed
problem $(P(\varepsilon))$, polynomials $b_i(\varepsilon)$ are positive (see Definition 3).

 This property is true at the beginning. Let us show that if it is true
at some iteration, it is also true at the next one. After a pivot operation,
we have

$$\bar{b}_r(\varepsilon) = b_r(\varepsilon)/A_r^S \succ 0$$

$$\bar{b}_i(\varepsilon) = b_i(\varepsilon) - A_i^S b_r(\varepsilon)/A_r^S \qquad \text{for} \quad i \neq r$$

From (10), these polynomials are positive or zero. Since $|L| = 1$ they are
strictly positive.

Remark 18: At each iteration of the simplex algorithm applied to the perturbed
problem $(P(\varepsilon))$, the value of the objective function corresponding to the basic
solution associated with the current feasible basis is

$$\zeta(\varepsilon) = \tilde{\zeta}^0 + \tilde{\zeta}^1 \varepsilon + \tilde{\zeta}^2 \varepsilon^2 + \ldots + \tilde{\zeta}^m \varepsilon^m$$

where coefficients $\tilde{\zeta}^k$ are defined by the succession of pivot operations of
Remark 15. The increase of the value of the objective function from one iteration to the next is thus

$$c^S b_r(\varepsilon)/A_r^S$$

which is -- from Remark 17 -- a positive polynomial.

Theorem 3: The simplex algorithm applied to perturbed program $(P(\varepsilon))$ is
always finite.

Proof: The argument is the same as the one used for the proof of Theorem 2.
The value of the objective function -- which is now a polynomial in ε -- strictly
increases from iteration to iteration. Thus one cannot meet a basis that was
found before. Since the number of bases is finite, so is the algorithm.

Remark 19: We now have a procedure that solves any linear program (written in
canonical form with respect to a feasible basis) in a finite number of iterations.

It suffices to solve the associated perturbed program $(P(\varepsilon))$ and to let $\varepsilon = 0$ when an optimal solution has been found.

Remark 20: What the artifact of "perturbed program $(P(\varepsilon))$" and definition of "positive polynomials" in fact brings is a more sensitive way of comparing rows in case of tie in the initial linear program (since the constant term of polynomials $b_i(\varepsilon)$ plays a dominant role in the comparison rule).

This method can be presented differently in terms of lexicographic ordering.   See Exercise 13.

EXERCISES

1. Let J be a feasible basis and linear program (P) be written in canonical form with respect to J. Assume that $s \notin J$ and $c^S > 0$. Show that if $A^S \leq 0$, $(PP(J,s))$ -- as defined in Remark 5 -- has no optimal solution and that the same is true for (P).

2. Solve completely the linear program of Exercise IV.1.

3. Solve the linear program

$$\begin{cases} 4x_1 + 4x_2 + 4x_3 + x_4 \leq 44 \\ 8x_1 + 6x_2 + 4x_3 + 3x_4 \leq 36 \\ 5x_1 + x_2 + 6x_3 + 2x_4 = z(\text{Max}) \end{cases} \qquad x_i \geq 0 \quad i = 1,2,3,4$$

Compare your result with what was obtained in solving Exercise IV.5.

4. Solve by the simplex algorithm

$$\begin{cases} 2x_1 + x_2 \leq 5 \\ x_1 - x_2 \leq 1 \\ x_1 + x_2 \leq 3 \\ 3x_1 + 2x_2 = z(\text{Max}) \end{cases} \qquad x_1, x_2 \geq 0$$

Give a graphic illustration.

5. Consider the linear program

$$(P) \begin{cases} 2x_1 + x_2 + 3x_3 + 2x_4 \leq 8 \\ 3x_1 + 2x_2 + 2x_3 + x_4 \leq 7 \\ 2x_1 + 3x_2 + 2x_3 + 3x_4 = z(Max) \end{cases} \qquad x_i \geq 0 \qquad i = 1,2,3,4$$

(a) Write the dual (D) of (P) and give a graphic solution of (D).

(b) Solve (P) by the simplex algorithm and check the solution of (D).

(c) Call E the matrix of coefficients of slack variables x_5 and x_6 in the canonical form relative to the optimal basis. Check that

$$E = \begin{bmatrix} 2 & 1 \\ 1 & 2 \end{bmatrix}^{-1}$$

and explain why.

(d) Check that $(-c^5, -c^6)$ is the optimal solution of (D) and explain why.

6. Solve the linear program

$$\begin{cases} 9x_1 + 6x_2 \leq 54 \\ x_1 + 2x_2 \leq 14 \\ 3x_1 - x_2 \leq 9 \\ 3x_1 + x_2 = z(Max) \end{cases} \qquad x_1, x_2 \geq 0$$

using the simplex algorithm.

7. Use the simplex algorithm to prove

$$\left. \begin{array}{l} 2x_1 + x_2 \leq 4 \\ 4x_1 - 3x_2 \leq 2 \\ -3x_1 + 2x_2 \leq 3 \\ x_1, x_2, \geq 0 \end{array} \right\} \Rightarrow x_1 + x_2 \leq 5$$

8. Use the simplex algorithm to prove

$$\left.\begin{array}{rcl} 2x + y & \leq & 3 \\ -2x + y & \leq & 1 \\ x & \leq & 1 \\ x, \ y & \geq & 0 \end{array}\right\} \quad \Rightarrow \quad (x + y) \leq 5/2$$

Show that we can obtain $(x+y) \leq 5/2$ using only part of the hypotheses. Weaken the hypotheses to obtain the strongest implication. Check on a graphic.

9.   Let

$$(P) \quad \begin{cases} Ax = b \qquad x \geq 0 \\ cx = z \,(Max) \end{cases}$$

be a linear program written in canonical form with respect to an optimal basis J.

(a)   Show that if $c^j < 0$ for $j \notin J$, then the optimal solution is unique.

(b)   Show on an example that the optimal solution may be unique with, at the same time, some $c^J = 0$ for $j \notin J$.

10.   Consider the linear program

$$\begin{cases} x_1 + 4x_2 + 2x_3 + 3x_4 & \leq & 20 \\ 2x_1 + x_2 + 3x_3 + x_4 & \leq & 6 \\ 7x_1 + 11x_2 + 12x_3 + 9x_4 & = & z\,(Max) \end{cases}$$

(a)   Find an optimal solution of (P). Is this solution unique?

(b)   The coefficient of x_3 in the objective function is changed from 12 to $12 - \delta$ $(\delta \geq 0)$. What is the variation of the optimal solution when δ varies?

(c)   The right-hand side of the first inequation changes from 20 to 19. What is the corresponding variation of the optimal solution?

11.   Show that if $\Lambda(\varepsilon)$ is not identically 0 and is not positive, then $-\Lambda(\varepsilon)$ is positive. Show that the sum of two positive polynomials is a positive polynomial. Show that the relation "$\succ$" is a total order on polynomials.

12.   Let (P) be a linear program written in canonical form with respect to a feasible basis J_0. Let $G = (X,U)$ be the directed graph defined in the following way:

(i) There is a one-to-one correspondence between nodes in G and the feasible bases of (P).

(ii) There is an arc from node x_J (corresponding to basis J) to node $x_{\bar{J}}$ (corresponding to basis $\bar{J}$) if and only if an iteration of the simplex algorithm (as presented in Section 3) may lead from J to $\bar{J}$.

    (a) Is it possible that graph G include directed cycles? What about directed cycles of length 2?

    (b) Show that there exists an elementary path in G from x_J to $x_{\bar{J}}$ where $x_{\bar{J}}$ corresponds to the optimal basis $\bar{J}$.

    (c) Show that if the rule of choice of the pivot row $r \varepsilon K$ is the following: *"Choose one r in K with equal probabilities among elements of K,"* the algorithm is finite with probability 1.

13. Indices of components of vectors of $\mathbb{R}^k$ are supposed to be ordered (take, for instance, "natural order" $1 < 2 < \ldots < k$). We defined the "lexicographic" order on vectors of $\mathbb{R}^k$ in the following way: $a \in \mathbb{R}^k$ is ℓ-positive if $a \neq 0$ and if the <u>first</u> nonzero component of a is positive. We note that

$$a \succ 0$$

a is ℓ-greater than b if $a - b \succ 0$. We note that

$$a \succ b$$

(a) Show that the order in which the words are written in a dictionary is the lexicographic order.

(b) Given a linear program written in canonical form with respect to a feasible basis J:

$$(P) \begin{cases} Ax = b \qquad x \geq 0 \\ cx = z\,(\text{Max}) \end{cases}$$

we associate with (P) an ℓ-linear program

$$(P_\ell) \begin{cases} AX = B \qquad X_j \succ 0 \qquad j = 1, 2, \ldots, n \\ cX = Z(\ell \cdot \text{Max}) \end{cases}$$

where X is the $m \times (m+1)$ matrix of unknowns

Z is a $(m+1)$-row vector (of unknowns).

$B = (b, U_m)$

Show that we can define (using lexicographic order of vectors of $\mathbb{R}^{m+1}$) a finite algorithm to solve (P_ℓ) .

(c) Show that if $\bar{X}$ is an optimal solution of (P_ℓ) , then $\bar{x} = \bar{X}^1$ is an optimal solution of (P) .

(d) Deduce a finite process to solve any linear program and show that it is identical to the method developed using perturbed programs.

(e) Solve example of Remark 12.

Chapter VI. The Two Phases of the Simplex Method: Theoretical Results Proved by Application of the Simplex Method

We now have to show how a given linear program can be written in canonical form with respect to a feasible basis (when the solution set is not empty). We then have to prove that a linear program with an optimal solution has a basic optimal solution. This result can be used to prove various theorems.

1. The Two Phases of the Simplex Method

Remark 1: Recall that a linear program

$$(P) \quad \begin{cases} Ax = b & x \geq 0 \\ cx = z\,(Max) \end{cases}$$

is said to be written in canonical form with respect to the feasible basis J if the following three conditions are satisfied:

(1) A^J is, up to a permutation of its columns, the unit matrix. This permutation is defined by the mapping "col" (cf. Remark V.1).

(2) $b \geq 0$.

(3) $c^J = 0$.

However, if conditions (1) and (2) are satisfied but not condition (3), we pose

$$y^i = c^{col(i)} \qquad i = 1, 2, \ldots, m$$

and the linear program

$$(P') \quad \begin{cases} Ax = b & x \geq 0 \\ (c - yA)\, x = z\,(Max) - yb \end{cases}$$

is equivalent to (P) and satisfies (1), (2), and (3). Thus we will consider that it suffices to fulfill conditions (1) and (2).

Definition 1: Let us consider the linear program

$$(P) \quad \begin{cases} Ax = b \quad\quad x \geq 0 \\ cx = z(Max) \end{cases}$$

We make no assumption on (P): linear system $Ax = b$ is not necessarily full rank and we do not assume that the set of feasible solutions to (P) is non-empty.

However, without loss of generality (by multiplying by -1 the equations for which $b_i < 0$), we assume that

(2) $$b \geq 0$$

We associate with linear program (P) an auxiliary linear program

$$(PA) \quad \begin{cases} Ax + Uv = b \quad\quad x, v \geq 0 \\ \sum_{i=1}^{m} v_i = \psi(min) \end{cases}$$

where U is the $m \times m$-unit matrix and $v_1, v_2, \ldots, v_m$ are called "artificial variables."

Remark 2: The ith constraint of (PA) is written

$$A_i x + v_i = b_i$$

i.e., v_i measures the difference between the right-hand side b_i and $A_i x$. When all artificial variables are equal to 0, x, the feasible solution of (PA), is thus a feasible solution of (P).

Remark 3: We apply to (PA) the process of Remark 1: let e be the m-row vector each component of which is equal to 1. (PA) is equivalent to

$$(PA') \quad \begin{cases} Ax + Uv = b \quad\quad x, v \geq 0 \\ -eAx = \psi(Min) - eb \end{cases}$$

(PA') is written in canonical form with respect to the feasible basis $J_0 = \{n+1, n+2, \ldots, n+m\}$.

Theorem 1: The simplex algorithm (as presented in Chapter V) can be applied to (PA'). In a finite number of iterations, we end up with an optimal basic solution.

Proof: The objective function of (PA') is

$$\psi = v_1 + v_2 + \ldots + v_m \geq 0 \qquad \text{since} \qquad v_i \geq 0 \qquad i = 1, 2, \ldots, m$$

Thus, the algorithm cannot terminate with a set of feasible solutions for which the objective function is unbounded ($\psi \to -\infty$ is impossible). From Chapter V, the algorithm terminates (in a finite number of iterations) with an optimal basic solution.

Theorem 2: Let $\hat{x}, \hat{v}$ be an optimal solution of (PA') (and thus of (PA)). A necessary and sufficient condition for (P) to have a feasible solution is that

(4) $\hat{v}_i = 0 \qquad i = 1, 2, \ldots, m$

Proof: If condition (4) is satisfied, $\hat{x}$ is obviously a feasible solution of (P). Assume that (P) has a feasible solution $\bar{x}$ and that condition (4) is not satisfied. $(\bar{x}, \bar{v} = 0)$ is then a feasible solution of (PA). And we have

$$\bar{\psi} = \sum_{i=1}^{m} \bar{v}_i = 0 < \hat{\psi} = \sum_{i=1}^{m} \hat{v}_i$$

which contradicts the fact that $(\hat{x}, \hat{v})$ was, by assumption, an _optimal_ solution of (PA).

Theorem 3: Let

$$(\hat{PA}) \quad \begin{cases} \hat{A}x + \hat{B}v = \hat{b} \qquad\qquad x, v \geq 0 \\ \hat{c}x + \hat{d}v = \psi(\text{Min}) - \hat{\zeta} \end{cases}$$

be the linear program (PA) written in canonical form with respect to an optimal basis (which we know to exist from Theorem 1). Then if

- $\hat{A}_i = 0, \ b_i = 0$
- v_r is the basic variable in the ith row,

the rth constraint of (P) (i.e., $A_r x = b_r$) was redundant.

Proof: Canonical form $(\hat{PA})$ has been obtained through a sequence of pivot operations. The ith equation of $(\hat{PA})$ can thus be considered as a linear combination of the equations of the linear system

$$Ax + Uv \; = \; b$$

the coefficient of the rth equation in this linear combination being different from 0. The very same linear combination applied to the linear system

$$Ax \; = \; b$$

gives the redundant equation

$$0x \; = \; 0$$

The theorem is proved.

Theorem 4: If (P) has a feasible solution, there exists an optimal basis for (PA) containing no index r corresponding to an artificial variable v_r.

Proof: Assume that v_r is a basic variable in $(\hat{PA})$. With no loss of generality, we can assume that $\hat{B}_r^r = 1$. From Theorem 2, we have

$$\hat{b}_r \; = \; 0$$

(a) If $\hat{A}_r = 0$, we know from Theorem 3 that the rth equation of (PA) was redundant. We can thus suppress the rth equation of $(\hat{PA})$.

(b) If $A_r \neq 0$, let $\hat{A}_r^s \neq 0$. We can then make a pivot operation on element $\hat{A}_r^s$: the variable v_r leaves the basis and variable x_s enters the basis (without change of the basic solution, since $\hat{b}_r = 0$).

We can repeat the process on all artificial basic variables.

Definition 2: The solution of linear program (PA), followed by the expulsion of artificial basic variables according to the process described in the proof of Theorem 4, is called "phase I of the simplex method." After phase I has been accomplished, the linear program (P) itself is written in canonical form with respect to a feasible basis (if a feasible solution exists) and the simplex

algorithm can be applied to (P): this part is called "phase II of the simplex
method."

   We follow here denominations proposed by G. Dantzig: The <u>simplex method</u>
is composed of two phases. In each of them the <u>simplex algorithm</u> can be applied
(to the auxiliary problem in phase I, to (P) in phase II).

<u>Remark 4</u>: Instead of (PA), we could have associated

$$(\widetilde{PA}) \quad \begin{cases} Ax + Uv & = b \\ -cx \quad\quad +z & = 0 \\ \displaystyle\sum_{i=1}^{m} v_i & = \psi(min) \end{cases} \quad\quad x,v \ge 0$$

as the auxiliary problem in which z is a nonconstrained basic variable (and
thus will never be candidate to leave the bases). If $(\widetilde{PA})$ is solved instead
of (PA), then at the end of phase I the linear program is written in canonical
form with respect to a feasible basis ((1), (2), and (3) are satisfied) and
the operations described in Remark 1 need not be performed. This is what is
generally done.

<u>Remark 5</u>: If (P) contains a variable, say x_1, which is not constrained to
be positive or zero, we can go back to the general case using the method of
Chapter I (see Remark I.10). This is correct but not very clever. We will prefer expressing x_1 as a function of the other variables in an equation where
x_1 has a nonzero coefficient, replace x_1 by this value in the other equations
and in the objective function, and solve the reduced linear program thus obtained. Finally, the value of x_1 for the optimal solution is computed from
the expression giving x_1 (see Exercise 3). If more than one variable is unconstrained, this procedure is extended naturally.

   To maintain the sparsity of matrix A, it might be advantageous not to
eliminate x_1 but to consider it as a basic variable from which, once entered,
the basis will never be a candidate to leave (the same argument as in Remark 4--
see Chapter VII).

<u>Remark 6</u>: In linear program (P), it may happen that a variable, say x_s, is
contained in only one equation, say the rth equation. Then if $A_r^s b_r > 0$, it
is not necessary (and in fact, it is rather clumsy) to introduce an artificial

variable corresponding to this equation. We prefer to consider x_s as the basic variable corresponding to the rth equation.

Examples: Assume that we have to solve

$$(P_\alpha) \begin{cases} \alpha x_1 + 2x_2 + x_3 && = 2 \\ x_1 + x_2 + 5x_3 && = 12 \\ x_1 + 2x_2 + 6x_3 + x_4 && = 13 \\ x_1 + x_2 + x_3 + x_4 && = z(Min) \end{cases} \quad x_1, x_2, x_3, x_4 \geq 0$$

We need only add artificial variables for the first and second equations; x_4 will be the basic variable associated with the third equation (see Remark 6). The auxiliary problem is written

$$(PA_\alpha) \begin{cases} \alpha x_1 + 2x_2 + x_3 && + v_1 && = 2 \\ x_1 + x_2 + 5x_3 && + v_2 && = 12 \\ x_1 + 2x_2 + 6x_3 + x_4 && && = 13 \\ x_2 + 5x_3 && + z & = 13 \\ v_1 + v_2 && = \psi(Min) \end{cases} \quad \begin{array}{l} x_i \geq 0 \quad i=1,3,4,5 \\ v_i v_2 \geq 0 \end{array}$$

In subtracting the first two equations to the objective function, we obtain

$$-(\alpha + 1)x_1 - 3x_2 - 6x_3 \qquad\qquad = \psi(Min) - 14$$

and (PA_α) is written in canonical form with respect to a feasible basis.

FIRST CASE: $\alpha = 1$. We apply the simplex algorithm to (PA_1) :

x_1	x_2	x_3	x_4	v_1	v_2	z	b
1	2	1		1			2 ←
1	1	5			1		12
1	2	6	1				13
	1	5				1	13
-2	-3	-6$_*$					-14
1	2	1		1			2
-4	-9			-5	1		2
-5	-10		1	-6			1
-5	-9			-5		1	3
4	9			6			-2

This basis is optimal. The corresponding value of ψ is positive. From Theorem 2, (P_1) has no feasible solution. Take an equation of $(\hat{PA}_1)$ where an artificial variable is basic and the right-hand side is nonzero:

$$-4x_1 - 9x_2 - 5v_1 + v_2 = 2$$

In terms of the initial variables, this equation becomes

$$-4x_1 - 9x_2 = 2$$

which is clearly infeasible. In other words, phase I of the simplex method has produced a linear combination of the equations of the system (subtract 5 times the first equation from the second one), which is an infeasible equation. (P_1) has no feasible solution. We stop.

SECOND CASE: $\alpha = 0$. We apply the simplex algorithm to (PA_0):

x_1	x_2	x_3	x_4	v_1	v_2	z	b
	2	1		1			2 ←
1	1	5			1		12
1	2	6	1				13
	1	5				1	13
-1	-3	-6 $_*$					-14
	2	1		1			2
1	- 9			-5	1		2
1	-10		1	-6			1 ←
	- 9			-5		1	3
-1 $_*$	9			6			-2
	2	1		1			2
	1		-1	1	1		1 ←
1	-10		1	-6			1
	- 9			-5		1	3
	-1 $_*$		1	0			-1
		1	2	-1	-2		0
	1		-1	1	1		1
1			-9	4	10		11
			-9	4	9	1	12
			0	1	1		0

Phase I is performed. We have found a feasible basis for (P_0):

$$
\begin{cases}
& x_3 + 2x_4 = 0 \\
& x_2 - x_4 = 1 \\
& x_1 - 9x_4 = 11 \\
& 9x_4 = z(\text{Min}) - 12
\end{cases}
\qquad x_1, x_2, x_3, x_4 \geq 0
$$

Here the initial basis found at the end of phase I is also optimal; i.e.,
phase II is finished at the same time as phase I. This is just due to good
luck.

Remark 7: Nonbasic artificial variables do not play any role. We can as well
forget them. Thus when an artificial variable leaves the basis, we will suppress it.

The Simplex Method

Phase I: The linear program (P) is written in standard form. Let us
multiply by -1 the equations for which the right-hand side is negative. Define the auxiliary problem as in Definition 1. The auxiliary problem is written
in canonical form with respect to a feasible basis.

Solve the auxiliary problem using the simplex algorithm. The auxiliary
linear program is then written in canonical form with respect to an optimal
basis.

(a) If the value of the objective function is positive, the
linear program (P) has no feasible solution. STOP.

(b) If the value of the objective function is equal to zero,
apply repetitively the following process until all artificial basic variables are eliminated:

Let v_r be a basic artificial variable. Perform a pivot
operation that leads v_r out of the basis. If such a
pivot operation is impossible, suppress the corresponding
equation.

When there is no more artificial variable in the basis, (P) is written in
canonical form with respect to a feasible basis.

Phase II: Apply the simplex algorithm to the linear program (P) as
written at the end of Phase I.

2. Results That Can Be Proved by the Simplex Method

The simplex method is a finite process since the simplex algorithm itself
is finite. From this finiteness, we deduce the following results:

Theorem 5   (Fundamental Theorem of Linear Programming): A linear program:

(a) Which has a feasible solution has a basic feasible solution.

(b) Which has an optimal solution has a basic optimal solution.

(c) Which has a feasible solution and the objective function of
which is bounded (upper bound if the objective function is
to be maximized, lower bound if the objective function is to
be minimized) has an optimal solution.

Theorem 6:   If two dual programs (P) and (D) both have a feasible solution,
they both have an optimal solution and the values of the objective function for
the optimums are equal.

Proof: Let $\bar{x}, \bar{y}$ be a couple of solutions of the dual linear programs

$$(P) \begin{cases} Ax \le b \qquad x \ge 0 \\ cx = z \ (Max) \end{cases} \qquad\qquad (D) \begin{cases} yA \le c \qquad y \ge 0 \\ yb = w \ (Min) \end{cases}$$

From Theorem II.2, the value of the objective function of (P) is bounded by
$\bar{y}b$ and the value of the objective function of (D) is bounded by $c\bar{x}$. From
Theorem 5, (P) and (D) both have a basic optimal solution. The property is
then a consequence of the corollary of Theorem IV.3.

Theorem 7 (Farkas' Lemma): Let A be an m×n-matrix and b be an m-column
vector. If for any m-row vector y such that

$$yA \le 0$$

we have $yb \le 0$,   then $x \ge 0$ exists such that

$$Ax = b$$

Proof: Let us consider the linear program

$$(P) \qquad \begin{cases} yA \le 0 \\ yb = z \ (Max) \end{cases}$$

(P) has a feasible solution $y = 0$. By assumption, the objective function is
bounded by 0. From Theorem 5, (P) has an optimal basic solution. From the
corollary of Theorem IV.3, its dual has an optimal (and thus a feasible) solution. The dual of (P) is

$$\begin{cases} Ax & = & b & \qquad x \geq 0 \\ 0x & = & w(Min) \end{cases}$$

Theorem 8   (Theorem of the Alternatives):   One and one only of the two following systems of constraints has a solution

$$(I) \quad \begin{cases} Ax = b \\ x \geq 0 \end{cases} \qquad\qquad (II) \begin{cases} yA \leq 0 \\ yb > 0 \end{cases}$$

Proof: (I) and (II) cannot both have solutions $\bar{x}$ and $\bar{y}$:

$$0 \geq \bar{y} A \bar{x} = \bar{y}b > 0$$

If system (II) has no solution, the hypotheses of Theorem 7 are fulfilled and thus (I) has a solution.

Remark 8:   Other theorems are presented as exercises.   Their proofs follow the same line.

EXERCISES

1. Solve the linear program

$$(P) \quad \begin{cases} x_1 + x_2 \geq 2 \\ - x_1 + x_2 \geq 3 \\ x_1 \qquad \geq 4 \\ 3x_1 + 2x_2 = z(Min) \end{cases} \qquad x_1, x_2 \leq 0$$

2. Solve the linear program

$$(P) \quad \begin{cases} x_1 + x_2 + 2x_3 \leq 6 \\ 2x_1 - x_2 + 2x_3 \geq 2 \\ 2x_2 + x_3 = z(Max) \end{cases} \qquad x_1, x_2, x_3 \geq 0$$

3. Solve the linear program

$$(P) \begin{cases} -x_1 + x_2 + x_3 - x_4 = 1 \\ 2x_1 + 7x_2 + x_3 + 8x_4 = 7 \\ 2x_1 + 10x_2 + 2x_3 + 10x_4 = 10 \\ 2x_1 + 18x_2 + 5x_3 + 14x_4 = z(\text{Max}) \end{cases} \qquad \begin{aligned} & x_1 \gtrless 0 \\ & x_2, x_3, x_4 \geq 0 \end{aligned}$$

4. Solve the linear program

$$(P) \begin{cases} 2x_1 + x_2 - x_3 \geq 4 \\ 4x_1 - 3x_2 \geq 2 \\ -3x_1 + 2x_2 + x_3 \geq 3 \\ -x_1 + 3x_2 - 3x_3 = z(\text{Max}) \end{cases} \qquad x_1, x_2, x_3 \geq 0$$

5. Consider the linear program

$$(P) \begin{cases} x_1 - x_2 \geq 1 \\ 2x_1 - x_2 \geq 6 \\ x_1 + x_2 = z(\text{Min}) \end{cases} \qquad x_1, x_2 \geq 0$$

and the associated problem

$$(PA) \begin{cases} x_1 - x_2 - x_3 + x_5 = 1 \\ 2x_1 - x_2 - x_4 + x_6 = 6 \\ x_1 + x_2 + Mx_5 + Mx_6 = z(\text{Min}) \end{cases} \qquad \begin{aligned} & x_i \geq 0 \\ & i = 1, \ldots, 6 \end{aligned}$$

where   M is a positive scalar.

(a) Explain the roles played by x_3, x_4, x_5, x_6, and M.   Show that if M is large enough, the solution of (PA) is equivalent to simultaneous application of phases I and II of the simplex method.

(b) Solve (PA) with M = 100.

(c) Can this method be generalized?

6. Does the following system have a solution?

$$\begin{cases} x_1 + 3x_2 - 5x_3 = 10 \\ x_1 - 4x_2 - 7x_3 = -1 \\ x_1 \geq -3, \quad x_2 \geq 2, \quad x_3 \geq -1 \end{cases}$$

7. Is it possible to find numbers a, b, and c such that

$$\begin{cases} a^2 + b^2 + 2c^2 = 8 \\ 8a^2 + 11b^2 + 10c^2 = 31 \end{cases}$$

8. Find a non-negative solution to the system

$$\begin{cases} x_1 + 2x_2 - 2x_3 + x_4 = 0 \\ -x_1 + 2x_2 + x_3 + 2x_4 = 21 \end{cases}$$

9. Prove the following forms of the theorem of the alternatives: One and only
one of the two following systems of constraints has a solution:

(a) (I) $Ax \leq b, \quad x \geq 0$ (II) $uA \geq 0, \ u \geq 0, \quad ub < 0$

(b) (I) $Ax = b$ (II) $uA = 0, \ ub < 0$

(c) (I) $Ax \leq b$ (II) $uA = 0, \ u \geq 0, \ ub < 0$

(d) (Gordan - 1873):

(I) $Ax = 0, \ x \geq 0, \ x \neq 0$ (II) $uA > 0$

(e) (Stiemke - 1915):

(I) $Ax = 0, \quad x > 0$ (II) $uA \geq 0, \quad uA \neq 0$

(f) (Motzkin- 1936):

(I) $\begin{cases} Ax + By + cz = 0 \\ x, y \geq 0 \quad x \neq 0 \\ (A \text{ nonempty}) \end{cases}$ (II) $\begin{cases} uA > 0 \\ uB \geq 0 \\ uC = 0 \end{cases}$

(g) (Motzkin-Tucker)

(I) $\begin{cases} Ax + By + Cz = 0 \\ x > 0, \ y \geq 0 \\ (A \text{ nonempty}) \end{cases}$ (II) $\begin{cases} uA \geq 0 \qquad uA \neq 0 \\ uB \geq 0 \\ uC = 0 \end{cases}$

10. Using the theorem of the alternatives, prove that the following systems have no solutions:

(a)
$$\begin{cases} x_1 + 3x_2 - 5x_3 = 2 \\ x_1 - 4x_2 - 7x_3 = 3 \end{cases} \qquad x_1, x_2, x_3 \geq 0$$

(b)
$$\begin{cases} 6x_1 - 5x_2 \geq 7 \\ -2x_1 - 7x_2 \geq 2 \\ -x_1 + 3x_2 \leq -1 \end{cases}$$

(c)
$$\begin{cases} -3x_1 - 2x_2 + x_3 + 2x_4 = 5 \\ -2x_1 - x_2 + 3x_3 + 5x_4 = 27 \\ x_i \geq i \qquad i=1,2,3,4 \end{cases}$$

11. Prove that if B is a square antisymmetric matrix, the following system has a solution:

$$\begin{cases} Bx \geq 0 \qquad x \geq 0 \\ Bx + x > 0 \end{cases}$$

Hint: Prove that
$$\begin{cases} -Bx \leq 0 \\ -Bx - Ux \leq -e \end{cases} \qquad x \geq 0$$
has a solution.

12. Show that if A is a square matrix such that
$$x^T Ax \geq 0 \qquad \forall x$$

then the system
$$Ax \geq 0, \quad x \geq 0, \quad x \neq 0$$

always has a solution.

Chapter VII. Computational Aspects of the Simplex Method: Revised Simplex Algorithm; Bounded Variables

Up to this point, we have introduced linear programming and its method of solution, the simplex algorithm, in a purely theoretical fashion. We paid no attention to the effectiveness of the algorithm nor to the fact that one has to face special problems (and in particular, numerical ones) when the algorithm is implemented on a computer. In this chapter, we give a brief account of the efficiency of the simplex algorithm (both from a theoretical and a practical standpoint). Then we show how harmful rounding errors may be for a practical application. In the third section, we describe the "revised simplex algorithm," which has essentially been designed for computer implementation. Finally, we describe how bounded variables can be taken care of in a way that reduces computation as much as possible.

1. Efficiency of the Simplex Algorithm

We mentioned in Section I.5 (and will prove in Chapter VIII) that simplex algorithm finds an "optimal" vertex of the polyhedron of feasible solutions of a linear program (P) after a journey along the edges of this polyhedron. This procedure may seem rather clumsy: why stay on the border of the domain of feasible solutions instead of going "directly" (but how?) to the optimal point?

However, the experience of solution of numerous linear programs leads to the conclusion that the algorithm is surprisingly efficient. For problems with $m \leq 50$ and $m+n \leq 200$, Dantzig reported (cf. [2]), that the number of iterations is of the order of magnitude of $3m/2$, rarely running over $3m$. More recent experiments conducted over problems of larger size lead to an analogous conclusion. The number of iterations depends very loosely on the number of variables: some authors suggest that, for fixed m, the number of iterations is proportional to the logarithm of n, on the average. This brilliant performance is certainly an important factor of the success that the simplex method has won even if no staisfying explanation has been given of this efficiency.

However, this rough estimate, which is of prime importance to the practitioner, does not give a bound of the number of iterations. Simplex algorithm is "nonpolynomial" in the sense that it is always possible to construct examples for which the number of iterations is not bounded by a polynomial in n and m (in fact, the precise meaning of nonpolynomial algorithm is slightly more sophisticated, but we will be content here with this approximation). We now present an example constructed by Klee and Minty (see Exercise 8):

$$(P_M) \quad \begin{cases} 2 \sum_{j=1}^{i-1} 10^{i-j} x_j \ + \ x_i \ \le \ 100^{i-1} & i = 1,2,\ldots,n \\[2mm] x_j \ \ge \ 0 & j = 1,2,\ldots,n \\[2mm] \sum_{j=1}^{n} 10^{n-j} x_j \ = \ z(\text{Max}) \end{cases}$$

which requires 2^{n-1} iterations of the simplex algorithm when the criterion to choose the entering variable is $c^s = \text{Max}[c^j]$. Actually, examples can be constructed that beat any rule. But these examples are of an academic nature. On "current" (note the lack of rigorous meaning of this term) problems, the algorithm works very well.

Recently [1979], Khachian proposed an algorithm that solves linear programs using a number of elementary operations (such as additions, comparisons, and multiplications), which is bounded by a polynomial in a quantity that expresses the size of the program. This beautiful mathematical result is very likely to be of moderate practical use. Although it is polynomial, Khachian's algorithm seems to be far less efficient than the simplex to solve most -- if not all -- linear programs.

2. Numerical Pitfalls

The presentation of the simplex algorithm in preceding chapters was completely abstract in the sense that we assumed that the calculations were conducted with a perfect precision. But it is well known that numbers in a computer are represented only with a certain precision (of d digits, say): they are rounded off.

To give an example of the type of problem rounding off can lead to, let us try and solve the following linear system by the Gauss-Jordan elimination method, assuming that numbers are represented with three significant digits:

$$\begin{cases} 0.001x_1 + x_2 = 1 \\ x_1 + x_2 = 2 \end{cases}$$

Using the first equation to eliminate x_1 and rounding off intermediate results to three significant digits, we obtain

$$x_1 = 0, \qquad x_2 = 1$$

a clearly improper result. The reason for this error is that we pivoted on 0.001, which is too small a coefficient relative to the other coefficients of matrix A and to the precision used. This difficulty is prevented by numerous tricks in linear programming computer codes (scaling, search for a pivot of reasonable size, etc.).

Another effect of rounding off is the problem of "recognizing zero." Numbers that are small in absolute value have an uncertain sign, and thus (for instance), the optimality condition

$$c^j \leq 0$$

will have no precise meaning. Thus in computer codes, zero must be defined through two small positive numbers, t_1 and t_2, called "zero tolerance." A scaler α is considered to be equal to zero if

$$-t_1 < \alpha < t_2$$

Other zero tolerance will be used: For instance, we will refuse introducing x_s in the basis if this introduction leads to a pivot on element A_r^s such that

$$A_r^s < t_3$$

(see above). Needless to say, a proper definition of these zero tolerances (which might be adaptative with the evolution of the algorithm), requires some skill and experience.

Finally, experience shows that for most practical linear programs, matrix A is very sparse (1% of nonzero terms, and even less is frequent for matrices of large size). If this sparsity is maintained, the number of operations can be drastically decreased, whereas if the problem is treated as in Chapter V,

there is no reason why the sparsity would stay (there will be "fill in").
Computer codes will use several devices (and in particular, the so-called
revised simplex algorithm) to take advantage of the built-in sparsity of
matrix A without destroying it.

The conclusion of this brief section is that practical implementation
of the simplex algorithm is far away from the elementary algorithm presented
in Chapter V. Codes have been written that are available on most computers.
These codes represent several person-years of work by specialists and can
handle linear programs with several thousand constraints and a quasi-unli-
mited number of variables. It is not advisable, when one has to solve a
linear program, to code the simplex algorithm from scratch. Utilization of
one of these codes will be preferred; user notice is easy to understand for
any reader of the present book.

3.   Revised Simplex Algorithm

As we announced in the preceding section, the simplex algorithm is, in
general, not implemented in the form under which it is presented in Chapter V.
To limit the propagation of round-off errors, to deal in a better way with
sparse matrices, and to decrease the number of operations, the "revised" form is
preferred. We insist on the fact that, basically, the algorithm remains the same
and that it is solely its implementation that changes. We refer to the simplex
algorithm as presented in Section V.3.

Remark 1: Let J be a feasible basis of the linear program

$$(P) \quad \begin{cases} Ax = b \qquad\qquad x \geq 0 \\ cx = z\,(Max) \end{cases}$$

We let

(1) $A(J) = (A^J)^{-1} A$ (we have $(A(J))^J = U_m$)

(2) $b(J) = (A^J)^{-1} b$

(3) $\pi(J) = c^J (A^J)^{-1}$

(4) $c(J) = c - \pi(J) A$

(5) $\zeta(J) = \pi(J) b$

Written in canonical form with respect to basis J, the linear program (P) becomes

$$(P_J) \quad \begin{cases} A(J)x = b(J) & x \geq 0 \\ c(J)x = z(\text{Max}) - \zeta(J) \end{cases}$$

In the revised simplex algorithm we know, at each iteration, the feasible basis J, but we do not know all the coefficients of linear program (P_J). The principle is to compute only those coefficients that are really needed.

For Step 1, we need $c(J)$. Then $\pi(J)$ is computed by (3) and $c(J)$ by (4). For Step 2, we need $(A(J))^s$, which is given by

$$(1') \qquad \qquad (A(J))^s = (A^J)^{-1} A^s$$

For Step 3, we need $b(J)$, given by (2). Then the new basis

$$\hat{J} = J \cup \{s\} \setminus \{\text{col}(r)\}$$

is determined. But *the pivot operation of Step 4 is not performed.*

Remark 2: The main advantage of the revised simplex algorithm is not so much a reduction in the number of operations (see Exercise 1) as the fact that round-off errors cannot propagate since we always work with the initial matrix of data A.

Linear programs in which n (number of variables) is much larger than m (number of equations) are frequently met. It may then happen that matrix A (or $A(J)$) cannot be held in the central memory of the computer, whereas A^J (or $(A^J)^{-1}$) is of sufficiently limited size to be contained in the fast memory. It suffices then to store on a peripheral device matrix

$$M = \begin{bmatrix} A \\ c \end{bmatrix}$$

by columns. Then if $\pi(J)$ has been computed by (3), we can compute -- using (4) -- successively coefficients of $c(J)$ by calling each column of M, one at a time. Recall that we do not have to look for $\text{Max}_j (c(J))^j$ since we can stop as soon as an index s (such that $(c(J))^s > 0$) has been found. Note that, very often, computer codes will look for the largest among the p first positive $(c(J))^j$ met; this type of heuristic approach may improve code efficiency.

Remark 3: The disadvantage of the revised simplex algorithm is that we have to
compute, for each iteration, the inverse of basic matrix $(A^J)^{-1}$ (which takes
a number of operations that is of the order of m^3). From what we have seen in
Chapter III, we know that

(6) $$(A^{\hat{J}})^{-1} = Pi(r,s) \; (A^J)^{-1}$$

where $Pi(r,s)$ is the pivot matrix (cf. Section III.4), which has a single
nontrivial column. It is easy to check that (6) can be performed with m^2
additions and m^2 multiplications.

If we call $D_1, D_2, \ldots, D_q$, the q first pivot matrices and J_q the
basis after the qth iteration, we have

(6') $$(A^{J_q})^{-1} = D_q * D_{q-1} * \circ \circ \circ * D_2 * D_1$$

and this matrix can be stored under a compact form (at least if $q < m$) using
nontrivial columns of matrices D_k. (6') is called, in linear programming
literature, "the product form of the inverse."

In fact, as soon as q reaches a certain value, this method is not very
good: round-off errors appear and the sequence of nontrivial columns is heavy
to take care of. Thus, in the computer codes that are available, the following
compromise is adopted: from time to time, the basic matrix A^J is completely
inverted and this allows a new start with fresh numerical data. The program
decides itself when to perform this reinversion. The decision is taken as a
function of:

(a) Controls that the code can do by itself; for instance, how far
     from zero is $(c(J))^J$?

(b) The value of q.

Remark 4: There is a very simple way to avoid inversion of matrix A^J at each
iteration without using (6) and (6'). It suffices to note that we do not really
need $(A^J)^{-1}$, but that we can obtain what we are looking for $(b(J), \pi(J),$
$(A(J))^S)$ by solving linear systems:

(2') $$A^J b(J) = b$$

(3') $$\pi(J) A^J = c^J$$

(1'') $A^J (A(J))^S = A^S$

     We now have three linear systems to solve. The loss[†] in number of opera-
tions is substantial since when we had $(A^J)^{-1}$, we needed only to perform
matrix multiplications (2), (3), (1'). But some advantages can compensate for
this loss:

> (i) No propagation of round-off errors.
>
> (ii) Nondestruction of sparsity; advantage can be taken
> of a particular structure of matrix A.

Revised Simplex Algorithm

Linear program (P) is not written in canonical form with respect to a feasible
basis, but a feasible basis J is known.

REPEAT the following procedure *until either an optimal basis* is obtained *or*
a set of feasible solutions for which z *is unbounded* is shown to exist.

    STEP 1: Solve the linear system

(3') $\pi(J) A^J = c^J$

    Let $c(J) = c - \pi(J)A$ and choose an s such that $(c(J))^S > 0$. If
such an s does not exist, the basis J is optimal. STOP.

    STEP 2: Solve the linear system

(1'') $A^J (A(J))^S = A^S$

    If $(A(J))^S \leq 0$, no optimal solution exists (z is unbounded). STOP.

    STEP 3: Solve the linear system

(2') $A^J_* b(J) = b$

    and let $I = \{i | (A(J))^S_i > 0\}$ ($I \neq \emptyset$ because of Step 2).
      Choose an r such that

[†]Note that when $(A^J)^{-1}$ is used, there is a gain with respect to simplex
algorithm.

$$(b(J))_r / (A(J))_r^S = \underset{i \in I}{Min} \ [(b(J))_i / (A(J))_i^S]$$

STEP 4: Let

$$J: = J \cup \{s\} \setminus \{col(r)\}$$

$$col(r): = s$$

END REPEAT

Example: To avoid complex notations, we write $\pi, \hat{c}, \hat{A}^s, \hat{b}$ instead of $\pi(J)$, $c(J)$, $(A(J))^S$, $b(J)$. Assume that we want to solve the linear program (program (P_2) of Chapter I -- see Exercise II.12).

$$\begin{cases} x_1 + x_2 + x_3 & = 550 \\ \qquad\qquad\quad x_4 + x_5 + x_6 = 350 & \qquad x_j \geq 0 \\ x_1 \qquad\qquad + x_4 \qquad\quad = 400 & \qquad j = 1, 2, \ldots, 6 \\ \quad x_2 \qquad\qquad + x_5 \qquad = 300 \\ -5x_1 - 6x_2 - 3x_3 - 3x_4 - 5x_5 - 4x_6 = z(Max) \end{cases}$$

we are given the feasible basis $J = \{1, 2, 4, 6\}$ with $col(1) = 1$, $col(2) = 2$, $col(3) = 4$, $col(4) = 6$. π is computed in solving

$$(\pi^1, \pi^2, \pi^3, \pi^4) * \begin{bmatrix} 1 & 1 & 0 & 0 \\ 0 & 0 & 1 & 1 \\ 1 & 0 & 1 & 0 \\ 0 & 1 & 0 & 0 \end{bmatrix} = (-5, -6, -3, -4)$$

We get

$$\pi^1 = -6, \quad \pi^2 = -4, \quad \pi^3 = 1, \quad \pi^4 = 0$$

$$\hat{c}^3 = -3 + 6 = 3, \quad \hat{c}^5 = -5 + 4 = -1; \quad \hat{c}^1 = \hat{c}^2 = \hat{c}^4 = \hat{c}^6 = 0$$

3 is the index that "enters" the basis. We solve

$$\begin{bmatrix} 1 & 1 & 0 & 0 \\ 0 & 0 & 1 & 1 \\ 1 & 0 & 1 & 0 \\ 0 & 1 & 0 & 0 \end{bmatrix} * \hat{b} = \begin{bmatrix} 550 \\ 350 \\ 400 \\ 300 \end{bmatrix}$$

and

$$\begin{bmatrix} 1 & 1 & 0 & 0 \\ 0 & 0 & 1 & 1 \\ 1 & 0 & 1 & 0 \\ 0 & 1 & 0 & 0 \end{bmatrix} * \hat{A}^3 = \begin{bmatrix} 1 \\ 0 \\ 0 \\ 0 \end{bmatrix}$$

We get

$$\hat{b}_1 = 250 \qquad \hat{b}_2 = 300 \qquad \hat{b}_3 = 150 \qquad \hat{b}_4 = 200$$

$$\hat{A}_1^3 = 1 \qquad \hat{A}_2^3 = 0 \qquad \hat{A}_3^3 = -1 \qquad \hat{A}_4^3 = 1$$

Thus, $K = \{4\}$, $\text{col}(4) = 6$. Thus, the new basis is $J = \{1,2,4,3\}$ with $\text{col}(1) = 1$, $\text{col}(2) = 2$, $\text{col}(3) = 4$, $\text{col}(4) = 3$. We compute η by

$$\eta * \begin{bmatrix} 1 & 1 & 0 & 1 \\ 0 & 0 & 1 & 0 \\ 1 & 0 & 1 & 0 \\ 0 & 1 & 0 & 0 \end{bmatrix} = (-5, -6, -3, -3)$$

We get

$$\pi^1 = -3, \qquad \pi^2 = -1, \qquad \pi^3 = -2, \qquad \pi^4 = -3$$

$$\hat{c}^5 = -5 + 4 = -1; \qquad \hat{c}^6 = -4 + 1 = -3; \qquad \hat{c}^1 = \hat{c}^2 = \hat{c}^3 = \hat{c}^4 = 0$$

The present basis is optimal.

4. Linear Programs with Bounded Variables

Definition 1: We consider, in this section, the linear program

$$(PB) \quad \begin{cases} Ax = b \qquad \alpha_j \le x_j \le \beta_j \qquad j = 1,2,\ldots,n \\ cx = z\,(Max) \end{cases}$$

with $\alpha_j \in \mathbb{R} \cup \{-\infty\}$, $\beta_j \in \mathbb{R} \cup \{+\infty\}$

Remark 5: The "usual" linear program under standard form (say (P) of Remark 1) is a special case of (PB) with

$$\alpha_j = 0 \qquad\qquad j = 1,2,\dots,n$$

$$\beta_j = +\infty \qquad\qquad j = 1,2,\dots,n$$

Remark 6: For the sake of simplicity in the presentation and without loss of generality (cf. Exercise 3), we will assume that

$$-\infty < \alpha_j, \qquad \beta_j < \infty \qquad\qquad j = 1,2,\dots,n$$

We pose

$$\hat{x}_j = x_j - \alpha_j$$

$$\hat{b} = b - A\alpha$$

(PB) can then be written in standard form:

$$(PB') \quad \begin{cases} A\hat{x} & = \hat{b} \\ \hat{x} + u & = \beta - \alpha \\ c\hat{x} & = z(\text{Max}) - c\alpha \end{cases} \qquad \hat{x},\ u \geq 0$$

(the u_j are slack variables). If A is a $m \times n$-matrix, we note that (PB') contains $m+n$ constraints and $2n$ variables. We will show now that (PB) can be solved as a linear program with m constraints and n variables only. Constraints $x_j \leq \beta_j$ can be taken care of in a direct way by a very slight modification of the simplex algorithm.

Definition 2: We assume that the linear system $Ax = b$ is full rank. (If this were not the case, we could deduce an equivalent full-rank system by applying phase I of the simplex method.) A set of indices J such that A^J is square nonsingular will be called a "basis" of (PB) (note that it is not a basis of (PB')). In this context, we say that

$$(PB_J) \quad \begin{cases} x_J + (A^J)^{-1} A^{\bar{J}} x_{\bar{J}} & = (A^J)^{-1} b \qquad \alpha_j \leq x_j \leq b_j \\ (c^{\bar{J}} - \pi A^{\bar{J}}) x_{\bar{J}} & = z(\text{Max}) - \pi b \end{cases}$$

with $\bar{J} = \{1,2,\dots,n\} \setminus J$, π solution of $\pi A^J = c^J$ is the linear program (PB) "written in canonical form with respect to the basis J."

A solution of the linear system $Ax = b$ such that

$$j \in \bar{J} \longrightarrow x_j = \alpha_j \qquad \text{or} \qquad x_j = \beta_j$$

is called a "basic solution associated with basis J." Note that to a given basis, there correspond 2^{n-m} basic solutions in this context.

Theorem 1: A basic feasible solution associated with basis J is an optimal solution of (PB), if the following conditions are satisfied:

(7')
$$c^j - \pi A^J > 0 \qquad \longrightarrow \qquad x_j = \beta_j$$

(7")
$$c^j - \pi A^j < 0 \qquad \longrightarrow \qquad x_j = \alpha_j$$

Proof: Let $\bar{x}$ be a basic solution relative to basis J and x be any feasible solution. We have

$$z = \pi b + \sum_{\{j \,|\, c^j - \pi A^j > 0\}} (c^j - \pi A^j) x_j + \sum_{\{j \,|\, c^j - \pi A^j < 0\}} (c^j - \pi A^j) x_j$$

$$\bar{z} = \pi b + \sum_{\{j \,|\, c^j - \pi A^j > 0\}} (c^j - \pi A^j) \bar{x}_j + \sum_{\{j \,|\, c^j - \pi A^j < 0\}} (c^j - \pi A^j) \bar{x}_j$$

$$z - \bar{z} = \sum_{\{j \,|\, c^j - \pi A^j > 0\}} (c^j - \pi A^j)(x_j - \beta_j) + \sum_{\{j \,|\, c^j - \pi A^j < 0\}} (c^j - \pi A^j)(x_j - \alpha_j) \leq 0$$

The last inequality is due to the fact that each term of the sum $z - \bar{z}$ is negative or zero. The reader will note the analogy of this proof with that of Theorem IV.3.

Remark 7: A basis J together with $\underline{a}$ basic solution, relative to J, can be found using phase I of the simplex method (see Exercise 4). Then we pose

$$|c^s - \pi A^s| = \text{Max}\{ \underset{\{j \,|\, x_j = \alpha_j\}}{\text{Max}} [c^j - \pi A^j]; \underset{\{j \,|\, x_j = \beta_j\}}{\text{Max}} [-c^j + \pi A^j]; 0\}$$

If $|c^s - \pi A^s| = 0$, relations (7') and (7") are verified and, from Theorem 1, the present basic solution is optimal. Assume that we have

$$c^s - \pi A^s < 0$$

and thus, $x_s = \beta_s$ (the case $c^s - \pi A^s > 0$ and $x_s = \alpha_s$ is similar). The idea consists -- as in the simplex algorithm -- of having variable x_s decrease from its present value β_s without changing the value of the other nonbasic variables and having the basic variables adjusted so that linear system $Ax = b$ remains verified. The diminution of x_s will be limited at the first occurrence of one of the following events:

(a) x_s reaches its lower bound α_s. The solution thus obtained is still
     a basic solution relative to J. For index s, relation (7") is
     now verified and we look for another index such that (7') or (7") is
     not satisfied.

(b) One of the basic variables x_r for $r \varepsilon J$ reaches either its lower or
     its upper bound. Then

$$J' = J \cup \{s\} \setminus \{col(r)\}$$

     is a new basis. The linear program is written in canonical form with
     respect to J' and the process is resumed.

Remark 8: We do not describe the simplex algorithm for linear programs with bounded variables with more details. The reader is invited to:

1. Express what happens when $c^s - \pi A^s > 0$ (cf. Remark 7) and how
    the algorithm proceeds.

2. Note that the proposed algorithm is the simplex if $(PB) \equiv (P)$,
    i.e., if the lower bounds are 0 and the upper bounds $+\infty$.
    Indicate how the algorithm is changed if some variables only
    are bounded.

3. Formulate the algorithm in its generality.

4. Verify that the procedure resulting from this algorithm is
    identical to the one obtained through the application of simplex
    algorithm to (PB') (see Exercise 5).

The economy of memory space and computer time that is obtained through this method of applying the simplex algorithm to linear programs having bounded variables is very important. Since many "real" linear programs have the values

of some of their variables bounded, commercial computer codes all work
according to the lines we just described. Moreover, the revised variant of the
simplex algorithm can be used here. This will be done in the following illus-
trative example.

Example: We will solve

$$\begin{cases} 6x_1 + 5x_2 + 3x_3 + x_4 + 2x_5 = 16 \\ 3x_1 + 2x_2 + 9x_3 + x_4 + 5x_5 = z \,(\text{Max}) \end{cases} \qquad 0 \le x_j \le j \qquad j=1,2,\ldots,5$$

The starting basis is $J = \{4\}$ and the basic solution is

$$x_1 = 1, \qquad x_2 = 0, \qquad x_3 = 0, \qquad x_4 = 0, \qquad x_5 = 5$$

First Iteration: $\pi = 1$

j	1	2	3	4	5
$c^j - \pi A^j$	-3	-3	6	0	3

$s = 3$.   If x_3 increases, x_4 must decrease. But x_4 is already at 0 . Thus,
the new basis is $J = \{3\}$ with the same basic solution.

Second Iteration: $\pi = 3$

j	1	2	3	4	5
$c^j - \pi A^j$	-15	-13	0	-2	-1

$s = 1$. x_1 decreases and x_3 increases $(x_3 = 2(1 - x_1))$. We are in case (a) of
Remark 7: we are blocked when x_1 reaches its lower value 0 . We still have
basis $J = \{3\}$.   The new basic solution is

$$x_1 = 0, \qquad x_2 = 0, \qquad x_3 = 2, \qquad x_4 = 0, \qquad x_5 = 5$$

Third Iteration: $s = 5$. x_5 decreases and x_3 increases:

$$x_3 = 2 + \frac{2}{3}\,(5 - x_5)$$

We are here in case b: we are blocked when x_3 reaches its upper bound 3 for
$x_5 = 7/2$.   The new basis is $J = \{5\}$ and the basic solution is

$$x_1 = 0, \qquad x_2 = 0, \qquad x_3 = 3, \qquad x_4 = 0, \qquad x_5 = \frac{7}{2}$$

Fourth Iteration: $\pi = 5/2$.

	1	2	3	4	5
$c^j - \pi A^j$	-12	-21/2	3/2	-3/2	0

The present solution is optimal.

EXERCISES

1. Count the number of operations (additions, multiplications, comparisons) needed for one iteration of the simplex algorithm and for one iteration of the revised simplex algorithm.

2. Consider the linear program

$$
\begin{cases}
x_1 + x_2 + x_3 = 6 \\
\quad\quad\quad x_4 + x_5 + x_6 = 4 \qquad x_j \geq 0 \\
x_1 \quad\quad + x_4 = 5 \qquad j = 1,2,\ldots,6 \\
\quad x_2 \quad\quad + x_5 = 3 \\
\quad\quad x_3 \quad\quad + x_6 = 2 \\
3x_1 + x_2 + 2x_3 + 6x_4 + 2x_5 + 4x_6 = z(\min)
\end{cases}
$$

   (a) Show that the constraint set is redundant. Assign the name (P) to the linear program obtained after deletion of a redundant constraint.

   (b) Show that $\{1,2,5,6\}$ is a feasible basis for (P).

   (c) Solve (P) using the revised simplex algorithm.

3. Write linear program (PB) of Section 4 in standard form without making the assumption that

$$
\alpha_j > -\infty \quad , \quad\quad \beta_j < \infty \quad\quad j = 1,2,\ldots,n
$$

   All cases will have to be taken care of.

4. How can phase I of the simplex method be extended to linear program (PB) with bounded variables? (See Section 4.)

5. Prove that the procedure presented to solve linear programs with bounded variables (PB) is identical to the one obtained through application of simplex algorithm to (PB'). In particular, give an interpretation, in terms of (PB'), of blocking case (a) of Remark 7.

6. Solve the linear program

$$\begin{cases} 4x_1 + 4x_2 + 4x_3 + x_4 \leq 48 \\ 8x_1 + 6x_2 + 4x_3 + 3x_4 \leq 72 \\ 1 \leq x_1 \leq 10 \\ 2 \leq x_2 \leq 5 \\ 3 \leq x_3 \leq 6 \\ 4 \leq x_4 \leq 8 \\ 5x_1 + x_2 + x_3 + 2x_4 = z(Max) \end{cases}$$

using the method of Section 3.

7. Consider the linear program

$$(K) \quad \begin{cases} a_1 x_1 + a_2 x_2 + \ldots + a_n x_n \leq b \\ c_1 x_1 + c_2 x_2 + \ldots + c_n x_n = z(Max) \end{cases} \qquad x_1, x_2, \ldots, x_n \geq 0$$

with $a_1, a_2, \ldots, a_n > 0$; $b > 0$; $c_1, c_2, \ldots, c_n \geq 0$. Without loss of generality, we also assume that

(1)
$$\frac{c_1}{a_1} \geq \frac{c_2}{a_2} \geq \ldots \geq \frac{c_n}{a_n}$$

(a)   Show assumption (1) can be done "without loss of generality."

(b)   Show, by a common-sense argument, that

$$x_1 = b/a_1, \qquad x_2 = x_3 = \ldots = x_n = 0$$

is an optimal solution to (K).
Prove the proposition by using linear programming theory.

(c)   Propose a very simple algorithm giving directly (without pivoting or iteration) an optimal solution of linear program (KB) obtained from (K) by adding constraints

$$\alpha_j \leq x_j \leq \beta_j \qquad j = 1, 2, \ldots, n$$

(d)   Check that the algorithm you found gives directly the solution of the problem solved as an example in Section 3.

8. Solve the Klee-Minty problem of Section 1 for $n = 3$.

Chapter VIII. Geometric Interpretation of the Simplex Method

1. Convex Programming

<u>Definition 1</u>: Recall that we denote by $\mathbb{R}^n$ the Euclidian n-dimensional space, i.e., the set of n-column vectors with real components. A "convex set" C in $\mathbb{R}^n$ is a set such that if two points p and q belong to C , then the whole segment [pq] belongs to C .

A closed set is one that includes its boundaries.

Example: The following sets are convex:

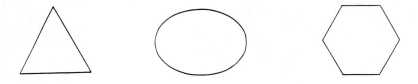

The following sets are not convex:

<u>Theorem 1</u>: The intersection of convex sets is a convex set.

<u>Proof</u>: Let F be a family of convex sets and let C be the intersection of the sets in F . Let p and q be two points in C ; p and q are in all

the convex sets of family F and thus segment [pq] is in all the sets of F
(since these sets are convex) and thus   [pq] is in the intersection C .

<u>Definition 2</u>: Let p and q be two points of $\mathbb{R}^n$; recall that x belongs
to segment [pq] if and only if

$$x_i = \lambda p_i + (1 - \lambda)q_i \qquad \text{for } i=1,\dots,n \qquad 0 \le \lambda \le 1$$

This set of equations, which can be written:

$$(1) \qquad x = \lambda p + (1-\lambda)q \qquad 0 \le \lambda \le 1$$

is the equation of segment [pq] . By this we mean that when λ varies between
0 and 1 , the point x varies along segment [pq]. Moreover, if $\ell(pq)$,
$\ell(px)$, $\ell(xq)$ denote the lengths of segments [pq], [px], [xq], respectively,
we have

$$(2) \begin{cases} \ell(xq) = \lambda\ell(pq) \\ \ell(px) = (1-\lambda)\ell(pq) \end{cases}$$

<u>*Example:*</u> Consider in R^2 (see Figure VIII.1)

$$p = \binom{1}{2}, \qquad q = \binom{3}{-1} .$$

$$x_1 = \lambda + 3(1 - \lambda)$$
$$\qquad\qquad\qquad\qquad 0 \le \lambda \le 1$$
$$x_2 = 2\lambda - 1(1 - \lambda)$$

When λ varies between 0 and 1 , point x varies along segment [pq] .
For instance, we have

$$\lambda = 1, \quad x = p; \qquad \lambda = 1/4, \qquad x = \begin{bmatrix} 5/2 \\ -1/4 \end{bmatrix}$$

$$\lambda = 1/2, \qquad x = \begin{bmatrix} 2 \\ 1/2 \end{bmatrix}; \qquad \lambda = 0, \qquad x = q$$

<u>Definition 3</u>: If c is an n-row vector and α a scalar, the equation

$$c^1 x_1 + c^2 x_2 + \dots + c^n x_n = \alpha$$

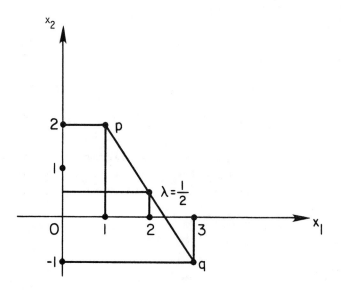

Figure VIII.1: An Example Illustrating Definition 2

defines a *hyperplane*. Note that in $\mathbb{R}^2$, a hyperplane reduces to a straight
line and in $\mathbb{R}^3$, a hyperplane is a plane.

The inequality

(4) $cx \leq \alpha$

defines a "closed half space." It is clear that (4) defines a closed set; it is
called a half space because a hyperplane (3) separates $\mathbb{R}^n$ into two regions and
the set of points that satisfy (4) all belong to the same region.

Theorem 2: A half space is a convex set.

Proof: Let p and q both belong to the half space (4), i.e.,

(4') $cp \leq \alpha$

(4'') $cq \leq \alpha$

Now, if x is a point of segment $[pq]$ we have, from (1),

$$x = \lambda p + (1 - \lambda)q \qquad\qquad 0 \le \lambda \le 1$$

$$c(\lambda p + (1 - \lambda)q) = \lambda cp + (1-\lambda)cq$$

Now since

$$0 \le \lambda$$

$$0 \le 1 - \lambda$$

we can multiply inequalities (4') and (4"), respectively, by λ and $(1 - \lambda)$ and get

$$cx = \lambda cp + (1 - \lambda)cq \le \lambda\alpha + (1 - \lambda)\alpha = \alpha$$

Thus x satisfies (4); any point of segment $[pq]$ belongs to half space (4); i.e., the half space is a convex set.

Definition 4: From Theorem 1 a set that is the intersection of half spaces is convex. Such a set will be called a "convex polyhedral set" or a "convex polyhedron."

Remark 1: The set $C = \{x \mid Ax \le b, \; x \ge 0\}$ of feasible solutions of the linear program

$$(P) \quad \begin{cases} Ax \le b & x \ge 0 \\ cx = z(\text{Max}) \end{cases}$$

is a convex polyhedral set since each constraint of (P),

$$A_i x \le b_i \qquad\qquad i = 1,2,\ldots,m$$

$$x_j \ge 0 \qquad\qquad j = 1,2,\ldots,n$$

defines a half space.

Definition 5: A real-valued function f defined on a convex set C is convex if

$$f(\lambda p + (1 - \lambda)q) \le \lambda f(p) + (1 - \lambda)f(q) \qquad 0 \le \lambda \le 1; \; p,q \in C$$

Note that a linear function defined on a convex set is a convex function.

<u>Definition 6</u>:   The optimization problem (mathematical program) *"Find the*
minimum of a convex function f *over a convex set* C" is a "convex program."

<u>Definition 7</u>:   Given a convex program

$$\underset{x \in C}{\text{Min}} \quad [f(x)]$$

$\bar{x}$ is called a "local optimum" if there exists an open set D containing $\bar{x}$
such that

$$f(\bar{x}) \leq f(x) \qquad\qquad \text{for all} \quad x \in D$$

Example: Consider the function shown in Figure VIII.2.

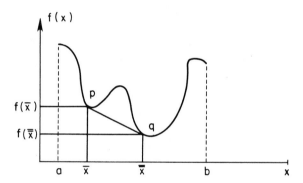

Figure VIII.2:   An Example of a Function Which is not Convex

It is not a convex function since the curve does not lie below the segment [pq].
In this example, $\bar{x}$ is a local minimum for f(x) but it is not a global minimum ($\bar{\bar{x}}$ is one).

<u>Remark 2</u>:   From Remark 1 we deduce that a linear program (which can always be
written under the form of a minimization problem) is a convex program.

<u>Theorem 3</u>:   For a convex program, a local minimum is a global minimum.

<u>Proof</u>:   Suppose that theorem is not true.   There exists

$\bar{x}$ a local minimum

$\bar{\bar{x}}$ a global minimum

i.e., $f(\bar{\bar{x}}) < f(\bar{x})$,

$x = \lambda\bar{\bar{x}} + (1-\lambda)\bar{x}$ is a point in C for $0 < \lambda < 1$,   since C is convex. (See Figure VIII.3). Moreover,

$$f(\lambda\bar{\bar{x}} + (1 - \lambda)\bar{x}) \le \lambda f(\bar{\bar{x}}) + (1 - \lambda)f(\bar{x}) \qquad \text{for}\; 0 \le \lambda \le 1$$

since f is a convex function. Now, for $0 < \lambda \le 1$, and since $f(\bar{\bar{x}}) < f(\bar{x})$, we have

$$\lambda f(\bar{\bar{x}}) + (1 - \lambda)f(\bar{x}) < \lambda f(\bar{x}) + (1 - \lambda)f(\bar{x}) \;=\; f(\bar{x})$$

Thus, for $0 < \lambda \le 1$ $f(x) < f(\bar{x})$. We have seen that

$$\ell(\bar{x}\; x) \;=\; \lambda\ell(\bar{x}\; \bar{\bar{x}})$$

so that if λ is small enough, x is as near as we want to $\bar{x}$;   thus there exists a set of points x,   as close as we want to $\bar{x}$,   for which

$$f(x) < f(\bar{x})$$

so that it is not true that $\bar{x}$ is a local minimum and the theorem is proved by contradiction.

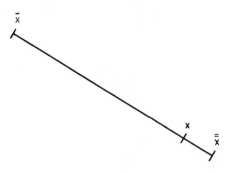

Figure VIII.3: $x = \lambda\bar{\bar{x}} + (1-\lambda)\bar{x}$

Remark 3: Theorem 3 is very important in practice. This property of convex programs, not permitting any local minima, makes solution algorithms reasonably simple. In effect, when we get a feasible point, it is sufficient to examine its neighborhood, and this usually can be done rather simply. On the other hand, the fact that Theorem 3 is not true for nonconvex programs makes the latter class of problems extremely difficult to solve. When we find a point that is suspected to be an optimal point, we have to compare it with all the other points to be sure that it is actually optimal. Integer programs (where the solution point must be an integer) are highly nonconvex and thus very difficult. Actually, no consistently "good" algorithm is known that solves integer programs.

2. Geometric Interpretation of the Simplex Algorithm

Example: Consider the linear program

$$(P) \begin{cases} -2x_1 + x_2 \leq 1 \\ x_1 - 2x_2 \leq 5/2 \\ x_1 - x_2 \leq 3 \\ \frac{1}{2}x_1 + x_2 \leq 3 \\ x_1 + 2x_2 = z\,(\text{Max}) \end{cases} \qquad x_1, x_2 \geq 0$$

which is solved by using the simplex algorithm in the succession of simplex tableaus shown below. (x_3, x_4, x_5, x_6 are the slack variables, which correspond to the 1st, 2nd, 3rd, and 4th constraints, respectively).

x_1	x_2	x_3	x_4	x_5	x_6	z	b
-2	1	1					1 ←
1	-2		1				5/2
1	-1			1			3
1/2	1				1		3
1	2 ↑					1	0

-2	1	1					1
-3		2	1				9/2
-1		1		1			4
5/2		-1			1		2 ←
5 ↑		-2				1	-2
	1	1/5			4/5		2 3/5
		4/5	1		6/5		6 9/10
		3/5		1	2/5		4 4/5
1		-2/5			2/5		4/5
		0			-2	1	-6

We have, successively, bases $J = \{3,4,5,6\}$, $J' = \{2,4,5,6\}$, and $J'' = \{2,4,5,1\}$; J'' is an optimal basis since the cost vector relative to J'' is nonpositive.

The three corresponding basic solutions are

$$(5) \begin{cases} x_1 = 0 \\ x_2 = 0 \\ x_3 = 1 \\ x_4 = 5/2 \\ x_5 = 3 \\ x_6 = 3 \\ z = 0 \end{cases} \qquad (5') \begin{cases} x_1 = 0 \\ x_2 = 1 \\ x_3 = 0 \\ x_4 = 9/2 \\ x_5 = 4 \\ x_6 = 2 \\ z = 2 \end{cases} \qquad (5'') \begin{cases} x_1 = 4/5 \\ x_2 = 2\ 3/5 \\ x_3 = 0 \\ x_4 = 6\ 9/10 \\ x_5 = 4\ 4/5 \\ x_6 = 0 \\ z = 6 \end{cases}$$

We can represent in the $x_1 x_2$ plane the feasibility domain for Problem
(P) . It is the convex polygon OABCDE shown in Figure VIII.4. In this figure,
we notice the following

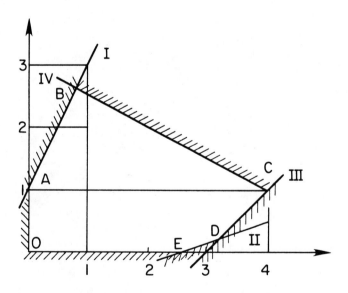

Figure VIII 4 : The Feasibility Domain for (P)

1. The points that correspond to basic solutions (5), (5'), (5") are vertices 0, A, B of the polygon.

2. In the application of the simplex algorithm, when one of the nonbasic variables increases, the others remaining at zero value, we go from one vertex of the polygon to an adjacent one. For instance, when one goes from basic solution (5') to basic solution (5"), the nonbasic variable x_3 remains nonbasic and thus 0, which means that the point moves along constraint I until constraint IV (which corresponds to the "blocking" row) is hit.

3. For the cost vector relative to basis J", we have $\hat{c}^3 = 0$, although $3 \notin J"$. This means that x_3 can increase without z decreasing and that the optimal solution may not be unique (see Exercise V.9). In effect, we can let x_3 increase from 0 up to $x_3^* = 8$. For $x_3 = x_3^*$, x_5 hits 0. We have a new basis $J''' = \{2,4,3,1\}$. The problem can be written in canonical form with respect to this basis:

$$\left\{ \begin{array}{l} x_2 \qquad\qquad \frac{1}{3} x_5 - \frac{1}{3} x_6 \;=\; 1 \\[2mm] \qquad x_3 \;+\; \frac{5}{3} x_5 - \; x_6 \;=\; 8 \\[2mm] \qquad\quad x_4 - \frac{4}{3} x_5 + \frac{2}{3} x_6 \;=\; \frac{1}{2} \\[2mm] x_1 \qquad\qquad +\, \frac{2}{3} x_5 + \frac{2}{3} x_6 \;=\; 4 \\[2mm] \qquad\qquad\quad 0\, x_5 \,-\, 2\, x_6 \;=\; z - 6 \end{array} \right.$$

The corresponding basic solution is

$$(5''') \quad \left\{ \begin{array}{lll} x_1 = 4 & x_4 = \frac{1}{2} & \\ x_2 = 1 & x_5 = 0 & z = 6 \\ x_3 = 8 & x_6 = 0 & \end{array} \right.$$

We see, moreover, that all the points that are on the segment defined by the two optimal basic solutions (5") and (5''') are optimal, namely all the points of segment [BC], the equation of which is

$$
(6) \qquad
\begin{cases}
x_1 = \dfrac{4}{5} + \dfrac{2}{5}\, x_3 \\[2mm]
x_2 = 2\dfrac{3}{5} - \dfrac{1}{5}\, x_3
\end{cases}
\qquad 0 \le x_3 \le 8
$$

These properties are general ones, as will be seen now.

Definition 8: Let C be a convex set; a will be called an "extreme point" of C (or a vertex if C is a polyhedral set) if

$$
\left.
\begin{aligned}
&p, q \in C \\
&a = \lambda p + (1 - \lambda)q \\
&0 < \lambda < 1
\end{aligned}
\right\}
\qquad \Rightarrow \qquad p = q = a
$$

Definition 9: Let C be a convex set; the segment $E \subset C$ will be called an "edge" if

$$
\left.
\begin{aligned}
&e \in E \\
&p, q \in C \\
&e = \lambda p + (1 - \lambda)q \\
&0 < \lambda < 1
\end{aligned}
\right\}
\qquad \Rightarrow \qquad p, q \in E
$$

Remark 4: Definitions 8 and 9 have the same form. They can be restated in the following way: "A point a (resp. a segment E) of a convex polyhedral set C is a vertex (resp. an edge) if every time this point a (resp. any point of this segment E) is the middle point of a segment contained in C, this segment is reduced to a (resp. is contained in E).

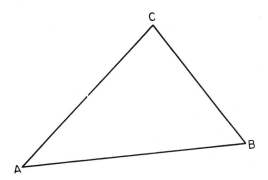

Figure VIII.5: An Illustration of Definitions 8 and 9

Example: Consider the triangle ABC shown in Figure VIII.5. It is clear that
the definitions just given are consistent with everyday language: The three
vertices of this triangle are A, B, and C and the three edges are [AB], [BC],
and [CA].

Definition 10: Two vertices of a convex polyhedral set are said to be "adjacent"
if there is an edge joining them.

Theorem 4: Let C denote the convex polyhedral set of feasible points of the
linear program

$$(P) \quad \begin{cases} Ax = b \qquad x \geq 0 \\ cx = z\,(Max) \end{cases}$$

A basic feasible solution of (P) is a vertex of C .

Proof: Let J be a feasible basis and $\bar{x}$ be the basic solution corresponding
to J :

$$(7) \qquad \begin{cases} \bar{x}_j = 0 \qquad\qquad j \notin J \\ \bar{x}_J = (A^J)^{-1} b \end{cases}$$

We apply Definition 8: let p, q$\in$C such that

$$\bar{x} = \lambda p + (1 - \lambda)q \qquad 0 < \lambda < 1$$

From (7), we have

$$\lambda p_j + (1 - \lambda)q_j \ = \ 0 \qquad\qquad j \notin J$$

Since $\lambda > 0$ and $(1 - \lambda) > 0$, this implies that

$$p_j \ = \ q_j \ = \ 0 \qquad\qquad j \notin J$$

and from the uniqueness of the basic solution (i.e., from the fact that J is a basis), we have

$$P_J \ = \ q_J \ = \ (A^J)^{-1}b \ = \ \bar{x}_J$$

Thus

$$p \ = \ q \ = \ \bar{x}$$

<u>Theorem 5</u>: An iteration of the simplex algorithm consists of changing current (feasible) basis J into basis $J' = J \cup \{s\} \setminus \{col(r)\}$. The basic solutions associated with J and J' correspond to adjacent vertices.

<u>Proof</u>: From one iteration to the next, the solution of the linear program varies in the following way (we assume (P) written in canonical form with respect to J):

$$(8) \qquad \begin{cases} x_j = 0 & j \notin J, \quad j \neq s \\ 0 \le x_s \le x_s^* = b_r/A_r^s \\ x_J = b - A^s x_s \end{cases}$$

We apply Definition 9. Let $\bar{x}$ be a point of the segment (8) and let p,q be feasible solutions of (P) such that

$$\bar{x} \ = \ \lambda p + (1 - \lambda)q \qquad\qquad 0 < \lambda < 1$$

Using the same argument as in the proof of Theorem 4, we show that

$$p_j \ = \ q_j \ = \ 0 \qquad \text{for} \qquad j \notin J, \quad j \neq s$$

Since p and q are feasible solutions, we have

$$\begin{cases} p_J = b - A^s p_s \\ q_J = b - A^s q_s \end{cases} \qquad\qquad \begin{aligned} 0 \le p_s \le x_s^* \\ 0 \le q_s \le x_s^* \end{aligned}$$

so that p and q satisfy (8). Thus (8) defines an edge of C .

Remark 5: Let us consider the following linear program in canonical form:

$$(P) \quad \begin{cases} Ax \le b & x \ge 0 \\ cx = z(Max) \end{cases}$$

which, by addition of slack variables y_i for $i = 1, 2, \ldots, m$ can be written

$$(P) \quad \begin{cases} Ax + Uy = b & x, y \ge 0 \\ cx = z(Max) \end{cases}$$

The set of feasible solutions

$$C = \{x \mid Ax \le b, \quad x \ge 0\}$$

is defined by the intersection of m+n half spaces (m half spaces $A_i x \le b_i$,
n half spaces $x_j \ge 0$). For a basic solution, we have at most m variables
x_j, y_i that are positive, thus at least n of them that are equal to zero.
When $x_j = 0$, the corresponding point belongs to the limiting hyperplane of the
half space $x_j \ge 0$. When $y_i = 0$, the corresponding point belongs to the
limiting hyperplane of the half space:

$$A_i x \le b_i$$

Finally, we see that a basic solution corresponds to the intersection of
at least n hyperplanes limiting the m+n half spaces the intersection of which
constitutes C . Note that:

(a) In general, n hyperplanes of $\mathbb{R}^n$ intersect at one point.

(b) The case where a basic solution corresponds to the intersection
     of more than n hyperplanes is the case of degeneracy of the
     basic solution.

We now get a geometric interpretation of the perturbation method we used
in Section V.4 to prove finiteness of the simplex algorithm. By moving the
limiting hyperplanes by infinitesimal and not commensurable quantities
$\varepsilon, \varepsilon^2, \ldots, \varepsilon^m$ we make sure that each basic solution is nondegenerate, i.e.,
corresponds exactly to the intersection of n limiting hyperplanes.

Remark 6: Consider the linear program

$$(P) \quad \begin{cases} Ax = b \qquad\qquad x \geq 0 \\ cx = z\,(\text{Max}) \end{cases}$$

written in canonical form with respect to feasible basis J. Let $s \notin J$. If $A^S \leq 0$, the set of solutions

$$(8') \qquad\qquad \begin{cases} x_j = 0 \qquad\qquad j \notin J \quad j \neq s \\ x_s \geq 0 \\ x_J = b - A^S x_s \end{cases}$$

is unbounded. It corresponds to an edge "which is infinite in one direction" (think of a triedron). We will call this type of edge with just one end point a "ray."

A basic feasible solution of (P) corresponds to a vertex of the domain C of feasible points. This vertex is the end point of $n-m$ edges or rays, corresponding to the $n-m$ nonbasic variables. The criterion

$$c^j \leq 0 \qquad\qquad j \notin J$$

for optimality is a local test that decides for optimality: if the objective function does not increase along the $n-m$ edges whose end points are the present basic solution, this solution is optimal. The choice

$$c^S = \text{Max}_{j \notin J}\ [c^j]$$

for the variable to enter the basis corresponds to the choice of the edge with the largest "slope," i.e., the largest increase of the objective function by unit increase of the entering variable. The exploratory variant (see Remark V.8) consists of examining all neighbors of the present basic solution and choosing the neighboring vertex for which the objective function is largest.

Remark 7: We can now summarize the results of this section.

    (a)   The constraints of a linear program (P) define a feasible domain that is a convex polyedron C.

    (b)   The basic solutions of (P) correspond to the vertices of C.

    (c)   A vertex of C is determined by the intersection of at least n limiting hyperplanes. A vertex determined by more than n limiting hyperplanes corresponds to a degenerate basic solution.

(d) The simplex algorithm can be interpreted as a journey along a chain of adjacent vertices of C.

(e) When we are at a vertex such that no edge corresponds to an increase in the value of the objective function, we stop: the present solution is optimal.

EXERCISES

1. In general, if C is a convex polyhedral set, a subset F of C will be called a face if

$$\left. \begin{array}{l} x \in F \\ p, q \in C \\ x = \lambda p + (1 - \lambda)q \\ 0 < \lambda < 1 \end{array} \right\} \implies p, q \in F$$

(a) Show that vertices and edges are faces of a convex polyhedral set. Namely, a vertex is a zero-dimensional face, an edge is a one-dimensional face.

(b) List all the faces of a cube.

(c) Show that the set of optimal solutions of a linear program is a face. Show that the vertices of this set are also vertices of the set of feasible solutions.

2. Consider the following linear programs:

$$x_1 \geq 0, \quad x_2 \geq 0, \quad \max z = x_1 + 2x_2 \text{ subject to}$$

(i) $\left\{ \begin{array}{l} -2x_1 + x_2 \leq 1 \\ x_1 - 2x_2 \leq 2 \\ x_1 - x_2 \leq 3 \end{array} \right.$

(ii) $\left\{ \begin{array}{l} -2x_1 + x_2 \leq 1 \\ x_1 - 2x_2 \leq 2 \\ x_1 - x_2 \leq 3 \\ \frac{1}{2} x_1 + x_2 \leq \frac{9}{2} \end{array} \right.$

$$(iii) \quad \begin{cases} -2x_1 + x_2 \leq 1 \\ x_1 - 2x_2 \leq 2 \\ x_1 - x_2 \leq 3 \\ \frac{1}{2} x_1 + x_2 \leq 3 \end{cases}$$

(a) Solve each of these problems using the simplex method. Follow the solution point on a diagram and give any relevant comments about the uniqueness of the solution.

(b) Write the duals of these linear programs. Give the solutions of the duals. With the help of the diagram you got in part (a), comment about the uniqueness of the solution of these dual programs.

3.   Give a method of finding the second-best basic solution, the third-best, ..., the pth best basic solution.

4. Consider the linear program

$$(P) \quad \begin{cases} x_1 - x_2 \leq 3 \\ x_1 + x_2 \leq 7 \\ x_1 - x_2 \geq 1 \qquad x_1, x_2 \geq 0 \\ x_1 \qquad \leq 5 \\ 2x_1 - x_2 = z \, (Max) \end{cases}$$

(a) By application of phase I of the simplex method with a *minimum* number of artificial variables, find a feasible basis.

(b) Apply the simplex algorithm and find the optimal solution.

(c) Draw the feasible region on a graph and show the path followed by the solution point in the application of the simplex algorithm to the preceding question.

(d) Comment on the graph about the uniqueness of the solution of the dual of (P).

(e) Write and solve the dual of (P). Give *all* the optimal solutions of the dual. How many basic optimal solutions are there?

5. Consider the set of points in R^3 that satisfy

$$-x_1 + 3x_2 + x_3 \leq 9$$
$$4x_1 - 2x_2 + x_3 \leq 4 \qquad x_1, x_2, x_3 \geq 0$$

(a) Compute the vertices of the polyhedron C.

(b) Find the set of points in C that maximize

$$z = 2x_1 + 2x_2 + 3x_3$$

6. Given a linear program

$$\begin{cases} Ax \leq b \qquad x \geq 0 \\ cx = z \, (\text{Max}) \end{cases}$$

show that

(a) If the optimal solution is not unique, there exists an edge of $C = \{x \mid Ax \leq b, \quad x \geq 0\}$ parallel to $cx = 0$.

(b) If a coefficient c^j, $j \notin J$, of the cost vector relative to an optimal basis J, is zero, this optimal basis is not unique.

(c) It is possible that (P) has several optimal bases but just one optimal solution. What can be said then of this optimal solution?

(d) A necessary and sufficient condition for the optimal basis of (P) (resp. of the dual (D) of (P)) not to be unique is that the optimal solution of (D) (resp. of (P)) is degenerate.

7. Given two nonempty, closed convex polyhedra C and C' with $C \cap C' = \phi$, show that there exists a hyperplane that strictly separates them.

HINT: Let $C = \{x \mid Ax \leq b\}$, $C' = \{x \mid A'x \leq b'\}$.

Show that one can find $\bar{y}, \bar{y}' \geq 0$ such that

$$\bar{y}A + \bar{y}'A' = 0 \qquad \bar{y}A \neq 0$$

$$\bar{y}b + \bar{y}'b' < 0$$

and that the hyperplane

$$\bar{y}Ax = \frac{1}{2} (\bar{y}b - \bar{y}'b')$$

answers the question.

Chapter IX. Complements on Duality: Economic Interpretation of Dual Variables

Duality is so essential to linear programming theory that we considered it important to introduce the concept as early as possible in this course. Some results on duality were proven in Chapters II, IV, and VI as soon as the tools to establish them were available. In particular, we have seen that as soon as a linear program has been solved by the application of the simplex method, an optimal solution for its dual has also been found (corollary to Theorem IV.3).

In the first section, we gather the most important of the results about duality that have been obtained and give a few extra theorems. In the second section we give some economic interpretations of linear programming and duality theory and comment on the concept of price.

1. Theorems on Duality: Complementary Slackness Theorem

We consider the following pair of dual programs:

$$(P) \begin{cases} Ax \leq b \qquad\qquad x \geq 0 \\ cx = z\,(\text{Max}) \end{cases} \qquad\qquad (D) \begin{cases} yA \geq c \qquad\qquad y \geq 0 \\ yb = w\,(\text{Min}) \end{cases}$$

and we refer the reader to Chapter II for the definitions and preliminary results about duality. Let us first recall here the most important theorems obtained so far.

__Theorem II.2:__ For every couple $\bar{x}, \bar{y}$ of feasible solutions to (P) and (D), respectively, we have

$$c\bar{x} \leq \bar{y}b$$

Corollary. Let $\bar{x}, \bar{y}$ be a couple of feasible solutions to (P) and (D), respectively, such that $c\bar{x} = \bar{y}b$. Then $\bar{x}, \bar{y}$ are a couple of optimal solutions to (P) and (D), respectively.

Corollary of Theorem IV.3: The multiplier vector relative to an optimal basis of linear program (P)[†] is an optimal solution of its dual (D).

Theorem VI.6: If two dual linear programs (P) and (D) both have a feasible solution, they both have an optimal solution and the values of the objective functions for the optimums are equal.

Remark 1: The following results can be considered as consequences of preceding theorems:

(i) If one of the problems has a class of unbounded solutions ($z \to \infty$ or $w \to -\infty$), then the other does not have a feasible solution.

(ii) If (P) (resp. (D)) has a feasible solution but not (D) (resp. not (P)), then (P) (resp. (D)) has a class of unbounded solutions.

(i) is a direct consequence of Theorem II.2. If (ii) was not true, from the fundamental theorem of linear programming (Theorem VI.5), (P) would have an optimal basis, and from the corollary of Theorem IV.3, we get a contradiction.

Remark 2: It may happen that neither (P) nor (D) has a feasible solution. Example:

$$(P) \begin{cases} x_1 - x_2 = 1 \\ x_1 - x_2 = -1 \\ x_1 + x_2 = z \text{ (Max)} \end{cases} \quad x_1, x_2 \geq 0 \qquad (D) \begin{cases} y_1 + y_2 \geq 1 \\ y_1 + y_2 \leq -1 \\ y_1 - y_2 = w \text{ (Min)} \end{cases}$$

These results are summarized in the following table:

[†] In Chapter IV, proof of this result is given when (P) is written in standard form. We leave as an exercise the extension of the proof to the case where (P) is in canonical form.

| | | (P) has a feasible solution | | (P) has no feasible solution |
		(P) has an optimal solution	(P) has no optimal solution	
(D) has a feasible solution	(D) has an optimal solution	$w_{min} = z_{max}$ Theorem VI-6	impossible	impossible
	(D) has no optimal solution	impossible	impossible	$w \to -\infty$
	(D) has no feasible solution	impossible	$z \to +\infty$	possible

Definition 1: Let $\bar{x}$ be a feasible solution of (P) . The ith constraint is said to be:

$$\text{"tight"} \qquad \text{if} \qquad A_i\bar{x} = b_i$$

$$\text{"slack"} \qquad \text{if} \qquad A_i\bar{x} < b_i$$

Theorem 1 (Complementary Slackness Theorem): A necessary and sufficient condition for a couple $\bar{x},\bar{y}$ of feasible solutions to (P) and (D) , respectively, to be optimal is that:

(a) Whenever a constraint of one of the problems is slack, then the corresponding variable of the other problem is zero.

(b) Whenever a variable of one of the problems is positive, then the corresponding constraint of the other is tight.

Proof: Let us write problems (P) and (D) with slack variables:

$$\text{(P)} \quad \begin{cases} Ax + U\xi = b \qquad x, \xi \geq 0 \\ cx \qquad = z\,(\text{Max}) \end{cases} \qquad \text{(D)} \quad \begin{cases} yA - \eta U = c \qquad y, \eta \geq 0 \\ yb \qquad = w\,(\text{Min}) \end{cases}$$

(in (P), U is the $m \times m$ unit matrix; in (D), U is the $n \times n$ unit matrix).

Let $\bar{x}, \bar{\xi}$ and $\bar{y}, \bar{\eta}$ be feasible solutions to (P) and (D), respectively. Let us multiply the ith constraint of (P) by the corresponding slack variable $\bar{y}^i$ and add up for $i = 1, 2, \ldots, m$. We get

$$(1) \qquad \bar{y}A\bar{x} + \bar{y}\bar{\xi} = \bar{y}b$$

Similarly, let us multiply the jth constraint of (D) by $\bar{x}_j$ and add up for $j = 1, 2, \ldots, n$. We get

$$(1') \qquad \bar{y}A\bar{x} - \bar{\eta}\bar{x} = c\bar{x}$$

Subtracting $(1')$ from (1), we have

$$(2) \qquad \bar{y}\bar{\xi} + \bar{\eta}\bar{x} = \bar{y}b - c\bar{x}$$

Necessary condition: Let $\bar{x}, \bar{y}$ be optimal solutions of (P) and (D), respectively. Then from Theorem VI.6, we have

$$\bar{y}b - c\bar{x} = 0$$

and from (2)

$$\bar{y}\bar{\xi} + \bar{\eta}\bar{x} = 0$$

But

$$\bar{y}\bar{\xi} + \bar{\eta}\bar{x} = \sum_{i=1}^{m} \bar{y}^i\bar{\xi}_i + \sum_{j=1}^{n} \bar{\eta}^j\bar{x}_j$$

Each term of this sum is nonnegative, so that the sum can be zero only if each term is 0. Thus we have

$$(3) \qquad \begin{cases} \bar{y}^i > 0 \Rightarrow \bar{\xi}_i = 0 \\ \bar{\xi}_i > 0 \Rightarrow \bar{y}^i = 0 \\ \bar{\eta}^j > 0 \Rightarrow \bar{x}_j = 0 \\ \bar{x}_j > 0 \Rightarrow \bar{\eta}^j = 0 \end{cases}$$

which is a statement equivalent to the last two sentences of the theorem.

Sufficient condition: If $\bar{x}, \bar{y}$ are a pair of feasible solutions to (P) and (D), respectively, and if the conditions of the theorem are fulfilled, then (3) is true, $\bar{y}\xi + \eta\bar{x} = 0$, and, from (2), we have that $c\bar{x} - \bar{y}b = 0$, so that $\bar{x}, \bar{y}$ are a pair of optimal solutions to (P) and (D).

Remark 3: The complementary slackness theorem is very important and is frequently used. Its interest lies in the fact that it permits to prove with a minimum amount of computation (without computing the primal or the dual objective function) that a given solution to a linear program is in fact an optimal one.

Example: Let us consider the pair of dual linear programs

$$(P) \quad \begin{cases} 3x_1 + x_2 \geq 4 \\ x_1 + 4x_2 \geq 5 \\ x_1 + x_2 = z\,(\text{Min}) \end{cases} \quad x_1, x_2 \geq 0 \qquad (D) \quad \begin{cases} 3y_1 + y_2 \leq 1 \\ y_1 + 4y_2 \leq 1 \\ 4y_1 + 5y_2 = w\,(\text{Max}) \end{cases} \quad y_1, y_2 \geq 0$$

and assume that someone tells us that $\bar{x}_1 = 1$, $\bar{x}_2 = 1$ might be an optimal solution. It suffices to check that the linear system

$$(*) \quad \begin{cases} 3y_1 + y_2 = 1 & (\text{since } \bar{x}_1 > 0) \\ y_1 + 4y_2 = 1 & (\text{since } \bar{x}_2 > 0) \end{cases}$$

has a nonnegative solution. Solving this system yields

$$\bar{y}_1 = 3/11, \quad \bar{y}_2 = 2/11$$

and this is sufficient to assure that $\bar{x}$ is an optimal solution to (P) (see also Exercises 4 and 5).

Remark 4: Theorem 1 is sometimes called the "weak" complementary slackness theorem. It may happen that for a couple $\bar{x}, \bar{y}$ of optimal solutions to (P) and (D), we have simultaneously tight constraint and the corresponding dual variable equal to zero.

However, the (strong) complementary slackness theorem (which we will not prove here -- see Exercise 3), states that there always exists a couple $\bar{x}, \bar{y}$ of optimal solutions to (P) and (D), respectively, with the implications:

(a)   Whenever a constraint of one of the problems is tight, the corresponding dual variable is positive.

(b)   Whenever a variable of one of the problems is zero, the corresponding constraint of the dual is slack.

Beware that this theorem does not assure that the optimal solutions in question are basic ones. It may happen that no couple of basic optimal solutions satisfies the strong complementary slackness theorem.

2. Economic Interpretation of Dual Variables

In Section II.3, we gave an economic interpretation of the dual of the transportation problem (P_2). We now give other illustrations.

(a) *The Pill Manufacturer's Problem*: Suppose that a housewife has to find a minimum-cost diet by buying a combination of five foods, subject to the constraints that the diet will provide at least 21 units of vitamin A and 12 units of vitamin B, the properties of the five foods under consideration being given by

Food	1	2	3	4	5
Vit. A content	1	0	1	1	2
Vit. B content	0	1	2	1	1
Cost	20	20	31	11	12

The housewife will have to solve the following linear program:

$$
(4) \quad
\begin{cases}
x_1 + x_3 + x_4 + 2x_5 \geq 21 \\
 x_2 + 2x_3 + x_4 + x_5 \geq 12 \\
20x_1 + 20x_2 + 31x_3 + 11x_4 + 12x_5 = z\,(\text{Min}) \\
 x_j \geq 0 \qquad j = 1, 2, \ldots, 5
\end{cases}
$$

Now assume that a merchant or pill manufacturer possesses pills of vitamin A and pills of vitamin B. He wants to know at which prices he must sell the pills in order to:

    (1)   Stay competitive with the diverse foods that are on the market
         (in terms of vitamin supply, not in terms of cooking).

    (2)   Make as much money as possible if he can sell his pills to
         the housewife.

    Calling y_1, y_2 the prices of a pill of 1 unit of vitamin A and of a
pill of 1 unit of vitamin B, respectively, the pill manufacturer's problem is

(5)
$$
\begin{cases}
y_1 \;\;\;\;\;\;\;\;\;\; \leq 20 \\
\;\;\;\;\; y_2 \leq 20 \\
y_1 + 2y_2 \leq 31 \\
y_1 + \;\; y_2 \leq 11 \\
2y_1 + \;\; y_2 \leq 12 \\
21y_1 + 12y_2 = w \text{ (Max)}
\end{cases}
\qquad y_1, y_2 \geq 0
$$

    The housewife problem (4) is solved in the succession of simplex tableaus
shown below.

x_1	x_2	x_3	x_4	x_5	s_1	s_2	b
1		1	1	2	-1		21 ←
	1	2	1	1		-1	12
*	*	-29	-29	-48 ↑	+20	+20	z - 660
1/2		1/2	1/2	1	-1/2		21/2
-1/2	1	3/2	1/2		1/2	-1	3/2 ←
24	*	-5	-5 ↑	*	-4	20	z - 156
1	-1	-1		1	-1	1	9
-1	2	3	1		1	-2	3
19	10	10	*	*	1	+10	z - 141

The optimal basis is $J = \{5,4\}$; we have

$$\pi A^J = c^J$$

so that π is found by solving the system

$$\begin{cases} \pi^1 + \pi^2 = 11 \\ 2\pi^1 + \pi^2 = 12 \end{cases}$$

$i.e.,$

$$\begin{cases} \pi^1 = 1 \\ \pi^2 = 10 \end{cases}$$

Thus, without doing any computation, we know that an optimal solution of the pill manufacturer's problem (5) is

$$y_1 = 1$$
$$y_2 = 10$$

It is easy to check that (1, 10) is feasible and we have

$$1 \times 21 + 10 \times 12 = 141$$

which is the cost of the minimum-cost diet found in solving (4). The solution of the pill manufacturer's problem could also have been found graphically.

(b) *Marginal Prices for Production Problem* (P_1): Assume that the manager of the firm that was depicted in Section I.1.a might buy some extra quantities of the different raw materials. The question we will try and answer now is: "What prices is the manager ready to pay for these extra quantities?" Recall that problem (P_1) was written in the following form:

$$(P_1) \quad \begin{cases} 2x_1 + x_2 \le 8 & (I) \\ x_1 + 2x_2 \le 7 & (II) \\ x_2 \le 3 & (III) \\ 4x_1 + 5x_2 = z\,(Max) \end{cases} \qquad x_1, x_2 \ge 0$$

and that the optimal solution was $\bar{x}_1 = 3$, $\bar{x}_2 = 2$, $\bar{z} = 22$.

It takes the manager very little thinking to discover that, given that for the optimal solution he has got 1 unit of raw material III in excess, he is not ready to buy any extra quantity of raw material III, whatever its price might be. In economic terms, we should say that a commodity that is in excess has a value equal to zero.

Now suppose that the supply of commodities II and III are held fixed and that we want to know whether it pays to buy extra quantities of raw material I. Not knowing the subtleties of sensitivity analysis for linear programs, the manager of the firm decides to try to solve his linear program with a supply of 9 (instead of 8) for raw material I. He actually finds that the same basis is optimal and that the solution is

$$\begin{cases} x_1 = 11/3 \\ x_2 = 5/3 \\ z = 22 + 1 \end{cases}$$

Thus it will be rewarding to buy extra quantities of raw material I if and only if its price is less than 1. For the manager of the firm, 1 unit of raw material is worth 1, whatever its real market price. Suppose that the market price of raw material I is less than 1 and that, desiring to earn much more money, the manager decides to buy 9 extra units. He expects his return to be increased in proportion. But solving

$$(P_1') \quad \begin{cases} 2x_1 + x_2 \le 8 + 9 \\ x_1 + 2x_2 \le 7 \\ x_2 \le 3 \\ 4x_1 + 5x_2 = z\,(Max) \end{cases} \qquad x_1, x_2 \ge 0$$

he finds that the optimal basis is $J = \{1,3,5\}$ and the optimal solution is

$$x_1 = 7, \quad x_2 = 0, \quad z = 28$$

$i.e.$, an increase of only 6. And increasing further the availability of raw material I would be of no use. Thus we conclude that the "internal" price we determined for raw material I is valid only if we stay "in the neighborhood" of the present production plan. This is why these prices are called "marginal."

What is the marginal price of raw material II now? Solving (P_1) with a supply of 8 units (instead of 7) for raw material II leads to the optimal solution

$$x_1 = 8/3, \quad x_2 = 8/3, \quad z = 22 + 2$$

The marginal price of raw material II ($i.e.$, the value for this production unit of an extra unit of raw material II) is thus 2.

Finally, we see that the marginal prices $(1,2,0)$ are equal to the optimal solution of the dual of (P_1). This result is not purely coincidental, as we will see now.

(c) *Marginal Prices and Dual Variables*: Let us consider the linear program

$$(P) \quad \left\{ \begin{array}{ll} Ax = b & x \geq 0 \\ cx = z \,(\text{Max}) \end{array} \right.$$

and let J be an optimal basis for (P). Let δb be an m-vector that we call a *variation* of b, and let us assume that δb is small enough so that

$$(A^J)^{-1} (b + \delta b) \geq 0$$

$i.e.$, J is also an optimal basis for

$$(P_\delta) \quad \left\{ \begin{array}{ll} Ax = b + \delta b & x \geq 0 \\ cx = z \,(\text{Max}) \end{array} \right.$$

The optimal basic solution of (P_δ) is then

$$x_J = (A^J)^{-1}b + (A^J)^{-1}\delta b$$

$$x_j = 0 \qquad\qquad\qquad j \notin J$$

$$z = \pi b + \pi \delta b$$

But from the corollary to Theorem IV.3, $\bar{y} = \pi$ is an optimal solution of the dual of (P). We thus have:

<u>Theorem 2</u>: The variation of the optimal value of the objective function of problem (P), for a variation δb of the right-hand side b sufficiently small for the optimal basis to remain the same, is $\bar{y}\delta b$, where $\bar{y}$ is an optimal solution of the dual of (P).

It often happens that linear programs come from economic problems. Take, for instance, problem (P) above:

1. b_i may represent the quantity of commodity i to be used if $b_i > 0$, or the quantity of commodity i to be produced if $b_i < 0$.

2. x_j represents the *level* of activity j.

3. c^j represents the profit produced by activity j operating at level 1 if $c^j > 0$.

4. $-c^j$ represents the cost of operating activity j at level 1 if $c^j < 0$.

5. A is called the "matrix of technological constraints."

6. y_i is the dual variable, which is a price attached to commodity i.

Then the problem (P) and its dual (D) may be expressed as follows:

(P): Given the availability (demand) for each of the m commodities i, and a profit (cost) for each of the n activities j, what is the level of each activity such that:

- supplied commodities will be consumed
- demanded commodities will be produced

for a maximum total profit (a minimum total cost)?

(D): Given a unit profit (cost) for each of the n activities j ,   and a
supply (demand) for each of the m commodities i ,   what must be the unit price
of each commodity i   such that the total value of commodities consumed minus
the total value of commodities produced be minimum, subject to the constraints
that for each activity j ,   the total value of consumed commodities minus the
total value of produced commodities -- for a level of activity j   equal to 1 --
will be greater than or equal to the unit profit of activity j ?

EXERCISES

1. What is the dual of

$$
(P) \begin{cases}
x_1 & + x_3 & & = 1 \\
& x_2 + x_3 & & = 2 \\
x_1 & & + x_4 & = 2 \\
& x_2 & + x_4 & = 4 \\
x_1 + x_2 & + x_3 + x_4 & & = z \, (\text{Max})
\end{cases}
$$

Solve the dual of (P).   From this solution, what can be said about (P) ?
Check directly on (P)   that what can be said about (P)   by studying its
dual is in fact true.

2. Write down the complementary slackness theorem in economic terms.

3. Prove the following "strong complementary slackness theorem": If both dual
    linear programs (P)   and (D)   have feasible solutions, it is possible to
    find a pair of optimal solutions such that:

    (i)   Whenever a constraint of one problem is tight,
          the corresponding variable of the other is positive.

    (ii) Whenever a variable of one problem is 0 ,   the
          corresponding constraint of the other is slack.

HINT: Use the result of Exercise VI.11. Take

$$B = \begin{bmatrix} 0 & -A & b \\ A^T & 0 & -c^T \\ -b^T & c & 0 \end{bmatrix} \qquad z = \begin{bmatrix} y^T \\ x \\ t \end{bmatrix}$$

4. Using the complementary slackness theorem, show that

$$x_1 = 1, \quad x_2 = 2, \quad x_3 = 0, \quad x_4 = 4, \quad x_5 = 0$$

is an optimal solution of

$$\begin{cases} x_1 + 2x_2 + 3x_3 - 4x_4 + 5x_5 \leq 0 \\ \qquad\qquad -2x_3 + x_4 + 3x_5 \leq 4 \\ 3x_1 \qquad + 4x_3 \qquad + x_5 \leq 3 \\ \qquad x_2 - x_3 \qquad + 2x_5 \leq 2 \\ x_1 - 4x_2 + 3x_3 + x_4 + 2x_5 \leq 1 \\ x_1 + 2x_2 + 3x_3 + 4x_4 + 5x_5 = z\,(\text{Max}) \end{cases} \qquad x_i \geq 0$$

5. Consider the linear program

$$\begin{cases} x_1 + 2x_2 \leq 14 \qquad\qquad x_i \geq 0 \qquad i = 1,2 \\ 2x_1 - x_2 \leq 10 \\ x_1 - x_2 \leq 3 \\ 2x_1 + x_2 = z\,(\text{Max}) \end{cases}$$

Is solution $x_1 = 20/3, \quad x_2 = 11/3$:

    (a)   Feasible?

    (b)   Basic?

    (c)   Optimal?

6. Show that $x_1 = x_2 = 0$, $x_3 = 4.5$, $x_4 = 6$ is an optimal solution of the linear program of Exercise IV.5.

7. Use the complementary slackness theorem to prove that the feasible solution of transportation problem of Exercise I.6 is in fact optimal.

8. What can be said of the marginal prices when the optimal solution of the linear program

$$\begin{cases} Ax \leq b \qquad x \geq 0 \\ cx = z\,(\text{Max}) \end{cases}$$

is degenerate? Give a geometric interpretation.

9. Let $\mathcal{D} \subset \mathbb{R}^n$ $\mathcal{D}' \subset \mathbb{R}^m$ and $F : \mathcal{D} \times \mathcal{D}' \to \mathbb{R}$. $\bar{x} \in \mathcal{D}'$, $\bar{y} \in \mathcal{D}'$ is a saddle point for F if:

(*) $F(x,\bar{y}) \leq F(\bar{x},\bar{y}) \leq F(\bar{x},y)$ $\forall x \in \mathcal{D}$, $\forall y \in \mathcal{D}$

Show that (Lagrangian theorem in linear programming) a necessary and sufficient condition for $\bar{x}, \bar{y} \geq 0$ to be a couple of optimal solutions of dual linear programs

$$(\text{P}) \begin{cases} Ax \leq b \qquad x \geq 0 \\ cx = z\,(\text{Max}) \end{cases} \qquad\qquad (\text{D}) \begin{cases} yA \geq c \qquad y \geq 0 \\ yb = w\,(\text{Min}) \end{cases}$$

is that $\bar{x}, \bar{y}$ is a saddle point of the Lagrangian:

$$F(x,y) \;=\; cx - y(Ax - b) \qquad\qquad x \geq 0, \; y \geq 0$$

The common value of the objective functions at the optimum is $F(\bar{x},\bar{y})$.

HINT: To prove sufficiency, use the fact that (*) is true for any x and any y.

Chapter X. The Dual Simplex Algorithm: Parametric Linear Programming

Consider the pair of dual linear programs

(PC) $\begin{cases} Ax \le b \qquad x \ge 0 \\ cx = z\,(\text{Max}) \end{cases}$ (DC) $\begin{cases} yA \ge c \qquad y \ge 0 \\ yb = w\,(\text{Min}) \end{cases}$

written in canonical form. If $b \ge 0$, then $x = 0$ is a feasible solution of (PC). We say in this case that (PC) is "primal feasible." If $c \le 0$, then $y = 0$ is a feasible solution of (DC). In this case, we say that (PC) is "dual feasible." Given a linear program written in canonical form with respect to a basis, we know (from Theorem IV.3) that this basis is optimal if and only if the linear program is at the same time primal and dual feasible.

The simplex algorithm can be characterized by saying that we look for dual feasibility while maintaining primal feasibility (which has been obtained through phase I of the simplex method). In some cases, the linear program is given dual feasible but primal infeasible. It would then be neither smart nor efficient to call for phase I and phase II of the simplex method. It is better to apply the dual simplex algorithm, which looks for primal feasibility while maintaining dual feasibility.

The dual simplex algorithm is presented in the first section. In the second section, we study the variations of the optimal solution of (PC) when some of the "data" vary. In effect, some of these data are often imprecise and it is thus interesting to see how an error would affect the solution. It also happens that market prices, for instance, vary and one wants to know how the optimal solution is sensitive to such variations. These studies are referred to as "sensitivity analysis" or "post-optimality analysis" and can be conducted in a systematic way through "parametric programming."

Another case where parametric programming can be used happens when we have two (or more) objective functions we want to maximize simultaneously. Then,

156

studying

$$(Q_\mu) \quad \begin{cases} Ax \leq b \qquad\qquad x \geq 0 \\ \\ (c + \mu f)x = z\,(Max) \end{cases}$$

(where c and f are n-row vectors and μ is a parameter) for various values
of μ -- i.e., for different relative weights of these objective functions --
gives some insight into the way the optimal solution depends on each objective
function.

1. Dual Simplex Algorithm

If the linear program

$$(P) \quad \begin{cases} Ax = b \qquad x \geq 0 \\ \\ cx = z\,(Max) \end{cases}$$

is written in canonical form with respect to basis J and is dual feasible,
we have

(1) A^J is, up to a permutation of columns, the unit matrix
(this permutation is given by the function "col").

(2) $c \leq 0$

(3) $c^J = 0.$

Each iteration of the dual simplex will consist mainly, as for the primal,
in a pivot operation on the coefficients of the linear program. After this
pivot operation, the linear program will be written in canonical form with
respect to the basis

$$\bar{J} \;=\; J \cup \{s\} \backslash \{col(r)\}$$

How will we determine on which indices r and s perform the pivot operation?

We begin by choosing a row index r such that $b_r < 0$. If such an index
does not exist, J is an optimal basis. We stop. Thus the index leaving the
basis will be col(r) . Let us call s the index entering the basis; we
examine now how s is chosen.

The cost vector $\bar{c}$ relative to the basis $\bar{J}$ will be equal to

$$\bar{c} = c - \pi A_r$$

In order that condition (3) be satisfied after pivoting, we must have

$$\bar{c}^s = c^s - \pi A_r^s = 0$$

and thus

$$\pi = c^s / A_r^s$$

In particular, for $j = col(r)$, we get

$$\bar{c}^j = -c^s / A_r^s$$

and thus, for condition (2) to be verified after pivoting, we need $\bar{c}^j \leq 0$, $i.e.$, $A_r^s \leq 0$ and then $A_r^s < 0$.

We now ask the question: What happens if no candidate column exists, $i.e.$, if $A_r \geq 0$? In this case, the rth constraint is

$$A_r x = b_r < 0$$

which clearly is an infeasible equation for all nonnegative x's. Our problem does not have a feasible solution.

Assume now that we pivot on $A_r^s < 0$. We get

$$\bar{c} = c - \frac{c^s}{A_r^s} A_r$$

By assumption we have

$$c \leq 0 ; \qquad c^s \leq 0 ; \qquad A_r^s < 0$$

Thus for all k such that $A_r^k \geq 0$, we have $\bar{c}^k \leq 0$. In order that condition (2) be satisfied after pivoting, we then take s defined by

$$(4) \qquad c^s / A_r^s = \underset{\{j | A_r^j < 0\}}{\text{Min}} [c^j / A_r^j]$$

Dual Simplex Algorithm

Linear Program (P) is written in canonical form with respect to basis J and $c \leq 0$. The mapping "col" is defined as in Remark V.1.

Repeat | the following procedure until either an optimal basis is obtained or it is shown that (P) does not have feasible solution.

Step 1: Choose an r such that $b_r < 0$. If such an r does not exist, the basis J is optimal. STOP.

Step 2: If $A_r \geq 0$, no feasible solution exists. STOP.

Step 3: Let $L = \{j \mid A_r^j < 0\}$ ($L \neq \emptyset$ because of Step 2)

Choose an s such that

$$c^s / A_r^s = \text{Min}_{j \in L} \ [c^j / A_r^j]$$

Step 4: Perform the pivot operation (defined by row r and column s) on the matrix of coefficients of linear program (P). After this pivot operation (P) is written in canonical form with respect to

$$\bar{J} = J \cup \{s\} \setminus \{col(r)\}$$

Let $J = \bar{J}$; $col(r) := s$.

end repeat

Remark 1: The reader will note how closely the dual simplex algorithm parallels (or mirrors) the (primal) simplex (see Section V.3). The fact that the dual simplex algorithm roughly reduces to the primal simplex performed on the dual will be apparent in the following example. The proof of this property is left as an exercise.

In Step 3, the choice of s in case of a tie can be made using a perturbation technique or lexicographic rule. The principles of the revised and the dual simplex algorithm can be combined.

EXAMPLE: Consider (D_1), the dual of linear program (P_1).

$$(D_1) \quad \begin{cases} 2y_1 + y_2 \qquad\quad \geq 4 \\ y_1 + 2y_2 + y_3 \geq 5 \\ 8y_1 + 7y_2 + 3y_3 = w(\text{Min}) \end{cases} \qquad y_i \geq 0 \qquad i=1,2,\ldots,3$$

which, after addition of the slack variables y_4, y_5 can be written in canonical form with respect to the basis $J = \{4,5\}$:

$$(5) \quad \begin{cases} -2y_1 - y_2 \qquad + y_4 \qquad\quad = -4 \\ -y_1 - 2y_2 - y_3 \qquad + y_5 = -5 \\ -8y_1 - 7y_2 - 3y_3 \qquad\qquad = z(\text{Max}) \end{cases} \qquad y_i \geq 0 \qquad i=1,2,\ldots,5$$

We now give the solution of this linear program using the dual simplex algorithm in tabular form:

y_1	y_2	y_3	y_4	y_5	z	b
-2	-1		1			-4
-1	-2	-1		1		-5 ←
-8	-7	-3 $\cdot *$			1	
-2	-1		1			-4 ←
1	2	1		-1		5
-5	-1 $_*$			-3	1	15
2	1		-1			4
-3		1	2	-1		-3 ←
-3 $_*$			-1	-3	1	19
	1	2/3	1/3	-2/3		2
1		-1/3	-2/3	1/3		1
		-1	-3	-2	1	22

Remark 2: The dual simplex algorithm is frequently used in "post optimization."
After having solved a linear program, it might happen that we want to add constraints that are not satisfied for the present "optimal" solution. These new
constraints are a source of "infeasibility." It is much more efficient to
apply a few steps of the dual simplex algorithm than to begin again the solution from scratch. This situation often occurs in combinatorial optimization
when one solves integer linear programs (*i.e.*, linear programs with integrity
constraints on the variables -- see Reference [4]).

2. Parametric Linear Programming

Parametric programming consists of studying how the optimal solution of the
linear program

$$(P) \quad \begin{cases} Ax = b \qquad x \geq 0 \\ cx = z\,(Max) \end{cases}$$

varies when components of b and/or c depend linearly on one or more parameters.
Study of the variation of the solution with the variation of some coefficients
of A is a more intricate matter and is not presented here.

We first study numerical examples and then give a few general results.

(a) A numerical example of variation of the solution of (P) as a
     function of c: We will study

$$(Q_\mu) \quad \begin{cases} 2x_1 + x_2 + x_3 = 8 \\ x_1 + 2x_2 + x_4 = 7 \qquad x_i \geq 0 \qquad i=1,2,\ldots,5 \\ + x_2 + x_5 = 3 \\ (4 + \mu)x_1 + 5x_2 = z\,(Max) \end{cases}$$

We recognize, for $\mu = 0$, problem (P_1). We write (Q_μ) in
canonical form with respect to the basis $\{5,1,2\}$:

$$(6) \begin{cases} \quad \frac{1}{3} x_3 - \frac{2}{3} x_4 + x_5 = 1 \\[2mm] x_1 \quad + \frac{2}{3} x_3 - \frac{1}{3} x_4 \quad = 3 \\[2mm] \quad x_2 - \frac{1}{3} x_3 + \frac{2}{3} x_4 \quad = 2 \\[2mm] \mu x_1 \quad - x_3 - 2x_4 \quad = z(\text{Max}) - 22 \end{cases} \qquad x_i \geq 0 \qquad i=1,2,\ldots,5$$

Actually, (6) is not very satisfactory since it gives the optimal solution only for $\mu = 0$. Let us subtract μ times the second equation from both sides of the objective function. We get

$$(7) \begin{cases} \quad \frac{1}{3} x_3 - \frac{2}{3} x_4 \quad + x_5 = 1 \\[2mm] x_1 \quad + \frac{2}{3} x_3 - \frac{1}{3} x_4 \quad = 3 \\[2mm] x_2 \quad - \frac{1}{3} x_3 + \frac{2}{3} x_4 \quad = 2 \\[2mm] - (\frac{2}{3}\mu + 1) x_3 + (\frac{1}{3}\mu - 2) x_4 = z(\text{Max}) - 22 - 3\mu \end{cases} \qquad x_i \geq 0 \qquad i=1,2,\ldots,5$$

With this form, we see that the present basis is optimal for

$$\frac{2}{3} \mu + 1 \geq 0 \qquad \text{and} \qquad \frac{1}{3} \mu - 2 \leq 0$$

i.e.,

$$-\frac{3}{2} \leq \mu \leq 6$$

So we are naturally led to examine what happens when μ goes over these bounds. For $\mu = 6$, the coefficient of x_4 is equal to zero in (7). We check that

$$(4 + 6)x_1 + 5x_2 = 10x_1 + 5x_2$$

is parallel to the constraint relative to raw material I. For $\mu > 6$, we let x_4 enter the basis. We perform a pivoting as usual except that the coefficient c^s is not a scalar but a function of μ:

$$c^4 \;=\; \tfrac{1}{3}\,\mu \,-\, 2$$

We get

(8)
$$
\begin{cases}
x_2 & & + x_5 & = 3 \\[4pt]
x_1 + x_2 + \tfrac{1}{2} x_3 & & & = 4 \\[4pt]
\tfrac{3}{2} x_2 - \tfrac{1}{2} x_3 + x_4 & & & = 3 \\[4pt]
-(\tfrac{1}{2}\mu - 3) - (\tfrac{1}{2}\mu + 2)x_3 & & & = z(\text{Max}) - 16 - 4\mu
\end{cases}
\qquad x_i \geq 0 \quad i = 1,2,\ldots,5
$$

This basic solution is optimal for $\mu \geq 6$. Let us come back to the case $\mu \leq -3/2$. We start from (7) and let x_3 enter the basis. We get

(9)
$$
\begin{cases}
x_3 - 2x_4 + 3x_5 = 3 \\[4pt]
x_1 + x_4 - 2x_5 = 1 \\[4pt]
x_2 + x_5 = 3 \\[4pt]
(-\mu - 4)x_4 + (2\mu + 3)x_5 = z(\text{Max}) - 19 - \mu
\end{cases}
\qquad
\begin{array}{l}
x_i \geq 0 \\[6pt]
i = 1,2,\ldots,5
\end{array}
$$

The basis $\{3,1,2\}$ is optimal for $-4 \leq \mu \leq -\tfrac{3}{2}$. For $\mu < -4$, x_4 enters the basis and we get

(9')
$$
\begin{cases}
2x_1 + x_3 - x_5 = 5 \\[4pt]
x_1 \qquad x_4 - 2x_5 = 1 \\[4pt]
+ x_2 + x_5 = 3 \\[4pt]
(\mu + 4)x_1 - 5x_5 = z(\text{Max}) - 15
\end{cases}
\qquad x_i \geq 0 \qquad i = 1,2,\ldots,5
$$

The basis $\{3,4,2\}$ is optimal for $\mu \leq -4$.

We can now summarize our results in the following table :

μ	$-\infty$		-4		$-3/2$		6		$+\infty$
x_1	0		1		3		4		
x_2	3		3		2		0		
x_3	5		3		0		0		
x_4	1		0		0		3		
x_5	0		0		1		3		
z	15		$19 + \mu$		$22 + 3\mu$		$16 + 4\mu$		

If we plot the value of z_{Max} as a function of μ we get Figure X.1.

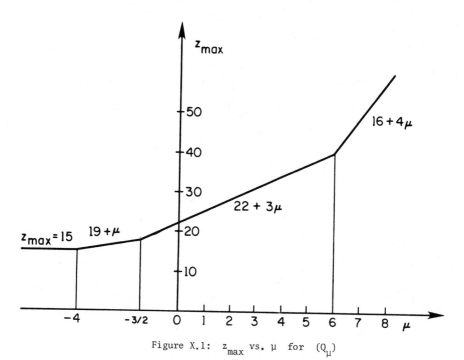

Figure X.1: z_{max} vs. μ for (Q_μ)

The geometric interpretation of these results shown in Figure X.2 is particularly enlightening.

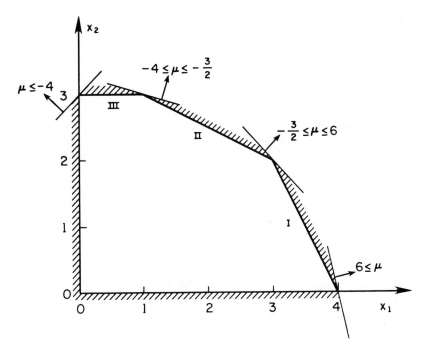

Figure X.2: Geometric Solution for (Q_μ)

(b) A numerical example of variations of the solution of (P) in the function of b: We consider the linear program

$$(P_\mu) \quad \begin{cases} 2x_1 + x_2 + x_3 & = 8 + 2\mu \\ x_1 + 2x_2 + x_4 & = 7 + 7\mu \qquad x_i \geq 0 \\ x_2 + x_5 & = 3 + 2\mu \qquad i=1,2,\ldots,5 \\ 4x_1 + 5x_2 & = z\,(\text{Max}) \end{cases}$$

We note that for $\mu = 0$, (P_μ) is problem (P_1). We write (P_μ) in canonical form with respect to the basis $\{5,1,2\}$:

$$(10) \quad \begin{cases} \dfrac{1}{3} x_3 - \dfrac{2}{3} x_4 + x_5 = 1 - 2\mu \\[2mm] x_1 + \dfrac{2}{3} x_3 - \dfrac{1}{3} x_4 = 3 - \mu \\[2mm] x_2 - \dfrac{1}{3} x_3 + \dfrac{2}{3} x_4 = 2 + 4\mu \\[2mm] - x_3 - 2x_4 = z(\text{Max}) - 22 - 16\mu \end{cases} \qquad x_i \geq 0 \quad i=1,2,\ldots,5$$

This basis is feasible, and thus optimal, for

$$1 - 2\mu \geq 0, \qquad 3 - \mu \geq 0, \qquad 2 + 4\mu \geq 0$$

i.e.,

$$-\frac{1}{2} \leq \mu \leq \frac{1}{2}$$

Let us explore what happens when $\mu > 1/2$. In this case, the first component of the right-hand side becomes negative. The basis $\{5,1,2\}$ stays optimal but is no longer feasible: (1) stays dual feasible. We are led to perform a step of the dual simplex algorithm. We pivot on the first row and fourth column and we get

$$(11) \quad \begin{cases} - 2x_3 + x_4 - \dfrac{3}{2} x_5 = - \dfrac{3}{2} + 3\mu \\[2mm] x_1 + \dfrac{1}{2} x_3 - \dfrac{1}{2} x_5 = \dfrac{5}{2} \\[2mm] x_2 + x_5 = 3 + 2\mu \\[2mm] - 5x_3 - 3 x_5 = z - 25 - 10\mu \end{cases} \qquad \begin{array}{l} x_i \geq 0 \\[2mm] i=1,2,\ldots,5 \end{array}$$

The basis $\{4,1,2\}$ remains feasible for all $\mu \geq 1/2$. Let us come back to (10) and try $\mu < -1/2$. Infeasibility appears in the third row and we perform again a step of the dual simplex algorithm. We get

$$(12) \quad \begin{cases} x_2 & + x_5 & = 3 + 2\mu \\ x_1 + 2x_2 & + x_4 & = 7 + 7\mu \\ - 3x_2 + x_3 - 6x_4 & & = -6 - 12\mu \\ - 3x_2 & - 8x_4 & = z - 28 - 28\mu \end{cases}$$

The basis $\{5,1,3\}$ remains feasible, and thus optimal, for $-1 \le \mu \le -1/2$. For $\mu < -1$, the second equation is infeasible.

These results can be summarized in the following table:

μ	-1		-1/2				1/2		$+\infty$
x_1	0	$7 + 7\mu$	$7/2$		$3 - \mu$	$5/2$		$5/2$	
x_2	0	0	0		$2 + 4\mu$	4		$3 + 2\mu$	
x_3	6	$-6 - 12\mu$	0		0	0		0	
x_4	0	0	0		0	0		$-3/2 + 3\mu$	
x_5	1	$3 + 2\mu$	2		$1 - 2\mu$	0		0	
z	0	$28 + 28\mu$	14		$22 + 16\mu$	30		$25 + 10\mu$	

And if we plot the value of z_{max} as a function of μ, we get Fig. X.3.

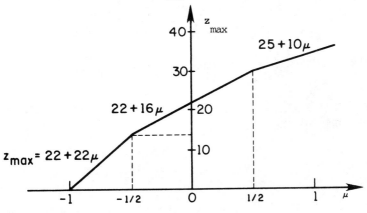

Figure X.3: z_{max} vs. μ for (P_μ)

On Figure X.4, we sketch the domain of feasible solutions for various
values of μ.

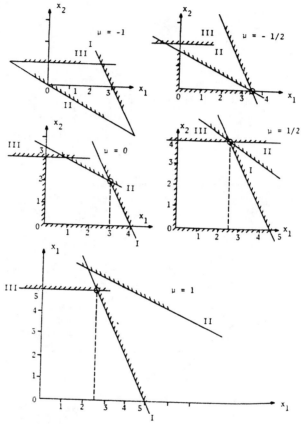

Figure X.4: The Domain of Feasible Solutions of (P_μ) for Various μ

(c) <u>General results in parametric programming</u>: Let us consider the following
linear programs:

$$(P_\mu) \begin{cases} Ax = b + \mu d \qquad x \geq 0 \\ cx = z\,(\text{Max}) \end{cases} \qquad (Q_\mu) \begin{cases} Ax = b \qquad\qquad x \geq 0 \\ (c + \mu f)x = w(\text{Max}) \end{cases}$$

where μ is a scalar, d is an m-column vector, and f is an n-row vector.

The domain of feasible solutions for (Q_μ) does not depend on μ. We assume that

$$\{x \mid Ax = b, \quad x \geq 0\} \neq \emptyset$$

We let $z(\mu)$ (resp. $w(\mu)$), denote the value of the objective function of (P_μ) (resp. of (Q_μ)) for an optimal solution.

Definition 1: Recall (cf. Definition VIII.5) that a real-valued function g defined on a convex set C is convex if

$$g(\lambda p + (1 - \lambda)q) \leq \lambda g(p) + (1 - \lambda) g(q) \qquad 0 \leq \lambda \leq 1; \quad p,q \in C$$

The function g is said to be "concave" if $-g$ is convex.

Theorem 1: We have the following properties:

(i)   The set of values of μ for which (P_μ) has a feasible solution is an interval $[a,b]$ (bounds of which may be infinite).

(ii) If for some $\mu_0 \in [a, b]$, (P_{μ_0}) has a finite optimal solution, the same is true for (P_μ) for all $\mu \in [a,b]$.

(iii) The set of values of μ for which a certain basis of (P_μ) (resp. of (Q_μ)) is optimal is an interval.

(iv) $z(\mu)$ is a piecewise linear concave function of μ.

(v) $w(\mu)$ is a piecewise linear convex function of μ.

Proof: (i) the set

$$\{(x,\mu) \mid Ax = b + \mu d, \quad x \geq 0\}$$

is a convex polyhedron of $\mathbb{R}^{n+1}$. Its projection on the μ-axis is thus an interval.

(ii) (P_μ^*), the dual of (P_μ), has a feasible solution or not independently of the value of μ. The property is then a consequence of duality theorem (see Section IX.1).

(iii) These sets are convex as can be seen by writing (P_μ) (resp. (Q_μ)) in canonical form with respect to an optimal basis.

(iv) Let J be an interval for which J is an optimal basis of (P_μ) (resp. (Q_μ)). In this interval $z(\mu)$ (resp. $w(\mu)$) is a linear function of μ, as can be seen in writing (P_μ) (resp. (Q_μ)) in canonical form with respect to J.

Let $\bar{\mu}$, $\bar{\bar{\mu}} \varepsilon [a,b]$ and let $\bar{x}, \bar{\bar{x}}$ be the corresponding optimal solutions of $(P_{\bar{\mu}})$ and $(P_{\bar{\bar{\mu}}})$, respectively. Let

$$x = \lambda \bar{x} + (1 + \lambda)\bar{\bar{x}} \qquad\qquad 0 \le \lambda \le 1$$

Then x is a feasible solution of (P_μ) for

$$\mu = \lambda\bar{\mu} + (1 - \lambda)\bar{\bar{\mu}}$$

And thus

$$(*) \qquad\qquad z(\mu) \ge cx$$

(v) The dual of (Q_μ) is a problem of type (P_μ) except for the objective function that is to be minimized.

EXERCISES

1. Use the dual simplex algorithm to solve

$$(P) \quad \begin{cases} 3x_1 + x_2 \ge 4 \\ x_1 + 4x_2 \ge 5 \\ x_1 + x_2 = z\,(Max) \end{cases} \qquad x_1, x_2 \ge 0$$

2. Solve, using the dual simplex algorithm, the linear program

$$\begin{cases} x_1 - x_2 \le 1 \\ x_1 \qquad \ge 1 \\ x_1 + x_2 \ge 3 \\ x_1 + 2x_2 = z\,(Min) \end{cases} \qquad x_1, x_2 \ge 0$$

3. Solve, using the dual simplex algorithm, the linear program

$$
\begin{cases}
x_1 + x_2 \geq 2 \\
-x_1 + x_2 \geq 3 \qquad\qquad x_1, x_2 \geq 0 \\
x_1 \qquad\;\; \geq 4 \\
3x_1 + 2x_2 = z\,(\text{Min})
\end{cases}
$$

4. Describe the lexicographic method applied to the dual simplex algorithm.

5. Consider the linear program

$$
(P) \quad
\begin{cases}
Ax \leq b \qquad x \geq 0 \\
cx = z\,(\text{Max})
\end{cases}
$$

which is neither primal feasible (some b_i are negative), nor dual feasible.
Let e be the m-column vector each component of which is equal to 1 and
$\bar{\mu} = -\,\text{Min}_i\,[b_i]$.

Prove that applying the technique of Section 2(b) to solve

$$
(P_\mu) \quad
\begin{cases}
Ax \leq b + \mu e \qquad x \geq 0 \\
cx = z\,(\text{Max})
\end{cases}
$$

starting with $\mu = \bar{\mu}$ and letting μ decrease to 0 gives an alternative
method of initialization (an alternative phase I).

Use this technique to solve

$$
\begin{cases}
x_1 + 2x_2 - 3x_3 - x_4 \leq -1 \\
2x_1 + x_2 + 2x_3 + 3x_4 \leq 3 \qquad x_i \geq 0 \\
x_1 + 3x_2 - x_3 + x_4 = z\,(\text{Max}) \qquad i = 1,2,\ldots,4
\end{cases}
$$

6. Solve the linear program

$$
\begin{cases}
x_1 + x_2 + 2x_3 \leq 6 \\
2x_1 - x_2 + 2x_3 \geq 2 \qquad x_i \geq 0 \qquad i = 1,2,3 \\
\alpha x_1 + 2x_2 + x_3 = z\,(\text{Max})
\end{cases}
$$

(a) For $\alpha = -1$.

(b) For all values of α .

7. Give all the optimal solutions of

$$(P_\alpha) \begin{cases} x_1 + x_2 \geq 2 \\ x_1 + 2x_2 \geq 3 \\ (2 + \alpha)x_1 + 4x_2 = z\,(\text{Min}) \end{cases} \qquad x_1, x_2 \geq 0$$

when α varies.

8. Give all the optimal solutions of

$$(Q_\alpha) \begin{cases} x_1 + x_2 \geq 3 - \alpha \\ x_1 + 2x_2 \geq 2 + \alpha \\ (2 + \alpha)x_1 + 4x_2 = z\,(\text{Max}) \end{cases} \qquad x_1, x_2 \geq 0$$

9. Solve the parametric program

$$(P_p) \begin{cases} -2x_1 + x_2 \leq 1 + \mu \\ x_1 - 2x_2 \leq 2 - 2\mu \\ x_1 + x_2 \leq 3 + 6\mu \\ x_1 + 2x_2 = z\,(\text{Max}) \end{cases} \qquad x_1, x_2 \geq 0$$

Chapter XI. The Transportation Problem

A large number of linear programs actually solved are transportation problems or possess a structure of the same type. This special structure allows very efficient implementation of the simplex algorithm (so that very large transportation problems can be solved). This structure also has a great theoretical interest since network flow problems present the very same structure. For these two reasons, the transportation problem deserves special study in a course on linear programming.

1. The Problem

Definition 1: We call the following linear program, the "transportation problem":

$$(T) \begin{cases} \sum_{\ell=1}^{q} t_{k\ell} = a_k & k=1,2,\ldots,p \\ \\ \sum_{k=1}^{p} t_{k\ell} = b_\ell & \ell=1,2,\ldots,q \\ \\ \sum_{\ell=1}^{q} \sum_{k=1}^{p} d_{k\ell} t_{k\ell} = z \text{ (Min)} \end{cases} \qquad t_{k\ell} \geq 0$$

where

- The $p \times q$ $t_{k\ell}$ are the variables or unknowns
- Coefficients a_k, b_ℓ, and $d_{k\ell}$ are given with

$$a_k > 0 \qquad \text{for} \quad k=1,2,\ldots,p$$
$$b_\ell > 0 \qquad \text{for} \quad \ell=1,2,\ldots,q$$

$$(1) \qquad\qquad \sum_{k=1}^{p} a_k \;=\; \sum_{\ell=1}^{q} b_\ell$$

<u>Remark 1</u>: If $a_k < 0$ (resp. $b_\ell < 0$), the kth constraint (resp. $(p+\ell)^{th}$ constraint) of (T) is infeasible. In addition:

$$a_k = 0 \;\rightarrow\; t_{k\ell} = 0 \qquad \text{for} \qquad \ell=1,2,\ldots,q$$

$$b_\ell = 0 \;\rightarrow\; t_{k\ell} = 0 \qquad \text{for} \qquad k=1,2,\ldots,p$$

Let us add up the p first constraints and the q last constraints of (T). We find

$$(1') \qquad\qquad \sum_{k=1}^{p} a_k \;=\; \sum_{k=1}^{p}\sum_{\ell=1}^{q} t_{k\ell} \;=\; \sum_{\ell=1}^{q} b_\ell$$

Thus, if (1) is not satisfied, (T) has no feasible solution.

Now assume that we add the same constant α to each coefficient $d_{k\ell}$. The value of the objective function of (T) will be increased by

$$\sum_{k=1}^{p}\sum_{\ell=1}^{q} \alpha t_{k\ell} \;=\; \alpha \sum_{k=1}^{p} a_k \;=\; \alpha \sum_{\ell=1}^{q} b_\ell$$

For every feasible solution of (T), its objective function is increased by a constant term: the value of the optimal solution does not change and we can assume, without loss of generality, that

$$d_{k\ell} \geq 0 \qquad\qquad k=1,2,\ldots,p; \qquad \ell=1,2,\ldots,q$$

<u>Remark 2</u>: Let us consider the problem met by an industrialist who wants to transport at minimal cost a certain commodity from p factories (in the kth factory a quantity a_k of this commodity is available) to q warehouses (the demand in the ℓth warehouse is b_ℓ); unit costs of shipping (i.e., the cost of shipping 1 unit) from factory k to warehouse ℓ is $d_{k\ell}$. Formulation of this problem is as follows ($t_{k\ell}$ denotes the amount of commodity shipped from factory k to warehouse ℓ):

$$
(2) \quad
\begin{cases}
\displaystyle\sum_{\ell=1}^{q} t_{k\ell} \;\leq\; a_k & k=1,2,\ldots,p \\[2em]
\displaystyle\sum_{k=1}^{p} t_{k\ell} \;\geq\; b_\ell & \ell=1,2,\ldots,q \\[2em]
\displaystyle\sum_{\ell=1}^{q}\sum_{k=1}^{p} d_{k\ell} t_{k\ell} \;=\; z\,(\text{Min})
\end{cases}
\qquad t_{k\ell} \geq 0
$$

Adding up the p first and the q last inequations, we get

$$
(1'') \qquad \sum_{\ell=1}^{q} b_\ell \;\leq\; \sum_{k=1}^{p}\sum_{\ell=1}^{q} t_{k\ell} \;\leq\; \sum_{k=1}^{p} a_k
$$

This relation has the following interpretation: in order that linear program (2) have a feasible solution, it is necessary that the total demand be not greater than the total availability of the commodity. We will thus assume that (1'') is satisfied.

Let us now add a fictitious warehouse of index 0 for which the demand is

$$
b_0 \;=\; \sum_{k=1}^{p} a_k \;-\; \sum_{\ell=1}^{q} b_\ell
$$

and assume that the transportation costs d_{k0} from the factories to this fictitious warehouse equal 0 . We then get a new linear program (2'). We leave it as an exercise (Exercise 2) to show that (2') is in fact equivalent to (2) and with the same form as (2).

For (2'), the double inequality (1'') is in fact an equality (due to the value we have given to b_0). From this can be deduced the fact that the inequalities in (2') can be replaced by equalities (there can be no feasible solution for which a single inequality is slack).[+] We conclude this remark by saying that (T) is an appropriate model for the transportation problem.

[+]The same argument was used in Exercise II.12.

Remark 3: A problem of this type has been investigated by Monge. The present formalism was first studied by Hitchcock, Kantorovitch, and Koopman. Problem (P_2) of Chapter I is a transportation problem.

The mathematical properties of linear programs that are transportation problems come from the fact that the matrix A has a very special structure. This special structure is due to the fact that there is a graph on which the problem is defined. Solution methods other than the revised simplex algorithm that we are about to present here exist to solve transportation problems. We can, in particular, cite the "*Hungarian method*" of H.W. Kuhn, a method that is also named "primal-dual" (see [6]).

2. Properties of the Transportation Problem

Remark 4: The transportation problem can be written

$$(T) \quad \begin{cases} Ax = f \\ cx = z(Min) \end{cases} \quad x \geq 0$$

where

- A is a $(p+q) * pq$-matrix

- $f = \begin{bmatrix} a \\ b \end{bmatrix}$ is a $(p+q)$-column vector

- c is a pq-row vector

- x is a pq-column vector.

To make the correspondence clear between c and d on the one hand, and x and t on the other hand, we pose

$$\begin{cases} c^j = d_{k\ell} \\ x_j = t_{k\ell} \end{cases}$$

for

$$(3) \qquad j = q(k-1) + \ell \qquad\qquad 1 \leq \ell \leq q$$

In the sequel, a column index of matrix A will sometimes be denoted by j, sometimes by the couple (k,ℓ). j and (k,ℓ) are related through (3).

Remark 5: Each variable $t_{k\ell}$ appears once and only once (with coefficient 1) in the group of the p first equations of (T) (actually in the kth equation of this group). Each variable $t_{k\ell}$ appears once and only once (with coefficient 1) in the group of the q last equations of (T) (actually in the ℓth equation of this group). Thus matrix A has the following properties:

(i)   A column of A has exactly two nonzero elements that are equal to 1.

(ii) One of these nonzero elements belongs to the group of the p first rows, the other to the group of the q last rows.

(iii) Any $(p+q)$-column vector with properties (i) and (ii) is a column of A.

Example: Matrix A for problem (P_2) is

$$
A = \begin{bmatrix}
1 & 1 & 1 & & & \\
 & & & 1 & 1 & 1 \\
1 & & & 1 & & \\
 & 1 & & & 1 & \\
 & & 1 & & & 1
\end{bmatrix}
$$

Definition 2: We will give the name "nonsingular triangular" matrix (in brief, "triangular" matrix) to a *square* nonsingular matrix B satisfying the following (recursive) definition:

(i)   A nonzero scalar is a triangular matrix of dimension 1.

(ii) B has a row with exactly one nonzero element. The submatrix obtained from B by deleting this row and the column containing the nonzero element is triangular.

Remark 6: This definition is a very slight extension of the usual concept of triangular matrix: given a triangular matrix as defined here, there exists a proper way of permuting its rows and columns that gives a triangular matrix as usually defined.

Remark 7: Note that if B is a triangular matrix, linear system

(4) $Bx = f$

can be solved very easily by substitution. Let i be a row of B containing just one non-zero element, say B_i^j. We have

(4')
$$x_j = f_i/B_i^j$$

Substituting x_j by its value (4') in the other equations of (4), we get a linear system of dimension n-1 (if B was of dimension n) the matrix of which is triangular.

Theorem 1: Every square nonsingular submatrix of A (the constraint matrix of linear program (T)) is triangular.

Proof: Let B be a square nonsingular submatrix of A of dimension k. Assume that B is not triangular but that every submatrix of A of dimension less than k is triangular (then $k \geq 2$ from the definition of a triangular matrix of dimension 1).

From Remark 5(i), every column of B contains at most two nonzero elements. Assume that there exists a row of B with just one nonzero element. Deleting this row and the column of B containing the nonzero element, we obtain submatrix of A of dimension k-1, which, by the assumption of minimality on k, is triangular. Thus B would be triangular. Consequently, every row of B contains at least two nonzero elements.

If we count the number of nonzero elements of B by looking at the rows, we find at least 2k elements. By looking at columns, we find at most 2k elements. Thus B has exactly 2k nonzero elements and exactly two nonzero elements in each row, two nonzero elements in each column.

From Remark 5(ii), each column contains a 1 in the group of the p first equations and another 1 in the group of the q last equations. We now consider the k-row vector y defined by

$$y^i = \begin{cases} +1 & \text{if the } i^{th} \text{ row of } B \text{ belongs to the group} \\ & \text{of the } p \text{ first rows of } A \\ -1 & \text{if the } i^{th} \text{ row of } B \text{ belongs to the group} \\ & \text{of the } q \text{ last rows of } A \end{cases}$$

We have $y \neq 0$, $yB = 0$. Thus B is singular and we have a contradiction.

Corollary:[†]   Matrix A is totally unimodular; i.e., every square submatrix of
A has a determinant that is equal to +1, -1, or 0 .

Proof: After a permutation on rows and columns (which does not change the
absolute value of the determinant), a triangular matrix can be written under
the classical Δ form with

$$\Delta_i^j = 0 \qquad\qquad if \qquad j > i$$

The value of the determinant of such a matrix is equal to the product of its
diagonal elements, which are all equal to 1 if B is a submatrix of A .

Remark 8:   The example of Section VII.3 consists of solving (P_2) by the
revised simplex algorithm. The reader will check that all basic matrices are
triangular and that this was a great help in actually solving the different
linear systems.

Remark 9:   The matrix

$$M = \begin{bmatrix} 1 & 0 & 1 \\ 1 & 1 & 0 \\ 0 & 1 & 1 \end{bmatrix}$$

has exactly two 1's in each column. It is not triangular since property (ii)
of Remark 5 is not satisfied.

Remark 10:   Every basic solution of linear program (T) will be integer valued
if components of vectors a and b are integers. Let I be a subset of the
set of rows of A such that

$$rank\ (A_I) \quad = \quad rank\ (A)$$

i.e., rows not belonging to I correspond to redundant equations of the set of
constraints Ax = f . Let J be a basis of (T) . The basic solution corresponding to J is

(4")

$$x_j \ = \ 0 \qquad\qquad j \notin J$$
$$A_I^J x_J \ = \ f_I$$

[†]This property will not be used in the sequel.

But A_I^J is a square nonsingular submatrix of A, i.e., A_I^J is triangular and all nonzero elements of A_I^J are equal to 1. Thus (4") is a system of type (4) that will be solved by additions and subtractions. If f_I has integer components, x_J will also have integer components.

Theorem 2: A possesses p+q-1 linearly independent columns. Any constraint of (T) is redundant. After deletion of a single constraint, the linear system thus obtained is full rank.

Proof: Let y be the (p+q)-row vector, the components of which are

$$y^i = \begin{cases} 1 & \text{if} \quad 1 \leq i \leq p \\ -1 & \text{if} \quad p+1 \leq i \leq p+q \end{cases}$$

From Remark 5(i) and 5(ii), we have

$$yA = 0$$

Thus the linear system Ax = f is redundant. Let

$$J = \{1,2,\ldots,q,q+1,2q+1,3q+1,\ldots,(p-1)q + 1)\}; \qquad |J| = p+q-1$$

$$I = \{1,2,\ldots,p-1, p, p+2,p+3, \ldots,p+q\}; \qquad |I| = p+q-1$$

It is easy to check that A_I^J is triangular.

Since all components of y are different from 0, any constraint can be deleted and the system thus obtained is nonredundant.

Example: For p = 4, q = 7, matrix A_I^J as the following shape:

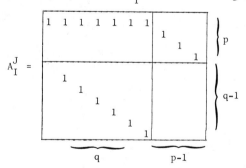

<u>Theorem 3</u>: A necessary and sufficient condition for a feasible solution of (T) to be an optimal solution is that one can find

$$u_1, u_2, \ldots, u_p$$
$$v_1, v_2, \ldots, v_q$$

such that

(5) $u_k + v_\ell \leq d_{k\ell}$ $k=1,2,\ldots,p; \quad \ell=1,2,\ldots,q$

(6) $u_k + v_\ell < d_{k\ell} \rightarrow t_{k\ell} = 0$ $k=1,2,\ldots,p; \quad \ell=1,2,\ldots,q$

<u>Proof</u>: The dual of (T) is

$$(T^*) \quad \begin{cases} u_k + v_\ell \leq d_{k\ell} & k=1,2,\ldots,p; \quad \ell=1,2,\ldots,q \\ \displaystyle\sum_{k=1}^{p} a_k u_k + \sum_{\ell=1}^{q} b_\ell v_\ell = w(\text{Max}) \end{cases}$$

Condition (5) guarantees that u_k and v_ℓ are a feasible solution of (T*). If (5) and (6) are satisfied, we have

$$t_{k\ell} > 0 \rightarrow u_k + v_\ell = d_{k\ell}$$

Thus we have a couple of feasible solutions to (T) and (T*) that satisfy the complementary slackness theorem.

<u>Remark 11</u>: If u_k, v_ℓ $(k=1,2,\ldots,p; \quad \ell=1,2,\ldots,q)$ satisfy constraints (5), so do

$$u_k + \alpha, \quad v_\ell - \alpha \qquad k=1,2,\ldots,p; \quad \ell=1,2,\ldots,q$$

for any α. Thus the solution of (T*) is defined up to an additive constant. Thus the solution of (T*) is defined up to an additive constant. This comes from the fact that, y being defined as in the proof of Theorem 2, we have $yA = 0$. We will take advantage of this fact in the sequel by systematically imposing $u_1 = 0$.

3. Solution of the Transportation Problem

Remark 12: Transportation problem (T) and its algorithm of solution are presented in the following table of dimensions $(p+1) \times (q+1)$:

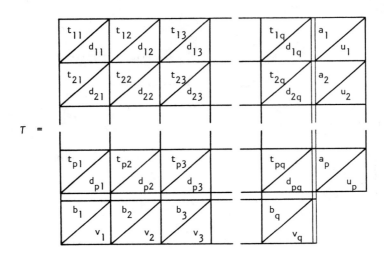

The problem consists of finding $t_{k\ell}$, u_k, v_ℓ such that:

   (i) The sum of $t_{k\ell}$ on the kth row is equal to a_k.

   (ii) The sum of $t_{k\ell}$ on the ℓth column is equal to b_ℓ.

  (iii) u_k and v_ℓ satisfy constraints (5).

  (iv) Relations (6) are satisfied.

We note that this presentation of the transportation problem is much more compact than the usual formalism since matrix A has $p+q$ rows and $p \times q$ columns, as opposed to the $p+1$ rows and $q+1$ columns of the preceding table. In fact, each entry of this table corresponds to a column of A.

Example: We consider the transportation problem defined by the table

$$T_0 \quad = \quad$$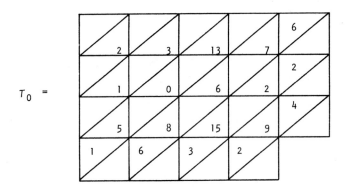

The corresponding linear program is

	x_1	x_2	x_3	x_4	x_5	x_6	x_7	x_8	x_9	x_{10}	x_{11}	x_{12}	b
	1	1	1	1									6
					1	1	1	1					2
									1	1	1	1	4
$(T_0) \quad =$	1				1				1				1
		1				1				1			6
			1				1				1		3
				1				1				1	2
	2	3	13	7	1	0	6	2	5	8	15	9	(Min)

Remark 13: As announced earlier, we will solve transportation problems through the revised simplex algorithm. This means that we will carry a primal, feasible solution and dual variables satisfying complementary slackness relations. When the dual variables provide a feasible solution of the dual problem, we will be done. In other words, after an initialization step, we will carry $t_{k\ell}$, u_k, and v_ℓ satisfying (i), (ii), and (iv) of Remark 12. We will stop when (iii) is also verified.

Remark 14: To initialize, we look for a feasible basis J and the corresponding basic solution. J will denote the set of couples (k,ℓ) in the basis. From Theorem 2, we have $|J| = p+q-1$. The procedure is the following:

(i)   If $p=1$, $q \geq 1$

$$J = \{(1,1),(1,2),\ldots,(1,q)\}$$
$$t_{11} = b_1, \quad t_{12} = b_2,\ldots,t_{1q} = b_q$$

(ii)   If $p > 1$, $q = 1$,

$$J = \{(1,1),(2,1),(3,1),\ldots,(p,1)\}$$
$$t_{11} = a_1, \quad t_{21} = a_2,\ldots,t_{p1} = a_p$$

(iii)   If $p > 1$ and $q > 1$, we choose an entry from table T, for in-
        stance[†], entry (r,s) such that

(7) $$d_{rs} = \text{Min}_{\{k=1,2,\ldots,p; \ \ell=1,2,\ldots,q\}}[d_{k\ell}]$$

We let

$$J: = J \cup \{(r,s)\}$$

(8) $$t_{rs} = \text{Min}[a_r, b_s]$$

(8) is the maximum amount of commodity that can be transported from
r to s without violating nonnegativity constraints on the other
variables (look at row sums and column sums in tableau T).

(iv)   If $a_r \leq b_s$, we have $t_{rs} = a_r$ and all the other variable $t_{r\ell}$
        for $\ell \neq s$ will be equal to 0. The rth row of tableau is
        saturated. We can now consider that we want to find a feasible
        solution for the transportation problem obtained from (T) by sup
        pressing the rth row of T and replacing b_s by

$$b_s - a_r$$

(In this new transportation problem, we ask that the
sum on column s be only equal to $b_s - a_r$.)

[†]Choice (7) is not essential. We can also take $r = s = 1$. We then have, for
evident reasons when one looks at table T , a method called the "north-
west corner method." (7) is a heuristic approach which in general will give a
starting solution closer to the optimal.

(v)   If $a_r > b_s$,   we have $t_{rs} = b_s$ and all the variables t_{ks} for
$k \neq r$ will be equal to 0 .   The sth column of table T is
saturated. We define a new transportation problem by suppressing
the sth column of table T and replacing a_r with $a_r - b_s$.

Example: We apply this procedure to find an initial solution to (T_0) .   The
solution is given in the following table:

$$T_0^{(1)} \quad = $$

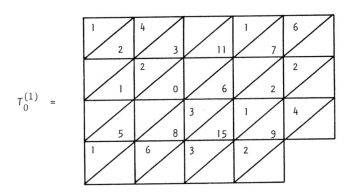

We begin by posing $t_{22} = 2$, $J = \{(2,2)\}$.   We suppress the second row and
b_2 changes from 6 to 4 .   Then we pose $t_{11} = 1$; $J: = J \cup \{(1,1)\}$,   we suppress the first column, and a_1 is decreased from 6 to 5 .   Then we pose
$t_{12} = 4$, $J: = J \cup \{(1,2)\}$,   we suppress the second column, and a_1 decreases
from 5 to 1 .   Then we pose $t_{14} = 1$, $J: = J \cup \{(1,4)\}$,   we suppress the
first row, and b_4 is decreased from 2 to 1 .

The reduced transportation table is then

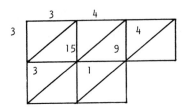

We have $p = 1$;   we let $t_{33} = 3$, $t_{34} = 1$, $J: = J \cup \{(3,3),(3,4)\}$.

We now present the initialization algorithm more formally:

Initialization routine

$t_{k\ell}$: = 0   for   k=1,2,...,p; ℓ=1,2,...,q

J: = $\emptyset$;   P: = {1,2,...,p}; Q: = {1,2,...,q}

while $|P|>1$ and $|Q|>1$ do

   d_{rs}: = $\underset{\{k\epsilon P;\ \ell\epsilon Q\}}{\text{Min}}$ $[d_{k\ell}]$;   J: = $J\cup\{(r,s)\}$

   /*   if more than one couple (r,s) is candidate, choose anyone */

   if $a_r \leq b_s$ then

      t_{rs}: = a_r ; b_s: = $b_s - a_r$;   P: = $P\setminus\{r\}$

   else

      t_{rs}: = b_s; a_r: = $a_r - b_s$;   Q: = $Q\setminus\{s\}$

   end if

end while

if $|P| = 1$ then

   let r be the unic element in P

   for all sϵQ   do

      J: = $J\cup\{(r,s)\}$; t_{rs}: = b_s

   end for all

else   /* then $|Q| = 1$ */ let s be the unic element of Q

   for all rϵP   do

      J: = $J\cup\{(r,s)\}$; t_{rs}: = a_r

   end for all

end if

end initialization routine

<u>Theorem 4:</u>   The set of indices found at the end of the initialization routine
is a feasible basis.

<u>Proof:</u>   Let   n   be the number of times we go through the "while" loop.   At each
step $|P| + |Q|$ is decreased by   1   unit.   At the exit of the loop we have,
say, $|P| = 1$.   Thus we will then have

$$|P| + |Q| = p + q - n$$
$$|Q| = p + q - n - 1$$

The loop "for all" that   follows will go through $|Q|$ steps.

For each iteration in the "while" loop and each iteration in the "for all"
loop, $|J|$ is increased by   1   unit.   Thus at the end of the application of
the routine, we have

$$|J| = n + |Q| = p + q - 1$$

If   J   is really a basis, the solution we have found (and which is feasible by
construction) is the basic solution associated with   J   since

$$(k, \ell) \notin J \rightarrow t_{k\ell} = 0 \qquad \text{(by construction)}$$

Let $I = \{2, 3, \ldots, p, p+1, \ldots, p+q\}$.   It remains to show that

$$B = A_I^J$$

is in fact a basis.   We just have to prove that

$$(*) \qquad\qquad A^J x_J = 0 \quad \rightarrow \quad x_J = 0$$

Consider the first index we introduced in   J ,   say (r, s) ,   and assume that
$a_r \leq b_s$ (the same argument in the other case).   Then

$$(r, \ell) \in J \rightarrow \ell = s \qquad \text{(by construction)}$$

and thus $x_{rs} = 0$ is the unique possibility for the rth equation of $(*)$.
The argument follows along this line on the successively reduced transportation
problems.

Corollary: Transportation problem (T), as defined in Definition 1, always has a feasible solution.

Remark 15: To apply the revised simplex algorithm, we need to know the multiplier vector π relative to basis J. Thus we have to solve the linear system

$$(9) \qquad\qquad \pi A_I^J = c^J$$

where π is the $(p+q-1)$-row vector $(u_2, u_3, \ldots, u_p, v_1, v_2, \ldots, v_q)$. From the structure of matrix A (see Remark 5), (9) can be written

$$(9') \qquad\qquad \begin{cases} u_1 = 0 \\ u_k + v_\ell = d_{k\ell} \qquad \text{for all } (k,\ell) \in J \end{cases}$$

A_I^J, being triangular (9) (or (9')), can be solved very easily, as we see in the next example.

Example: Entries corresponding to columns in J are those where the value of $t_{k\ell} \neq 0$ (the other entries correspond to nonbasic columns). Looking at table $T_0^{(1)}$, we begin with $u_1 = 0$. We find immediately

$$v_1 = 2, \qquad v_2 = 3, \qquad v_4 = 7$$

since

$$u_1 + v_1 = 2, \qquad u_1 + v_2 = 3, \qquad u_1 + v_4 = 7 \qquad \text{(from (6))}$$

Then, from $v_2 = 3$, we deduce that $u_2 = -3$ and from $v_4 = 7$ that $u_3 = 2$. Finally, from $u_3 = 2$ we get $v_3 = 13$. And we get the table $T_0^{(2)}$ shown on the next page.

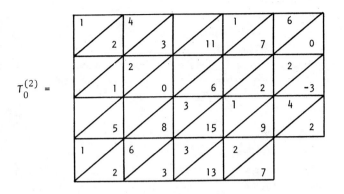

$$T_0^{(2)} =$$

Next, this procedure is presented more formally.

Dual variables computation routine

$u_1 := 0$; $P := P' := \{1\}$; $Q := Q' := \emptyset$

while $|P| < p$ and $|Q| < q$ do

for all $k \in P'$ and $\ell \in \{1,2,\ldots,q\} \setminus Q$ such that $(k,\ell) \in J$ do

$v_\ell := d_{k\ell} - u_k$; $Q' := Q' \cup \{\ell\}$; $Q := Q \cup \{\ell\}$

end for all

$P' := \emptyset$

for all $\ell \in Q'$ and $k \in \{1,2,\ldots,p\} \setminus P$ such that $(k,\ell) \in J$ do

$u_k := d_{k\ell} - v_\ell$; $P' := P' \cup \{k\}$; $P := P \cup \{k\}$

end for all

$Q' := \emptyset$

end while

end routine

Remark 16:   We will not give a formal proof of this routine. P' and Q' are the set of indices for which values of u_k and v_ℓ have been computed in the pre- ceding step.   The reader will understand the mechanism of the algorithm by applying it to the preceding example.

Remark 17:   if constraints

(5)
$$u_k + v_\ell \leq d_{k\ell}$$

are satisfied for all $(k,\ell) \notin J$, the current solution (basic solution relative
to basis J) is optimal (see Theorem 3). If this is not the case, we choose a
column index, for instance the couple (r,s) given by

(10)
$$d_{rs} - u_r - v_s = \underset{\{(k,\ell) \notin J\}}{Min} [d_{k\ell} - u_k - v_\ell]$$

for the column index to enter the basis. We now have to decide which index
will leave the basis. Before giving a general answer, we will go back to our
example.

Example: If we look at table $T_0^{(2)}$ and if we apply criterion (10), we find
that $(2,3)$ is the entering variable. Denote by θ the value of t_{23}. What
is the maximum possible value of θ when we adjust the basic variables? We
consider the table

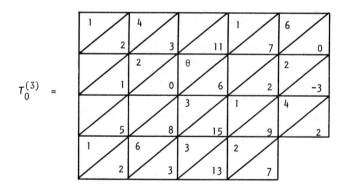

$$T_0^{(3)} =$$

Since we want to leave the nonbasic variables different from t_{rs} at their
zero level, we see that t_{11} must stay equal to 1 for any value of θ. Considering the second row and the third column, the adjustment leads us to

$$t_{22} = 2 - \theta$$
$$t_{33} = 3 - \theta$$

This implies, in considering the second column and the third row, that

$$t_{12} = 4 + \theta$$
$$t_{34} = 1 + \theta$$

Finally, considering first row and fourth column, we have

$$t_{14} = 1 - \theta$$

We have described a sort of a cycle. The maximum possible value for θ is $\theta = 1$: in effect, for $\theta > 1$, t_{14} would go negative. Thus, index $(1,4)$ goes out of the basis. We thus have the new basis, the new basic solution, and -- by calling the "dual variables computation routine" -- the new values of dual variables. These results are given in the following table:

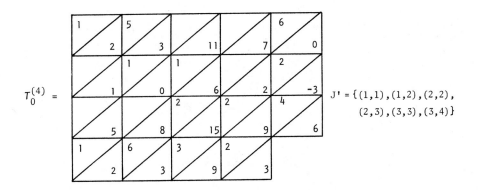

$$T_0^{(4)} = \qquad\qquad\qquad\qquad\qquad\qquad J' = \{(1,1),(1,2),(2,2),$$
$$(2,3),(3,3),(3,4)\}$$

Now $(3,1)$ is a candidate to enter the basis. We see that if $t_{31} = \theta$, there will be some adjustments in all the basic variables except t_{34}, which is the only basic variable in its column that will not be able to change. We write, in the following table (shown on the next page), the adjustments of basic variables.

$$T_0^{(5)} =$$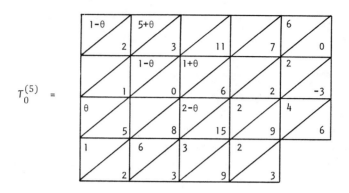

The maximum possible value for θ is $\theta = 1$. For $\theta = 1$, we have two basic variables that reach 0 simultaneously: t_{11} and t_{22}. This is a case of degeneracy. We will choose (arbitrarily) one of those indices as the leaving index: let $(2,2)$ leave the basis. $(1,1)$ is still in the basis, but $t_{11} = 0$ for the basic solution. Calling the "dual variables computation routine," we get

$$T_0^{(6)} =$$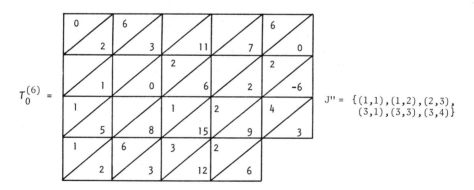

$$J'' = \{(1,1),(1,2),(2,3),\\ (3,1),(3,3),(3,4)\}$$

(Note that 0 in entry (1.1) means that $(1,1)$ is a basic index even if $t_{11} = 0$.) Index $(1,3)$ is now a candidate to enter the basis. The chain of adjustments on the basic variables is given by the following table:

$$T_0^{(7)} =$$

The maximum possible value for θ is $\theta = 0$:   (1,3) enters the basis and (1,1) leaves the basis, but the basic solution does not change. We get

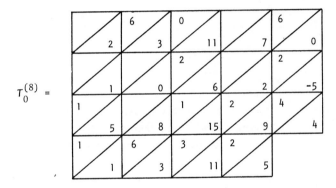

$$T_0^{(8)} =$$

This solution is optimal. We are done.

Remark 18:   Let us go back to the general case of Remark 17 and let σ be the index of the variable entering the basis $(\sigma = q(r-1) + s)$.   To find the index that leaves the basis, we study the variation of the basic solution x_J when $x_\sigma = \theta$ varies.   We have

(11) $A^J x_J + A^r \theta = f$

and we look for

$\bar{\theta}$ = maximum value of θ for which (11) is satisfied and $x_J \geq 0$.

For $\theta = \bar{\theta}$, one of the basic variables (at least) will cancel. We choose this one (or one of these) to leave the basis.

The next step is a study of the way x_J depends on θ in (11). To make things clear, call $\bar{x}_J$ the (unique) solution of

$$A^J x_J = f$$

Here, we just give the results of the study of this dependence (these results are a consequence of the structure of matrix A or, said in another way, of the network problem which is embedded in the transportation problem).

(i) $J \cup \{\sigma\}$ can be partitioned into three subsets: J', J^+, J^- with

$$x_j \in J' \qquad\qquad x_j \text{ does not depend on } \theta$$

$$x_j \in J^+ \qquad\qquad x_j = \bar{x}_j + \theta$$

$$x_j \in J^- \qquad\qquad x_j = \bar{x}_j - \theta$$

(ii)   The indices of J' can be found in the following way. First look for a row or a column of T that contains a single element of $\hat{J} = J \cup \{\sigma\}$. The corresponding variable cannot vary. Delete these indices (which are alone in their rows or columns) from $\hat{J}$ and start again. Repeat until no further deletion is possible.

(iii)   Let $\tilde{J} = J^+ \cup J^-$. For each row or column of T we have exactly 0 or 2 indices of $\tilde{J}$, one belonging to J^+, the other to J^-. Since $\sigma \in J^+$, determination of J^+ and J^- is an easy task.

Remark 19: Once we have determined J', J^+, and J^-, we have

$$\bar{\theta} = \underset{j \in J^-}{\text{Min}} [\bar{x}_j]$$

and the index of the variable to leave is

$$\tau \in J^- \qquad \text{with} \qquad \bar{x}_\tau = \bar{\theta}$$

We now give more formally the procedure of change of basis.

Change of basis routine

```
/* (r,s) is the index of the variable to enter the basis */
```

$J' := \emptyset;$ $J^+ := \{(r,s)\};$ $J^- := \emptyset;$ $P := \{1,2,\ldots,p\};$
$Q := \{1,2,\ldots,q\};$ $J := J \cup \{(r,s)\}.$

repeat

   EXIST: = FALSE

   for all $k \in P$ do

   | if $|\{\ell' | (k,\ell') \varepsilon J \setminus J'\}| = 1$ then
   | | $\ell :=$ unic element $(\{\ell' | (k,\ell') \varepsilon J \setminus J'\})$
   | | $J' := J' \cup \{(k,\ell)\};$ $P := P \setminus \{k\};$ EXIST: = TRUE
   | end if

   end for all

   for all $\ell \varepsilon Q$ do

   | if $|\{k' | (k',\ell) \varepsilon J \setminus J'\}| = 1$ then
   | | $k :=$ unic element $(\{k' | (k',\ell) \varepsilon J \setminus J'\});$
   | | $J' := J' \cup \{(k,\ell)\};$ $Q := Q \setminus \{\ell\};$ EXIST: = TRUE
   | end if

   end for all

until EXIST = FALSE

$k := r;$ $j := s$

iterate

   | $\ell :=$ unic element $(\{\ell' | (k,\ell') \varepsilon J \setminus J'; \ell' \neq j)\});$ $j := k$

exit $\ell = s$

   | $J^- := J^- \cup \{(k,\ell)\};$ $k :=$ unic element $(\{k' | (k',\ell) \varepsilon J \setminus J': k' \neq j\});$ $J^+ := J^+ \cup \{(k,\ell)\}$

end iterate

Find $(\hat{r},\hat{s})$ such that $t_{\hat{r}\hat{s}} = \underset{\{(k,\ell) \varepsilon J^-\}}{\text{Min}} [t_{k\ell}];$ $\bar{\theta} := t_{\hat{r}\hat{s}}$

   $t_{k\ell} := t_{k\ell} + \bar{\theta}$ $\forall (k,\ell) \varepsilon J^+$

   $t_{k\ell} := t_{k\ell} - \bar{\theta}$ $\forall (k,\ell) \varepsilon J^-$

$J := J \setminus \{(\hat{r},\hat{s})\}$

end routine

We let the reader check that this routine performs the change of basis and the change of basic solution as indicated in Remarks 18 and 19. The solution algorithm for the tranportation problem is given next.

Algorithm PRIMAL TRANSPORTATION

> Call Initialization routine
> iterate
>> Call dual variables computation routine
>> Find (r,s) such that $d_{rs} - u_r - v_s = \text{Min}_{(k,\ell) \not\in J} [d_{k\ell} - u_k - v_\ell]$
> exit: $d_{rs} - u_r - v_s \geq 0$
>> Call change of basis routine
> end iterate

end algorithm

4. The Assignment Problem

Definition 3: Let us consider the following problem. n persons must be assigned to n jobs (one job for one person). There is a cost $d_{k\ell}$ associated with the assignment of person k to job ℓ (think of a training cost). The problem consists of assigning each person to a job (and each job to a person) at a total minimum cost. This problem, known in the literature as the "assignment problem," can be formulated as a $\{0,1\}$ integer programming problem by posing

$$t_{k\ell} = \begin{cases} 1 & \text{if the } k^{th} \text{ person is assigned to the } \ell^{th} \text{ job} \\ 0 & \text{if not} \end{cases}$$

and

$$(A) \begin{cases} \sum_{k=1}^{n} t_{k\ell} = 1 & \ell = 1, 2, \ldots, n \\ \\ \sum_{\ell=1}^{n} t_{k\ell} = 1 & k = 1, 2, \ldots, n \\ \\ \sum_{k=1}^{n} \sum_{\ell=1}^{n} d_{k\ell} t_{k\ell} = z \, (\text{Min}) \end{cases} \qquad t_{k\ell} \in \{0,1\}$$

Theorem 5: Problem (A) can be solved in ignoring integrity constraints $t_{k\ell} \in \{0,1\}$. More precisely, every basic optimal solution of

$$
(A') \begin{cases}
\sum_{k=1}^{n} t_{k\ell} = 1 & \ell = 1, 2, \ldots, n \\[2mm]
\sum_{\ell=1}^{n} t_{k\ell} = 1 & k = 1, 2, \ldots, n \\[2mm]
\sum_{k=1}^{n} \sum_{\ell=1}^{n} d_{k\ell} t_{k\ell} = z \, (\text{Min})
\end{cases}
\qquad t_{k\ell} \geq 0
$$

is an optimal solution of (A) .

Proof: (A') is a transportation problem. From Remark 10, every basic solution of (A') is integer valued. Now constraints

$$
\sum_{k=1}^{n} t_{k\ell} = 1 \qquad t_{k\ell} \geq 0
$$

of (A') imply that $t_{k\ell} \leq 1$. Thus every basic feasible solution of (A') is a feasible solution of (A) . Hence every basic optimal solution of (A') is an optimal solution of (A) (since constraints of (A') are included in constraints of (A)).

Remark 20: Because of Theorem 5, the tradition is that problem (A') itself is called an assignment problem.

Remark 21: For any basic solution of the assignment problem, we will have 2n-1 variables in the basis and only n variables equal to 1 (corresponding to the assignment chosen). The assignment problem will be very degenerate (at each step, n-1 variables equal 0). However, no perturbation method or lexicographic variant is necessary. But it is of prime importance to keep continuously a basis of appropriate dimension with basic variables at level 0 .

EXERCISES

1. Show that linear program (T̄) obtained from (T) of Definition 1 by changing "Min" into "Max" in the objective function is a transportation problem.

   How is the "PRIMAL TRANSPORTATION" algorithm to be changed to solve (T̄) ?

2. Prove that linear programs (2) and (2') (see Remark 2) are equivalent.

3. We consider transportation problem (T) defined by the table

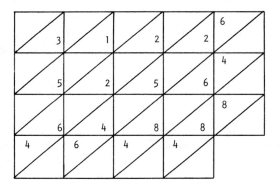

(a) Show, without doing any calculation, that this transportation problem has an optimal solution with even components.

(b) Show that the solution

$$x_{11} = x_{12} = x_{21} = x_{24} = x_{33} = x_{34} = 0; \quad x_{13} = x_{22} = x_{23} = 2; \quad x_{14} = x_{31} = x_{32} = 4$$

is optimal. Is it unic?

(c) a_1 and b_2 are changed simultaneously and their value is increased by δ. How do the solution and the value of the objective function vary as functions of δ ?

(d) Was it possible to foresee that in some domain the value of the objective function would decrease when δ increases?

4. Solve the transportation problem

11	7	6	9	13
8	6	4	7	14
5	3	2	3	8
10	8	12	5	

5. Solve the transportation problem (example of [6])

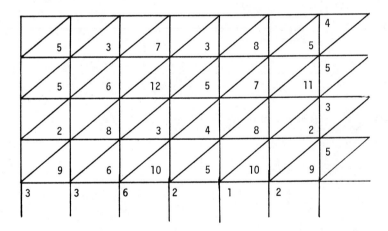

5	3	7	3	8	5	4
5	6	12	5	7	11	5
2	8	3	4	8	2	3
9	6	10	5	10	9	5
3	3	6	2	1	2	

6. Consider the transportation problem

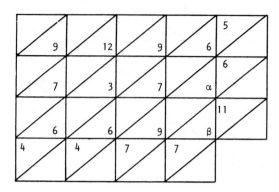

(a) Find a solution of this problem for $\alpha = 7$, $\beta = 8$.

(b) What is the optimal solution for $\alpha = 3$, $\beta = 8$?

(c) For $\alpha = 7$, give the set of values of β for which solution of question (a) is optimal.

(d) What is the set of values of (α, β) for which solution of question (a) is optimal?

(e) Give all the solutions of this transportation problem for all values of (α, β).

7. Solve the assignment problem defined by the cost matrix

$$
\begin{bmatrix}
2 & 5 & 4 & 4 \\
0 & 9 & 3 & 7 \\
1 & 8 & 8 & 9 \\
9 & 4 & 1 & 6
\end{bmatrix}
$$

8. We consider an assignment problem for which the objective function is to be maximized (think of $d_{k\ell}$ as returns instead of costs)

Solve the example defined by the return matrix.

$$\begin{bmatrix} 13 & 16 & 7 & 12 \\ 6 & 10 & 2 & 5 \\ 4 & 7 & 0 & 4 \\ 12 & 14 & 6 & 10 \end{bmatrix}$$

9. Consider the assignment problem with the cost matrix

$$\begin{bmatrix} 1 & 5 & 5 & 2 & 3 \\ 1 & 5 & 3 & 1 & 4 \\ 4 & 1 & 0 & 2 & 0 \\ 1 & 4 & 5 & 3 & 3 \\ 2 & 5 & 4 & 6 & 6 \end{bmatrix}$$

(a) Give an optimal solution.

(b) Give all optimal solutions.

References

[1] Chvatal, V., *Linear Programming,* W.M. Freeman & Co., 1982.

[2] Dantzig, G.B., *Linear Programming and Extensions,* Princeton University Press, 1963.

[3] Gale, D., *The Theory of Linear Economic Models,* McGraw Hill, New York, 1960.

[4] Garfinkel, R.S. and G.L. Nemhauser, *Integer Programming,* John Wiley, 1972.

[5] Gass, S., *Linear Programming, Methods and Applications,* McGraw Hill, New York, 1958.

[6] Ford, L.R. and D.R. Fulkerson, *Flows in Networks,* Princeton University Press, 1962.

[7] Simonnard, M., *Linear Programming,* Prentice Hall, Englewood Cliffs, New Jersey, 1965.

Aide Memoire and Index of Algorithms

Given a linear program in standard form

$$(P) \quad \begin{cases} Ax = b & x \geq 0 \\ cx = z \ (\text{Max}) \end{cases}$$

where A is an m×n matrix, we call:

Feasible solution: A vector x such that

$$x \geq 0$$
$$Ax = b$$

Optimal solution: A feasible solution which maximizes z.

Basis: A set J of m indices such that A^J is nonsingular.

Basic variables: The variables whose indices are in the basis.

Basic solution corresponding to basis J : The solution obtained with the non-basic variables equal to 0, *i.e.,*

$$\begin{cases} x_j = 0 & j \notin J \\ x_J = (A^J)^{-1} b . \end{cases}$$

The basic solution which corresponds to a given basis is unique.

Feasible basis: A basis such that the corresponding basic solution is feasible, *i.e.,* a basis J such that

$$(A^J)^{-1} b \geq 0 .$$

Multiplier vector relative to a basis I (or simplex multipliers):

$$\pi = c^J (A^J)^{-1} .$$

Cost vector relative to a basis J :

203

$$\hat{c} = c - \pi A .$$

Optimal basis: A basis such that the corresponding basic solution is optimal; by virtue of theorem IV.3, a basis is optimal if and only if

$$\hat{c} = c - \pi A \leq 0 .$$

Basic optimal solution: A basic feasible solution which is optimal, or in other words, a basic solution which corresponds to an optimal basis.

INDEX OF ALGORITHMS

1. Pivot operation: how to perform a pivot operation on the coefficient of a linear system - p. 49.

2. Simplex algorithm: how to solve a linear program when it is written in canonical form with respect to a feasible basis - p. 81.

3. Phase I of simplex method: how to write a linear program in canonical form with respect to a feasible basis - p. 103.

4. Revised simplex algorithm: another way of implementing the simplex algorithm - p. 115.

5. Simplex algorithm with bounded variables: how to provide, in a compact way, for bounds on the values of variables - p. 119.

6. Dual simplex algorithm: how to solve a linear program which is dual feasible but primal unfeasible - p. 159 .

7. Transportation algorithm: how to solve the transportation problem - p. 186, 189, 195 and 196.

Index